INDEPENDENCE HALL

in American Memory

INDEPENDENCE HALL

in American Memory

Charlene Mires

PENN

University of Pennsylvania Press
Philadelphia

Copyright © 2002 University of Pennsylvania Press
All rights reserved
Printed in the United States of America on acid-free paper

10 9 8 7 6 5 4 3 2 1

Published by
University of Pennsylvania Press
Philadelphia, Pennsylvania 19104-4011

Library of Congress Cataloging-in-Publication Data

Mires, Charlene.
  Independence Hall in American memory / Charlene Mires.
    p.   cm.
  Includes bibliographical references and index.
  ISBN: 0-8122-3665-3 (acid-free paper)
  1. Independence Hall (Philadelphia, Pa.)—History.
2. Memory—Social aspects—United States. 3. Public history—
United States. 4. Historic sites—Social aspects—United States.
5. National characteristics, American. 6. Philadelphia (Pa.)—
Buildings, structures, etc. 7. Philadelphia (Pa.)—History. I. Title.
F158.8.I3 M57   2002
974.8'11 21   2002069583

Title page illustration: "The Boys in Blue," commemorative
lithograph, 1866 (see page 115)

CONTENTS

INTRODUCTION

On fine summer afternoons in Philadelphia, I sit among the bench-warmers of Independence Square. We carry books or newspapers, cold drinks or carry-out lunches, and like the pigeons of the square we roost around one of the most significant historic structures in the United States—Independence Hall. In 1776, the Continental Congress adopted the Declaration of Independence here; in 1787, delegates from the new nation drafted the U.S. Constitution. The United States and the city of Philadelphia have far surpassed their eighteenth-century proportions, but Independence Hall has survived under the protection of historically minded Philadelphians and later the federal government. It is a place both local and national, present and past, alive with activity and frozen in time. Tourists and schoolchildren continually file through the famous building, affirming its importance as the birthplace of the nation's founding documents. In its preservation and interpretation at the beginning of the twenty-first century, Independence Hall seems to have passed directly from the eighteenth century to the present. Inside, George Washington's chair seems to stand just where he left it. The silver inkstand gathers no dust. The clock in the distinctive steeple seems to keep steady time. How remarkable, how inspiring it can be.

Across the United States, hundreds of historic sites and monuments remind and reassure Americans of the presence of the past. We can visit the homes of Jefferson and Washington, the battlefields of Manassas and Gettysburg, and the places that incubated the African American and women's civil rights movements. We can envision Thomas Edison in his workshop or remember Davy Crockett at the Alamo. But most encounters with such places are brief stops on school field trips or summer vacations. Visitors step momentarily into an illusion of the past, consume a carefully carved slice of history, purchase a postcard or two, and move on. Such historical tourism has become an essential contributor to Americans' perceptions of their history. More than textbooks, more than history courses, Americans value museums and historic sites as opportunities for experiencing the past.[1] The significance of history in the public mind has been demonstrated in recent years by the popularity of historical documentaries and by such controversies as how to teach history in the public schools, how to display the *Enola Gay* at the National Air and Space Museum, and whether to allow a "Disney's America" to be built amid the Civil War landscape of Virginia.[2]

Because historic places play such a significant role in our sense of a shared national past, they deserve attention beyond the scope of a standard tour or guidebook. Historic places may seem to have obvious stories to tell (what could be more evident than associating Independence Hall with the Declaration of Independence and the Constitution?). However, such places have histories beyond the obvious. If the nation's historical memory is built upon fragmented, tightly edited stories, we risk losing touch with the greater complexity of national life. We may gain a sense of national unity, but depending on the historic places we choose to visit, we may lose sight of the diversity and conflicts that have characterized the nation's history. We may gain a surface understanding of events and a feeling of historic ambiance, but at the expense of full engagement with the deeply rooted issues that define the nation's civic life.[3]

In this book, I am getting off the tourist bus and stepping back from one historic place—Independence Hall—to see what can be learned from a broader, deeper history. Although the Declaration of Independence and the U.S. Constitution rightfully prevail at Independence Hall, I argue that the significance of the building cannot be fully understood without incorporating the complex cultural and social history that has inhabited and surrounded it for nearly three centuries. This does not require abandoning the traditional associations of Independence Hall, but rather reaching across arbitrary boundaries of time and space. The significance of Independence Hall includes the history of the nation's founding, to be sure, but it also extends to the ways Americans have remembered that history at its place of origin. It is a nation's history, but it is also a history embedded in one of the nation's oldest and largest cities, with a diverse population and a changing urban environment. To see Independence Hall as a place with a long history in an American city does not diminish its significance, I would argue, but rather enhances it. In a more fully articulated history, Independence Hall emerges as a place where successive generations have struggled to define the essence of American national identity.

Buildings, Nations, and Memories

To understand Independence Hall, and potentially other historic places, this book is concerned with three interlocking processes: the construction of a building, a nation, and memory.[4] Buildings, nations, and memories share an important characteristic—they all involve processes of remembering and forgetting, preserving some aspects of the past while obscuring others. Such remembering and forgetting is fundamental in the formation of individual and collective identities.[5] At the most self-evident level, we know from personal experience that we retain some memories but not others. As we retell stories about our own lives, some aspects of the stories become prominent and embellished while others are downplayed or omitted. Scholars have identified similar processes at work in the construction of national identities. How is it that nations, which encompass diverse populations and histories of conflict as well as harmony, manage to remain unified? In a classic statement, "What Is a Nation?" (1882), French historian Ernest Renan argued that the survival of nations depended on remembering characteristics of unity while suppressing memories of conflict that could threaten a sense of shared national identity.[6] Among those who later extended Renan's analysis, international studies scholar Benedict Anderson has advanced another influential definition of nation as "an imagined political community." To imagine a nation as a community requires forgetting as well as remembering. "Regardless of the actual inequality and exploitation that may prevail," Anderson has written, "the nation is always conceived as a deep horizontal comradeship."[7] In this view, nations are defined by beliefs (illusions, some might say) in shared characteristics among citizens. Nations are not fixed entities, defined only by geography; rather, they are continually redefined through processes of reimagining the nation and what it represents.

Where do buildings come in? Certainly they are not the only contributors to national identity, but they have the capacity to facilitate remembering and forgetting.[8] We build, adopting architectural styles of the past or striking out in new directions. We inhabit, investing buildings with experiences to be remembered or forgotten. We remodel, preserve, neglect, restore, or demolish, manipulating aging structures to suit changing needs. These processes are common to all structures, not just places regarded as historic. All around us, buildings communicate a sense of where we stand in relation to the past and present. But when buildings such as Independence Hall are associated with events or people important to the nation's past, they take on enhanced significance—not only because of the famous people or events, but because they allow individuals to participate in the processes of remembering and forgetting aspects of the nation's history. The remembering is often intentional, enacted through historic preservation, interpretation, commemorations, or heritage tourism. Such activities help to bolster a sense of the nation's stability and endurance. But to achieve such an aura of permanence virtually *requires* forgetting—not necessarily in the form of intentional lies about the past, but often through a less calculated letting-go of ephemeral events, controversies, or eras that do not fit a selected vision for preservation.[9] To fully understand the significance of a building, I argue, requires considering the forgetting as well as the remembering. Indeed, aspects of a building's past that have been obscured by historic preservation may hold the richer story of the construction of national identity. A carefully tended building may belie the conflicts and activity of everyday life that have surrounded it over time.

To think of buildings in terms of the processes of remembering and forgetting is a departure from the usual practice for considering the significance of historic buildings in the United States. Questions about the significance of buildings often arise in the context of decisions about preservation or official historic designation. Should a building be preserved? Does it deserve to be recognized on the National Register of Historic Places? If so, why? The issue of significance is thereby framed as a quest to define what is memorable. This framework, codified in the United States by the Historic Preservation Act of 1966, directs our collective attention toward readily identifiable historic contexts, notable people, events, and architectural distinctiveness.[10] Certainly, associations such as these help to mark a building's place in history. To stop at this point, however, is to risk overlooking more complex meanings. If memories of famous events and notable people have survived, it is likely that other aspects of the building's history have been forgotten along the way. The forgotten history, if recovered, may contribute to a richer understanding of the building's history, potentially revealing changing meanings of the building over time. With this, it is possible to detect how and why successive generations used, changed, restored, or preserved the building in keeping with their regard for its historical associations. This process is a valuable record of interactions between past and present.

As places for remembering and forgetting, buildings are workshops of public memory. In using this term, I follow historian John Bodnar's definition of public memory as "a body of beliefs and ideas about the past that help a public or society understand both its past, present, and by implication, its future."[11] Scholars exploring this topic have traced the changing understandings of historic figures such as George Washington, events such as the Civil War and the American Revolution, and documents such as the U.S. Constitution. They have shown how the present influences interpretations of the past, how traditions emerge and change, and how competing versions of the past are promoted and contested.[12] While significant attention has been given to the historic preservation movement, scholars have not fully considered the networks of interaction between past and present that individual buildings represent.[13] Buildings, I argue, provide a public stage for enacting beliefs and ideas about the past. As places of memory, buildings are depositories, providing places to create and store material connections to the past. They are conduits, communicating perceptions of the past into the future. Paradoxically, buildings also act as filters, preserving some aspects of the past while allowing others to be forgotten. To understand these processes, this book crosses disciplinary boundaries to view relationships between buildings and public memory in five principal ways.[14]

First, in their original design, buildings capture and project the values of their builders. As in architectural history, this book will be concerned with choices of materials, architectural style, and construction techniques. In contrast to many building histories, however, this history of Independence Hall will consider these structural choices in light of what they may reveal about public memory.[15] A building may embody a cherished past or discard previous practices in favor of something new. As a result, buildings are more than artifacts of style and taste. To the extent that buildings perpetuate the past or abandon it, they provide snapshots of public memory at the moment of their design. They reflect attitudes toward the past held by their designers or sponsors. As long as the original characteristics of the building survive, this record of public memory is projected into the future.[16]

Second, buildings are not just structures but places with histories that extend beyond their walls into the surrounding environment. They exist in the context of landscapes—not in the static sense of a building standing on a plot of ground, but in a more dynamic interchange between buildings and their surroundings. If buildings are understood only as structures in isolation, we risk losing sight of their significance within the communities they occupy. As cultural geographers, historians, and urban studies scholars have shown, landscapes can be understood as expressions of meaning created by humans as they interact with the physical environment.[17] Regard for the past may be a factor in this interaction. For example, preservation interests may challenge plans to change a landscape valued for its historical associations. As we will see in the case of Independence Hall, buildings valued for their architectural or historical significance also may exert a strong influence on their environments by dictating the appearance of nearby structures or claiming enlarged public spaces for purposes of commemoration. This book will consider the significance of a historic building within an urban environment, looking especially for the ways that changes in the environment have reflected and contributed to the shaping of public memory.

Third, as they age, buildings dare us to make choices. Buildings deteriorate, presenting dilemmas of preservation, adaptation, or destruction. They fall out of architectural fashion, tempting us to remodel or demolish. We may choose to embrace the past that a building represents, discard that past, or alter it. Whatever the choice,

buildings draw us into interaction with the past. When they are considered particularly historic, as in the case of Independence Hall, such choices have widespread impli-
cations, challenging one generation after another to define its regard for the nation's
history. These are the issues at the heart of the historic preservation movement, which
in recent years has attracted the attention of academic historians as well as practi-
tioners. Recent books have focused on the activities of preservationists, making a connection to public memory by showing how individuals and groups use buildings to
construct desired images of the past.[18] The impact of such activities has been demonstrated by histories of historic preservation in cities such as Boston, Seattle, San Antonio, and Charleston, South Carolina.[19] In contrast to this body of scholarship, the
central focus of this work is not an individual or an organization, but a single building. With the building at the center of analysis, this book will address issues of historic
preservation, but as one aspect of a more complex relationship between buildings and
public memory.

Fourth, buildings have social histories which contribute to the construction of
public memory. Buildings are places where people interact, by choice or by chance,
contributing to a building's history. As hubs of human activity, buildings such as the
White House, Thomas Jefferson's Monticello, the Empire State Building, and the World
Trade Center (even before September 11, 2001) have inspired biographical works that
trace the interconnected histories of structures, people, and events.[20] This book is also
a building "biography," in that it traces events at Independence Hall from the time of
its construction until the recent past. However, to pursue the connection between
buildings and public memory, activities in and around Independence Hall will be considered for what they may reveal about the meaning of the building to diverse groups
and individuals. At various times in its history, people have gathered at Independence
Hall to socialize, to vote, to stand trial, to demonstrate against the actions of government, and to celebrate moments of national triumph. They have made Independence
Hall the center of a web of traditions that articulate an appreciation as well as a critique of the nation's founding principles.[21] Interactions such as these become factors
in public memory as they reflect or redefine ideas about the past that the building represents. The history of such changing interactions is less easily recovered than the
structural history of a building, but it is essential to understanding the character and
meaning of buildings as they change over time.

Finally, entwined with all of the above, buildings have cultural significance. If we
know a building's structural, environmental, and social history, so what? Why is a
building valued (or not)? What does it represent? What associations with the past does

it bring to mind? This elusive, ever-changing quality is potentially the most revealing statement of public memory, but it is also the most difficult to pin down. Because historic preservation has often been the purview of elite, homogeneous groups, the appearance of a building may communicate a constricted sense of its cultural significance. To achieve a more complete understanding of the cultural significance of Independence Hall, this book builds on the scholarship on public memory. Buildings have made only occasional appearances in such scholarship, but concepts have been developed that help in understanding the relationships between buildings and public memory.

The French historian Pierre Nora has introduced a phrase for places of particular importance to national identity: *lieux de mémoire*—sites of memory. These are places that allow individuals to connect with a past that lies beyond personal memory and to form a collective perception of the nation.[22] Independence Hall is an especially rich example of Nora's concept because it embodies such a powerful array of memories. There is the building itself, a fine example of Georgian architecture that exemplifies elite taste in colonial America. There are two very different documents, the Declaration of Independence and the Constitution, each full of memorable phrases that have remained in our national consciousness: *Life, liberty, and the pursuit of happiness. We the people.* There are the people behind the documents—George Washington, Thomas Jefferson, John Adams, Benjamin Franklin, and the other members of the Second Continental Congress and delegates to the Constitutional Convention. There is the Liberty Bell, offering another memorable phrase, *Proclaim liberty throughout all the land unto all the inhabitants thereof.* Independence Hall has allowed Americans to grasp any of these memories, in any combination. As we will see, these memories have been put to work in many ways to address changing needs.

To explore Independence Hall as a site of remembering and forgetting, this book will engage especially with two concepts: memory as *contested* and memory as *collective.* To think of public memory as contested is to recognize the existence of competing versions of the past.[23] In the case of buildings, this provides a framework for looking beyond the product of historic preservation and considering other perspectives that might be revealed by the building's history. The process of preservation itself may provide a record of contested memory, as individuals or groups vie to perpetuate their particular versions of the past. In cases of politically charged places like Independence Hall, activities such as demonstrations and commemorations also may reveal a prism of meanings, changing over time. Approaching Independence Hall from the standpoint of contested memory allows us to see the building not only as a place to celebrate the famous events of 1776 and 1787, but also as a place defined by the political, social, and cultural struggles over the memory of those events.

The second concept, collective memory, provides a framework for distinguishing among the divergent memories that may be attached to a single place. As defined by sociologists, a collective memory is formed within a group of people who occupy a shared time and place.[24] The characteristics of sharing, time, and place are all important considerations. With regard to sharing, decisions about buildings are often made within definable groups—civic organizations, for example, or government agencies. If we can define the shared characteristics and life experiences of the individuals who comprise these groups, then we may also discern the extent to which collective memory was constructed around factors such as class, gender, race, or ethnicity. If we know the shared characteristics of people who have influenced a building's appearance and interpretation, then we can also look to people who do not share those characteristics to explore the possibilities of other perceptions and interpretations of the building.

Applying the concept of collective memory to buildings also requires consideration of time and place. Collective memory fades as group members depart or die; the memory does not outlast the group. Here, however, buildings have an important role to play. They provide groups with an opportunity to embed their collective memory in a physical entity, potentially creating a version of the past that will survive from one generation to the next. In this way, buildings provide a conduit by which the collective memories of one group may contribute to others' ideas about the past, thereby contributing to long-lasting public memory. However, even as buildings extend collective memory by allowing it to be communicated across time, they place limitations on collective memory by anchoring it in place. Perception may be tied to proximity. Even a place as famous as Independence Hall varies in meaning for people from different regions of the country and different parts of the world. Considering the meanings of buildings requires being alert for a geography of memory, where distance from the structure becomes a significant factor.

These issues of public memory provide a conceptual frame for this book, but Independence Hall provides the historical record to be explored and the story to be told. From our vantage point in the twenty-first century, the building is inextricably linked to the American Revolution, offering an opportunity to explore public memory as it relates to the founding events and ideals of the nation. Given its powerful associations and a history even longer than the United States, reaching from 1732 to the present, Independence Hall is arguably the best possible case study of the simultaneous processes of constructing and preserving a building, the nation, and memory.[25] Examining these processes at one eighteenth-century building in the heart of Philadelphia may open doors toward a greater understanding of the meanings and significance of buildings, especially those considered historic.

Independence Hall: Untold Stories

Having spent some time thinking about buildings and public memory, I have been reaching back into my own memory to try to reconstruct how this project began. This is treacherous, I know, because our memories are not simply snapshots of the past preserved intact, but ideas about the past that we subconsciously reassemble to meet present needs.[26] Looking back, this project may have begun in the bicentennial year, 1976, during a vacation stop in Philadelphia—but I don't think so. In my album from that trip, I have one photograph of Independence Hall's iconic steeple, but there are three of the Liberty Bell and two of the newly constructed Visitor Center. I do not have a distinct memory of standing in the room occupied by the Second Continental Congress and the Constitutional Convention, although I know that I did. More than this, I recall a park ranger playing the harpsichord on the second floor, the disorientation of navigating my way around the unfamiliar city, and the difficulty of finding a parking space. I experienced Independence Hall as a tourist, taking away an impression of the place but not a full appreciation of its history.

It was not Independence Hall that pulled me back to Philadelphia in 1984, but a job at the *Philadelphia Inquirer* and a feeling of connection to a family history that included an Irish weaver who immigrated to the city in 1783, at the first possible opportunity after the American Revolution. I rented an apartment in a rehabilitated industrial building not far from Independence Hall, and I felt pleased to live in a neighborhood that several million people each year had to travel to see. I began to experience Independence Hall as a new resident of its home city. I noted the contrasts between the symbols of American ideals and the presence of the homeless who occupied steam grates on corners adjacent to Independence National Historical Park. For the first time, I saw photographs of the area around Independence Hall before the park was created, when the building was surrounded by a cityscape of nineteenth-century industry. In the photographs, Independence Hall seemed surprisingly small and out of place among factories, banks, and office buildings. This may have begun my awareness that Independence Hall might be more than it appeared to be.

In a more definitive way, this project began in 1993, on a typically sweltering Philadelphia Fourth of July. That morning, I joined the thousands who gathered on the plazas north of Independence Hall to watch as Nelson Mandela and F. W. de Klerk of South Africa accepted the Liberty Medal, an award given annually to recognize champions of freedom and to draw international attention to Philadelphia. Like many others, I could not get within a block of the ceremony because of the crowd. Standing in the second block, I could only watch President Clinton award the medals by looking at a wide, overhead screen. Most of us in the general public saw the event the same way that we might have watched it at home, on television. But Independence Hall and the adjacent park provided an opportunity to connect the present to the past and ourselves to the nation and the world. We felt the need to be at that historic place, on a historic day, watching (however distantly) a historic event of our times.

I noticed a change in the appearance of Independence Hall on that Fourth of July morning. To create a more attractive image on television, the scaffolding that had supported the building's steeple for much of the year had been removed. The scaffolding indicated that long-needed repairs were being made to the steeple, which dates to 1828. The work followed a wave of unflattering publicity about conditions in and around Independence Hall. For two years running, in 1991 and 1992, the National Trust for Historic Preservation had placed Independence National Historic Park on its "most endangered historic places" list to call attention to outmoded infrastructures such as utility and fire protection systems. The National Parks and Conservation Association claimed that because of an antiquated sprinkler system, a fire could level Independence Hall in thirty minutes. Finally, the federal government agreed to a $75 million, ten-year rehabilitation program for Independence Hall and other historic buildings in the park.[27] This series of events, more than anything else, prompted the questions that led to this book. When and why are societies willing to spend the money necessary to keep historic buildings in repair? If we could chart this, would we learn something about the public's changing regard for the history that the building represents?

Remarkably little has been published about the history of Independence Hall, and even less has addressed the building's history beyond the eighteenth century. The building is so tightly associated with the Declaration of Independence and the Constitution that it perhaps has seemed to have no other history worth pursuing. Since assuming management responsibility for Independence Hall in 1951, the National Park Service has undertaken prodigious research on the events of the late eighteenth and early nineteenth centuries and the structural history necessary to restore the building to its eighteenth-century appearance. The most important "publication" of this research, of course, takes place every day in the on-site interpretation of Independence Hall. However, given the numbers of people who come to see the building and the limits of time and space, building tours present only the proverbial tip of an informational iceberg. In printed form, Park Service research is contained primarily in internal reports, a handful of articles and book chapters (most published during the 1950s), two collections catalogs, and guidebooks for tourists.[28] Although an institutional history of Independence National Historical Park was published in 1987, the last history of Independence Hall intended for the general public was written in 1954.[29]

Outside the National Park Service, Independence Hall has attracted little serious interest among historians. Scholars have produced an immense body of work about the Declaration of Independence, the Constitution, and the activities of the federal government during the 1790s, when Philadelphia was the nation's capital, but they have shown little interest in the building at the center of these events.[30] Unlike other buildings viewed as national symbols, such as the White House or the U.S. Capitol, Independence Hall does not have a historical society that convenes conferences and encourages scholarship. Beyond the work of the park staff, it is not a center for study of the American Revolution. The building is so utterly successful as a shrine to the nation's founding, and so completely dedicated to heritage tourism, that it perhaps has seemed too mundane or too thoroughly understood to warrant scholarly investigation. Even in works devoted to the memory of the American Revolution, the Declaration of Independence, and the Constitution, Independence Hall has played a limited role.[31]

In fact, Independence Hall has a long and complex history, especially as a place where Americans have gathered to honor and debate the ideas expressed in the Constitution and the Declaration of Independence. The building did not automatically become a shrine after the departure of the Second Continental Congress and the Constitutional Convention. More than two centuries of effort have gone into perpetuating the memory of the nation's founding. The building originated in the 1730s as the Pennsylvania State House and continued that function until 1799; it served as a public building for the city of Philadelphia for most of the nineteenth century. Only gradually, as the events of 1776 and 1787 faded into the past, did the building become recognized as "Independence Hall." Over time, the space identified as "historic" inside and outside the building has become larger, more elaborate, and more distinctly dedicated to the purpose of commemoration. Beginning with the 1820s, when one room inside the building became regarded as "Hall of Independence" and Philadelphians named the surrounding city block "Independence Square," the historic space expanded to include a first-floor museum (1876), a restoration of the second floor (1897), restoration of the adjacent meeting places of Congress and the Supreme Court

(1890s–1920s), and the creation of state and national parks (1948–present). By the turn of the twenty-first century the historic space was being elaborated once again with construction of a new Visitor Center, a National Constitution Center, and an enlarged pavilion for Independence Hall's most famous artifact, the Liberty Bell. The more Americans have become separated in time from their nation's founding, it seems, the more necessary it has been to sustain a material connection to that past. As the famous events have become more distant, increasingly elaborate means have been devised to recall and honor them.

In the process of preserving these vital national memories, other aspects of the history of Independence Hall were cast aside. The building became separated from its early history as the capitol of Pennsylvania and from its significant place in the history of the city of Philadelphia, particularly during the nineteenth century. In its lifetime, Independence Hall has functioned as a cultural center, a courthouse, a political arena, and a gathering place for public demonstrations. Its story includes artists and scientists who defined a national culture, accused fugitive slaves who faced the loss of freedom, nativist politicians determined to limit the influence of immigrants and Catholics, and protesters demanding civil rights. As much as the acts of creating the Declaration of Independence and the Constitution, these events tell us about life, liberty, and the pursuit of happiness in the United States of America. Although it is not readily apparent, Independence Hall has been a place of contesting, defining, and expanding the promises of the nation's founding documents. More than previously acknowledged, Independence Hall has served as workshop for constructing and defending national identity.

When I sit in Independence Square these days, I am distracted not only by the activity of tourism, but also by the things that I cannot see. In this manicured park, I cannot see the dust and ruts created by soldiers mustering for the War for Independence. I feel alone in recognizing the place where Frederick Douglass stood in 1844 to denounce slavery and in envisioning the crowds of African Americans who waited to hear if federal courts would return their neighbors to bondage. I doubt that anyone around me can hear the echoes of mourning for deceased American presidents or the drifting chants for women's suffrage, for free speech, and for enforcement of the full rights of citizenship for all Americans. As you read this book, I invite you to join me in the square, in your imagination if not physically seated among the bench-warmers, to contemplate this place which seems to me very crowded with history, memory, and the struggles of constructing and preserving a nation.

Chapter 1

LANDMARK

A British Home for the American Revolution

Finding the origins of Independence Hall requires excavation, not through rock and soil, but through time and memory. Forget about guided tours, the Liberty Bell, and the Fourth of July. Forget about the Constitution, the Declaration of Independence, and the United States of America. Before all of these, a two-story brick outpost of British gentility stood on Chestnut Street in Philadelphia, between Fifth and Sixth Streets, then the outskirts of the city. "It is a fine, large building having a tower with a bell, and is the greatest ornament in the town," botanist Peter Kalm, touring North America for the Swedish Academy of Sciences, observed in 1748.[1] Shortly thereafter, surveyors Nicholas Scull and George Heap featured the same building—the Pennsylvania State House—on their new *Map of Philadelphia and Parts Adjacent*. Although the map showed only faint beginnings of organized settlement in Pennsylvania, Heap's drawing of the State House stood boldly at the top like a crown. Stately and substantial, the Pennsylvania State House represented the steady grasp of British culture on life in the American colonies. The image was reproduced widely on maps and in magazines, in the colonies and in Europe.[2]

Even in the twenty-first century, the building pictured on the Scull and Heap map is instantly recognizable. To us, it is not the Pennsylvania State House, but Independence Hall, a place valued for its associations with the founding of the United States. Our perception of this place has been constructed from our lessons in American history and our experiences as participants in the life of the nation. At Independence Hall, our historical memory is refreshed by the narratives of the Second Continental Congress and the Constitutional Convention. We feel transported to the past. However, it is an edited past, emphasizing nation over locality, consensus over conflict, and clarified

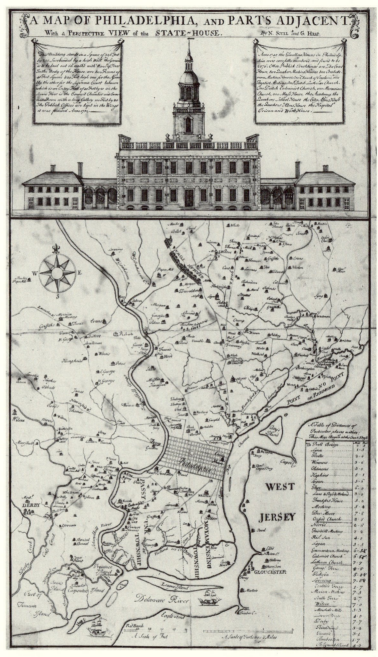

1. With the Pennsylvania State House displayed prominently at the top, Nicholas Scull and George Heap's *Map of Philadelphia and Parts Adjacent* (1752) communicated to the world that European civilization had been successfully transplanted to William Penn's colony. (Courtesy of John Carter Brown Library at Brown University)

narrative over the complexity of eighteenth-century life. A more fully articulated history allows us to see not only the Declaration of Independence and the Constitution, but also the social and intellectual currents from which they emerged. In this history, the Pennsylvania State House does not stand alone, but rather in the context of a growing city, an extended British empire, and an emerging nation. Only with this foundation is it possible to investigate the later processes of constructing, remembering, and forgetting the history of Independence Hall.

Origins

The history of the Pennsylvania State House begins in 1729, at the close of a tense, tumultuous decade in the colony founded by William Penn nearly fifty years before. The colony had grown quickly, with a bustling port at Philadelphia and a rich hinterland yielding grains for market. However, Pennsylvania's prosperity fluctuated with the vagaries of overseas commerce. In the 1720s, not for the first time, international trade conditions thrust Pennsylvania into economic depression. Grappling with the crisis, the Pennsylvania Assembly and Governor Patrick Gordon deadlocked, especially over the Assembly's desire to bolster the economy by issuing paper money. In the streets of Philadelphia, riots erupted sporadically over bread prices, and the lower classes attacked the stocks and pillories, the instruments of legal authority. Even when the province regained its financial footing, a surge in immigration seemed to present a renewed threat to social cohesion.[3] Throughout this turbulent decade, the Assembly, controlled mostly by English Quakers from the upper ranks of society, struggled to maintain order. The Assembly passed laws to regulate trade, to safeguard public health and safety, to discourage immigration, and to govern the behavior of slaves. Operating within a frame of government established by William Penn, the elected Assembly had the authority to initiate laws for the province, subject to approval by the governor. However, like so many other aspects of Pennsylvania life in the 1720s, the Assembly lacked stability, convening in rented or borrowed rooms for lack of a permanent meeting place.[4]

In 1729, the Pennsylvania Assembly authorized construction of "a House for the Assembly of this Province to meet in."[5] While this action addressed a practical problem, it also entwined closely with the Assembly's concerns over political control and cultural identity. Like other provincial assemblies in the mainland British colonies, the Pennsylvania Assembly had developed by the 1720s into a sophisticated political institution, capable of resisting the will of its appointed governor.[6] Its decision to create a permanent meeting place coincided with a break in its long deadlock with Governor Gordon over issuing paper money. When the governor finally authorized £30,000 in paper money in 1729, the Assembly immediately designated £2,000 for its own meeting house. Tellingly, the action specified a building for use by the Assembly, making no mention of the colony's executive officer.[7] This new structure in Philadelphia would represent the authority of the people's representatives, not the appointed officials who held power over them. By the time construction began in 1732, the Assembly's records referred to the "State-house" rather than "House for the Assembly," reflecting the significance of the structure and the political maturity of Pennsylvania.[8]

In addition to reinforcing its political authority, the Pennsylvania Assembly in 1729 acted within an atmosphere of anxiety over the cultural identity of the province. Pennsylvania had originated as an English colony, but William Penn's principle of religious tolerance, combined with abundant land and opportunity, had attracted a diverse population, including Germans, Swedes, Dutch, Scots-Irish, and Africans whom the European colonists acquired as slaves. Still, eighteenth-century Pennsylvanians lived under British law, engaged in British commerce, and celebrated birthdays of British sovereigns. During the 1720s, an unprecedented number of new immigrants, predominantly Germans and Scots-Irish, challenged this prevailing British identity. The surge in immigration alarmed the leaders of the Pennsylvania Assembly, most of whom were born in England. Just as far-flung subjects of the British empire had developed a sense of shared nationhood in response to French enemies, the perceived threat of unfamiliar, unwanted immigrants elevated British identity among the resident leaders of Pennsylvania.[9] The Assembly commissioned an investigation of the new immigrants, and in 1729, in the same session in which the State House was authorized, approved a tax to discourage more.

At the center of both the immigration issue and the proposal to build a State House stood Assembly Speaker Andrew Hamilton, a lawyer who later became famous as the defense attorney in the libel case of John Peter Zenger. Born and educated in Scotland, Hamilton had become a man of the British empire by gaining power and prestige in Great Britain's North American colonies.[10] His career in the colonies began in 1696 at the age of twenty-one. After reading law and beginning his practice in Virginia and Maryland, he attracted the notice of the Penn family, who engaged him to defend their claims in Delaware. On behalf of the Penns, he traveled twice to London, becoming a barrister at Gray's Inn in 1713.[11] By the time of the immigration outcry and the State House proposal, Hamilton had risen in provincial politics to become Speaker of the Assembly, and he lived on a country estate, Bush Hill, north of Philadel-

phia. Immersed in elite British culture, transplanted to America, Hamilton took leading parts in curtailing new immigration and creating a State House. He coauthored
legislation that temporarily imposed a duty of forty shillings on immigrants to Pennsylvania, and he served on the committee to select a site for the State House, eventually guiding its design.[12] Linked through the initiative of Andrew Hamilton, the
immigration measure and the State House served a common purpose: to stabilize and
protect British cultural identity.

For Philadelphia, seat of the provincial government, a new State House had the
potential to change the physical and social organization of the city. William Penn had
intended Philadelphia to be a "green country town," but by the 1720s, Philadelphians
had thwarted the orderly grid envisioned in the original city plan. Where Penn had
hoped to see orderly, spacious estates, two-story brick houses stood shoulder-to-shoulder in tiny alleys that subdivided the original lots. The city's population had grown to
nearly five thousand, but even the broad main streets remained unpaved, and animals
foraged through strewn garbage. Rather than spread across the two-mile width of the
city plan, Philadelphians clustered close to the Delaware River, near the bustle of
waterfront commerce.[13] By the 1720s, the heart of the city stood just two blocks inland,
at Second and High Streets, the location of the city's courthouse and principal market.
Young Benjamin Franklin encountered this crossroads when he arrived in the city
from Boston on October 6, 1723, at the age of seventeen. Walking into the city from the
wharf on the Delaware, he encountered a boy with bread near Second and High Streets,
then detoured onto Second Street in search of the bakery. The next day, Franklin
applied for work at Andrew Bradford's printing office on Second Street.[14] In addition to
being the business and governmental center, the Second and High Streets intersection *Market*
was a religious anchor of the city. On one corner stood the Friends Meeting House,
where Franklin fell asleep after walking through Philadelphia on his first day in town.
By the end of the decade, the new Christ Church—the Church of England—was under
construction on Second Street, just north of the courthouse.[15]

Locating a new State House within this urban environment presented challenges,
but also opportunity. The State House would have consequences beyond its function as
a meeting place for the Assembly. As a public gathering place, it would draw Philadelphians to whatever location was chosen. As the largest building in the city, the State
House would be the dominant example of architectural style and taste projected within Philadelphia and beyond. The site selection as well as the building's design once
again defined the State House as a place of cultural significance. Again, Andrew
Hamilton took the lead. Prevailing over vigorous argument to place the building at

Second and High Streets, Hamilton selected a slightly sloping, vegetation-covered site at the outskirts of the city, across the street from property he owned on Chestnut Street between Fifth and Sixth Streets.[16] Long before the arrival of William Penn, the site had been a camp for American Indians.[17] In the original surveys for the city, Penn's surveyors had drawn eight building lots on this block, but by the 1730s, only a few small houses existed on the south side, facing Walnut Street. When Hamilton's plan was endorsed by the Assembly, lots for the State House were acquired on the Chestnut Street side, facing north.[18] Through Hamilton's efforts, Pennsylvania gained a State House that was more suburban than urban, looking more like a gentleman's country seat than a house of state. As it took form beginning in 1732, the Pennsylvania State House projected to the world that proper British gentlemen remained at the helm of William Penn's province.

Although it seems ironic in hindsight, given the building's later association with American independence, the Pennsylvania State House of the eighteenth century was a memory of Great Britain made real on American soil. The State House embraced the transformation in British architecture that had occurred early in the eighteenth century, when British architects rediscovered Andrea Palladio, an Italian Renaissance architect. Turning to the architectural practices of ancient Rome, Palladio espoused principles of careful mathematical proportions and triadic arrangements of central buildings with flanking wings. Beauty, in Palladio's view, derived from the harmony of ideal forms. His principles were popularized in England through a translation of his *I Quattro Libri dell' Architettura* (*The Four Books of Architecture*) in 1715, and were transferred from there to the British colonies in America, where Palladian-style buildings became known as Georgian, corresponding with the reign of the British king. Traveling merchants (and lawyers like Andrew Hamilton) helped to transfer the style to America, as did James Gibbs's *Book of Architecture,* published in 1728 and widely used by American builders. In Philadelphia, the Carpenters' Company, a building trades guild founded in 1724, disseminated Georgian design principles among its members, who applied them to the homes, churches, and public buildings under construction throughout the city.[19]

Because the Pennsylvania State House has long been regarded as a leading example of public architecture in the Colonial period, it may be difficult to perceive the building as domestic in design. However, the building created in the 1730s lacked the brick tower and steeple that made the State House so distinctive for later generations. These were added between 1750 and 1753, then made widely recognizable by the

Scull and Heap map of Philadelphia. With a cupola instead of the tower and steeple, the State House plan attributed to Andrew Hamilton resembled the country houses for British nobility reproduced in Gibbs's *Book of Architecture*.[20] Within the British empire, such country houses functioned as symbols of power and wealth, identifying their owners as persons of high social standing and members of the ruling class.[21] With dimensions of nearly 107 by 45 feet, the Pennsylvania State House was by far the grandest house in Pennsylvania, more than twice the length of Stenton, the country house built in 1728 for James Logan, a high-ranking associate of the Penn family. Built to the scale of Gibbs's house designs, the State House reproduced the magnitude and style of British country houses. Like other provincial capitols built during the eighteenth century in Virginia, Maryland, and Massachusetts, the Pennsylvania State House projected a sense of order and purpose.[22] In the spirit of the eighteenth-century Enlightenment, its symmetry and ornament embodied reason, not emotion. It was stylish, but not ostentatious.

The project of creating a building from the plan approved by the Pennsylvania Assembly fell to Edmund Woolley, a master carpenter and member of the Carpenters' Company, well versed in Georgian architecture. Under Woolley's direction, beginning in 1732, laborers sunk a foundation of rubble stone and lime mortar into the sandy clay soil along Chestnut Street. Carpenters and masons then constructed the interior frame and exterior shell. The carpenters erected wooden girders and beams and framed interior walls and roof trusses. For every joint, they carved mortise holes into one piece of wood and corresponding tenons on the other. For the main girders, they reinforced joints with iron plates and pins. Meanwhile, the masons built the exterior shell from hard-burned brick laid in the Flemish bond pattern, twenty-two to twenty-three inches thick. Under the direction of the builder, covered walkways that Hamilton had sketched between the State House and its flanking wings became graceful, arched piazzas. The piazzas sheltered stairways that led to the second floor of the two wing buildings.[23]

The interior followed Hamilton's scheme. On the first floor, on either side of a central hall, the carpenters framed two rooms approximately forty feet square with ceilings twenty feet high. With a hallway nearly twenty feet wide in between, one room was designated for the Pennsylvania Assembly, the other for the provincial Supreme Court. The interior plan allowed the largest possible space for the Assembly Room, but in doing so, it created an awkward intersection between the interior hallway walls and the two exterior windows closest to the front door. As part of the builders' solution, the

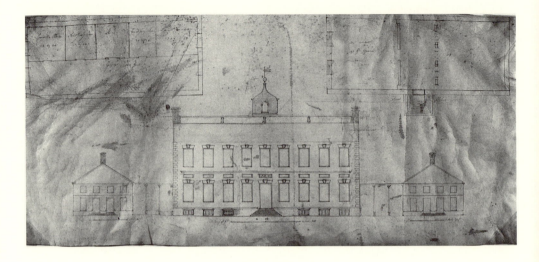

windows remained forever blind, visible on the exterior of the building, but hidden by the walls inside. Upstairs, the interior plan divided the second floor in half lengthwise, with a "long room" fronting Chestnut Street and the remaining space divided into chambers for the Provincial Council and committee meetings of the Assembly.[24]

The Pennsylvania Assembly moved into the State House in 1736, with construction still under way. In 1749, in the midst of a building boom brought on by the colony's continued growth, the Assembly called on Woolley once again, to "carry up a Building on the South-side" of the State House "to contain the Staircase, with a suitable Place thereon for hanging a Bell."[25] The resulting masonry tower, sixty-nine feet high with a wooden steeple rising still higher, replaced the cupola in Hamilton's design and transformed the appearance of the State House from a gentleman's country house to a public landmark.[26] With this addition, the State House had two distinctive facades, the original house-like facade facing Chestnut Street and a new, more church-like facade facing the State House yard. The tower and steeple resembled the church steeples of the time, as illustrated in Gibbs's *Book of Architecture*. Inside the State House, the new tower housed a grand staircase bathed in light from a large Palladian window, like the window of Christ Church on Second Street. The State House steeple provided a place for a new bell that the Assembly ordered from England. Isaac Norris, a successor to Hamilton as Speaker of the Pennsylvania Assembly, placed the order and specified that the bell be cast with a biblical inscription that later became viewed as prophetic: "Proclaim liberty thro' all the land to all the inhabitants thereof" (Leviticus 25:10). When the bell arrived, it cracked when tested and had to be recast twice to achieve a satisfactory tone.[27]

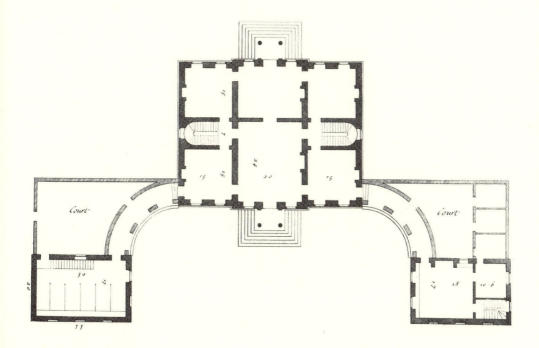

2. (*facing page*) A sketched plan for the Pennsylvania State House, attributed to Andrew Hamilton, directed builders to create a symmetrical, triadic structure in the Palladian architectural style, known in the American colonies as Georgian, after the British monarch. (Courtesy of the Historical Society of Pennsylvania)

3. (*above*) In style and scale, the Pennsylvania State House resembled the country houses which symbolized wealth, power, and social standing in Great Britain. The designs were known in the American colonies through *A Book of Architecture*, by James Gibbs, which included this house plan in 1728. (Courtesy of the Library Company of Philadelphia)

With its State House and fine churches, Philadelphia reassured visitors that European civilization had been successfully transplanted to America. Lord Adam Gordon, an officer of the Sixty-sixth Regiment of Foot, traveled through the colonies while stationed in the West Indies from 1764 to 1765. Passing through Philadelphia, he admired "the regularity of its Streets, their great breadth and length, their cutting one another at right Angles, their Spacious publick and private buildings, Quays and Docks, the Magnificence and diversity of places of Worship." He considered Philadelphia "the first Town in America, but one that bids fair to rival almost any in Europe."[28] Another visitor from England in the late 1760s noted, "Their public buildings make a good appearance, many of which are not to be exceeded in this country. . . . The State House is a noble edifice, with two wings, one of which is for the reception of the friendly Indians when they come down from the woods."[29]

The State House changed the physical and social geography of Philadelphia, exerting a westward pull on the activities of government, commerce, and civic life. While William Penn's original plan for the city had designated five public squares, by the 1770s the State House had become the site of a sixth, as the Assembly acquired the entire block around the building and enclosed the square with a seven-foot-high brick wall.[30] Although the Assembly considered creating a park in front of the State House as well, the property across Chestnut Street developed instead into a cluster of taverns and stables. The presence of the State House transformed one of these buildings, a small two-story tavern built in the 1690s, from a travelers' wayside to a gathering place for entertainment and discussions of politics and commerce. By 1736, Evan Powel operated this tavern under the Sign of the Thistle and Crown, and by 1738, Henry Clark had renamed it the Coach and Horses. Along with other businesses and property owners near the new State House, Powel and Clark acknowledged the importance of the building by advertising their proximity to it in the *Pennsylvania Gazette*.[31] The new State House, conceived as a sign of British culture, quickly became a social and political landmark for a growing American city.

Building on the Enlightenment: Government, Religion, and Science

The Pennsylvania State House was emblematic of its time, both in its architecture and in the activities that took place in and around the building. The intellectual currents of the Enlightenment, emanating from Europe, flowed in and around the State House. Even the site of the building, on the undeveloped fringe of the city, presented a near equivalent of John Locke's conception of the mind—a blank slate, to be defined only by the experiences and sensations of life. For four decades before 1776, when the Declaration of Independence captured the essence of Enlightenment thought to define a new nation, the Enlightenment animated the State House and its surroundings. Just as the State House stood at the edge of the growing city of Philadelphia, activities in and around the building pushed at the frontiers of human understanding in science, government, and religion. Old ideas withered, sometimes slowly and painfully, while new ideas took root. Within an urban setting, the effervescent ideals of liberty and self-determination coexisted with the realities of imprisonment, slavery, and servitude.[32]

The events of the American Revolution created for later generations an image of the State House as a sedate meeting place for serious, white-wigged gentlemen. But at this public building of the eighteenth century and in the space around it, people from all walks of life met and mingled. There were assemblymen, but also doorkeepers and attendants such as Mary Burden, who earned £5 in 1753 for sweeping and airing the rooms. There were Englishmen, but also Indian chiefs who came to negotiate treaties and visiting foreign dignitaries, including a sheik from Syria. Lawyers came to the courts, but so did their clients, the accused criminals. One of the convicted, John Holland, was branded in the hand at the State House as punishment for manslaughter. The State House was the scene of brilliant parties, but also gory spectacles, such as the display of the bodies of two men and a boy that were brought into the city dead, scalped by Indians. People gathered in the streets outside the State House to hear the winning numbers drawn in city lotteries. They also came for religious purposes, to attend the Philadelphia Yearly Meeting in 1751 and to hear the introduction of Methodism to the city in 1769, when the Reverend Joseph Pilmore preached from the steps of the State House on a mission from John Wesley.[33]

In this building that reflected the architectural style of Great Britain, Americans also participated in the intellectual transformation that had occurred among educated elites in western Europe. By the early eighteenth century, learned Europeans on both sides of the Atlantic viewed scientific knowledge as the key to understanding and improving the world. Not limited to the laboratory, the scientific revolution permeated the culture of Europe and the Americas with the conviction that human knowledge and reason could overturn long-held assumptions. The language of science, stressing the laws of nature, provided a foundation for Enlightenment philosophies of society and government. Within this cultural context, science and politics coexisted easily in and around the Pennsylvania State House.[34]

Although built for the Pennsylvania Assembly, the State House accommodated two of the leading learned societies of the American colonies—the Library Company of Philadelphia, which occupied the west wing from 1739 through 1772, and the American Philosophical Society, which held a series of meetings in the State House in 1768.[35] Like similar societies in Europe, these organizations promoted Enlightenment culture among the educated elite in the American colonies.[36] The Library Company, devoted to science and philosophy, grew to include a museum of natural history and a collection of the latest scientific apparatus. Both the Library Company and the Philosophical Society sponsored scientific lectures and experiments. In 1752, for example, Ebenezer Kinnersley performed a series of electrical experiments at the State House; he charged a half-dollar for each lecture and limited his audience to twenty people at a time.[37] In 1762, Doctor William Shippen, Jr., offered an introductory anatomy lecture, using anatomical paintings from London to teach medical students unable to go abroad for training and "for the entertainment of any Gentlemen, who may have the Curiosity to understand the Anatomy of the Human Frame." Such events at the State House extended scientific knowledge to a somewhat broader public of specially interested individuals with sufficient money for admission and leisure time to attend.[38]

As an ongoing pursuit at the State House, science interacted with government. Benjamin Franklin was among the most prominent Pennsylvanians to cross between the worlds of science and politics, but many others took active roles in the scientific community as well as the provincial government. As in Europe, Pennsylvania's scientific societies operated with official patronage. Governor John Penn provided the Library Company with equipment from Europe, including a precious air pump for conducting experiments with air pressure.[39] In 1769, the Pennsylvania Assembly appropriated funds for a telescope to allow scientists to participate in the international effort to observe the transit of Venus moving across the background of the sun. Reinforcing the connection between government and science, the telescope financed by the Pennsylvania Assembly tracked the transit of Venus from an observatory constructed in the State House yard.[40]

Foremost, the State House was a center of politics where Pennsylvanians defined their relationship with the governing Penn family and their place within the British empire. In the middle decades of the eighteenth century, well before the convening of a Continental Congress, the State House echoed with themes later associated with the American Revolution—the struggle for control of government, for example, and arguments over liberty and power. For four decades before the Declaration of Independence, Pennsylvanians struggled over issues of individual conscience, the collective needs of a colony, and their strained relationship with the Penn family proprietors. Acknowledging this earlier, provincial history, the State House can be seen as a stage for a series of revolutionary changes, beginning with a wrenching transition from Quaker to non-Quaker control of Pennsylvania.

The Assemblies that convened in the State House in the middle decades of the eighteenth century were predominantly Quaker, sustaining the Quaker leadership that had dominated the colony since the days of William Penn. However, the needs of a growing province provoked a crisis of conscience that reflected the questioning of authority which characterized the Enlightenment era. The Quakers were pacifists, but they were subjects of an empire battling France for control of North America. They were lawmakers for a province in which Europeans and Native Americans clashed on the western frontier. How could Quakers in good conscience raise armies for the king or for domestic defense? Indeed, they could not. In the room where the Second Continental Congress later debated independence, Quaker assemblymen argued bitterly that duty to their religious conscience outweighed demands from their proprietary governors or even the British king. Ultimately, the conflict pushed many out of the Pennsylvania Assembly. In 1756, ten Quakers resigned their seats. Although Quakers did not retire entirely from government, political domination of the province shifted into non-Quaker hands.[41]

During the eighteenth century, Pennsylvanians also struggled to define their place within the British empire. They filled the State House with declarations of their rights to liberty, but ironically, given later events, they sought greater unity with Great Britain, not separation. Pennsylvanians gathered in the Long Room of the State House for elegant parties toasting the health of King George II or celebrating British military victories over France, but they chafed under the proprietary control of the Penn family. Several times during the decades before the American Revolution, the Assembly pursued the possibility of making Pennsylvania a crown colony, rather than a possession of the descendants of William Penn. This campaign reached its height in the 1760s even as resistance to British authority was growing in other colonies and among the lower and middle ranks of Pennsylvanians. In 1764, led by Benjamin Franklin and Joseph Galloway, antiproprietary assemblymen conducted an intense public relations campaign that emanated from the State House into the countryside through newspaper reporting and pamphleteering.[42]

In this odd juxtaposition of events, the political vocabulary of the Enlightenment animated the arguments of both the antiproprietary movement and the emerging resistance to British authority. Embracing language that came to represent one of the great contradictions of the American Revolution, both movements framed their protests with the opposition of "liberty" and "slavery"—"slavery" referring to their own loss of independence to an excess of power, not to the condition of African slaves. In a mass meeting in the State House yard in 1764, in the midst of the antiproprietary campaign, Galloway exhorted fellow Pennsylvanians to embrace "Royal Liberty" rather than "Proprietary Slavery." The contrasting use of "liberty" and "slavery" also appeared in arguments against British taxation, including the famous *Letters from a Farmer in Pennsylvania*, written in 1767 and 1768 by Galloway's colleague John Dickinson. In his letters, Dickinson argued that taxation without representation constituted slavery for British subjects in America.[43] As Pennsylvanians simultaneously confronted British taxation and their own place within the empire, the State House echoed with Enlightenment philosophy, marshaled for different purposes.

In the four decades that preceded the Declaration of Independence, the Pennsylvania State House and the city growing around it reflected not only the achievements of the Enlightenment but also its limitations.[44] Although Enlightenment thinkers promoted the ideas of freedom that ignited the American Revolution, most continued to accept fundamental inequalities within society. Enlightenment-era concern with order and subordination could be seen in the urban landscape of Philadelphia, especially in the new Walnut Street Jail built in the early 1770s in the block south of the State House. Like its neighbor, the prison was built in the Georgian style by a member of the Carpenters' Company, but it was much larger than the State House. The prison, built of cut stone rather than brick, extended 184 feet along Walnut Street with wings 90 feet southward on both ends. Through the barred windows, inmates would extend baskets and caps at the ends of long poles to beg food from passersby. Through those windows, prisoners had a view of events that promoted liberty for the British colonies in America.[45]

Degrees of freedom and servitude also were apparent in the city's working population, which included indentured servants and African American slaves. Many members of the Pennsylvania Assembly had owned at least one slave at some point in their lives.[46] Indentured servants and slaves worked in the taverns on Chestnut Street across from the State House. Freedom could be seized in these circumstances, but it could also be lost. In 1738, a forty-year-old Irish servant named Margaret McClenny staged a personal revolution by running away from the Chestnut Street tavern of Henry Clark, who offered twenty shillings reward for her return. In 1761 and 1762, Thomas Lennon, identifying himself by location "opposite the State House" offered for sale first "a hearty Negroe wench, very fit for Town or Country Business" and later four years' service by "a servant lad . . . strong and healthy, very fit for a Farmer."[47] The indentured laborers, prisoners, and slaves of eighteenth-century Philadelphia comprised an urban environment which contrasted sharply with events that we have come to associate with the building later known as Independence Hall.

Revolution in the Streets, Conflict in the Corridors

We hold these truths to be self-evident; that all men are created equal, that they are endowed by their Creator with certain unalienable Rights, that among these are Life, Liberty, and the pursuit of Happiness.—That to secure these rights, Governments are instituted among Men, deriving their just powers from the consent of the governed,— That whenever any Form of Government becomes destructive of these ends, it is the Right of the People to alter or to abolish it.

From the Declaration of Independence (1776)

Thomas Jefferson's words in the Declaration of Independence, approved by the Second Continental Congress at the Pennsylvania State House on July 4, 1776, captured the essence of Enlightenment philosophy. Jefferson himself acknowledged that this fusion of political philosophy, science, religion, and individual rights did not spring from his pen alone, but rather captured the "harmonizing sentiments of the day."[48] In this sense, the Declaration of Independence represented continuity with activities at the Pennsylvania State House in the previous four decades. But in many other ways, of course, the Declaration of Independence marked a point of departure. Most significantly, thirteen British colonies broke from Great Britain and formed an independent nation. To the delegates meeting at the State House, the document's opening flourish of philosophy was less significant (and less dangerous) than its list of grievances against the king, which formed the justification for independence. However, the opening lines of the Declaration of Independence presented the new United States with a set of guiding ideals.[49] As the place that echoed such powerful dedication to life, liberty, and the pursuit of happiness, the Pennsylvania State House was forever changed, marked as a place where Americans could celebrate, challenge, and redefine the founding ideals as the nation grew.

The Declaration of Independence was a singular event in the history of the nation, and the Second Continental Congress gathered together the leading men of the age—Thomas Jefferson and Richard Henry Lee of Virginia, John Hancock and John Adams of Massachusetts, Benjamin Franklin and John Dickinson of Pennsylvania were among the fifty-five delegates who came to be regarded as the nation's founding

4. Although not begun until 1785, John Trumbull's *Declaration of Independence* created a lasting image of the significance of the State House in the American Revolution. Like other artists of his time, Trumbull valued accuracy in his portraits of the signers more than authenticity in his portrayal of the State House interior. (Courtesy of Yale University Art Gallery)

fathers. However, if our perception of the Pennsylvania State House during the American Revolution is limited to the actions of the Second Continental Congress, we fail to recognize the complex struggle that gave birth to the nation.[50] The Continental Congress met inside the State House, but so did the Pennsylvania Assembly, dominated by conservatives who opposed independence from Great Britain. Men of high social rank constituted both the Assembly and the Continental Congress, but while they deliberated in the State House, people of lower and middle rank demonstrated in the State House yard and created a revolutionary movement that challenged established authority. The landmark State House in Philadelphia gathered these activities together, forcing them into interaction, into conflict, and eventually to a resolution that changed the course of history.

The American Revolution grew from social as well as political conflict, particularly in port cities such as Philadelphia. In these cities, with rapidly growing populations and increasing gaps between rich and poor, economic conditions politicized people who were far removed from the usual practice of colonial politics.[51] While the Pennsylvania Assembly during the 1760s sought unity with Great Britain and tried to quell disorder, lower- and middle-ranking Philadelphians joined their counterparts in other colonies in a growing resistance to British policies. In the process, the State House yard became contested ground which surrounded the Assembly but also served as a forum for public dissent. Demonstrations in Philadelphia were tame in comparison to Boston, the cauldron of American radicalism, but nevertheless they brought as many as eight thousand people at a time to the State House yard. Crowds packed into the square to protest the series of taxes levied by Great Britain on the colonies: the Stamp Act, the Townshend Revenue Acts, and the Tea Act. In 1765, a mass meeting at the State House dispatched a committee to demand that the Stamp Act commissioner resign (he did not, but agreed to postpone his duties until neighboring colonies began to enforce the act). Under pressure from mechanics and artisans, reluctant Philadelphia merchants gathered at the State House to sign nonimportation agreements to protest the Townshend duties on glass, lead, paint, paper, and tea. Philadelphians massed at the State House again in 1773 to decide on a response to the arrival of a shipment of British tea. They sent instructions to the ship captain to sail away (he did).[52]

At the State House, a crossroads for Philadelphians of divergent social classes, resistance to taxation coexisted with a continuing allegiance to Great Britain. When news of the repeal of the Stamp Act arrived in Philadelphia in May 1766, the city's leading citizens celebrated at a grand dinner at the State House, where they toasted the king and queen to the sounds of cannon salutes in the State House yard. In 1773, as Philadelphians were objecting to the Tea Act, provincial leaders gave a testimonial dinner at the State House for Thomas Penn, the departing governor of Pennsylvania. At the banquet, the diners raised their glasses to the British monarch while a brass band played "God Save the King." Among twenty toasts, the Philadelphians drank to "Prosperity to and Unanimity between Great Britain and the Colonies," "The British Navy and Army," and "General Gage." There followed, however, a toast to "The Friends of American Freedom."[53]

By 1774, when the American conflict with Great Britain reached new heights with the Boston Tea Party and the subsequent closing of Boston Harbor by the British, the lower and middle ranks of Pennsylvanians had gained sufficient political experience to challenge the authority of the conservative Assembly. Following the closing of Boston Harbor, Paul Revere rode into Philadelphia on May 19, carrying a message that asked Pennsylvania to join in a unified response to British policies. Pennsylvanians waited for a month for their new governor, John Penn, to call the Assembly into session to consider such action. When he refused, thousands of people gathered in the State House yard on June 18. Acting outside the governmental structure of the colony, the mass meeting called upon Pennsylvania counties to organize committees of correspondence and to send representatives to a convention in Philadelphia in July. Like other colonies where governors had suspended representative assemblies, Pennsylvanians now had an extralegal government to organize resistance to the British. Unlike other colonies, the extralegal government in Pennsylvania acted not in place of the legal Assembly, but in opposition to it. While many members of the Pennsylvania Assembly clung to the hope of reconciliation, new political leaders emerged in the extralegal convention, which in July 1774 drew seventy-five delegates to Carpenters' Hall, two blocks from the State House.[54]

Relations with Great Britain remained a point of contention within the legally constituted Assembly. Revolutionary forces gained sufficient strength in the Assembly to add Pennsylvania's support for calling a Continental Congress to deliberate responses to British policies.[55] Still, the pro-British Joseph Galloway remained Speaker of the Assembly, and the legislators ignored the extralegal convention's instructions for delegates to the Congress and its suggestions for who should represent Pennsylvania. The Assembly remained so adverse to conflict with Great Britain that the First Continental Congress declined to meet in the State House when it convened in Philadelphia in September 1774.[56] Reflecting the continued divided sentiment in Pennsylvania, the First Continental Congress met at Carpenters' Hall, but the delegates were entertained at the

State House in the style to which Philadelphians had become accustomed. Five hundred people attended a welcoming dinner on September 16, 1774; music, toasts, and cannon salutes honored the occasion. In keeping with precedent, the toasts began with the king, the queen, and the prince of Wales. As the toasts progressed, the new political dynamics that arrived in Philadelphia with the Congress also became clear: "Perpetual Union to the Colonies"; "Much injured town of Boston"; and "May Great Britain be just and America free." But just as the First Continental Congress did not take the final step of declaring independence, toasts also offered hope of a continued union: "A happy reconciliation between Great Britain and her Colonies, on a constitutional ground."[57]

Between the First Continental Congress and the convening of the Second Congress in May 1775, opposition to Great Britain intensified in the public space around the State House more than in the legislative chambers inside. The first shots of the War for Independence, fired in the Battle of Lexington on April 19, 1775, prompted another massive gathering in the State House yard. Called together by the bells of the city, thousands of people met "to consider the measures to be pursued in the present critical situation of the affairs of America," the *Pennsylvania Gazette* reported the next day. Speakers roused the crowd. Without waiting for action by the Assembly, "the company unanimously agreed to associate for the purpose of defending with ARMS their property, liberty and lives, against all attempts to deprive them of them."[58] Soldiers began to drill in open spaces everywhere around the city, including the State House yard. Men unfamiliar with firearms learned to use them. Men unaccustomed to military discipline learned to march in formation. While the Assembly once again stood adjourned, the yard outside the seat of the provincial government became a place characterized by shouting, sweat, gunfire, and dust.[59]

The Pennsylvania State House gained its opportunity for a lasting place in American history in May 1775 with the arrival of the Second Continental Congress in Philadelphia. This time, with Galloway no longer occupying the speaker's chair in the Assembly, the Congress agreed to meet in the State House.[60] For the next year, with fighting under way between the Americans and the British in New England, the Second Continental Congress and the Pennsylvania Assembly shared Pennsylvania's capitol building.[61] Although disagreeing on the prospect of breaking from Great Britain, delegates and assemblymen had ample opportunity to interact within the State House. From time to time, formal communications passed from one body to the other. Delegates to Congress and members of the Assembly could cross paths in the central hallway. At the State House, members of either group might encounter Governor Penn, who met periodically with representatives of the Assembly on the second floor to tend to the routine business of the province.[62]

The sequence of events in the Second Continental Congress is well known: John Hancock of Massachusetts presided, and the delegates selected George Washington of Virginia to be commander in chief of the Continental Army. For nearly a year, the Congress wrestled with the question of independence. Then, in June 1776, Richard Henry Lee of Virginia offered a resolution for independence from Great Britain. A committee including Thomas Jefferson—another Virginian—retired to draft the Declaration of Independence. On July 2, 1776, the Congress took the definitive step of resolving to separate from Great Britain. Two days later, on the Fourth of July, the delegates amended and accepted Jefferson's declaration. Then, on July 8, Philadelphia Sheriff John Nixon stepped onto a platform in the State House yard to read the Declaration to the public. Philadelphians gathered in the square, as they had so many times before, at the sound of the bells of the city—perhaps including the State House bell, but perhaps not, given the structural deterioration of the State House steeple by 1776.[63]

As significant as this narrative of the Continental Congress is, it is only part of the story of the Pennsylvania State House and its place in the American Revolution. In retrospect, knowing that the collective action of the colonies created the United States of America, the actions in the Assembly Room rightfully dominate our perception. However, these actions took place in a statehouse, and the emerging states of the union were the laboratories of revolution.[64] The Pennsylvania State House served as a stage for national events, but it also functioned as workshop for breaking away from England and establishing an independent state.

To the aggravation of the more radical members of the Congress, the Pennsylvania Assembly in 1775 and early 1776 remained dominated by members with strong allegiance to Britain.[65] At the outset of the Second Continental Congress, the Assembly instructed Pennsylvania's delegates to take actions that would best restore "Union and Harmony between Great-Britain and the Colonies."[66] As conflict intensified during 1775, the Congress began to talk of independence, but the Assembly insisted on reconciliation. Even though American and British troops were at war, the Assembly instructed its delegates to "dissent from, and utterly reject, any Proposition . . . that may cause, or lead to, a Separation from our Mother Country, or a Change in the Form of this Government."[67]

The tension between the Congress and the Assembly reached a breaking point on May 15, 1776. On that day, in an action that John Adams called "the most important resolution that was ever taken in America," the Congress recommended that the colonies should form new governments if their present governments were not "sufficient to the exigencies of their affairs."[68] Within the walls of the Pennsylvania State House, the action meant that the Congress had invited the extralegal government of Pennsylvania to replace the Assembly meeting upstairs.[69] With the leaders of Pennsylvania's committees of correspondence laying groundwork for a new state government and with rising public sentiment for independence, the Assembly could no longer resist the pressure to change its instructions to Pennsylvania's representatives in the Congress. Still, it was not until June 1776, as Richard Henry Lee offered the resolution that "these united colonies are, and of right ought to be, free and independent states," that Pennsylvania removed its order for its delegates to oppose independence. The Assembly conceded, "All Hopes of a Reconciliation, on reasonable Terms, are extinguished."[70] But even then, the instructions left it up to the delegates to vote for independence or not, as they chose. Pennsylvania cast its vote for independence only when two members of the delegation abstained from voting and two others stayed away. The remaining three—Benjamin Franklin, James Wilson, and John Morton—decided the question for Pennsylvania.[71]

The Declaration of Independence for the United States also triggered the culmination of the internal revolution in Pennsylvania. The Pennsylvania Assembly did not officially adjourn until the following September, but the work of creating a new state government began in the State House on July 15 with the convening of the Pennsylvania Constitutional Convention, an outgrowth of the extralegal committees of correspondence that had been active for the last two years. Signifying the revolution that had occurred in Pennsylvania politics, many of the convention delegates were farmers, artisans, or soldiers, with only a few delegates of the type of gentlemen who previously occupied the Assembly. Now, seated in the State House, the convention not only worked on the constitution, but also acted as the governing authority of Pennsylvania. The convention issued orders for military defenses and gave new instructions to the state's delegates to Congress: "The present necessity of a vigorous exertion of the United force of the Free States of America, against our British Enemies, is the most important object of your immediate regard."[72] Stripped of its power, the old Pennsylvania Assembly came back to the State House briefly in August and September to attend to routine financial matters upstairs while the convention and the Continental Congress met below. But from July onward, revolutionary governments at the Pennsylvania State House wielded authority for both state and nation.[73]

In an action seldom memorialized by later generations who preserved the building where it occurred, the Pennsylvania Constitutional Convention of 1776 enacted the most radically democratic constitution of all the thirteen states in the union. Officers of the convention began by pledging to "oppose the tyrannical proceedings of the king and Parliament of Great Britain against the American Colonies and support a government in the Province on the authority of the people only."[74] Before considering a new frame of government, the convention first drafted a bill of rights to protect individual liberties against encroachment by government authority. Based in part on an earlier bill of rights written for Virginia, and similar to the later Bill of Rights added to the federal Constitution, "A Declaration of the Rights of the Inhabitants of the Commonwealth of Pennsylvania" has remained ever since part of the state's constitution.[75]

Among the thirteen new state constitutions, Pennsylvania's took the most democratic stance in extending the vote, granting authority to the legislature, and limiting the power of the executive. The constitution ended property qualifications for voting and granted suffrage to all freemen who had been residents and taxpayers in Pennsylvania for at least one year. To safeguard against accumulations of political power, it established annual elections for representatives to a unicameral Assembly. Instead of a governor, an elected Supreme Executive Council held executive authority. At least once every seven years, an elected Council of Censors would convene to review the effectiveness of the rest of the government. Even with the War for Independence in full force, and with the Continental Congress meeting across the hall, the Pennsylvania Constitution of 1776 was controversial from the start. The convention proclaimed it in force without putting it to a public vote, and twenty-three of the convention's ninety-six delegates refused to sign it. Its radicalism provoked a strong reaction in Philadelphia, reviving and strengthening Loyalist sentiment and opening a chasm that defined state and local politics for more than a decade.[76]

In its exuberance for liberty, the new Pennsylvania government also addressed the most blatant contradiction of the Revolutionary era: the persistence of slavery in a new nation founded on the ideals of liberty. Thomas Jefferson, a slaveholder, had blamed Great Britain for slavery in his original draft of the Declaration of Independence, but the issue proved too volatile for the Second Continental Congress, which struck out that paragraph. Still, the contradiction was clear, prompting increasing numbers of Americans to free their slaves, especially in the North. Slaves also pursued their own liberty by fighting for independence or by crossing British lines to claim promises of freedom in exchange for fighting against the Americans. At the Pennsyl-

5. Although published in 1778 in the midst of the American Revolution, this view of the State House offers no clues to the conflicts of the era. The engraving by James Trenchard, based on a drawing by Charles Willson Peale, appeared in the *Columbian Magazine*. (Courtesy of the Library Company of Philadelphia)

vania State House in 1780, taking another step in extending the ideals of the Declaration of Independence, the state Assembly passed America's first law ordering the abolition of slavery. It was a gradual abolition law, however, freeing no slave immediately. Freedom was granted only to the children born to slaves after March 1, 1780, and even those children were not to be freed until they reached the age of twenty-eight. As a result, Pennsylvania did not achieve total abolition until 1847. Despite the gradualism of the law, Pennsylvania voters responded by sweeping its supporters out of office in the Assembly elections of 1780.[77]

Throughout the War for Independence, Pennsylvania's political disputes coexisted with the dangers of warfare, especially the advance of British troops toward Philadelphia. In 1777, Congress, the Assembly, and many of the city's inhabitants fled. That September, British troops defeated the Americans at Brandywine, southwest of Philadelphia. Soon after, Philadelphians could hear British artillery pounding at Fort Mifflin, which stood south of the city on an island in the Delaware River. Anticipating

British occupation, they spirited away the bells of the city, including the State House bell, lest they fall into enemy hands. General William Howe and his army occupied Philadelphia, including the State House, from September 1777 until June 1778. While redcoats camped in the State House yard, wounded British and American soldiers were dumped inside the building to await the attention of surgeons. Indicative of conditions inside the State House, soldiers of the British Royal Artillery had to be ordered not to urinate in the stairways. American officers were jailed on the second floor. Their conditions were at least better than prisoners of lower rank, who were imprisoned behind the State House in the Walnut Street Jail. From the State House windows, the officers could see bodies being carted from the disease-ridden prison to the nearby potter's burial ground.[78]

By the time the British left Philadelphia, a devastated city lay behind. Everywhere, the city was "excessively Dirty & disagreeable," one returning Philadelphian observed. Houses had been converted to barracks, and the city's usual street-cleaning practices had been suspended. Conditions were especially bad at the State House, where the British "had opened a large square pit near the State House, a receptacle for filth, into which they had also cast dead horses and the bodies of men."[79] The State House had lost any luster that it might have had in the heady days of the Declaration of Independence. Soldiers had trampled and littered the yard. The steeple was rotting into ruin. The stench of the place, inside and out, kept Congress away until the building could be thoroughly cleaned.[80]

As the city recovered, the State House regained its standing as a place of protest and celebration. In protest, Philadelphians gathered to demand government action against high wartime prices. In celebration, they came to hear the news of the British surrender to George Washington's army at Yorktown in 1781. Even after the war, the State House yard remained an arena for attracting the attention of government and townspeople. In 1783, long after the surrender of the British, soldiers of the Pennsylvania Line marched on the State House to demand pay from the Supreme Executive Council of Pennsylvania. The drunken row that resulted prompted Congress to move its meetings from Philadelphia to Princeton and to stay away for the next seven years.[81]

Constitutions: Wrestling with Democracy

We the People of the United States, in Order to form a more perfect
Union, establish Justice, insure domestic Tranquility, provide for the
common defense, promote the general Welfare, and secure the Bless-
ings of Liberty to ourselves and our Posterity, do ordain and establish
this Constitution for the United States of America.

Preamble to the Constitution (1787)

The American Revolution had been waged on the principle of republicanism—a belief that effective government depended on virtuous leaders who could subordinate self-interest to the public good, thereby assuring a necessary balance between liberty and power. Too much liberty could lead to a collapse of public order; too great a concentration of power could breed corruption and conspiracy. Americans' grievances against Great Britain had been driven by the conviction that the British Parliament had become corrupt, exercising excessive power by levying taxes on the colonies. When King George III did not respond to the Americans' appeals, he too was seen as corrupt, drawn into a conspiracy that ruined the balance of power among British commoners, nobility, and the sovereign. Condemning excessive power, Americans fought for liberty. Gaining liberty, however, they faced their own challenge of balancing their hard-won freedom with the need to maintain order in the new United States. In the Pennsylvania State House during the 1770s, the balance tipped toward the greatest degree of liberty—the Pennsylvania Constitution of 1776 granted widespread democracy, and the Articles of Confederation drafted by the Continental Congress linked the former colonies in loose cooperation rather than binding them to a strong central government. Once the War for Independence ended, Americans found that building a nation involved a continuing struggle to frame state and national governments with sufficient power to maintain public order, but power sufficiently limited to ensure the people's liberty.[82]

The quest for order in the 1780s extended to landscapes and buildings scarred by damage and neglect during the Revolution. In Philadelphia, the new Pennsylvania Assembly acted to restore a sense of serenity to the State House yard, which had been defined by the prewar Assembly as "a public open green and walk for ever." In 1784, the Assembly hired Samuel Vaughan, a merchant recently arrived from England, to landscape the war-torn square. Vaughan created a genteel park with gravel walks, Windsor benches, and garden seats of red cedar. When spring arrived in 1785, he planted more than one hundred elm trees, nearly that many holly bushes, and a lawn of clover.[83] "When thus improved, it became a place of general resort as a delightful promenade," an early historian of Philadelphia recorded. "It was something in itself altogether unprecedented, in a public way, in the former simpler habits of our citizens."[84] In place of the protest ground and military camp of earlier years, Vaughan installed a landscape intended for quiet repose. Lawns and trees transformed a place of war into a haven of peace.

Although the State House yard assumed a pastoral appearance, construction projects in the 1780s and early 1790s defined the space as a urban square. One project involved demolition: the State House steeple erected in the 1750s had irretrievably deteriorated, and so was taken down in 1781, six years before the federal Constitutional Convention convened. The other construction projects produced new buildings for the square, increasing its centrality in the public life of Philadelphia. For the east side, facing Fifth Street, Vaughan designed a building for the American Philosophical Society, ensuring the continuing presence of scientific inquiry near the State House. Construction began in 1785 and continued for the next four years. Meanwhile, on either side of the State House facing Chestnut Street, the city and county governments of Philadelphia acted on long-delayed plans for a county courthouse (1787–89) and City Hall (1790–91).[85] To build the courthouse, the Walnut Street Jail supplied convict laborers, who were distinguished from the general population by their shaved heads and clothing made distinctive by mismatched sleeves and pants legs of red and green, black and white, or blue and yellow.[86] The new buildings, brick and symmetrical, harmonized with the State House but featured the more delicate architectural detail of the Federal style.[87]

The political landscape proved more difficult to define, for the nation as well as the state of Pennsylvania. For the nation, weaknesses in the Articles of Confederation and a perceived threat to public order after Shays's Rebellion in Massachusetts spurred a movement for a stronger national government. Meanwhile, Pennsylvanians hotly debated constitutional issues raised by their 1776 constitution. Throughout the 1780s, critics argued for a greater balance of powers and a stronger state executive. As in the American Revolution, the Pennsylvania State House brought the controversies of state and nation together. The Philadelphia Convention of 1787, which convened at the State House to amend the Articles of Confederation but which ultimately produced a new U.S. Constitution, took place in the milieu of Pennsylvania politics. Opponents of the Pennsylvania constitution formed arguments that contributed to drafting the new federal constitution. The ratification of the federal constitution, in turn, helped Pennsylvanians overturn the 1776 constitution in favor of a less radical document in 1790.[88]

Like the narrative of the Declaration of Independence, the sequence of events during the Constitutional Convention has become a well-known chapter in American history. The delegates arrived in Philadelphia in May 1787 and selected George Washington to preside. Meeting behind closed doors in the Assembly Room of the State House, they soon abandoned the Articles of Confederation and instead began to draft an entirely new frame of government. They wrestled with balancing the interests of small states and large states. They developed a system of checks and balances among the legislative, executive, and judicial branches of government; they created a two-house legislature and a chief executive elected not by popular vote, but by electors chosen by the voters. Without mentioning slavery explicitly, the new Constitution affirmed its existence by providing for the return of fugitives, allowing the slave trade to continue until 1808, and counting three-fifths of persons who were not free in determining a state's population (and, therefore, its strength in the House of Representatives). In place of the loose union of states under the Articles of Confederation, the convention created a strong national government.[89]

In many ways, the U.S. Constitution that emerged from the federal convention was the opposite of the Pennsylvania Constitution of 1776, with its powerful one-house Assembly and executive committee. As a result, the proposed federal Constitution, approved on September 17, 1787, quickly became a new flash point for conflict within the Pennsylvania State House.[90] Would Pennsylvania ratify the new federal Constitution, which had been drafted within the walls of its own State House? Even mustering enough votes in the Assembly to call a ratifying convention required force. Members who supported the Pennsylvania Constitution of 1776 tried to block the new federal document by staying away from the Assembly and preventing the quorum necessary to call the ratifying convention. To break the deadlock, a band of determined Federalists led by naval Commodore John Barry tracked the absent assemblymen to their boardinghouse on Sixth Street and by force escorted two of them to the State House. In this manner, the Assembly mustered its quorum and called a ratifying convention for November.[91]

Conflict and even violence continued when the ratifying convention convened. Supporters of the federal Constitution attacked the Sixth Street boardinghouse once again before the convention began, breaking windows and pounding on the house as a warning to their opponents lodged inside. Angry crowds also shouted at and bombarded homes of others known to support the 1776 state constitution and thus oppose the far different federal document.[92] At the State House from November 21 to December 12, 1787, spectators packed into the Assembly Room and the hall to witness the debates over ratification. Delegates argued the merits of the new federal Constitution and, implicitly, issues that had consumed Pennsylvania politics for more than a decade. Was a balanced, two-house legislature preferable to a more powerful, single-house Assembly? Was a single executive preferable to distributing executive power to a committee? Furthermore, should a constitution include guarantees of the people's rights? Like anti-Federalists elsewhere, Pennsylvania opponents of the federal document decried its lack of a bill of rights. A guarantee of individual rights had been a priority when Pennsylvania's constitution was drafted in 1776. Within the federal convention, however, delegates felt that it was not necessary to define individual rights because the Constitution allowed the federal government only those powers explicitly stated in the document.

In the end, the absence of a bill of rights did not stop ratification in Pennsylvania. The political factions that had battled over constitutional issues since 1776 dictated the vote: forty-six votes in favor of the new federal Constitution, and twenty-three against. With that, Pennsylvania became the second state to ratify the U.S. Constitution.[93] A Grand Federal Procession marched through Philadelphia on July 4, 1788, appropriating Independence Day for a celebration of ratification that betrayed none of the preceding controversy. After the procession, Federalists memorialized the new frame of government by depositing the *Union*, a ship which had been pulled as a float in the parade, at the front door of the State House.[94] Within two years, opponents of the Pennsylvania Constitution of 1776 overhauled the structure of state government that they had long despised. In its place, the Pennsylvania Constitution of 1790 established a bicameral legislature and a governor with the power to veto legislation and make government appointments. Resembling the federal constitution in these respects, the new state plan retained widespread male suffrage and, with minor changes, the Declaration of Rights from 1776.[95]

The achievements of the Second Continental Congress in 1776 and the Constitutional Convention in 1787 have traditionally defined Independence Hall as a historic landmark. Undeniably, these proceedings placed the Pennsylvania State House in the spotlight of the nation's history. However, looking back on events at the State House during the eighteenth century, we also find that a great deal of history has become detached from the building. Topics such as the social conflict of the American Revolution, the political history of Pennsylvania, the role of science in the Enlightenment, and the contentious process of ratifying the U.S. Constitution are familiar to scholars who specialize in eighteenth-century history. However, these aspects of history have become obscured at the place where they occurred. Because the eighteenth-century history of Independence Hall is so complex—incorporating locality as well as nation, conflict as well as consensus, and social and cultural history along with politics—it offers a rich opportunity for investigating the processes of remembering and forgetting as they relate to places considered historic.

The events that transpired at the Pennsylvania State House from the time of its construction through the ratification of the U.S. Constitution suggest a number of ways that this place and this era can be remembered: The State House might be interpreted as an embodiment of European culture and intellectual traditions which, ironically, provided the rationale for independence and national government. It might be remembered as the building that reshaped the city of Philadelphia and created a public forum where people from all walks of life participated in political expression. It might be seen as the place where loyalty and resistance to Great Britain wrestled for control of the future of the British colonies in America. In addition to the achievements of the Declaration of Independence and the Constitution, the State House might be remembered as a place of continuing struggle to create state and national governments that defined suitable boundaries between liberty and authority.

These are all valid interpretations of the building known today as Independence Hall, but such tensions, actions, and ideas are not easily represented by architectural restoration and historic furnishings. Such complexities do not fit easily into a tour or rest comfortably with a public memory of Independence Hall as a place of national consensus. In service to the nation, buildings like Independence Hall allow history to be captured and compartmentalized, facilitating appreciation of the past but also allowing memory to be selective. People and events wash in and out of buildings like the tide, perhaps leaving bits of material evidence behind, like the inkstand that may have been used to sign the Declaration of Independence or the chair from which George Washington presided over the Constitutional Convention. Around such evidence, narratives can be created to make sense of the past. In the case of Independence Hall, we will see construction of a memory of national consensus despite the conflicts and uncertainties that have characterized much of the building's history. We will see how generations of restoration and preservation projects have rendered these aspects of the building's history invisible.[96]

As a Georgian-style building, the Pennsylvania State House was indelibly stamped with a time and place—the eighteenth-century British empire. The architectural style pulls public memory back to colonial America, regardless of the later history of the building. In this way, architecture facilitates public memory and gives it definition. However, from the inception of the State House through the ratification of the Constitution, the building's rooms and public spaces accommodated a great variety of activity. In the more than two centuries that have elapsed since then, Americans have chosen how to use these spaces, how to furnish them, and how to communicate their significance. Given the importance of the State House in the creation of the United States, these choices represent not only the regard that later generations attached to the place, but also their memory of the nation, its founders, and the meaning of the American Revolution. The history of the Pennsylvania State House—in 1790, not yet known as Independence Hall—did not end with the ratification of the U.S. Constitution. In many ways, it had barely begun.

Chapter 2

WORKSHOP

Building a Nation

Step into the State House yard in Philadelphia in the 1790s and witness the work of building a nation: three governments occupy the buildings facing Chestnut Street. The United States Congress convenes in the County Court House, the Pennsylvania Assembly meets in its customary rooms in the State House, and the municipal government of Philadelphia shares City Hall with the Supreme Court of the United States. Among these lawmakers from North and South, East and West, there is no certainty about the future. At the State House, you might encounter a meeting called by Federalists to maintain their hold on the state and national governments, but you might also find a demonstration by the Federalists' critics, who in this decade will create the nation's first political party system. In the din of politics, do not be surprised by the growling of bears or the calls of eagles, because the American Philosophical Society has rented most of its building on the State House square to Charles Willson Peale who, assisted by his large family and one slave, manages a museum of art and natural science. The society and the museum draw the intellectually curious to the square, and the federal officeholders attract artists, who arrive to paint portraits of the aging heroes of the American Revolution and the rising generation of new national leaders. The State House square is a workshop of culture as well as politics.

Such a panoramic view—the State House, the adjacent buildings, the public space, and the surrounding city—is essential for understanding this period in the history of Independence Hall. In the first decades after the Declaration of Independence and the Constitutional Convention, Americans arranged no commemorative plaques, honorary statues, or Colonial furnishings to recall the events of 1776 and 1787. Instead, from the 1790s through the 1820s, the memory of the American Revolution was kept alive in the anxious, strenuous activity of constructing and sustaining a nation. This was the work of the government, but also the occupation of individuals creating their roles as citizens of the United States. Political conflict, enacted in the streets as well as in legislative halls, turned on issues rooted in the Revolutionary-era fixation on the balance between liberty and order. Would the nation best be preserved by a strong national government or by widespread participation by engaged citizens, even those from the lower ranks of society? Under what conditions—if any—should liberty be curtailed? Every controversy seemed to raise the possibility that factionalism or sectionalism would doom the republic.[1]

In these uncertain times, activities in and around the Pennsylvania State House contested the legacy of the American Revolution. Politically, the United States had an ideology preserved in the Declaration of Independence and a government designated by the new Constitution, but Americans disagreed sharply on how to carry out the vision of the founders. Socially, the future of the nation depended on finding common ground, or at least a peaceful coexistence, for a population that did not share equally in the fruits of the Revolution. Culturally, the cultivation of an educated, enlightened citizenry seemed essential to sustaining the republic. The work of nation-building was not confined to one square block in Philadelphia, but it was uniquely concentrated at this place defined not only by politics but also by the arts and sciences and the constant presence of urban life.

The Nation's Capital

Because Philadelphia served as the temporary seat of the national government from 1790 to 1800, it is tempting to shift our historical focus from the Pennsylvania State House to adjacent Congress Hall (then the newly built County Court House), where the U.S. Congress convened. This is the natural path of the twenty-first-century tourist, who can walk from the setting of the Constitutional Convention in 1787 at Independence Hall to the scene of Congress in the 1790s. However, such a physical and temporal distinction masks the interactions that defined these places during this crucial decade in American history. True, while Congress debated national economic plans and international treaties, the State House continued to be "a public mart for the negotiation of state business," as a letterwriter observed in the *Pennsylvania Gazette*.[2] But officeholders at all levels lived and worked in close proximity, and issues such as federal financing and foreign policy permeated state and local elections. During Philadelphia's decade as the nation's capital, the states ratified the Bill of Rights, but by the end of the decade Congress passed the Alien and Sedition Acts, severely limiting freedoms of speech and press. Northern states gradually abolished slavery, but in 1793 Congress passed a law enforcing the return of fugitive slaves to their masters. In the urban environment of Philadelphia, no elected official could escape day-to-day exposure to public opinion about such issues, whether in the newspapers, in the streets, or on election days when Philadelphia voters passed their ballots through the windows of the Pennsylvania State House. Rather than a memorial to the past, the State House and its surroundings served as an active workshop of practical politics.[3]

For the U.S. Congress in 1790, the question of where to place a national capital tapped into deep sectional conflicts among the states and competing philosophical visions for the nation's future. Since leaving Philadelphia in 1783, Congress had met in Princeton, Annapolis, and other locations before settling in New York City in 1785. In New York, national officeholders quarreled over whether to place the permanent capital in the North or South and whether the government would function best in a commercial city or removed from economic interests. In this debate, Philadelphia did not emerge as a sentimental choice tied to the memory of the American Revolution or the recent Constitutional Convention. In fact, many in Congress disliked the city for its hot summers, outbreaks of disease, and the locals' penchant for mixing in the affairs of the national government. In the end, Philadelphia became part of a political bargain that settled another vexing question—the balance of financial power between the national government and the states. Needing votes from North and South to empower the national government to assume the Revolutionary War debts of the states, Treasury Secretary Alexander Hamilton tied his plan to legislation establishing the future capital. The seat of government would move for one decade to Philadelphia, then relocate to a new federal district on the Potomac River in Virginia.[4]

A city of more than 42,500 people by 1790, Philadelphia embraced its place as national capital with conviviality and elegance reminiscent of the days before the Revolution. The neighborhood around the Pennsylvania State House became devoted to the comfort and entertainment of the national officeholders. On Chestnut Street in the block west of Congress Hall, Oellers' Hotel opened in 1791 to house and feed legislators in high style. Across the street from Oellers', the new Chestnut Street Theatre began performances in 1793. By 1795, Ricketts' Circus had erected a circular amphitheater ninety-seven feet in diameter at Sixth and Chestnut, just across from Congress Hall. With light from a giant chandelier, the circus performed both day and night to audiences of up to 1,200 people. Crowds also gathered in the State House yard to watch balloon ascensions, beginning with J. P. Blanchard's ascension from the yard of the Walnut Street Jail in 1793. To add to the spectacle, Blanchard at times released parachutes from his balloons, sending dogs, cats, or squirrels floating back to earth. For more sedate edification, congressmen could stroll across the State House yard to Philosophical Hall and Peale's museum of art and natural sciences. Peale's wild animals grazed on the State House lawn.[5]

Despite its many attractions, Philadelphia also realized some of the worst fears of its critics during its decade as the nation's capital. Virulent epidemics of yellow fever periodically ravaged the city, most dangerously in 1793. While many of Philadelphia's more affluent citizens fled to the countryside, doctors and some city officials stayed behind, turning the new City Hall into a headquarters for maintaining civil order and combating the disease. Congress stood in recess. The Pennsylvania Assembly adjourned, but not before a young man collapsed from the disease on the west side of the State House. The mayor of Philadelphia ordered the streets cleaned and asked citizens to bring spare linens to the State House for the use of fever victims. Coffin-sellers displayed their grim wares on the sidewalks in front of the City Hall. Mounted on wheels, coffins bearing the dead were transported to the square diagonally southwest of the State House to join the remains of the poor and the soldiers of the Revolution already interred. More than five thousand people died in 1793, and the disease recurred with nearly equal strength five years later.[6]

Although city, state, and national officeholders met in separate buildings on the State House square, they were linked in webs of political and social activity that blurred jurisdictional boundaries. They attended the levees at the residence of President George Washington, one block north of the State House on High Street, and they talked politics in the drawing rooms of the social circle known as the "Republican Court."[7] They lived together in boardinghouses and taverns, and they assembled for concerts, theatrical performances, and to worship in the city's churches. Congressmen and state legislators could follow each others' actions in the local press or walk a few steps between their meeting halls to observe debates in person. National officeholders such as rivals Thomas Jefferson and Alexander Hamilton kept keen watch on local elections as indicators of the political winds.[8]

Consider, for example, the activities of Jacob Hiltzheimer, who represented Philadelphia in the Pennsylvania Assembly for most of the decade but crossed frequently into the realms of city and national government. Hiltzheimer attended legislative sessions at the State House, but he also observed debates in the U.S. Congress in the County Court House next door. He witnessed historic rites of passage for the young nation, including the first peaceful transfer of presidential power from George

Washington to John Adams in 1797. Hiltzheimer traveled to the seashore with Governor Thomas Mifflin of Pennsylvania, and he occasionally dined with other lawmakers at the residence of President Washington. In his official duties, Hiltzheimer conferred with city officials about Philadelphia's new municipal corporation, authorized by the Pennsylvania Assembly in 1789, and he attended meetings at the State House to plan canals and turnpikes linking Philadelphia to the state's interior. He also supervised construction of a presidential mansion, which Pennsylvanians hoped would help persuade the national government to make Philadelphia its permanent home. As an assemblyman, he helped to elevate selected colleagues to the U.S. Senate and to choose the electors who would cast Pennsylvania's votes for president of the United States.[9]

The convergence of three strata of government on one city block created a cauldron of politics that simmered with the hopes, anxieties, and turmoil of the times. Leading Federalists, fresh from the successful ratification of the Constitution, hoped to govern on the classical republican model, by consensus achieved among a select group of virtuous citizens. Instead, they encountered in Philadelphia a lively political culture of dissent, where critics were quick to call mass meetings and draft petitions to Congress or even to the President of the United States. Widespread popular interest in politics characterized the United States of the 1790s, but in Philadelphia, everyday people demonstrated their views within close range of state and federal officeholders. The Pennsylvania State House and its square provided places where local citizens could participate in national affairs. Although the State House yard functioned as a garden for public recreation, a view captured in scenes published by William Birch between 1798 and 1800, politics often punctuated the tranquility.[10]

With the principles of the republic at stake, even the procedures for choosing candidates for public office provoked discord. At the State House in 1792, for example, a series of meetings to organize a statewide convention to nominate candidates for Congress broke down in disagreement. Critics regarded the convention plan, advocated primarily by Federalists known in Philadelphia as "the junto," as undemocratic. By the third meeting, attendance outgrew the State House and forced debate into the State House yard. There, on July 31, 1792, two factions gathered in separate areas of the square and noisily shouted down nominations for chairman of the meeting. When the organizers attempted to select a chairman in private, the meeting erupted in disorder. "They rushed forward, seized the chair and table, and tore them to pieces," James Hutchinson, a critic of the junto's methods, wrote to an ally shortly afterward, "And it was with difficulty violences of a more serious nature were prevented."[11] After the disorder of the public meeting in July, both the junto and its critics met privately to craft tickets for the fall

BACK of the STATE HOUSE, PHILADELPHIA.

6. *Birch's Views of Philadelphia*, published in the late 1790s, sustained an image of the Pennsylvania State House as a place of pastoral serenity, despite its place at the center of national and local politics. (Courtesy of Independence National Historical Park)

election. The junto proceeded to hold its convention in Lancaster, but the meeting drew little support or attendance from counties distant from Philadelphia.[12]

Just as taxes had driven Americans to revolt against Great Britain, new federal excise taxes provoked political passions in the early republic. Governments meeting simultaneously on the State House square took opposing positions. In 1791, as Congress debated a proposed excise tax on distilled liquor to finance the national debt, the Pennsylvania Assembly worked in the State House on a memorial against the tax. U.S. Senator William Maclay, a Pennsylvanian who opposed the tax, heard echoes of the Revolution in the dissent of his state. "I feel sincere pleasure that so much independence has been manifested by the Yeomanry of Pennsylvania," he wrote in his diary after attending the state lawmakers' debate about the memorial. "Indeed I am fully satisfied that if a Spirit of this kind was not manifested from Some Quarter or other our liberties would soon be swallowed up."[13] Congress proceeded to adopt the tax, but Philadelphia citizens carried on with the dissent, circulating a petition that protested the tax as an infringement on the people's liberties. Additional federal excise taxes in 1794 incited renewed protests. The new taxes on sugar, snuff, and other products struck at the livelihoods of Philadelphians who owned and worked in the city's sugar refineries and tobacco processing plants. In a mass meeting behind the State House in May 1794, Philadelphians who opposed the federal taxes declared it "the inalienable right and bounded duty of all freemen vigilantly to observe the operations of government." Denouncing the taxes as an unfair burden on manufactures, they resolved to meet any additional taxes with protests and public demonstrations in the State House yard.[14]

In a nation born from international conflict, foreign policy also consumed the attention of officeholders and excited the public. Great Britain was a recent enemy, but a dominant force in international trade. France was a recent ally, but inflamed during the 1790s with its own revolution. The French Revolution seemed to carry forward the ideals of the American Revolution, but it also rushed dangerously into violence. In the United States, events in France exacerbated the existing divide between defenders of liberty and proponents of order maintained by a strong central government. In the shadow of the Federalist Congress, Philadelphia champions of the French cause met at the State House in 1793 to draft a warm welcome for the celebrated but controversial French minister Edmond Genêt. In 1795, Philadelphians gathered at the State House to voice their objections to Jay's Treaty with Great Britain, which critics viewed as too favorable toward the British.[15] Agitation over foreign policy spilled into the State House yard again in 1797 and 1798, when French privateering at sea drew the United States into a quasi-war, although none had been officially declared. After the XYZ Affair, in which the foreign minister of France demanded bribes in exchange for talks to end the conflict, Philadelphians took sides in what seemed to be an imminent conflict. In the State House yard, young men wearing black cockades (symbolizing opposition to France) scuffled with others wearing red and blue cockades (symbolizing the American Revolution, but resembling the tricolor of France). With the State House fracas just one episode in a series of violent outbursts, armed troops patrolled the streets of Philadelphia. Congress voted new funding for national defense. Fulfilling the suspicions of critics, Congress took federal authority to a new extreme by passing the Alien and Sedition Acts of 1798, aimed at silencing enemies of the government, especially Philadelphia's vociferous anti-Federalist newspapers.[16]

Enveloped by such national and international controversies, politics in Philadelphia revolved around the affairs of the nation rather than local concerns. Philadelphians were the first to organize Democratic-Republican societies, which turned to the language of the Declaration of Independence to rouse opposition to Federalist control during the Washington and Adams administrations.[17] Even the Fourth of July, ostensibly a celebration of national unity, became politically charged in Philadelphia and elsewhere as opposing factions organized separate events.[18] Policies emanating from Congress Hall prompted Philadelphia critics of the Federalists to organize slates of candidates not only for Congress but also for the Pennsylvania Assembly and the Philadelphia City Councils.[19] Casting off the Federalist ideal of government by a virtuous few, Democratic-Republicans in Philadelphia reached out to artisans, laborers, and the ethnic diversity of the state's population for support. Elections in Philadelphia became increasingly competitive, driving voter turnout in the city up from 26 percent of eligible voters in 1790 to about 50 percent by 1800.[20]

In Philadelphia and beyond, the fevered politics of the 1790s crested with the presidential election of 1800. Nationally, the opposition rooted in the decade's Democratic-Republican societies grew into the Republican Party, which supported Thomas Jefferson for the presidency. Jefferson's candidacy encouraged American voters to reject the Federalists and embrace a vision of the United States as an agrarian republic. By supporting Jefferson with votes cast at the Pennsylvania State House, Philadelphians involved the building in yet another revolution—the revolution of 1800 that overturned a decade of Federalist control.

The election of Thomas Jefferson and the end of the eighteenth century also marked a turning point in the history of the Pennsylvania State House and the city of Philadelphia. By the time Jefferson took office, Philadelphia had lost its status as a dual capital. The governments of Pennsylvania and of the United States both turned away from urban tumult to more bucolic settings that seemed more conducive to the nurturing of a peaceful agrarian republic. In 1799, in keeping with the westward expansion of the state's population, Pennsylvania moved its capital to Lancaster, vacating the State House occupied by the government since the 1730s.[21] A year later, despite efforts of Philadelphians to retain the national capital, the federal government moved on schedule to the new District of Columbia which had been carved from lands belonging to Maryland and Virginia along the Potomac River. Further signaling that an era in the history of Philadelphia had passed, a great fire in 1799 burned the popular Ricketts' Circus to the ground. And in December, Philadelphians learned of the death of George Washington, the revered first president of the United States who even in life had achieved the status of symbol of the new nation. In one of its last acts in Philadelphia, Congress assembled at Congress Hall to join a procession of mourning through the streets of the city.[22]

If further proof were needed that the Pennsylvania State House held little sentimental attachment for Americans at the turn of the new century, the public buildings designed for the new national capital provided it. In the competition to design the new U.S. Capitol, the government rejected Georgian designs similar to the old State House in favor of buildings that evoked the classical past.[23] Architecturally, the United States distanced itself from the British past (represented by the red-brick State House) to a style reminiscent of Greece and Rome, more ancient, but symbolic of the birth of a new republic. Public buildings in Philadelphia also turned away from the architectural style of the city's British past. The First Bank of the United States, built between 1795 and 1797 at Third and Chestnut Streets, two blocks east of the State House, made the transition clear. In the back, the building was faced with brick and retained many characteristics of Georgian style; but for the front facade, businessman-architect Samuel Blodgett created a Roman temple featuring a two-story portico. In contrast to the State House, which embodied memories of Great Britain, the First Bank of the United States, like the buildings proposed for the new District of Columbia, linked the fortunes of the new nation to ancient republics.[24]

Center of Arts and Science

In the late eighteenth century, as politics converged on the State House square, Philadelphia also emerged as a cultural capital, regarded by the artist Gilbert Stuart as the "Athens of America." A community of artists migrated to the city to paint portraits of the city's wealthiest families, then grew and flourished with the presence of the national government. For the young United States, they fulfilled a yearning for cultural expressions that would both rival Europe and be distinctly American.[25] Our understanding of the State House and its environment would be incomplete without artists such as Robert Edge Pine, whose studio occupied the Assembly Room during the late 1780s; Gilbert Stuart, who lived on the block east of the State House while painting portraits of George Washington during the 1790s; and Thomas Sully, whose studio in Philosophical Hall attracted aspiring artists in the early nineteenth century. The historical picture of the State House would be especially incomplete without Charles Willson Peale, who merged the arts, sciences, and the public interest with his museums in Philosophical Hall and, from 1802 through 1827, in the Pennsylvania State

7. In a self-portrait, *The Artist in His Museum* (1822), Charles Willson Peale displays his museum of art and natural science, a powerful expression of cultural nationalism which occupied the second floor of the State House from 1802 until 1827. (Courtesy of the Pennsylvania Academy of Fine Arts)

House. Although the State House lost its status as a political center at the end of the eighteenth century, it remained a workshop for American culture.[26]

Like others of his generation, Peale had a vision of nationhood that was both political and cultural, with the success of the republic dependent on a virtuous, well-educated citizenry. As a young man, he fought in the American Revolution, helping to secure independence from Great Britain. Joining the most radical revolutionaries in Pennsylvania, he supported the Pennsylvania Constitution of 1776, and he served one year in the Pennsylvania Assembly while Congress still resided in the State House.[27] He became acquainted with the new nation's political leaders, most notably George Washington, whose portraits he painted, and Thomas Jefferson, who shared Peale's interest in natural history and served on the Board of Visitors for Peale's first museum.[28] A prolific and highly regarded portrait artist, by the 1780s Peale had produced a notable series of "Illustrious Personages" of the Revolutionary era. His natural science museum began in 1785 as an adjunct to his painting room, but as his collection grew, Peale began to envision a national public institution that would contribute to the nation by entertaining and educating the public.

In 1790, the year that Philadelphia became the temporary capital of the nation, Peale announced his plans for the museum in a broadside addressed boldly to the "Citizens" of the United States of America. The artist explained that he had perfected techniques of preserving animal specimens, and he encouraged the public to add to the museum "all that is likely to be beneficial, curious or entertaining to the citizens of the new world." In the spirit of the eighteenth-century Enlightenment, he expressed hope that the collection would diffuse "an increase of knowledge in the works of the Creator—God, alone wise!" Ambitiously, he proposed that the collection in his house at Third and Lombard Streets might "grow into a great national museum, or repository of valuable rarities." Weaving together appeals grounded in science, religion, and national progress, the broadside implied that the obligations of citizenship in the new nation included supporting cultural enterprises such as Peale's museum.[29]

The museum gained a foothold in the web of political and social activity on the State House square in 1794, when Peale moved his growing collections and his family into rented rooms in Philosophical Hall. For two weeks, neighborhood boys trooped from the old museum to the State House square carrying animal specimens on their shoulders. The Peale family was a troop in itself: in addition to Peale and his wife Elizabeth, there were six children ranging from newborn to age sixteen and one slave. The boys organized an imaginary militia in the State House yard, which also became home for Peale's menagerie of live animals. An American bald eagle, already an adopted symbol of the new nation, occupied a cage mounted on Philosophical Hall. Once, a bear penned in the yard escaped and broke into the Peale family kitchen in the cellar.[30] Despite the commotion it brought to the State House yard, Peale's museum was a serious scientific enterprise which became a site of interaction for officeholders of the city, state, and nation. During the museum's first year in Philosophical Hall, subscribers for year-long passes included 122 elected or appointed public officials, among them eighty-eight U.S. senators and representatives.[31]

Envisioning his museum as a national institution, Peale constantly lobbied for government funding, but he found the Enlightenment-era bond between public patronage and the pursuit of knowledge fading by the end of the eighteenth century.[32] His greatest support from government came not in financial aid, but in new space for his museum—in the Pennsylvania State House, after it was abandoned by the state government. In 1802, the Pennsylvania Assembly allowed Peale the use of the second floor and the east room on the first floor—the room the Second Continental Congress and the Constitutional Convention had occupied. In exchange, the Assembly required Peale to maintain the building and the square, which after the departure of the national government had declined into a place of "vice and indecorum," especially at night.[33] Peale also agreed to accommodate the city's annual elections, which depended on using the east room for collecting and counting ballots. As a tenant of the state, and later the city government, Peale's museum occupied the State House for the next twenty-five years.[34]

In contrast to the surrounding city and the turmoil of politics, the exhibits that Peale installed in Philosophical Hall and the abandoned State House projected a sense of order and harmony. His "world in miniature," classified according to the system of Swedish botanist Carolus Linnaeus, assured visitors that nature could be controlled and that hierarchy prevailed.[35] First in the Linnaean scheme were humans, represented by Peale's portraits and by life-sized wax figures. (In the early years, he contemplated representing humans with preserved bodies, and he wished that he had proposed such preservation to Benjamin Franklin before his death.) Humans occupied a hierarchy of their own, as Peale distinguished between those of European descent and "the Indian, African, or other savage people." After humans, in descending order, Peale exhibited preserved large animals, birds, amphibians, fish, insects, and worms.[36] He also showed fossils and minerals. In 1801, Peale added a new prize to his collection: the skeleton of a mastodon, excavated from a field in Newburgh, New York. It was the first complete mastodon skeleton excavated in the United States, and only the second in the world.[37]

Expanding his exhibits into the State House, Peale transformed the house of government into a center for natural science. Despite his personal experience with the events of the American Revolution, he did not call attention to the events that had transpired in his new exhibit space. His museum was a place for contemplating the timeless wonders of nature, not the events of the past. Signs over the Chestnut Street entrance identified the State House as a "MUSEUM and GREAT SCHOOL OF NATURE." Facing the State House yard, another sign identified the building as a "SCHOOL OF WISDOM." Upon entering, visitors were directed up the stairs by an additional sign that advised, "Whoso would learn Wisdom, let him enter here."[38] Although concerned with building attendance for the museum, Peale did not turn the east room on the first floor into a historical attraction. He placed most of his collection on the second floor, and the Assembly Room for a time became a studio and gallery for his son Rembrandt.[39] He continually sought bigger and better quarters, demonstrating a willingness to leave the State House behind.[40]

Peale displayed portraits of many of the leading figures of the American Revolution, not solely because of their achievements in creating the nation, but because in his view they represented the best of the human species. Portraits in this era were a means of preserving the memory of individuals for posterity, and Peale had selected many of his subjects because of their noteworthy roles in the Revolution and early nation.[41] However, in his exhibit upstairs at the State House, most of the portraits hung above eye level, positioned in the natural hierarchy above cases of animals, birds, and insects. They merited one paragraph in the published guide:

> Over the Birds, in handsome gilt frames, are two rows of Portraits of dis-
> tinguished Personages, painted from the life, by C. W. Peale and his Son
> Rembrandt. This collection was begun in 1779, and contains various
> other characters of distinction beside civil and military; such as Franklin,
> Priestley, Rittenhouse, Sir Joseph Banks, Humboldt, &c.——Their several
> names are in frames over each Portrait, yet there is a number which refers
> to a concise account of each person in small frames on the opposite cases.
> Of seventy persons here portrayed, forty are dead——Some portraits of a
> larger size adorn each end of the room. One of J. Hutton, of Philadelphia,
> who died aged 108 years and 4 months.[42]

As the description in the guide indicates, the portrait collection was not intended to serve as an exhibit of the political history of the State House. Even subjects such as

Benjamin Franklin and David Rittenhouse were noted for accomplishments "beside civil and military"—that is, for their work as scientists. The portraits were not only of Americans, but included the British chemist Joseph Priestley, British botanist Joseph Banks, and German naturalist Alexander von Humboldt. The aged Philadelphian J. Hutton gained special notice for his significance as a phenomenon of nature, having lived to the age of 108 years, four months.

Visitors to Peale's museum in the early nineteenth century walked up the stairs of the State House to the second floor and paid twenty-five cents admission, less than the least expensive tickets for the theater or the circus, but still out of reach for many in the laboring class.[43] In the lobby at the top of the steps, they might encounter one of Peale's sons operating an electrical apparatus that produced shocks and flying sparks. Emerging into the Long Room, visitors beheld the collection that Peale had amassed over the previous twenty years. Walls lined with glass cases contained more than seven hundred mounted birds from throughout North America and elsewhere in the world. Cases projecting from the walls displayed four thousand insects and numerous mineral specimens and fossils.[44]

Surrounded by the birds, insects, rocks, and portraits, a working artist amused visitors by cutting their silhouettes using a physiognotrace, a device that allowed the artist to trace a profile from a shadow cast onto the machine. The artist was Moses Williams, who had been given to the Peale family as a slave but was not listed on tax records as property after 1802, suggesting that he had been freed. Working at prices set by Peale, Williams charged eight cents each for the silhouettes, which were highly popular among museum visitors (although at least one Southerner recoiled at having his profile made by a black artist). By Peale's account, 8,800 people had their silhouettes made at the museum in 1803 alone. Williams's subjects included many of the women of Philadelphia as well as visiting Indians.[45]

In addition to the attractions of the Long Room, Peale's museum in the State House consisted of the Quadruped Room, where more than 190 mounted animal specimens included a grizzly bear, a buffalo, and an anteater that measured seven feet, seven inches from snout to tail. Up a narrow stairway into what was left of the State House tower, Peale's Marine Room displayed mounted fish, amphibious animals, snakes, and sea shells. From these experiences, which might be accompanied by a scientific lecture or music on the concert organ installed in the Long Room, visitors could continue to Philosophical Hall. There, for an additional fifty cents, they could view the mastodon skeleton, standing nearly twelve feet tall and nineteen feet long. Beyond that, the Model Room contained archaeological specimens, Indian objects, models of machinery, and wax models of humans from various parts of the world, including a Chinese laborer, an African, a Sandwich Islander, and a South American. Finally, the Antique Room displayed casts of classical statuary.[46]

Advertised nationally, Peale's museum drew out-of-town visitors to Philadelphia. The appeal of the collection, rather than the building it occupied, is suggested in a series of detailed journal entries and letters written in 1808 by John Stevens Cogdell of Charleston, South Carolina. Cogdell, a thirty-year-old sculptor, artist, and lawyer, was the son of a Revolutionary War veteran, but he either did not notice or did not consider it notable that in visiting Peale's museum, he was also entering the building where the Declaration of Independence and the U.S. Constitution were issued. He found the museum "highly interesting—& worthy the patronage of the government and of the citizens." The natural history collection gave "an insight . . . into the wonders of nature," but as an artist, Cogdell was more interested in the portraits of military officers and statesmen. Some he pronounced excellent, but he was not impressed by the two portraits of George Washington. Only one of the two portraits of Jefferson was "excellent as to likeness and execution." However impressive the collection, Cogdell felt it paled in comparison to museums in Europe. During his tour through the State House, he was most impressed with the Court Room on the first floor, which "by far exceeds any I have ever seen."[47]

Cogdell's journal and letters also place Peale's museum in the context of other attractions for out-of-town visitors to Philadelphia. As an artist, Cogdell was particularly drawn to the Pennsylvania Academy of Fine Arts, founded by Charles Willson Peale and others in 1805 and situated in a new building on Chestnut Street west of the State House. By the early nineteenth century, public institutions also were becoming tourist attractions for travelers fascinated by the latest approaches to curing society's ills.[48] Cogdell visited both the Pennsylvania Hospital, where he saw the surgical amphitheater and heard the wailing of insane inmates, and the Walnut Street Jail, which had recently adopted the new penitentiary system of placing prisoners in isolation. The South Carolina lawyer also attended trials, went to services at churches of different denominations, and walked to the Schuylkill River to examine the latest in bridge technology.

Other visitors did come to Philadelphia because of its role in the American Revolution, and local citizens did not forget that the State House had been the scene of momentous events. Frances Wright, an Englishwoman who later became known as a vocal freethinker and founder of an interracial utopian community, toured America in 1819 with her sister. Twenty-three years old at the time of her tour, she had developed an enthusiastic devotion to the American Revolution from reading histories published in England. Arriving in Philadelphia, she was surprised to find Peale's natural history collection occupying the Pennsylvania State House. "I know not but that I was a little offended to find stuffed birds, and beasts, and mammoth skeletons filling the place of senators and sages," she wrote in a letter to a friend in England. Nevertheless, she took some solace in the behavior of local residents toward the building. "Every friend or acquaintance that ever passed it with me paused before it to make some observation. 'Those are the windows of the room in which our first Congress sat.' 'There was signed the declaration of our independence.' 'From those steps the Declaration of Independence was read in the ears of the people.' Ay! and deeply must it have thrilled to their hearts."[49]

By the time of Wright's visit, Peale had consolidated his museum, including the mastodon, into the State House. Beginning in 1812, Philosophical Hall gained a new tenant who drew an expanded community of artists to the square. Thomas Sully, who occupied the hall for the next ten years, was a prolific painter who during his lifetime produced more than two thousand works, three-fourths of them portraits. Sully, born in England in 1783 and raised primarily in Charleston, South Carolina, moved to Philadelphia in 1807. In Philadelphia and on travels in the United States and Europe, he honed his talents under the tutelage of Gilbert Stuart, Benjamin West, Charles Willson Peale, and others. At his studio in Philosophical Hall, he taught the techniques of the eighteenth century masters to the emerging artists of the nineteenth century.[50]

Among the artists who joined Sully's sketch club was John Lewis Krimmel, a young German immigrant who specialized in genre scenes of Philadelphia street life.[51] His *Election Day 1815* captured the State House in a commotion of democratic politics that had been absent from the William Birch scenes of the 1790s. In Krimmel's portrayal, the State House is a cultural center marked by the museum sign over its front door, but it remains a place of politics for the city of Philadelphia. Voters pass their ballots through the windows of the State House, but Krimmel gives prominence to the raucous activity in Chestnut Street, placing voting in the background of the lively political culture of the street. Well-dressed men cluster in conversation, politicos engage in last-minute arm-twisting, and partisans parade with a marching band. Children frolic, breaking free from attentive republican mothers. African American vendors peddle oysters and oranges in Chestnut Street. Amid the campaigning, a fight breaks out in a tavern.

Krimmel's work reflects a nation of young and old, black and white, men and women, laborers and employers, all participating in civic life. The painting captures the essence and the challenge of nationhood, the messy convergence of diverse inter-

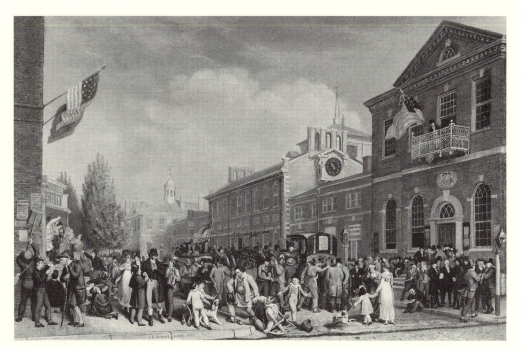

8. Of all the artists who worked in the vicinity of the State House during the late eighteenth and early nineteenth centuries, John Lewis Krimmel produced the only visual record of urban street life, *Election Day 1815*. (Courtesy of the Winterthur Museum)

ests within a community. As the painting suggests, the work of nation-building continued in and around the State House long after the national government departed. Krimmel provides an image of lively political participation, but he punctuates the scene with reminders that the rights of citizenship were limited in the early nineteenth century. The women in Krimmel's painting were responsible for rearing a new generation of American citizens, but they could not vote. In Pennsylvania, free black males in this period could vote, but Krimmel's election scene places them in service to others. All are united in the rituals of democracy, but like the hierarchy of nature displayed inside the State House in the exhibits of Peale's museum, the Philadelphians in the street occupied a social and political hierarchy that did not yet fulfill the ideals expressed by the nation's founding documents.[52]

Africans in America: Defining and Defending Liberty

Of all of the individuals in Krimmel's painting, the African American vendors deserve close attention because the Pennsylvania State House stood adjacent to one of the early nation's fastest growing communities of people of African descent. Since its earliest days, the State House had stood amid a population comprised of Africans as well as Europeans. Diagonally southwest of the State House yard, the potter's field in the city's southeast square had long served as an African burial ground. Although people of African descent lived throughout the city of Philadelphia, in the 1790s they began to cluster in the blocks just south of the State House, choosing to live near newly established African churches. Long-time residents of Philadelphia were joined by recently freed slaves from the South, who came in search of economic opportunity and security, drawn to Philadelphia by its reputation of Quaker abolitionism and by Pennsylvania's 1780 law for the gradual abolition of slavery. People of African descent also arrived from Saint Domingue with French refugees who fled with their slaves from the Haitian Revolution.[53] Even as Philadelphia lost its place as a center of state and national government, it became a magnet for African Americans seeking freedom. In the neighborhood south of the State House, African Americans struggled to define and defend the rights of American citizenship promised by the Constitution and the Declaration of Independence. In parallel to events on the State House square, sometimes engaging directly with officeholders, African Americans engaged in their own acts of independence, constitution-writing, and representation. If we enlarge our view of the history of Independence Hall to include these activities, we gain a greater understanding of nation-building in the early republic.[54]

If nationhood depends on a sense of shared community among citizens, the process of nation-building was especially complex among black Philadelphians. They were both Americans and Africans, some free and some slave, hopeful that the new nation would extend liberty to all, but conscious that freedom could be limited by race. Many black Philadelphians were former slaves who had been freed during the American Revolution. Between 1765, the year of the Stamp Act crisis, and 1783, the end of the war, the population of free black people in Philadelphia increased from 100 to more than 1,000 while the number of slaves in the city fell from 1,400 to about 400.[55] The language of the Declaration of Independence, the Constitution, and the Pennsylvania abolition law gave African Americans hope. Still, under Pennsylvania's gradual abolition law, freedom was promised only to slave children born in 1780 and after, and then only after the children had reached the age of twenty-eight. For others, freedom depended on the willingness of masters to grant freedom or allow slaves to purchase it. For example, Absalom Jones, who emerged as a religious leader by the end of the eighteenth century, was manumitted in 1784, but only after six years of petitioning his master for permission to purchase his own freedom.[56] For Jones and other Philadelphians of African descent, the events at the State House that created a nation independent of Great Britain coincided with countless personal acts of negotiating independence for themselves and others.

Within the new nation, many black Philadelphians forged a collective identity as descendants of Africa, but with the expectation that the strength and moral conduct of their community would help to secure their rights as American citizens. Voluntary associations and churches served as the foundation for community. In 1787, while delegates gathered to write a U.S. Constitution, a group of black Philadelphians founded the Free African Society; by 1794, the Society had given birth to two African churches, with more to follow. Within the many associations formed to further religion, education, and moral reform, African Americans engaged in their own acts of constitution-writing in the late eighteenth and early nineteenth centuries:

> We, the free Africans and their descendants, of the City of Philadelphia, in the State of Pennsylvania, or elsewhere, do unanimously agree, for the benefit of each other, to advance one shilling in silver Pennsylvania currency a month; and after one year's subscription from the date hereof, then to hand forth to the needy of this Society. (1787)[57]

> We the Founders and Trustees of the African Church of Philadelphia . . . ordain and decree, that none among us, but men of color, who are Africans, or the descendants of the African race, can elect, or be elected into any office among us, save that of a minister or assistant minister; and that no minister shall have a vote in our elections. (1794)[58]

> We the Subscribers, persons of colour of the city of Philadelphia, in the State of Pennsylvania, sensibly impressed with the high importance of education towards the improvement of our species . . . have resolved to unite and form ourselves into a society, to be known by the name of the Augustine Education Society of Pennsylvania, for the establishment and maintenance of a Seminary, in which children of colour shall be taught all the useful and scientific branches of education. (1818)[59]

The constitutions written in Philadelphia by African Americans communicated their strength of purpose within their own community, but also demonstrated the exertion required to maintain a place in the larger community of blacks and whites. In addition to their bold preambles, African American constitutions, beginning with the Free African Society in 1787, stressed propriety and humility, attempting to stifle behavior that might attract negative attention from their white neighbors. Rules for behavior showed both a desire to be accepted into the larger community and an awareness of the marginal place that African Americans occupied in the social structure of the nation.

Philadelphia's yellow fever epidemic in 1793 provided a vivid example of the position of African Americans as part of the population yet regarded as inherently different. When wealthier citizens fled, leaving the city in an urgent public health crisis, the mayor of Philadelphia called on the Free African Society to help bury the dead. Doctors, believing people of African descent to be immune to the disease, recruited black Philadelphians to provide medical attention to the sick. For their service, the black nurses and carters were accused of price-gouging and stealing from the sick and the dead. Community leaders acknowledged that some relief workers, black and white, had profited as desperate citizens bid for their services. But collectively, accounts kept by leaders of the Free African Society showed that African Americans had spent far more in providing service than they had earned.[60]

While serving Philadelphia during the yellow fever epidemic, African Americans were strengthening their own community by building the nation's first independent African church one block south of Independence Hall. The creation of African churches in Philadelphia grew from an incident that African Americans of later generations viewed as an exercise of civil rights in the spirit of the Declaration of Independence. In 1792, black Philadelphians walked out of St. George's Methodist Church when white trustees of the congregation demanded that they move from their customary seats to the rear of the balcony. Prompted by this action, all of the black worshipers rose and left the church. "We all went out of the church in a body, and they were no more plagued with us in the church," Richard Allen, a former slave and lay preacher, recalled.[61] A black clergyman of a later generation viewed the walkout from St. George's as a natural extension of the devotion to liberty that emanated from the Pennsylvania State House in 1776. "A moral earthquake had awakened the slumber of the ages," the Reverend William Douglass wrote in 1862, linking the removal from St. George's to the American Declaration of Independence. "The spirit stirring notes that pealed out from Independence Hall, proclaiming 'LIBERTY THROUGHOUT THE LAND TO ALL THE INHABITANTS THEREOF,' and causing the most humble to lift up his head with higher hopes and nobler aspirations, were yet echoing through every nook and corner of the land."[62] In 1792, the echoes were heard in St. George's and acted upon by the Free African Society, led by Absalom Jones and Richard Allen.

9. African Americans signaled their presence in Philadelphia and the new nation through the placement and design of the St. Thomas African Episcopal Church, which opened in 1794. "A Sunday Morning View of the African Episcopal Church of St. Thomas in Philadelphia" depicts worshipers arriving in 1829. (Courtesy of the Historical Society of Pennsylvania)

The first independent African Church in America, opened in Philadelphia in 1794, was both an expression of group identity and a statement of inclusion. The church, soon named St. Thomas African Episcopal, limited its voting membership to Africans and people of African descent. Its pastor was the former slave Absalom Jones. However, with a new building on Fifth Street south of Walnut, the congregation placed itself in close proximity to the Pennsylvania State House and established an architectural continuity between the African church and the halls of government on the State House square. From two available sites south of the State House, the founders of the first African Church in America chose the site closest to the square, just a half block south. Architecturally, the church they built in 1794 resembled the new City Hall recently completed on the State House square. The African church was somewhat smaller than City Hall, forty feet by sixty feet instead of fifty by sixty-six, but it was similar in materials, height, symmetry, and the Federal style evident in its windows.[63] The central window over the door of the church was Palladian, a smaller version of the window in the State House tower. On the eastern, most visible facade of the building, indicating their religious devotion but perhaps also their act of independence from white religious supervision, the congregation inscribed in marble: "The people that walked in darkness have seen a great light" (Isaiah 9:2).[64]

In 1794, black Philadelphians gained not one new church, but two. Although Richard Allen had been a leader in building the African church on Fifth Street, he was unwilling to give up his devotion to Methodism to adopt the congregation's choice to become Episcopalian. Moving a blacksmith shop to vacant land at Sixth and Lombard Streets, Allen founded Bethel Church, later the mother church of the African Methodist Episcopal denomination. One block west and three blocks south of St. Thomas, Allen's church provided another anchor for the African American community south of the State House. Combined with a wave of speculative housing construction in the district, Bethel Church and other African churches that soon followed made the neighborhood a center for African American life in Philadelphia and a destination for recently freed slaves from the South and the Pennsylvania countryside.[65]

Free black Philadelphians and their white allies maintained a vigilant watch on government activities on the State House square, calling attention to actions that seemed to contradict the promises of the Declaration of Independence and the Constitutions of Pennsylvania and the United States. In 1782, when the Pennsylvania Assembly considered amending the abolition law in ways that would have returned some freed slaves to bondage, African Americans responded with petitions against this proposed threat to their liberty. The proposal failed. In 1788, the Pennsylvania Abolition Society pressured the Assembly to close loopholes in the abolition law, limit shipbuilding for the slave trade, and increase fines for kidnapping slaves.[66]

During the 1790s, exchanges between African Americans and the national government confronted the continuing contradictions of slavery in a nation based on ideals of freedom and equality. In these exchanges, free black people acted as representatives for those who were still enslaved. In 1792, a pamphlet published in Philadelphia reprinted a letter in which Benjamin Banneker, a free African American in Maryland, questioned Thomas Jefferson about the disparity between his words in the Declaration of Independence and his practices as a slaveholder. In 1797, four former slaves living in Philadelphia petitioned Congress to call attention to the plight of slaves in their former home state of North Carolina, where state laws made manumission illegal. Slaves who had been freed, despite the law, were being captured and re-enslaved. "May we not be allowed to consider this stretch of power, morally and politically, a Governmental defect, if not a direct violation of the declared fundamental principles of the Constitution?" the petitioners asked. In 1800, when Congress moved to the new District of Columbia, a petition from free black Philadelphians followed, asking the government to end the slave trade and to reconsider the federal Fugitive Slave Act of 1793. Slaves, said the Philadelphians, should be "conceived equal objects of representation and attention . . . under the Constitution."[67]

In Philadelphia during the late eighteenth and early nineteenth century, events demonstrated that vigilance was necessary to secure the rights of citizenship for African Americans. Increasingly, as former slaves migrated into the city from the South and as some free black people prospered, black Philadelphians found their place in Pennsylvania and in the nation threatened. In 1813, the Pennsylvania Assembly considered banning further migration of African Americans into Pennsylvania. Although the state government had left Philadelphia, the free black community in the city maintained its vigilance. James Forten, a prosperous owner of a sail-making business, drafted an impassioned letter calling attention to the bitter irony of the proposed restriction in Pennsylvania, the birthplace of the Declaration of Independence and the first state to begin the process of abolishing slavery. He began his letter with irrefutable language: "We hold this truth to be self-evident," he wrote, "that God created all men equal, is one of the most prominent features in the Declaration of Independence, and in that glorious fabric of collected wisdom, our noble Constitution." The self-evident truth of the Declaration applied to all, he argued. "This idea embraces the Indian and the European, the savage and the Saint, the Peruvian and the Laplander, the white man and the African." To subvert the principle of equality would be a "direct violation of the letter and spirit of our Constitution."[68]

Forten's letter reflected the frustration of African Americans who lived in the nation, strived to be citizens, but faced firm and even violent resistance. In Philadelphia, the gulf between black hopes and the social reality of the city turned ugly each Fourth of July, the day dedicated to celebrating the nation. On at least one Independence Day early in the nineteenth century, white Philadelphians chased blacks out of the State House yard on Independence Day. By 1813, when Forten wrote his letter, black people risked attack if they ventured into the streets at all on July Fourth. African Americans had fought in the American Revolution, Forten reported, but the celebration of the Declaration of Independence had become a festival of violence against them. "Are not men of color sufficiently degraded?" he asked. "Why then increase their degradation?" On the Fourth of July, he wrote, "It is a well known fact, that black people . . . dare not be seen after twelve o-clock in the day, upon the field to enjoy the times; for no sooner do the fumes of that potent devil, Liquor, mount into the brain, than the poor black is assailed like the destroying Hyena or the avaricious Wolf!"[69] As their alternative to the Fourth of July, black Philadelphians gathered in their churches each January 1 to commemorate the date in 1808 when the United States ended its participation in the international slave trade.[70]

Living in the neighborhood south of the State House, African Americans also mobilized against their removal from the nation by resisting the American Colonization Society's project to transport free black Americans to Africa. The society's prominent founders, including Henry Clay, promoted colonization as beneficial for former slaves. However, a majority of the black population in Philadelphia viewed the project as a transparent attempt to deport free African Americans from the nation while retaining those who remained enslaved. In January 1817, a mass meeting of about three thousand people at Richard Allen's Bethel Church gave voice to the community's dissent. The resolutions adopted at the meeting pointed out that America had been cultivated by Africans—literally. "We their descendants feel ourselves entitled to participate in the blessings of her luxuriant soil, which their blood and sweat manured," the Philadelphians resolved, "and that any measure . . . having a tendency to banish us from her bosom, would not only be cruel, but in direct violation of those principles, which have been the boast of this republic." They declared that they would never be separated voluntarily from the nation, or from the people of African descent who remained in slavery in America.[71]

For African Americans in the late eighteenth and early nineteenth century, the significant national events that had taken place at the Pennsylvania State House had produced a mixed legacy. At this place in 1780, the Pennsylvania Assembly had passed the first law for the gradual abolition of slavery, but freedom from slavery did not translate into equality. The Declaration of Independence seemed to guarantee a future of equality for all, but the actions of government in later decades seemed to betray the promise. The language of the Declaration could be invoked in arguments for the full rights of citizenship, but it was clear to African Americans that gaining freedom was an incomplete process, not a reality achieved in 1776 or 1787. They believed that whatever progress had been made had been the work of God, not men. They established their place in the nation first by building strength in community in the blocks south of the State House, then reaching for inclusion in the nation.

In the history of Independence Hall, the years from 1790 to 1820 traditionally have been viewed as a time when the nation's history moved next door to Congress Hall, then departed Philadelphia altogether.[72] If we limit our attention to the State House alone and to the activities of national government, this is the history that emerges. However, if we choose instead to extend our field of vision to take in a greater area and a wider range of political, social, and cultural activity, a more complex history unfolds. Rather than standing in isolation, frozen in its Revolutionary past, the Pennsylvania State House in these decades occupied a place in the ongoing activity of nation-building. The nation was built not only from the top down, but from the bottom up. In and around the State House, ideas of what the nation could be—what it should be—spurred local activism, from the political battles of the 1790s to Charles Willson Peale's dream of a national museum to the tenacity of African Americans. Individually, these events have been written about at length by scholars, but except for Peale's museum, they have received limited attention as contributors to the meaning of Independence Hall.

If we organize our understanding of history around buildings, the past that we perceive may be limited by the boundaries that we establish. Buildings allow us to draw those boundaries tightly, creating concise, easily digestible stories. The more we push back the boundaries, taking in other buildings, public spaces, people, and neighborhoods, the more complex the story is likely to become. But the complexity may be a better reflection of events as they occurred. The politics of the 1790s occurred not only in the debates of Congress, but in the exercise of citizenship, through voting and voicing public opinion. The Declaration of Independence and the Constitution were interpreted not only in the halls of government, but among the people, including those of African descent who lived nearby. The nation was built not only through politics, but through cultural institutions such as Peale's museum.

Activities in and around the State House articulated competing traditions of memory associated with the American Revolution. In one view, the Revolution had logically and rightfully culminated in the Constitution. The champions of the Constitution, the Federalists, envisioned a nation kept in order by a strong central government led by a natural aristocracy of virtuous citizens. Opposing them, however, the Democratic-Republicans who supported Thomas Jefferson looked back to the spirit and language of the Declaration of Independence to stress a Revolutionary legacy of individual liberty. The American Revolution was not a moment of the past, but a living idea to be carried into the future. Peale's museum looked toward that future by fostering a national culture of enlightened citizens. The African Americans who lived in close proximity to the State House also looked toward the future, but with the stark realization that participating fully in the American nation would require continuing struggle. Later generations, looking back on these times, might embrace any combination of these traditions to construct a public memory of the early national era at the building later known as Independence Hall.

By the nineteenth century, the Pennsylvania State House had a rich and varied history. As a structure, however, its eighteenth-century British architectural identity worked against its emergence as a national symbol. In a nation trying to secure its future, the building was a material remnant of the past. Later generations would value the Georgian building for its evocation of colonial America, but citizens of the early republic did not need a building to recall the legacy of the American Revolution. For them, the events of 1776 and 1787 lived in the political, social, and cultural challenges of creating and sustaining a nation.

Chapter 3

RELIC

Survival in the City

In the first decades following independence from Britain, the United States was the epitome of youth—a new nation, growing, prospering, looking anxiously but optimistically toward the future. By the 1820s, however, a generational shift was at hand. Americans of the nineteenth century, engaged in enlarging the nation's cities, tilling new countryside, and pushing into the continent's interior, also confronted a dilemma in national identity.[1] What would become of the nation as it aged? What could succeeding generations do to renew the ideals of the American Revolution, which was fast fading from recent experience into history? A dwindling number of aged Americans sustained the only living memories of 1776, reminding younger generations that an era was slipping away. Funerals confirmed the fact. In Philadelphia, when a group of young men raised their glasses on the Fourth of July of 1824, their toasts mixed veneration, determination, and regret. "To the departed heroes of '76," they said, "tho' their clay cold corpses be mouldering in the dark and dreary mansions of death, the memory of their heroic achievements shall live in the hearts of their countrymen." And then, "To the Surviving Heroes of the Revolution—the scatter'd remnant of a gallant band. Their deeds are recorded on tablets of immortal adamant,—never—never—to be erased."[2] The legacy of the American Revolution was passing to generations born after the illustrious events toasted on the Fourth of July. How could they honor and sustain it?

In this transitional period in American history, the Pennsylvania State House presented a challenge to its caretakers in Philadelphia. Like the veterans of the American Revolution, the State House had seen glorious days, but time had diminished its luster. Despite being the birthplace of the Declaration of Independence and the Constitution, the Georgian-style State House was an unlikely candidate to be a symbol for the nation. The aging building did not inspire the reverence accorded to the nation's founders or brim with symbols of republican nationalism like the new U.S. Capitol created for the District of Columbia. The building occupied a prime location in the growing city of Philadelphia, but it belonged to the state government, which had moved westward at the turn of the century. The old State House was a Colonial-era relic, surviving the passage of time but not yet cherished for its historic associations.

Americans of the early nineteenth century recalled the American Revolution in art, histories, memoirs, and commemorations, but this memory work focused on the people, events, and principles of the nation's founding, not on the building in which it occurred. As long as the Revolution remained in living memory, even Philadelphians showed little regard for the fate of the Pennsylvania State House. By the 1820s, however, they began to embrace the State House as a means of preserving a past that was slipping away. From the many events that had transpired at the State House since its construction nearly a century before, Philadelphians selected the achievements of 1776 as the memory they would hold. The Pennsylvania State House became a place worthy of preservation, and for the first time, one room inside the State House became regarded as "Independence Hall."

Displacing Memory: Architecture and Iconography

By the early nineteenth century, perceptions of the Pennsylvania State House followed divergent paths, none of which contributed to elevating the structure to a national symbol. In its local context, the significance of the State House was complicated by the multiple functions of the building, including the presence of criminal courts and Charles Willson Peale's museum. Furthermore, significant gaps persisted between the ideals of the American Revolution and the reality of everyday life, especially for Philadelphia's growing population of African Americans. Although important events had occurred at the State House, it remained a public building in a growing city. For some Philadelphians, the State House served as a reminder of the American Revolution, but for others, it represented the difference between freedom and incarceration or the unrealized promises of the Declaration of Independence. [3]

Beyond Philadelphia, meanwhile, Americans memorialized the nation's founding in ways that detached the memory of the eighteenth-century events from the building in which they occurred. Rather than preserving historic buildings, Americans adopted national symbols that animated or personified the principles associated with the American Revolution.[4] National imagery reached to antiquity for the Roman goddess of Liberty, who appeared on maps, in allegorical paintings, and on coins produced by the first U.S. Mint. Liberty's distinguishing characteristic was the liberty cap, derived from the cap awarded to Roman slaves who gained freedom. In American images, Liberty often appeared with the national flag or with shields adorned with stars and stripes. Liberty might also be accompanied by the American bald eagle, the national symbol designated by Congress in 1782 which also became a highly popular symbol. The eagle was both a public and personal expression of patriotism, not only appearing on outdoor signs, the sterns of ships, and in advertisements, but also being drawn, painted, and carved into household furnishings.[5]

Nineteenth-century Americans also recalled the origins of their nation through the memory of George Washington, the commander of the Continental Army in the War for Independence and the first president of the United States. The veneration of Washington originated with his military leadership, which prompted the creation of coins, prints, and portraits that preserved an image of the virtuous citizen-soldier. By the 1790s, during Washington's first term as president, Americans began to celebrate his birthday on February 22. At his death in 1799, the outpouring of national grief included the declaration in Philadelphia that Washington stood "first in war, first in peace, and first in the hearts of his countrymen." The Washington legend became elaborated in the early nineteenth century in artistic works such as David Edwin's *Apotheosis of Washington* (1800), which completed the sanctification of the hero by showing Washington ascending to heaven, and in Mason Weems's biography, which introduced the story of the youthful Washington declaring, "I cannot tell a lie." Through the life and legend of Washington, Americans associated their memory of the American Revolution with a man more than with places such as the Pennsylvania State House.[6]

In addition to symbols of nationhood, Americans developed nationalist rituals, most notably the celebration of the Declaration of Independence each Fourth of July. But even in Philadelphia, the State House did not play a major role in commemorations during the late eighteenth and early nineteenth centuries. On some Independence Days, the Revolutionary War officers of the Society of Cincinnati met in the State House, and militia groups mustered in the State House yard before parading elsewhere. However, in the nineteenth-century city, such a heavily used public building did not lend itself to the preferred rituals of dinners, toasts, and fireworks. Celebrations dispersed into homes and taverns around the city, and Philadelphians watched fireworks in spacious Market Street or at Center Square, where the pyrotechnics would be less likely to set buildings on fire. The wealthiest families routinely left the city during the summer, getting away from the heat by escaping to their country homes or the seashore. For them, the place of commemoration mattered less than the sentiment.[7]

In the early nineteenth century, Philadelphians did not hesitate to alter the State House to meet local needs. As John Lewis Krimmel's *Election Day 1815* (see page 47) shows, the original piazzas and wings of the State House had been replaced by rows of office buildings. The steeple taken down in the 1780s had not been replaced. The eighteenth-century interior of the Assembly Room also had been stripped away. Who would guess that this was the Pennsylvania State House so proudly displayed on Scull and Heap's map of Pennsylvania sixty-five years before? In such disregard for preservation, the Pennsylvania State House did not differ markedly from other Colonial public buildings or places associated with the American Revolution. In Philadelphia, Benjamin Franklin's house was converted into a hotel in 1802 and then demolished by his heirs in 1812 to allow development of the property as building lots.[8] In New England, the Connecticut State House became a museum in 1797. Boston's Faneuil Hall, scene of some of the earliest mass meetings of the American Revolution, continued to be a city market and meeting hall, and the first Massachusetts State House was rented to merchants and tradesmen after a new State House was constructed in 1798.[9] As Americans looked toward the future, they adapted buildings of the past to serve present needs.

Altering the Pennsylvania State House to the needs and tastes of the nineteenth century began in 1812, when the Philadelphia city government obtained permission from the state to demolish the original piazzas and wing buildings to make way for new, fireproof office buildings. To design the buildings, the city called upon Robert Mills, a protege of Benjamin Henry Latrobe whose later work would include the Washington monuments in Baltimore and the District of Columbia.[10] Mills, who believed that designs should recognize prevailing regional styles and the tastes of his clients, created the State House office buildings to suit early nineteenth-century Philadelphia. By this time, the city was known for its rows of connected houses designed and built not individually, but as a unified whole. Mills's mentor, Latrobe, had designed an elegant rowhouse block of twenty-two houses for the 700 block of Walnut Street, two blocks west of the State House, in 1799.[11] From 1809 to 1810, Mills designed Franklin Row, a line of eleven houses on Ninth Street. In 1812, under Mills's direction, the government buildings along Chestnut Street also took on the character of a Philadelphia rowhouse development. [12]

In keeping with the principles of rowhouse design, in place of the original triadic structure of the State House flanked by two wing buildings linked by piazzas, Mills made the central structure the anchor of a unified row. For both ends of the State House, Mills designed connected office buildings with roof lines that extended from the stringcourse below the second-floor windows of the central structure. Like the State House, the buildings were brick, incorporated keystones as design elements, and had doors spaced at intervals similar to the windows in central building. To these borrowings, Mills added recessed doorways. From the choices that Mills presented, the city chose rectangular rather than arched recesses. The buildings stopped short of connecting with the City Hall and County Court House (Congress Hall), but otherwise presented a unified facade along Chestnut Street.[13]

With the eighteenth-century appearance of the State House substantially obscured, art rather than architecture allowed Americans to visualize the events of the nation's founding. In history paintings, however, the State House played a supporting rather than featured role. Artists focused on the act of declaring independence, not on the building. The action took place indoors, giving artists no reason to portray the State House as it appeared from the street or the square. Sharing an intense admiration for the leaders of the American Revolution, the artists were more concerned with producing accurate portraits for the benefit of future generations than with portraying an exact image of the events of July 1776 or the room where the events occurred. These artists were not in Philadelphia in 1776. Some had not yet arrived from Europe. Their paintings, produced beginning in the 1780s, were works of imagination, not documentation. However, they contributed to an iconography of the Revolutionary era that shaped public memory in the early nineteenth century.

Among the first artists to re-create the scene of the Declaration of Independence had been Robert Edge Pine, an artist from England who arrived in Philadelphia in 1784. An established portrait artist in his sixties, Pine had been sympathetic to the American cause and came to the United States to embark on a series of historical paintings of the American Revolution. As a friend of Samuel Vaughan, who was then landscaping the State House square, Pine soon was granted the Assembly Room of the State House—the room where the Second Continental Congress met—as a studio and gallery. He paid no rent (to the dismay of some members of the Pennsylvania Assembly) and charged visitors twenty-five cents admission. During the two years and two months that Pine occupied the State House studio, he produced his series of large historical paintings, incorporating portraits painted during trips to Virginia and Maryland. The series included *Congress Voting Independence*, which, although unfinished, was sold by lottery after his death in 1788 and is believed to have been

10. Although not painted until the late 1780s or early 1790s, *Congress Voting Independence*, by Edward Savage, offers the most accurate depiction of the interior of the Assembly Room at the time of the Declaration of Independence. Savage's work is believed to be based on the work of Robert Edge Pine, who occupied the room as his studio in the early 1780s. (Courtesy of the Historical Society of Pennsylvania)

destroyed in a museum fire in Boston in 1803.[14] Its value in presenting an accurate view of the Assembly Room may have been preserved by another artist, Edward Savage, whose own *Congress Voting Independence* may be a copy of Pine's earlier work.[15] Savage, born in New Jersey, lived in Philadelphia during the late 1790s. Occupying a house on South Fourth Street a block from the State House, he could have had first-hand knowledge of the building's interior. The Savage painting later became an important guide for twentieth-century preservationists, who found that the painting matched surviving architectural details inside the Assembly Room.[16]

The most widely circulated image of the Declaration of Independence in the early nineteenth century was a work of history, memory, and imagination conceived by an American artist in Europe with the help of such notable participants as Thomas Jefferson and John Adams. John Trumbull's *Declaration of Independence* (see page 16), the largest version of which hangs in the U.S. Capitol in Washington, D.C., has adorned postage stamps, currency, and commemorative china, not only in the United States but elsewhere in the world. Trumbull, who served as an aide to George Washington during the War for Independence, embarked on his series of historical paintings in a conscious effort to transmit a memory of the American Revolution to future generations. He wanted to "preserve and diffuse the memory of the noblest series of actions which have ever presented themselves in the history of man," he wrote in his autobiography. He was concerned not with the places where events of the Revolution occurred, but with actions, the spirit of the times, and the accurate portrayal of "the great actors in those illustrious scenes."[17] Trumbull began *The Declaration of Independence* in 1785 in Paris, where he consulted with Thomas Jefferson and obtained from him a sketch from memory of the Assembly Room.[18] After composing the painting, Trumbull embarked on the massive project of painting portraits of all of the men who attended the Second Continental Congress, voted for the Declaration, or signed it later. He worked on the portraits intermittently for more than twenty years, painting Jefferson in Paris, Adams in London, and sitting members of Congress in New York and Philadelphia.

Trumbull's painting, completed in 1818, deviated from the event of 1776 in several respects. His portraits, all created at least ten years after the fact, pictured his subjects as older than they were at the time of the Declaration. The content of the painting also reflects Trumbull's choices about who should be remembered in connection with the famous event. For example, his portrayal of the Declaration includes Pennsylvania delegate John Dickinson, who opposed independence and explicitly declined to be included in Pine's *Congress Voting Independence*.[19] Trumbull also portrayed men who signed the Declaration but were not in attendance when it was presented to Congress. Conscious of these interpretive choices, he consulted with Jefferson and Adams and later cited their advice to those who criticized his painting as inaccurate.[20] As for the Assembly Room, Jefferson's sketch from memory misrepresented some elements, such as the location of doors, and Trumbull freely created other embellishments. In Trumbull's depiction, the room became richly decorated, including military battle trophies and flags, upholstered chairs, and thick draperies. With artistic license, Trumbull produced an environment he believed suitable for such a magnificent event.[21]

As representations of events at the Pennsylvania State House, these early history paintings emphasized the Declaration of Independence and Revolutionary War heroes, but they paid little attention to the federal Constitutional Convention of 1787. As a writer in the *Portfolio*, published in Philadelphia in April 1824, observed, "The names

11. Porcelain hand-painted in China during the nineteenth century demonstrates the widespread imitation of the Trumbull image, as well as its adaptation. Here, not only has the Declaration of Independence been put to decorative use on dinner plates, but the signers have also acquired Asian features. (Courtesy of the Winterthur Museum)

and characters of those devoted republicans who signed the Declaration of Independence have been perpetuated in every form of illustration by the press and the graver, as well as the pencil and the pen." Meanwhile, "The patriots who framed the present Constitution of the United States, and the head of whom was Washington himself . . . are unknown or at least unthought of."[22] The Constitution had yet to achieve the veneration accorded to it later in the nineteenth century. No artist of the late eighteenth or early nineteenth century produced a major, lasting image of the Constitutional Convention to compare with the Declaration paintings of Pine, Savage, or Trumbull.[23] Philadelphians did not forget the convention that gathered in the State House in 1787.

Memorials to the Constitution appeared among the many tavern signs of the city, and the writer in the *Portfolio* noted that the Convention of 1787 met in the same State House "council chamber" where the Declaration had been approved.[24] However, local tavern signs made far less of an impression on public memory than the history paintings of the Declaration of Independence.

Mostly ignored by artists, the Pennsylvania State House in the early nineteenth century stood unvenerated, remodeled, and occupied primarily by Peale's museum. More than a place of the nation, it was a place of the city of Philadelphia. The state government, which had moved westward once again to Harrisburg, viewed the old State House as surplus property. As early as 1802, and again in 1813 and 1816, the Pennsylvania Assembly contemplated selling the State House and dividing the rest of its square into building lots.[25] The ensuing debate forced Philadelphians to define the significance of the building and adjacent public space. In these early decades of the nineteenth century, before the advent of public interest in historic preservation, the issue was not only—or even primarily—the history of the structure. Although defenders of the State House invoked its history, the two sides debated the future of the building in terms of property rights, legal precedents, and the proper relationship between state and city governments.

Was the building "historic"? In 1813, the Philadelphia City Councils argued against the state plan to sell the State House and square, noting, "The spot which the Bill proposes to cover with private buildings is hallowed . . . by many strong and impressive public Acts . . . which embrace the whole United States and which have given birth to the only free Republic the world has seen."[26] The statement is notable for its identification of the State House as a sacred place with global significance, and it has been regarded as an important precedent for the historic preservation movement that emerged later in the nineteenth century.[27] However, the Councils seemed to recognize that historic significance alone would not persuade state lawmakers to spare the building. Before invoking the building's history, they offered a series of practical reasons for preserving the State House and its square. In a city that had experienced severe outbreaks of yellow fever, the Councils argued that the open square was necessary for air circulation, believed essential to public health in the increasingly crowded city. The Councils also reminded the Assembly that the State House and yard served as the polling place for general elections. The loss of this public gathering place, especially as the city's population was growing, would impede voting.

Finally, the Councils raised an argument that persisted throughout nineteenth-century debates about Independence Hall. As early as 1735, the Provincial Assembly of

Pennsylvania had declared that the State House yard "should remain a public open green and walk for ever." Subsequent legislatures had echoed this language as they acquired property rights to the entire block between Chestnut and Walnut Streets and Fifth and Sixth Streets. Could an Assembly in the nineteenth century overturn these acts that defined the square as open space "for ever"? The City Councils and letter writers to the *United States Gazette* argued that "for ever" meant exactly that.[28] Shortly after the Councils' petition reached Harrisburg and the letters to the newspaper appeared, the Pennsylvania Senate called on the Secretary of the Commonwealth to gather together all titles, deeds, and papers related to the State House and the adjacent lot. The Senate voted 16–11 to postpone acting on the future of the State House and grounds.[29]

Although temporarily reprieved, the State House came dangerously close to demolition in 1816, when state lawmakers revived their hope for selling the property. In February and March of that year, first the Senate and then the House passed legislation creating an elaborate procedure for dividing the State House square into building lots, selling them, and using the proceeds to finance a new capitol building in Harrisburg. The city and county governments would keep the buildings on the northeast and northwest corners of the square, and the American Philosophical Society would remain in its headquarters on Fifth Street. However, two intersecting streets, each twenty feet wide, would be constructed through the square, with the remaining open spaces divided into building lots. It is difficult to imagine how the State House would have survived under such an arrangement. Furthermore, Philadelphia's interests would not have been represented on the commission empowered to sell the property. Appointed by the governor, none of the commissioners could be residents of the city or county of Philadelphia.

Deep in the bill, however, the lawmakers offered an alternative: the city of Philadelphia could purchase the property for $70,000, a sum inserted into the legislation by Nicholas Biddle, future president of the Second Bank of the United States and then a state senator representing Philadelphia. The selling price, based on land value, was a matter of controversy in the General Assembly, where some lawmakers tried unsuccessfully to raise the price to $125,000 or $200,000.[30] It also generated disagreement in Philadelphia, where some thought the price too high, especially since in exchange for selling the property, the state legislation continued the condition that none of the land south of the State House "be made use of for erecting any sort of buildings thereon; but that the same shall be and remain a publick green and walk forever."[31] If Philadelphians were going to argue the precedent of this language from 1735, legislators were going to hold them to it.

In any case, did the state have a legal right to demand money from the city in order to spare the State House? The question reopened the historic conflict between liberty and power which continued to define Pennsylvania politics. William Duane, publisher of the *Aurora* and a sharp critic of the Federalist majority in the state legislature, printed two editorials that thundered with indignation at the prospect that the city should have to purchase the State House and its yard from the state. It was "as if the city was no part of the *commonwealth*; or that the city had no right to those properties which belonged to it before the revolution; in fact, as if the city was part of another nation!"[32] Although he primarily argued the questions of state power and property rights, Duane also invoked the historic associations of the building to justify its preservation. After noting that Switzerland had preserved William Tell's cottage and that England had commemorated the Magna Carta with a monument, Duane turned to the subject at hand: "But in Pennsylvania, under the *Gothic mist of ignorance and vice,* by which it is now governed—everything is to be *pulled down. . . .* In the spirit of ancient times, or of that virtue which ought to govern all times, the *building* in which the *Declaration of Independence* was deliberated and determined, would obtain veneration the most sensible and endearing, as a monument of that splendid event; but this is not the spirit of the rulers of Pennsylvania now—the *state house must be sold*—for every thing now in political affairs is *barter and sale!*"[33]

Bound by the action of the Pennsylvania Assembly, the Philadelphia City Councils swiftly settled the fate of the State House by agreeing to buy the building and the square.[34] The city of Philadelphia borrowed $70,000 and paid the state in three installments, as specified in the state law. On June 29, 1818, the city took possession of the Pennsylvania State House on Chestnut Street, ensuring the survival of a significant building in the nation's history and placing its future in the hands of local citizens.

Stirring Memory: The Visit of Lafayette

At the moment when the American Revolution was fading from living memory into the distant past, Americans seized an opportunity to lavish gratitude on a surviving hero. The Marquis de Lafayette, the French nobleman who had volunteered his services and fortune to the Revolution at the age of nineteen, returned to the United States in 1824 at the invitation of the U.S. Congress. For thirteen months, traveling through every state in the nation, the seventy-six-year-old former general inspired massive parades and grand receptions. Lafayette was hailed as the "son of Washington" (whom he honored in an emotional pilgrimage to the first President's tomb at Mount Vernon) and as a patriot who gave selflessly to a country not his own.[35] The great effort devoted to receiving Lafayette, in Philadelphia and elsewhere, reverberated long after he moved to his next destination. Around the country, Americans devoted renewed attention to the relics of the American Revolution. Lafayette could provide only momentary euphoria, and mortality would doom his aging comrades in arms. But relics—rifles, uniforms, flags, and even buildings—could be tended and preserved. More than people, artifacts could withstand the tests of time.[36]

In Philadelphia, Lafayette's arrival focused attention on the old Pennsylvania State House and intensified regard for the former meeting room of the Pennsylvania Assembly as a place connected to the Declaration of Independence and the men of the Second Continental Congress who signed it in 1776. Through word and image, Lafayette's visit reinforced the State House as a significant bridge between past and present. The connections were evident in a souvenir handkerchief produced for the occasion which showed Lafayette's procession arriving at the State House. Ignoring buildings that stood across the street, the artist imagined the State House on a spacious plaza, a perspective that allowed the triumphal arch erected for the occasion to be pulled into the foreground. Lafayette, arriving in a grand barouche pulled by six horses, was the primary subject of this image; the State House was secondary but, nevertheless, integral. Furthermore, the caption announced "General La Fayette's arrival at Independence Hall"—among the earliest uses of "Independence Hall" to indicate the room in which independence was declared.[37]

Although Philadelphians had demonstrated some regard for the historic associations of the State House earlier in the nineteenth century when they acquired the building and its square from the State of Pennsylvania, in 1824 the State House was not treated as a historic site in any formal way. Charles Willson Peale's museum continued to occupy the second floor. A guide to Philadelphia published shortly before Lafayette's visit identified the east room of the first floor as "Court Room," with only a footnote to the text adding that this was the room in which the United States had declared independence from Great Britain.[38] Across the hall from the east room, the Mayor's Court dispensed punishment for civil disorders. Six months before Lafayette's arrival, the court was targeted by arsonists, who might have sent the entire structure up in flames. Four men entered through a window, piled chairs and books in the southeast corner of the room, and set the fire. Fortunately for the fate of the building, the windows of the Mayor's Court had no shutters, and the blaze was quickly detected from outside and extinguished.[39]

Philadelphians learned in July 1824 that Lafayette would visit Philadelphia, and

12. General Lafayette's tour of the United States in 1824–25 marked a turning point in the history of the Pennsylvania State House, which is identified as "Independence Hall" on this souvenir handkerchief printed at the Germantown Print Works, northwest of Philadelphia. (Courtesy of the Winterthur Museum)

they spent August and September preparing for his arrival. The greatest public attention focused on the procession that would accompany Lafayette into the city: military and civil groups organized units for the parade, and residents of the city campaigned to have their streets designated for the parade route. However, city officials also decided that the east room of the State House would serve as Lafayette's reception room and appointed architect William Strickland to redecorate the long-neglected chamber.[40] Strickland, born the year after the Constitutional Convention, had recently ascended to prominence as designer of the Greek revival Second Bank of the United States in the block east of the State House. Immersing himself in preparations for Lafayette's visit, Strickland drew heavily upon his earlier experience as a theatrical set designer.[41] By the time Lafayette arrived, Strickland had created a highly embellished State House setting to receive the general.

As planned, Lafayette entered the city on September 28 accompanied by an elaborate military and civic parade led by one hundred citizens and one hundred military officers on horseback, a band of musicians, a corps of cavalry, and a brigade of nearly two thousand infantrymen. Calling attention to the historical associations of the visit, three decorated carts loaded with Revolutionary War veterans followed General Lafayette's barouche. As one of Lafayette's traveling companions observed, "No one could, without emotion, behold these veterans of liberty whose eyes are half extinguished by age, [who] still poured forth tears of joy at their unexpected happiness, in once more beholding their ancient companion in arms." Traveling in the procession, "Their feeble and trembling voices were reanimated by the sounds of the martial music which accompanied them, and [they] acquired a new vigor in blessing the names of Washington and Lafayette."[42] Veterans too frail to travel in the parade viewed the general from the steps of the Second Bank of the United States as he neared the State House.

Reaching the State House, Lafayette entered the building through a triumphal arch created by Strickland from canvas painted to look like stone. Inside, in the room where independence had been declared, Philadelphia dignitaries received Lafayette in a chamber furnished with mahogany sofas and chairs and redecorated with red and blue carpet, with draperies of the same colors and studded with stars. Spending $230 on repairs and $2,708 on decor and furnishings, Strickland had created a room far different from the space occupied by the Continental Congress.[43] An eighteenth-century legislative hall furnished with Windsor chairs would not have been grand enough to match the exuberance that greeted Lafayette or to honor the cherished memory of the American Revolution. In the newly decorated chamber, the living hero was surrounded by memorials of his departed comrades: a wood sculpture of George Washington carved by William Rush and portraits of Revolutionary heroes by Charles Willson Peale, now eighty-three years old, and several of his artist sons. The setting suited Americans' sentimentality toward the memory of the American Revolution and its heroes.[44]

The ceremonial reception of Lafayette communicated Philadelphians' perception of the State House as a place made sacred by the heroic deeds of the Revolutionary generation. Welcoming Lafayette, Philadelphia Mayor Joseph Watson demonstrated that public memory of the Declaration overshadowed all other events in the history of the State House, including the Constitutional Convention that met in the same room. Mayor Watson described the old Assembly Room as a "hallowed hall, which may emphatically be called the Birthplace of Independence." Here, he said, "a convention of men, such as the world has rarely seen, pre-eminent for talents and patriotism, solemnly declared their determination to assume for themselves the right of Self Government, and that they and their posterity should thenceforth assert their just rank among the nations of the world."[45] Lafayette replied in kind: "Here within these sacred walls . . . was boldly declared the independence of these United States," and "Here, sir, was planned the formation of our virtuous, brave, revolutionary army, and the providential inspiration received that gave the command of it to our beloved, matchless Washington."[46]

With Lafayette's visit, Philadelphians created a reception ritual that prevailed throughout the nineteenth century and continually reinforced the definition of the east room of the State House as a historic place. Significantly for public memory, the ritual identified the State House as the place where solemn founding fathers arrived at a courageous consensus and declared independence from Great Britain. For Americans of the 1820s, especially in the presence of the great Lafayette, this memory surpassed all others. Frequently in succeeding decades, Philadelphians reenacted the ritual and the memory of 1776 when they welcomed visiting dignitaries to the room where independence was declared. Visitors echoed the honor paid by their hosts, reinforcing and perpetuating the room's sacred associations.

During preparations for Lafayette's visit, Philadelphians also named the east room of the State House to identify the space explicitly with the Declaration of Independence. During the weeks leading to the general's arrival, the phrase "Hall of Independence" emerged as a common reference. It was perhaps a convenient shorthand that evolved amid the intensity of preparations. At the outset, in July and August 1824, Philadelphia newspapers reported plans for decorating "the room in the State House in which the Declaration was signed."[47] The committee overseeing the plans spoke of the "East Room," the "drawing room," or the "hall prepared for his reception." By three weeks before Lafayette's arrival, however, the committee's records began to refer to the "Hall of Independence."[48] The new identification appeared on the printed invitations to Lafayette's reception and, perhaps as a result, appeared consistently in newspaper reports of the event.[49] For years afterward, "Hall of Independence" or, in shorter form, "Independence Hall," remained the appellation attached to the east room on the first floor of the State House. By extension, during the middle decades of the nineteenth century, "Independence Hall" sometimes served as a reference for the entire State House.

Lafayette's visit to Philadelphia transformed the State House into a place where citizens from many walks of life could connect with the American Revolution, thereby making the past part of their own experience. Lafayette's public reception in the Hall of Independence "presented a picture of the most perfect equality that can be imagined," the general's traveling companion observed. During several hours of greetings, "Mechanics with their hardened hands and unrolled sleeves advanced to Lafayette; the magistrate and plain clad farmer stood together; the clergymen and player stood side by side, and children sure of having their rights and feebleness respected marched boldly along before soldiers and sailors." Ensuring that the combined memory of 1824 and the American Revolution would be carried into the future, Lafayette returned to the State House yard several days later to extend additional greetings to thousands of Philadelphia schoolchildren.[50]

Although the feverish enthusiasm for Lafayette brought new attention to the old Pennsylvania State House, the Hall of Independence remained a room in a public building for the city of Philadelphia. Through rhetoric and ritual, Philadelphians recognized the room as a historic space, but they quickly removed its splendid decorations to make room for the October municipal election. The Mayor's Court continued in session across the hall, and Peale's museum stayed on the second floor until 1827. Nevertheless, Lafayette's visit had focused renewed attention on the historic associations of the State House. In 1825, as part of the official renaming of Philadelphia's public squares, the State House yard was designated Independence Square, extending the commemoration of the American Revolution from the building into the adjacent public space. Adding to the city's recognition of its Colonial and Revolutionary-era history, other major squares were designated Penn, Logan, Rittenhouse, Franklin, and Washington. The space named Washington Square, diagonally southwest of the State House, had been the burial ground for paupers, Revolutionary War casualties, yellow fever victims, and people of African descent. In naming the square for Washington, other histories became subsumed by the association with the Revolution and reverence for the first president of the United States.[51]

Public memory of the American Revolution, especially the Declaration of Independence, intensified further with the fiftieth anniversary of the United States in 1826 and the coincident deaths of John Adams and Thomas Jefferson on July Fourth of that year. Upon learning about Adams and Jefferson, Philadelphians fell into mourning and set aside July 24 as a day of remembrance. At the State House where Lafayette had been celebrated, the city eulogized the two former presidents from the generation of 1776. The rooms on the first floor were draped in black; the old State House bell was muffled and tolled. In Independence Square on July 24, a military and civic parade entered through the Walnut Street gate and marched in slow cadence to a platform erected behind the hall. Around the platform, which had been draped in black and decorated with flags, Philadelphians gathered to listen to a memorial oration for the two founding fathers who had expired, providentially it seemed, on the fiftieth anniversary of the Declaration of Independence. The older mourners might have remembered that in 1799, when Philadelphians learned of the death of George Washington, they had processed from Congress Hall to a memorial service at a nearby church. Now, in 1826, Philadelphians turned to the State House as a place of memory of the American Revolution and the departed members of the founding generation.[52]

Rebuilding the Past

By saving the State House from destruction, welcoming the Marquis de Lafayette, and participating in the events of 1826, Philadelphians had demonstrated the increasing value that they placed in preserving the memory of the American Revolution. To this point, they perpetuated memory more through their actions than by attempting to re-create the physical surroundings of the people and events that they revered. However, the elaborate reception of Lafayette and the memorial gathering for Jefferson and Adams had long-lasting effects on the people who participated, and in turn, a significant impact on the future of the State House. With the building so closely associated with the Declaration of Independence, Philadelphians took the first steps toward restoring its 1776 appearance.

The State House had been without its wooden steeple for more than forty-five years when, in 1828, the Philadelphia City Councils decided to replace it. The new steeple began as a project to meet practical needs, with the Councils calling for a new "turret" atop the truncated State House tower to provide the city with a new clock, fire watchtower, and bell. These were necessities at a time when early industrialization required the regulation of time and fires occurred with devastating frequency in densely populated urban areas. Although the project was born of necessity, the process of selecting a design for the new steeple became a debate about the merits of historic restoration. More than twenty years before the restoration of Washington's home at Mount Vernon, widely credited as launching the historic preservation movement in the

United States, Philadelphians grappled with the merits of rebuilding a structure of the past as a means of preserving historical memory.[53] Their recent experiences—the deaths of Revolutionary-era citizens, the desire to sustain and honor the memory of the nation's founders, and the fervor generated by the visit of Lafayette—influenced their decision about the State House steeple.

To design the new extension for the original brick tower that remained from the 1750s, city officials called once again upon William Strickland, the architect who had decorated the State House for Lafayette's reception. Strickland produced a plan at first regarded as a "restoration of the spire originally erected with the building, and standing there on the 4th of July, 1776." However, as council members soon pointed out, Strickland's design was not an exact copy of the original. Where the earlier steeple had been constructed of wood and designed in stacked tiers culminating in a cupola, Strickland's plan called for building up the surviving tower twenty-eight to thirty feet higher in brick, extending the tower straight upward rather than in tiers, with a cupola and spire at the top. Strickland said the tower needed the additional brick to support the weight of the new fire bell and the vibration from the desired clock.[54]

Most members of the Philadelphia City Councils in 1828 had been born after the original steeple was demolished, but a drawing produced at their meeting of February 28 demonstrated the differences between Strickland's plan and the original. Despite the practical necessities of housing the clock and bell, some council members argued that the tower project had a historic purpose as well. Their discussion demonstrated the reverence they attached to the building for its association with the Declaration of Independence. "It is a sacred spot—a sacred building," said Benjamin Tilghman, a Chestnut Street lawyer who had served on the committee that prepared for Lafayette's visit in 1824. "I regret that unhallowed hands were ever permitted to touch it, and I regard the rebuilding of the steeple as an entering wedge for restoring the building to the state in which it stood in 1776." Another council member, Henry Troth, a druggist whose business stood in nearby High Street, added, "By carrying up the turret two stories higher with brick . . . instead of the old wood work, the effect of the original is entirely destroyed." The issue was not just a matter of city services and architecture, he said: "Our character is at stake, as men of taste, and as admirers of antiquity, and I hope we will not proceed hastily in this business." The councilmen also recognized that they had a unique opportunity to bridge the past and present. "The restoration . . . is now possible, as persons are now living who remember the exact appearance of every part," Tilghman commented. "Fifty years hence it will be impossible."[55]

Discussion of the steeple design demonstrated how attitudes toward the State

House had changed in the fifteen years since parts of it had been demolished to make room for new office buildings. Arguing against the Strickland design, John C. Lowber, a lawyer with an office on Walnut Street, appealed to his fellow council members to consider the role of the State House in preserving the memory of the events that had taken place there. "No man will be able to look at that building with its new steeple and be able to persuade himself that it represents the ancient State House," Lowber said. "If the original features of the building cannot be preserved, I would much rather the whole were demolished." A monument at the site of the building would be preferable to the Strickland design, he said.[56]

In the face of Council opposition, Strickland changed his plan. He reduced the height of the masonry portion of the tower and more closely approximated the steeple of 1776. The resulting steeple housed the clock and bell necessary to regulate the nineteenth-century city, but it also fulfilled Philadelphians' desires for a material representation of the past. Although Strickland is frequently credited with being America's first restoration architect because of his State House steeple, the record shows that the will of his clients significantly influenced his plans.[57] The new steeple, designed to overcome the objections of the Philadelphia Common Council, was in place in time for the 1828 Fourth of July celebration. The new bell, cast by John Wilbank of Philadelphia, took its place in the steeple the following September. The old State House bell, with the inscription "Proclaim liberty throughout all the land" remained suspended in the brick tower below the steeple.[58]

The alteration of the Pennsylvania State House in 1828 had great significance for the evolving recognition of the building as a historic place. The Common Council debate showed that Philadelphians were beginning to think of the State House as a building that should be preserved as a historic landmark. In making a decision about the steeple design within this context, the Philadelphians of 1828 shaped the feature that prevailed in representations of the State House into the twenty-first century. Even though the tower and steeple are at the back of the structure, this was the side later depicted on coins and postage stamps; the tower side has often been depicted as the "front" in architectural copies of Independence Hall.[59] Facing onto the open space of Independence Square, with its lawn, walks, and trees, the tower side of the building presented a more pleasing appearance than the intended front of the building on Chestnut Street. In contrast to the pastoral appearance of the tower side, the Chestnut Street facade faced a highly urbanized landscape of storefronts, office buildings, and as the nineteenth century progressed, omnibuses and street cars.

The steeple project provided the opening wedge for restoration that Councilman

Benjamin Tilghman had envisioned. As with the tower project, however, a lack of reliable information combined with the practical needs of the growing city constrained other attempts to keep alive the memory of the founders by re-creating their material surroundings. In 1831, the City Councils hired architect John Haviland, designer of the admired Eastern State Penitentiary, to restore the Hall of Independence to its 1776 appearance, but Haviland acknowledged that precise information was difficult to come by. He surmised that the room must have been similar to the courtroom across the hall and, as a result, his "restoration" gave the east room the aura of an eighteenth-century court.[60] Along with Haviland's project, city officials for the first time acknowledged the historic associations of the space with a marker, a brass plaque engraved with the Declaration of Independence.[61] Beyond the Hall of Independence, however, the State House continued to be pressed into government service. The Mayor's Court continued to meet on the first floor. After Charles Willson Peale fulfilled his long-held wish to move out of the State House to more spacious quarters, city officials ordered the second floor remodeled and leased to the U.S. Marshal and U.S. District Court.[62]

Despite the growing recognition of the historic associations of the State House—one room of it, at least—the Hall of Independence was not yet a major destination for travelers or for Philadelphians showing the sites of the city to visitors. Travelers were drawn not to the old, but to the new. As unlikely as it seems in retrospect, the primary attraction for leisure travelers to Philadelphia in the middle decades of the nineteenth century was the new Eastern State Penitentiary, where visitors were admitted for a glimpse of the solitary-confinement method of reforming criminals. The penitentiary was the prime attraction in Philadelphia for Alexis de Tocqueville, who visited in 1831 on the journey that led to his *Democracy in America*, and Charles Dickens, whose visit in 1842 is described in his *American Notes*.[63]

Across town at the State House, the city opened the Hall of Independence to the public after the Haviland restoration, but visitors gained entrance only by summoning a janitor from the tower to descend and open the chamber with his key. The greater attraction of the building was the new steeple, which afforded the highest available view of the city.[64] Standing ninety-five feet above street level, safeguarded by railings, visitors overlooked an astonishing scene. The city and county of 160,000 people stretched north and south along the Delaware River for five miles; to the west, Philadelphians had also settled a mile and a half along the Schuylkill River. Furthermore, the population was spreading into the land between the two rivers, finally beginning to fill in the boundaries of the city envisioned by William Penn. Most astounding was the activity directly north of the State House: "It extends, as it were, in an unbro-

13. The State House steeple, restored in 1828, afforded aerial views of the city that had grown up around the old state capitol. *North View from Independence Hall Steeple* (1838) depicts a district evolving from an old artisan neighborhood into a dense area of small factories. In the twentieth century, these blocks became part of Independence National Historical Park. (Courtesy of Independence National Historical Park)

ken assemblage of bustling streets, churches, gardens, banks, and public edifices of every description, for nearly three miles," one viewer recorded in 1829. From the height of the State House steeple, the writer observed the traffic below on Chestnut Street—"the care-worn merchant at his bales, the laborer at his toil, the rich man's coach . . . upon its gilded wheels"—and reflected on the illustrious figures of the past who had traversed the same ground.[65]

Although Independence Hall was a place of importance in the nation's history, its survival in the early nineteenth century depended on the guardianship of citizens who lived in close proximity to the building. Practical considerations pressed against the old Pennsylvania State House, prevailing in 1812 when parts of the building were demolished, but giving way by 1828, when the new steeple was built. During the 1820s and 1830s, the building became more than a courthouse and rental property. As caretakers of the State House, Philadelphians could demonstrate their regard for the memory of the American Revolution by acts of commemoration and restoration, thereby bolstering its identity as a place of importance to the nation. The building was a bridge between past and present, but it was also a bridge between individual and nation—a connection forged by citizens, not by the state.[66]

With potentially longer life spans than human beings, buildings have the capacity to function as repositories of collective memory.[67] Before the last living memories of the American Revolution could pass away, Philadelphians created memorials to 1776 at Independence Hall. Preserving their collective memory of the past, they built a new steeple to look like the old, renovated a room, and placed a historical marker calling attention to the Declaration of Independence. By embedding their regard for the past in a building, they established a means for communicating their view of history to future generations. Tied to a building, this particular vision of the past would be restricted to place, communicated only to those who visited Independence Hall. However, with a life span potentially longer than any single generation, a building can conceivably extend the range of collective memory across time. As long as Independence Hall survived, so might the memory of the American Revolution deposited there. The collective memory forged among individuals who were united by their experience in early nineteenth-century Philadelphia might continue to contribute to the ideas and beliefs about the American Revolution that would constitute public memory in the future.

Buildings may hold memories, but they also allow those memories to be selected and compartmentalized. During the 1820s, Philadelphians identified the old Pennsylvania State House as a place associated with the American Revolution, particularly the Declaration of Independence. The association was natural, given the visit by Lafayette, the jubilee year of the Declaration, and the deaths of Jefferson and Adams. However, the process of memorializing the events of 1776 allowed other aspects of the building's past to fade away. The building reflected no memory of the Constitutional Convention or the more than sixty-year occupancy of the Pennsylvania state government. Rooms vacated by Charles Willson Peale were quickly put to different use, erasing the building's association with art and science. With attention focused on the room of the Declaration of Independence, the memory of the American Revolution was attached to revered founders and an act of political consensus, thereby obscuring conflict.

Nations are built through such processes of remembering and forgetting, striking a balance between those things that pull citizens together and the more divisive issues that may drive them apart.[68] If buildings project an aura of stability, preserving a history of consensus while obscuring conflict, then they may contribute to a sense of national community. However, to obscure conflict is also to minimize the complexity of national life. In the tension that preceded the Civil War, Philadelphians found new motivations for transforming their relic of the American Revolution into a national shrine.

Chapter 4

SHRINE

Slavery, Nativism, and the Forgotten History of the Nineteenth Century

Consider two fictional portrayals of Independence Hall from the 1840s: in one short story, the old Pennsylvania State House is portrayed as a place of the nation and the past, the scene of the triumph of the Declaration of Independence. The story takes place on the Fourth of July, 1776, as citizens wait anxiously for a decision from the Second Continental Congress. Above them, in the State House steeple, the old bell-ringer awaits the word. Finally, the news comes from a small boy who cries up to the steeple, "Ring!" With that, the Liberty Bell announces the birth of an independent nation.[1] Now, turn to a novel of the same decade. Here, the State House stands in nineteenth-century Philadelphia, its bell incessantly tolling the hours to a citizenry consumed by debauchery, corruption, and greed. In one episode, the character Devil-Bug falls into a drunken sleep, and the State House inhabits his nightmare. He finds he has been transported forward in time more than one hundred years, to 1950, and he discovers the State House in ruins and Philadelphians preparing to build a king's castle in its place. A ghostly figure confirms: "Yes! It is old Independence Hall! The lordlings of the Quaker City have sold their fathers' bones for gold! . . . The spirit of the old Republic is dethroned, and they build a royal mansion over the ruins of Independence Hall!"[2]

In these literary works of the 1840s, Independence Hall has multiple personalities, attached to past and present, representing not only patriotic enthusiasm but also fatalistic gloom. Remarkably, both the short story and the novel were the work of the same author, Philadelphian George Lippard, one of the most popular writers of his day.

GRAHAM'S MAGAZINE.

Vol. XLIV.   PHILADELPHIA, JUNE, 1854.   No. 6.

The Bellman informed of the passage of the Declaration of Independence.   (See page 562.)

14. Perpetuating George Lippard's fictional account of the Liberty Bell ringing to announce the Declaration of Independence, *Graham's Magazine* featured this illustration based on the story on its cover of June 1854. The accompanying article incorporated the story into its historical account of July 4, 1776. (Courtesy of the Library Company of Philadelphia)

His novel *The Quaker City: or, The Monks of Monks Hall*, serialized in 1844–45, was a torrid critique of the corruption of ruling elites. In book form, it was the best-selling novel in the United States until *Uncle Tom's Cabin* (1852), selling sixty thousand copies in its first year and going through twenty-seven printings thereafter.[3] Lippard's short story about the Declaration of Independence, set in the same city but so different in tone, appeared in Philadelphia's *Saturday Courier* in 1847 as part of a series of "Legends of the American Revolution." Quickly accepted as fact rather than fiction, the story of the bell-ringer at Independence Hall elevated the historical associations of the building and perpetuated a long-lasting association between the Liberty Bell and the Fourth of July.[4]

In the middle decades of the nineteenth century, Independence Hall simultaneously occupied a place in public memory and a place within a major American city, in a nation wrestling with sectional, racial, ethnic, and class conflict. In these contentious times, Independence Hall did not stand sealed in eighteenth-century splendor. How could it? This was where George Washington, Thomas Jefferson, Benjamin Franklin, and other revered founders conceived the nation, which nativist Americans of the mid-nineteenth century feared would crumble from the influence of immigrants, particularly Roman Catholics. This was the place that issued the Declaration of Independence, which seemed to promise life, liberty, and the pursuit of happiness— conditions that were elusive to laborers whose lives were being transformed by industrialization. The Declaration and the U.S. Constitution were also at the heart of the national debate about slavery. Such controversies inhabited and surrounded Independence Hall, creating tensions that both challenged and propelled its evolution as a historic shrine. In and around this historic building, Americans grappled with how ideals such as liberty and equality would be defined as the United States grew and changed.

Conflict and Commemoration

Americans in the second quarter of the nineteenth century created a political culture that reached to the past to define patriotism for a new age. Like President Andrew Jackson, who invoked the legacy of Thomas Jefferson to champion the rights of the "common man," Americans demonstrated a keen interest in constructing a nation that maintained a strong relationship with its revolutionary past. However, they envisioned that past in differing ways and for differing purposes. Events of the 1820s, especially the visit of the Marquis de Lafayette, contributed to a public memory of the nation's founding centered on revered heroes, particularly George Washington. However, by the

1830s, the economic upheavals of national expansion and industrialization stirred unrest, especially among laborers whose lives seemed to fall short of the ideals of liberty and equality expressed in the Declaration of Independence. In the nation's evolving industrial centers, workers adopted the language of the Declaration to call attention to aspects of the founding ideology that remained unfulfilled for nineteenth-century Americans.[5]

In this turbulent period in American history, Philadelphians used the old Pennsylvania State House and its public square in ways that reflected contested memories of the American Revolution and the tensions of sustaining the nation in the decades prior to the Civil War. Inside the building, rituals in the first-floor Hall of Independence memorialized the American Revolution by creating tableaus of national harmony. The Hall that received Lafayette in 1824 continued to function as a place for receiving and honoring national, international, and local heroes. Its rituals were formal, scripted by public officials. Independence Square, meanwhile, was a more contentious place where mass meetings and demonstrations often underscored the political, social, economic, and racial divisions that persisted within the nation. Like the officials who received honored guests in the Hall of Independence, Philadelphians who gathered in the square forged connections between the present and the nation's past. However, in contrast to the sedate rituals inside the State House, activities in the square seized upon the revolutionary language of the Declaration of Independence to challenge the nation to live up to its founding ideology.

While still a center of government and a place for public assembly, the old Pennsylvania State House by the 1830s stood in an urban environment marked by economic transformation. With the political revolution of the eighteenth century fading into history, Americans were swept into a "market revolution" driven by rapid expansion, new transportation systems, and the rise of manufacturing. The transformation could be seen north of the State House, where city blocks evolved from rows of artisan-occupied houses into a dense manufacturing district that employed wage laborers and marketed products across the nation. One block east of the State House, meanwhile, the imposing Second Bank of the United States exercised power over the nation's money supply, triggering bitter controversy in the 1820s and 1830s. Raising issues of liberty, equality, and power, the upheavals of the market revolution confronted Americans with the challenge of interpreting the nation's founding ideals for a new age.[6]

Liberty and power lay at the heart of the "Bank War" of the 1830s, which spilled from the Second Bank of the United States into the nearby State House and Independence Square. For Andrew Jackson, the Bank represented a bastion of power and a threat to American liberty. Battling the Bank became a crusade and hallmark of Jackson's presidency. In 1832, Jackson vetoed renewal of the Bank's charter. The next year, on a victory tour following his reelection, the president came to Philadelphia to mark the first anniversary of his Bank veto with a reception in the Hall of Independence. The event on June 10, 1833, erupted in a display of the diverging commemorative practices of the era. Although city officials had planned a solemn ritual welcome for a national dignitary, the reception turned into a raucous citizens' celebration of Jackson. In a scene reminiscent of the public's rush into the White House to celebrate Jackson's first inauguration, enthusiastic supporters surged into the Hall of Independence. The room became so packed that some Jackson partisans escaped the stifling chamber through the open windows, tumbling six feet down onto the square. Jackson was as controversial as he was popular, however, especially among Philadelphia manufacturers and financiers. The next year, after Jackson withdrew federal deposits from the Bank, Philadelphia employers and bankers organized a massive anti-Jackson demonstration in Independence Square, marshaling thousands of workers to carry banners and join in protesting the president's action and the financial panic that followed.[7]

Workers also marched in Independence Square in their own behalf, calling attention to growing class conflict in an industrializing city. The market revolution transformed the lives of working people, pushing them from an artisan-based economy of individual producers and small shops into larger-scale manufacturing. The transformation left many workers with less control over their labor, greater dependence on employers, and increased regulation of their behavior on the job. Excluded from financial or political power, workers of this era often expressed their grievances in the streets, parading with militia groups, striking for better wages or working conditions, or at times rioting through urban areas. Often during the 1820s, 1830s, and 1840s, laborers in cities including Boston and New York invoked the language of the Declaration of Independence in their quest for improved working conditions. In Philadelphia, Independence Square offered a place where workers could contrast their grievances with the rights they expected in a nation founded with the Declaration's ideology of liberty and equality.[8]

Labor grievances echoed in Independence Square during the 1830s, when Philadelphia workers acted on their changing circumstances by organizing unions and staging strikes over working conditions. In 1834, skilled and semiskilled workers formed the General Trades Union of the City and County of Philadelphia, which grew within two years from about two thousand to ten thousand members. When the union engaged in nation's first general strike in 1835, laborers paraded to Independence

Square to demand a ten-hour work day. The next year, after leaders of a dockworkers' strike were arrested by order of the mayor of Philadelphia, workers gathered in Independence Square—the seat of city government—to demonstrate for the right to set the prices for their own labor.[9] The square served as a physical connection between nineteenth-century grievances and the nation's founding ideals. The *Public Ledger* echoed the language of the meeting when it reported, "The workingmen, the pillars of the country, know their rights, and knowing them, will maintain them."[10] Although the economic depression of the later 1830s undercut the nascent labor movement, Independence Square remained a place for labor protest. In 1847, workers paraded into the square, accompanied by fife and drum, to protest competition by immigrant laborers. In 1857, an estimated ten thousand unemployed laborers gathered in the square to call attention to their hardships.[11]

While often an arena of conflict, Independence Square also drew Philadelphians together in patriotic support of the nation. When the United States went to war with Mexico in 1846, Philadelphians gathered in the square with nationalist enthusiasm. Responding to the declaration of war, a public meeting in the square adopted supportive resolutions that recalled the dedication of the signers of the Declaration of Independence. "Should the emergencies of our nation require it," the resolution declared, "our services, our fortunes, and our lives are now voluntarily pledged for the preservation of the integrity of the national domain, the security of the liberties and the conservation of the rights of our fellow citizens, and the honor of our country." To honor American victories, Philadelphia city officials illuminated the buildings on the State House square with candles in every window pane. When the war ended in 1848, Philadelphians welcomed home their local military heroes with a reception in the Hall of Independence. For the occasion, the Philadelphia Gas Works configured gas pipes into figures representing victory and peace, thereby embellishing the State House with a flaming Goddess of Peace, holding an olive branch, seated among emblems of American manufacturing and beneath a hovering eagle. Four thousand burners lit the display.[12]

Public demonstrations in Independence Square showed a sustained recognition of the ideology of the Declaration of Independence and hope for extending the promise of liberty. In a city with a high immigration rate, aspirations for freedom had an international flavor. In an extraordinary demonstration in April 1848, a multinational group of European immigrants showed support for the 1848 revolutionary movements against European monarchies by gathering in Independence Square, the birthplace of American independence. The *Public Ledger* reported, "The concourse was immense, and exceeded any demonstration which has been held in the same enclosure for many years." The demonstrators set up three stands: a main stage decorated with American and French flags and two speaker's stands where orators addressed the crowds in French, German, and English. A German band played in the square, and patriots paraded with flags of the republican movements of France, Germany, and Italy.[13]

Although intended as a demonstration for freedom in Europe, the gathering unexpectedly became a forum for protesting the limits of liberty in the United States as well. The demonstration had been advertised in the newspapers as a call for universal liberty, and in Philadelphia in the 1840s, the most passionate activists for liberty did not have far to walk to get to Independence Square. Unexpectedly, the European immigrants found themselves joined by a group of African Americans who had read about the demonstration for liberty and were determined to be part of it. They entered through the south gate of the square and gathered around their own orators. Philadelphia police at first tried to eject the black participants, but the Europeans insisted that they be allowed to stay. Like the European immigrants, African Americans living in Philadelphia knew that liberty remained a distant goal.

While public activities animated by the ideology of the Declaration of Independence defined Independence Square, the historical space inside Independence Hall remained largely the domain of city officials who defined the "Hall of Independence" on the first floor as a place for scripted ceremonial occasions. In the tradition of Lafayette's visit in 1824, the Hall richly fulfilled its ritual function as a reception room for the city of Philadelphia. As Andrew Jackson's reception of 1833 indicates, the room was a place for welcoming presidents and other prominent politicians, including Henry Clay, Martin Van Buren, William Henry Harrison, James K. Polk, and John Tyler. Philadelphians also used the Hall for welcoming European visitors such as Louis Kossuth, a revolutionary escaped from Hungary; Prince de Joinville, son of King Louis Philippe of France; and Granville John Penn, great-grandson of the founder of Pennsylvania. As railroads made travel easier and more accessible to the wider public, city officials also greeted visiting businessmen, newspaper editors, militia companies, and volunteer firefighters. Exchanges of welcome within the Hall of Independence reinforced its association with the nation's founders for both local officials and visitors. The setting allowed people of the nineteenth century to connect with national heroes of the past.[14]

Although Philadelphians received political dignitaries in the Hall of Independence, they tried to safeguard the historical aura of the room from practical politics as well as commercial exploitation. In 1836, city officials took steps to protect the room from "purposes inconsistent with the feeling cherished by the people towards this consecrated place." The City Councils outlawed "public exhibitions, or any display for which money should be demanded for admittance."[15] The city also barred activities of political parties, which engaged in particularly raucous electioneering during the Jacksonian era. Although Independence Square and the buildings flanking the old State House accommodated political rallies, party meetings, and torchlight parades, such explicit partisanship was not allowed into the Hall of Independence.[16] Citing long-standing practice, city officials declined requests to use the Hall from both the Native American Party in 1844 and the Whig Party in 1848, the year the Whig national convention met in Philadelphia. Whigs in the City Councils argued that because of its historical associations, the Hall would be an appropriate setting for all political conventions "appointed for so grave and important a purpose" as nominating a future president of the United States. However, they failed to gain admission for the Whig National Convention, which met instead in an auditorium several blocks away.[17]

Through rituals of reception, the Hall of Independence functioned as a place for recalling heroes of the present as well the past, living as well as dead. Beginning in the 1840s, Philadelphians expressed their respect for nationally prominent men who had died by offering their families use of the Hall, thus surrounding the newly departed with the aura of reverence attached to earlier heroes. John Quincy Adams, the former president who died at work in the House of Representatives in 1848, was the first to lie in state in the Hall of Independence. En route from Washington to Massachusetts, the Adams funeral train stopped in Philadelphia, where the casket was moved from the train to a hearse and pulled to the State House by six white horses with black plumes. The casket remained overnight in the Hall of Independence, draped in black for the occasion, before continuing its solemn journey to Massachusetts.[18] Four years later, Henry Clay also was brought to the State House after his death in Washington. The public was permitted to file by his closed casket. "The doors of the hall were thrown open, and the people to the number of thousands, of both sexes and of all ages, hues and conditions were admitted to take a last look of the magnificent coffin," the *Evening Bulletin* reported. After several hours of viewing, the casket was returned to the funeral train bound for Clay's home state of Kentucky.[19]

Philadelphians also used the Hall of Independence to honor a deceased native son. Elisha Kent Kane, a member of a prominent local family, was a physician and world explorer, most famous for his expeditions to the Arctic in search of a route to the North Pole. After he died in 1857 from disease contracted during one of his Arctic jour-

15. Viewings of honored, recently deceased heroes of the nineteenth century forged connections with the legacy of the nation's founders. Here, Philadelphians gather in the Hall of Independence in 1857 to pay their respects to the Arctic explorer Elisha Kent Kane, whose body lies in the company of the Liberty Bell and portraits of Revolutionary-era heroes. (Courtesy of Independence National Historical Park)

neys, the thirty-seven-year-old Kane was returned and honored as a hero in his hometown. Philadelphians paid their respects to the remains at the Hall of Independence. "Long before the hour for the starting of the procession the principal thoroughfares were crowded with citizens hurrying towards Independence Hall for the purpose of getting a glimpse of the coffin," the *Public Ledger* reported. Eulogizing Kane inside the hall, the Reverend C. W. Shields united Kane's memory with the historic associations where he lay: "Fittingly we have suffered his honored remains to repose a few pensive hours at the shrine where patriotism gathers its fairest memories and choicest honors," he said.[20] The Revolutionary War generation had passed away, but heroism had continued. A new hero joined the heroes of old in the Hall of Independence.

Freedom and Slavery

While nineteenth-century Americans commemorated the nation's founders and pursued the ideals expressed by the Declaration of Independence, they also grappled with the issue of slavery, the dilemma left unresolved by the heroes of the American Revolution. As a place central to the nation's early political history, the old Pennsylvania State House had a long association with debates over slavery, which took place within the Second Continental Congress, the Constitutional Convention, the United States Congress of the 1790s, and the Pennsylvania Assembly. As we have seen, the State House stood near one of the early nation's vibrant communities of African Americans, who maintained a vigilant watch for potential threats to their own independence. For this community, the decades prior to the Civil War brought alarming developments that stood in stark contradiction to the ideals of the Declaration of Independence and the Constitution. For the Pennsylvania State House, which functioned in part as a federal courthouse, the continuing controversy of slavery precipitated a startling series of events that have long been obscured in the public memory of Independence Hall as a place for commemorating the achievement of American freedom.

Although Pennsylvania had begun gradual abolition of slavery by law in 1780, African Americans living south of the State House in the mid-nineteenth century found freedom to be fragile and subject to threats beyond their control. Whatever prosperity or influence they achieved met with a backlash from whites fearful of losing their own economic or political ground. During the 1830s and 1840s, danger appeared in the streets as well as legislative halls. As African Americans migrated from the South in increasing numbers, and as some prospered, black Philadelphians were targeted repeatedly by white rioters who attacked people in the streets and invaded homes and churches. Making matters worse, in 1838 a revised Pennsylvania constitution took away African Americans' right to vote. That same year, within sight of the Independence Hall steeple, an angry white mob torched the new Pennsylvania Hall, which had been built by abolitionist groups as a forum for free speech. Still concerned with freeing their Southern brethren from slavery, free black people in Philadelphia and elsewhere found their own liberty endangered.[21]

As the home of the nation's leading free black community, Philadelphia became a capital of resistance against attempts to exclude African Americans from the full rights of American citizenship. Beginning in 1830, the black churches in the blocks south of Independence Hall hosted a series of national conventions of free people of color. Prompted at first by events in Cincinnati, Ohio, where local officials demanded that African Americans register with authorities, the conventions advocated a range of initiatives to build security for free black people and to work toward the abolition of slavery. Out of necessity, the conventions supported a colony in Canada as a refuge for African Americans fleeing from Ohio or other states, but they firmly resisted projects to transport free black people to Africa. The convention messages emphasized the United States as "our country" and the "land of our nativity" and asserted African Americans' allegiance to the nation. They invoked the Declaration of Independence to make the point that efforts to deport people of color from the United States contradicted the nation's founding principles. Considering the Declaration to be a statement of "incontrovertible facts," convention delegates advised free blacks throughout the United States, "that our forlorn and deplorable situation earnestly and loudly demand of us to devise and pursue all legal means for the speedy elevation of ourselves and brethren to the scale and standing of men."[22]

Free black Pennsylvanians also fought, in vain, against a new state constitution that for the first time excluded blacks from voting. With one word, "white," inserted into the qualifications for voting, the Pennsylvania Constitution of 1838 took away the voting rights that had been open to free blacks since 1790. Attempting to block ratification, free black Philadelphians organized a mass meeting at the Presbyterian Church on Seventh Street and endorsed an impassioned "Appeal of Forty Thousand Citizens" to be distributed throughout the state. Written by black abolitionist Robert Purvis, the appeal proclaimed "WE ARE CITIZENS" and challenged Pennsylvanians to live up to the legacy of the American Revolution, especially the acts of Pennsylvania that had abolished slavery and allowed all free men the right to vote. "We honor Pennsylvania and her noble institutions too much to part with our birthright, as her free citizens, without a struggle," the resolution declared.[23] Such determination could not overcome white perceptions of blacks as impoverished, unschooled, and disorderly, despite the appeal's presentation of statistics to disprove each point. African Americans in Pennsylvania lost the vote until after the Civil War.

During the conventions and the constitution fight of the 1830s, African Americans invoked the words of the Declaration of Independence and the Constitution, but they apparently did not take their appeals to nearby Independence Square. This is not surprising, given that blacks were targets of white violence and ridicule, and whites controlled the city and county governments meeting on the square. Nevertheless, Independence Hall as well as its bell with the inscription, "Proclaim liberty throughout all the land unto all the inhabitants thereof," entered into antislavery arguments in the decades preceding the Civil War. The "Liberty Bell," as the abolitionists called the old State House bell, emerged as an antislavery symbol, and Independence Hall functioned as a place for calling attention to the contradictions between the nation's founding ideals and the persistence of slavery in the United States.

In the 1830s, when New York and Boston abolitionists began referring to the "Liberty Bell" in antislavery literature, they were inspired by the inscription of the Philadelphia bell. However, the "Liberty Bell" soon developed into a symbol detached from the State House bell in Philadelphia. In the *Liberty Bell,* a periodical published in Boston beginning in 1839, the phrase was often used metaphorically, rather than in reference to a specific bell. The title page of each issue established more ancient origins for the bell symbolism, quoting a passage from a tale published in England in the late fifteenth or early sixteenth century.[24] The quotation, published with archaic spellings as if to emphasize the historic depths of the antislavery cause, spoke of bells ringing to drive away evil spirits. Inside nearly every issue, an illustration of a bell appeared with a poem titled "The Liberty Bell." Although the illustrations displayed part of the Philadelphia bell's inscription, "Proclaim Liberty . . . All the Inhabitants," they were not identified in print as the Pennsylvania State House bell. When pictured on the periodical's cover, the "Liberty Bell" hung suspended from a tree. The periodical's poems invoked "the Liberty Bell" but also "Liberty's Bell" and "Liberty Bells." Through the metaphor of bells, the verses extolled the joy that would accompany the end of slavery.[25]

While Boston abolitionists transformed the Liberty Bell into a symbol, antislavery activists in Philadelphia used Independence Hall to call attention to the contradictions between slavery and the language of equality in the Declaration of Independence. Pennsylvania Hall, which opened in 1838 at Sixth and Cherry Streets, about two and a half blocks north of Independence Hall, helped to facilitate the connection. With the motto "Virtue, Liberty, and Independence" in gold letters in its second-floor meeting hall, Pennsylvania Hall was built by antislavery activists, but they declared it to be a forum for the free speech of all. Before and after the Hall's destruction by an anti-abolitionist mob on May 17, 1838, speakers called attention to its proximity to the birthplace of the Declaration of Independence. Among the speakers prior to the attack, the Reverend Alvan Stewart of Utica, New York, declared that tolerating slavery at any time after the Declaration of Independence constituted "base hypocrisy," and he imagined a scenario of fugitive slaves arriving in Philadelphia from Maryland in search of freedom. Turned away from the city's churches, the fugitives in Stewart's story resorted to Independence Hall, where they encountered a common argument against confronting the issue of slavery:

> "Let us" they said, "go to the Hall of Independence, and see if the ghosts
> of Hancock, and Rush, and Franklin still hover there!" But the door of
> that old Hall was barred and bolted. . . . They were told ". . . if we of the
> North should listen to you, the two hundred and fifty thousand slavehold-

ers would knock this Union into fragments, so there would not be enough left of our common country to make a school district. Get you gone, there is no place for you here."[26]

Stewart's address reflected the dual character of Independence Hall in the middle nineteenth century. As a place both past and present, the Hall recalled eighteenth-century promises of freedom, but represented the denial of that freedom to nineteenth-century fugitives from slavery. Rather than positioning Independence Hall as a symbol of liberty, allowing the fugitives of his tale to find refuge, Stewart defined the Hall as a symbol of exclusion. In parallel to the U.S. Congress in these years, he presented Independence Hall as a place that denied discussion of the issue of slavery, lest the controversy fracture the nation.

For abolitionists, the perception of Independence Hall as a place of empty promise grew with the attack on their own hall dedicated to free speech. With Pennsylvania Hall in flames, mobs also set fire to a new Shelter for Colored Orphans north of the city and damaged the Bethel Church. In the aftermath, the Pennsylvania State Anti-Slavery Society pleaded with Philadelphians to recognize the significance of their actions. "In the heart of your free city—within view of the Hall of Independence, whose spire and roof reddened with the flame of the sacrifice—the deed has been done,—and the shout which greeted the falling ruin was the shout of Slavery over the grave of Liberty," the society exclaimed. "We ask of you as men jealous of your own rights, and your own liberties, to reflect upon the inevitable consequences which must follow the toleration of such an outrage." Like Stewart, the society envisioned dire results and warned Philadelphians that denying rights to any citizen could endanger the republic.[27]

In 1844, abolitionists turned the contradictions represented by Independence Hall to their advantage by staging an antislavery event in Independence Square. On a Saturday evening in August, Frederick Douglass, then in his early years as an antislavery speaker, stepped onto a stand near the building and addressed about two hundred people, both men and women, one-third of them African Americans. "At first he seemed embarrassed and spoke with some hesitancy; but soon his embarrassment disappeared," the *Pennsylvania Freeman*, newspaper of the Anti-Slavery Society, reported. The continuing description reflected the gulf between blacks and whites, even those joined in the abolitionist cause, as the newspaper expressed admiration but also surprise at Douglass's oratorical skill. "His heart began to play, and he poured forth a stream of glowing thought and thrilling eloquence, which, coming from an unlettered colored man, seemed to many of the audience utterly amazing."[28]

Douglass's text was not preserved, but he clearly took advantage of the contrast presented by Independence Hall and the persistence of slavery in the South. "The stand which Douglass occupied was close by the old Hall in which the Declaration of Independence was adopted, and he made one or two allusions to this circumstance with thrilling effect," the *Freeman* reported. The Philadelphia *Public Ledger* did not report the allusions to Independence Hall but noted that during his speech Douglass adopted the role of a master preaching a sermon to his slaves, describing the relative duties of the master and slave "in a bitter strain of sarcasm." The newspaper noted that "of course" not everyone in the square approved of Douglass's speech. According to the *Freeman*, the disapproval came primarily from city police, who muttered curses, cleared the square after one hour, and closed the gates to guard against a riot.[29]

As he became a celebrated orator in later years, Douglass invoked the contrast between the ideals of the Declaration of Independence and the persistence of slavery in the United States. Although he did not mention Independence Hall in his well-known 1852 address, "What to the Slave Is the Fourth of July?" his associations with events at the Philadelphia landmark were apparent. He recounted the events leading to the Declaration of Independence and spoke admiringly of the Declaration's ideals. Nevertheless, he pointedly criticized the continuing contradiction of slavery, telling his white audience in Rochester, New York: "The rich inheritance of justice, liberty, prosperity and independence, bequeathed by your fathers, is shared by you, not me. The sunlight that brought life and healing to you, has brought stripes and death to me. This Fourth [of] July is *yours*, not *mine*. *You* may rejoice, *I* must mourn" (emphasis in original).[30] African Americans in the nineteenth century debated whether they should commemorate the Fourth of July, given the continuing contradictions between the document's ideology and the persistence of slavery in America. In 1831, one of the national conventions of free blacks that met in Philadelphia recommended that people of color "set apart the fourth day of July, as a day of humiliation, fasting and prayer, that the shackles of slavery may be broken, and our sacred rights obtained." Some African Americans commemorated the nation's birthday on July 5, calling attention to the distance between the Declaration of Independence and the reality of American society in the nineteenth century.[31]

While Douglass's speech in 1844 brought the slavery debate into Independence Square, changes in federal law under the Compromise of 1850 injected racial and sectional conflict into the courtrooms inside the old Pennsylvania State House. From the 1830s until 1854, the building's second floor was rented to the U.S. Marshal and District Court. As a result, after the Compromise of 1850, the State House for four years became the center for enforcing the new, tougher Fugitive Slave Law enacted under the Compromise.[32] As in other northern cities, fugitive slave cases in Philadelphia were few, but they focused intense local attention on the issue of slavery.[33] Within the first six months after the law took effect in 1850, six accused fugitives faced hearings and sometimes temporary incarceration on the second floor of the State House. Other cases followed intermittently thereafter.[34] The events that transpired in the rooms above the Hall of Independence showed that liberty in the United States was not only a principle, but also a point of legal contention and a commodity that could be bought and sold.

Throughout the deepening sectional crisis of the early nineteenth century, the legal response to escapes from slavery rested upon the fugitive slave clause of the United States Constitution and the Fugitive Slave Law of 1793, enacted by Congress while it met in Philadelphia. As part of the Compromise of 1850, a new Fugitive Slave Law strengthened enforcement by requiring that fugitives be returned to masters who could properly document their identity. Under the law, the fates of the accused could be decided by federal judges (in Philadelphia, U.S. District Court Judges Robert C. Grier and John K. Kane) or by commissioners appointed specifically to uphold the Fugitive Slave Law (in Philadelphia, attorney Edward D. Ingraham). The law awarded commissioners five dollars for every accused fugitive determined to be free, but ten dollars for each person remanded to slavery.

For the nation, enforcement of the Fugitive Slave Law represented an attempt to balance the interests of North and South, but for free black people in the North, every accused fugitive represented a fate that could be their own. In Philadelphia, anxious African Americans gathered in Independence Square to await the outcome of each hearing held to establish an accused fugitive's identity. Inside, the accused had the support of abolitionists and vigorous defense by a group of Philadelphia lawyers who opposed the Fugitive Slave Law. While the issues of slavery were constitutional, African Americans noted the irony of such proceedings occurring in the birthplace of the Declaration of Independence. The *National Era*, an African American newspaper published in Washington, D.C., emphasized to its readers that the hearings in Philadelphia "took place in INDEPENDENCE HALL . . . on the very spot where the immortal words, fresh from the pen of Jefferson, that 'all men are created free and equal; that they were endowed by their Creator with certain unalienable rights; that among these are life, *liberty*, and the pursuit of happiness;' were proclaimed to the world as the platform of universal man, and the basis of his eternal right to resist oppression."[35] Philadelphia newspapers detailed the fugitive slave cases, including the following.

Henry Garnet, in his late twenties, was taken into custody on October 18, 1850, as he walked near Poplar Street and Ridge Road, on his way to work as a hod carrier. Accused of being a fugitive from slavery in Cecil County, Maryland, Garnet spent a night in custody in the U.S. Marshal's Office in the State House, where he met until 10 P.M. with friends and abolitionist lawyers. The next day, as a crowd of black Philadelphians gathered in Independence Square, a parade of witnesses attested to Garnet's identity as the fugitive. Judge Grier, rather than Commissioner Ingraham, took charge of the Garnet hearing, declaring that the court needed to establish procedure with the first case under the new law. Despite the testimony supporting Garnet's identity, Grier ruled that the documents presented to establish his accusers' ownership had not been properly attested in Maryland. Therefore, Grier ruled, Garnet would not be turned over to the accusers. Assured of his freedom, Garnet bolted from Independence Hall and dashed through a cheering throng outside in the square. Garnet's triumphal run momentarily placed him at risk again as Philadelphia police officers rushed to stop what they believed to be an attempted escape. An ensuing scuffle with the crowd resulted in the arrest of two black Philadelphians on charges of assault and battery.[36]

Adam Gibson, about twenty-four years old, was apprehended at Second and Lombard Streets on December 21, 1850, ostensibly on a charge of stealing chickens. Forced at gunpoint to the U.S. Marshal's Office, he was accused of being "Emery King," an escapee from Cecil County, Maryland. After a hearing to establish his identity, this time held before Commissioner Ingraham, it was ordered that Gibson be returned to slavery. In Maryland, however, his reputed owners found that Gibson was not the man whom they sought after all. They freed him, and by Christmas Day, Gibson was back in Philadelphia.[37]

On January 23, 1851, Stephen Bennett was seized in the midst of a job sawing wood in Columbia, Pennsylvania, a key location on the Underground Railroad and therefore a target for slave-catchers. Accused of being a fugitive from slavery in Baltimore, Bennett was taken to Philadelphia for his hearing. Beginning with Bennett's case, abolitionist lawyers routinely sought and won writs of habeas corpus to remove hearings from Ingraham, whom some perceived as pro-Southern, and place the accused in the jurisdiction of the district court.[38] Despite this maneuver, Judge Kane found that Bennett's identity had been sufficiently established and ordered him returned to his master. Before Bennett's departure for the South, however, his Columbia neighbors raised enough money to purchase his freedom. In a transaction completed in the U.S. Marshal's Office on January 25, Bennett was freed for the price of $700. In the building where liberty had been declared in 1776, it was purchased in

1851 for an African American who would have been returned to slavery under the law.[39]

On February 6, 1851, Tamor Williams, a married woman between thirty and thirty-five years old with five young children, was captured at her home at Fifth Street and Germantown Road and accused of being a slave named Mahala who had escaped from Worcester County, Maryland, more than twenty years earlier. Such an accusation against a mother of young children aroused intense interest. "All the seats in the court room were filled at an early hour, and the stair-case and avenues leading to the room were densely crowded," the *Pennsylvania Freeman* reported, "while large numbers of colored persons were assembled in Independence Square, during the whole of the intensely cold day." In the crowded U.S. district courtroom, witnesses from Maryland attested to Williams's identity. However, their testimony did not persuade Judge Kane, who ruled that there were no distinguishing characteristics to prove that the woman under arrest was the girl who had disappeared from slavery so many years earlier. Black Philadelphians celebrated the victory at the Philadelphia Institute at Seventh and Lombard Streets and escorted Williams, now reunited with her children, by carriage to her home. En route, the procession stopped to cheer the lawyers who represented Williams at the hearing and to direct "hideous groans" at the hotel of her kidnappers.[40]

On March 7, 1851, while four other family members escaped, Hannah Dellam and her son, Henry, were captured in Columbia, Pennsylvania, on suspicion of being fugitives from slavery in Baltimore. About forty years old and in an advanced stage of pregnancy, Hannah Dellam was doing wash at an employer's house when captured. Her son, about nine years old, was found hiding beneath hay in a barn. Taken to the district court in Philadelphia, the pair heard witnesses who attested to their identity as slaves as well as neighbors from Columbia who swore to their status as free citizens. Court observers, white and black, filled the district courtroom and spilled into the hallway, where their discussions at times turned to Hannah Dellam's pregnancy and the future of her unborn child. In the end, the claimants from Maryland established the identity of Dellam and her son, and Judge Kane ordered them transported to the South. A tense night followed around the State House as clusters of black Philadelphians who had heard of the decision gathered on the corners of Chestnut Street at Fifth and Sixth. The police, fearing a last-ditch attempt to liberate the accused fugitives, arrested about a dozen young men and boys, some carrying slingshots, knives, canes, or razors.[41]

As dramatic and unnerving as the first fugitive slave cases were, they were preludes to the celebrated treason trial that followed the so-called "Riot of Christiana," in which a Maryland slaveowner with the legally required warrants was killed while in pursuit of suspected fugitives in Lancaster County, Pennsylvania. In the aftermath of the confrontation on September 11, 1851, thirty-three blacks and five whites were charged with treason for interfering with the Fugitive Slave Law. Those who did not manage to escape arrest were taken to Philadelphia for trial. Charged with a federal offense, the defendants faced judge and jury in the second floor of the State House. The setting provided lawyers with the opportunity to link their arguments to the memory of the signers of the Declaration of Independence and the framers of the Constitution.

Amid the sectional tension of the 1850s, the Christiana shootout drew national attention and unleashed public debate that resonated with the historic associations of the old Pennsylvania State House. Were the Christiana men defenders of liberty in the tradition of the Declaration of Independence? Or were they the worst sort of criminals, defying the authority of the Constitution by refusing to comply with the law? At the Pennsylvania Anti-Slavery Society's annual meeting in West Chester, a speaker declared, "Those colored men were only following the example of Washington and the American heroes of '76."[42] In Philadelphia, on the other hand, a mass meeting in Independence Square supported swift punishment of the Christiana defendants "to prevent the recurrence of so terrible a scene upon the soil of Pennsylvania, to ferret out and punish the murderers thus guilty of the double crime of assaulting the Constitution, and of taking the lives of men in pursuit of their recognized and rightful property."[43]

With one defendant, a white man named Castner Hanway, brought to trial first as a test case, panels of prominent attorneys assembled for the prosecution and defense. The team of five defense lawyers included Thaddeus Stevens, an antislavery activist and congressman from Pennsylvania. The seven prosecution lawyers included U.S. Senator James Cooper of Pennsylvania, the U.S. attorney of the Eastern District of Pennsylvania, and the attorney general of Maryland. On November 24, the first day of the trial, the *National Era* noted that "an immense crowd of blacks and whites blocked up the passage-way through Independence Hall, leading to the Court-room. At half past ten o'clock the doors were opened and the crowd rushed in, filling the room to suffocation." In the course of the three-week trial, spectators included such prominent abolitionists as Lucretia Mott. At one session, twenty-four of Hanway's alleged accomplices were brought to court so that one of them could be identified by a witness. To the disgust of the chief prosecutor, they wore red, white, and blue scarves around their necks, and black defendants sat with white female supporters.[44]

During the trial, connections between the issues of the Christiana case and the history of Independence Hall were both explicit and implied. In addition to the prevailing association of the building with the Declaration of Independence, the trial arguments recalled the building as the meeting place of the Constitutional Convention. When the U.S. attorney argued for conviction on the charge of treason, he invoked the history of the Hall of Independence, asserting, "This venerated hall from which the Declaration of Independence was first proclaimed to an admiring world, never can be the scene of the violation of the Constitution, the noblest product of that Independence."[45] Legal arguments turned on the Constitution's fugitive slave clause and its definition of treason. Although the case at hand involved only Hanway's alleged role at Christiana, the lawyers injected emotional orations about the prospects that the nation founded in 1776 could disintegrate in the conflict over slavery. "I tell you, gentlemen, much as the Union is venerated and beloved, North and South, East and West, there are some things that may precipitate ruin and disaster upon that Union," Maryland Attorney General Robert J. Brent, a member of the prosecution team, said in his closing argument. Ruin would come, he said, if the Constitution were not upheld, including its provision for the return of fugitives. Citing George Washington's farewell admonition that the Constitution could only be altered by the whole people, not a few, Brent continued, "We have fallen upon evil times—upon wicked times—when this doctrine left to us as a sacred legacy to posterity, is here in the very building where the 'Declaration of Independence' first went forth to cheer and enlighten mankind, when that doctrine is here denied, scoffed at and denounced by counsel."[46]

The prosecution's arguments failed to convince either the judge or the jury that the shooting at Christiana constituted treason against the United States. Instructing the jury, Judge Grier characterized the shooting as an "insurrection for a private object" that did not "rise to the dignity of treason or a levying of war." Given that instruction, the jurors deliberated for just fifteen minutes across the street from the State House at the American Hotel, where they had stayed during the trial. Their verdict: "Not guilty." With treason ruled out as a charge for the Christiana shootings, Hanway and his fellow defendants were returned to Lancaster County for possible trial on state charges of riot and murder.[47]

Although never included in published histories of Independence Hall, and treated only in passing in histories of Philadelphia, the cases that transpired under the Fugitive Slave Law were searing experiences for African Americans who witnessed the capture of others and feared for their own freedom. The fact that the hearings took place in the birthplace of the Declaration of Independence and the Constitution underscored the contradictions between the founding documents and the experiences of nineteenth-century African Americans. Their perspective on Independence Hall was recorded in a pamphlet containing speeches given in Philadelphia on the Fourth of July in 1859 at the Banneker Institute, an African American society. On this Independence Day, speakers argued that African Americans should celebrate the Declaration of Independence because of its high ideals, even if those ideals had not been achieved. They emphasized a distinction between the Declaration of Independence and the Constitution, which they identified as contradicting the ideals of 1776 by providing for return of fugitive slaves.

One of the speakers, William H. Johnson, noted the irony of events in the 1850s, calling attention to both the Hall of Independence and the Liberty Bell. "There are tories today," he said, "and their business is to hunt down the poor fugitive negro, and to handcuff and drag him hundreds of miles from his home to be tried as a slave, and to be remanded . . . under the sound of the old State House bell, and within sight of the hall where independence was declared." The assembled black Philadelphians adopted their own declaration, saying in part, "that we do hold it to be a self-evident truth . . . that all men, irrespective of colour or condition, by virtue of their constitution, have a natural indefeasible right to life, liberty, and the possession of property."[48] For African Americans, the 1850s had marked the Pennsylvania State House as a place where liberty could be jeopardized, even as the language of the Declaration of Independence remained a source of hope and determination.

Nativist Shrine

During the middle decades of the nineteenth century, Philadelphia and other northern cities were caught in a period of incessant disorder, often fueled by racial and ethnic conflict.[49] Cities grew rapidly, drawing in newcomers from the countryside, the South, and Europe. Economic competition and cultural differences wracked crowded urban neighborhoods, often igniting violence, as the experience of African Americans in Philadelphia attested. Similar outbreaks of violence marked the relationship between native-born Americans and immigrants, especially the Irish Catholics who arrived in great numbers in the 1830s and 1840s. Nativist reaction against immigrants prompted not only riots in major American cities but also a political movement aimed at keeping the nation under the control of the native-born. This was especially true in Philadelphia, a nativist stronghold since the 1830s. The city exploded with anti-immigrant violence twice in 1844, and a decade later, nativist politicians surged into state and local elective offices. The election of the nativist candidates to the mayor's office and the City Councils in 1854 had significant consequences for the old Pennsylvania State House, including the first-floor "Hall of Independence." Although lost from the public memory of Independence Hall constructed in later years, nativist politics contributed to elevating the State House to a national shrine.

Nativists viewed their cause as a defense of the nation left to them by the founding fathers. Rising to prominence under the banners of the American Republican, Native American, and American Parties, they adopted Revolutionary-era rhetoric and symbols in their campaigns to require twenty-one years' residence in the United States before naturalization and to exclude immigrants from holding public office. In Philadelphia, an early constitution drafted by a nativist organization urged native-born Americans to "come forward . . . and prove that the spirit of '76 is not extinct, and that we are not degenerate sons of worthy sires."[50] In 1844, a year marked by nativist riots that torched two Catholic churches and left sixteen people dead, nativists paraded on Independence Day carrying Liberty figures, images of American eagles, portraits of George Washington, and the slogans "Beware Foreign Influence" and "Virtue, Liberty, and Independence."[51] During the rioting, Independence Square became an arena for inciting violence as well as attempting to keep the peace. On the first day of rioting in May, the nativists called a mass meeting in the square to decry what they viewed as an unwarranted attack by the Irish. Inciting an already angry crowd to new violence against Irish neighborhoods, one speaker declared that he "hoped yet to witness the eradication of every party principle or institution in the land which was not purely American." Two days later, Independence Square filled again with Philadelphians, this time summoned by the mayor and City Councils to appeal for peace.[52]

Nationally, nativist politicians swept into state and local offices in 1852 and 1854, benefiting as the second party system of Democrats and Whigs collapsed under the weight of the slavery conflict.[53] In Philadelphia, nativists also gained political advantage from a changed political landscape created in 1854 by the consolidation of the city and county into one municipal unit. Although the annexed territory included Democratic strongholds, voters surprised the Democrats by embracing the anti-immigrant message of the Native American Party. The nativists won the mayor's office as well as a majority of the new City Councils.[54] In control of city government, they acted on long-held convictions by barring foreign-born men from public office and the police force. Given their attachment to the memory of the founding generation, the new city officials also turned their attention to the old Pennsylvania State House. The significance of the building to the new officeholders was evident in a memoir of a

Native American Party supporter who visited Philadelphia in 1854. He recalled walking across Independence Square on election night, pondering the city's political affairs and the danger of foreign-born officeholders, and visiting Independence Hall:

> As I entered the beautiful enclosure, pregnant with so many stirring memories, and hallowed by the most sacred associations, the old clock pealed out the hour of ten. From the same point issued, seventy-eight years ago, those notes of liberty which swept on angel wings over this land—from that sacred place the proclamation went forth, that no foreign despot should oppress Americans. It seemed as though there were something mournful in those vibrations which announced the hour; and I almost imagined that the faithful chronicler of time was conscious that true patriotism had sadly declined.[55]

In the view of nativists, the Hall of Independence was a sacred place, and during their brief years in city office, they took steps to make it a shrine.

The mayor of Philadelphia elected in 1854 was Robert T. Conrad, who ran with support from the Native Americans as well as the Whig and Temperance parties of the city. Although nominated by the Whigs, he enthusiastically embraced the nativists' positions. Conrad, forty-four years old at the time of his election, was trained as a lawyer and had served as a judge, but he devoted himself most energetically to journalism, playwriting, and poetry.[56] In his literary endeavors as well as his politics, Conrad demonstrated a determination to sustain the principles and memory of the nation's founders. In the decade before his election, he produced an abridged version of John Sanderson's five-volume *Lives of the Signers to the Declaration of Independence* in order to make the work more accessible to a wide audience. In his introduction, Conrad stressed that the majority of the signers were native born, well educated, and affluent. If not native born, they came from the best possible place: England. They were men of virtue, models to be followed by succeeding generations.[57]

As they took their new offices in City Hall, Conrad and his nativist colleagues on the Philadelphia City Councils brought reverence for the Hall of Independence, but they also faced the practical demands for city office space. Since the 1830s, city officials had complained that the old buildings on Independence Square were inadequate. Committees commandeered meeting space wherever it could be found—the city treasurer's office, the county commissioner's rooms, or even the mayor's private room. Juries deliberated in taverns, and the State House basement served as the municipal dog pound. Public documents were carelessly catalogued and often stored in private homes. The city and county offices housed in the row buildings adjacent to the State House were so crowded that officials worried that the whole complex might go up in flames.[58] With consolidation in 1854, the City Councils' chambers in the City Hall were also too small to accommodate their increased membership.

To address the space problem, Philadelphia's newly elected officials looked next door to the State House. In the year after the nativists took office, they changed the interior of the State House in both form and function. They installed new council chambers on the second floor, displacing the U.S. Marshal's Office and District Court. The space that had been the banquet hall of colonial Philadelphians, a prison for Revolutionary War officers, the museum of Charles Willson Peale, and most recently the scene of enforcement of the Fugitive Slave Law, was divided into two council chambers painted in imitation of oak, richly carpeted, and lit by chandeliers. The earlier history of the space had not been forgotten; in fact, workmen found reminders of the building's past as they tore apart walls and erected new ones. They found a brick stamped "Nicholson, 1731" and numerous signs of aging, including rats' nests in wainscoting and wooden cornices.[59] Philadelphia newspapers reported the discoveries and recounted the varied history of the second floor, but for Philadelphians of 1854, these were not calls to restoration. The second floor took on an appearance wholly different from any before and, judging from council members' expense reports, acquired a thick cloud of cigar smoke as well.[60]

More significant to the evolution of the building as a shrine, the new city officials redecorated the first-floor Hall of Independence. Although valued for its association with the Declaration of Independence, the room by the 1850s represented a broader past that spanned from the founding of Pennsylvania to the return of Lafayette in 1824. The Hall displayed William Rush's sculpture of George Washington, which had been the centerpiece of Lafayette's reception; full-length portraits of Lafayette and William Penn; a chair believed to have been used by John Hancock during the signing of the Declaration of Independence; and a wooden step believed to have been used for the Declaration's first public reading. The art and relics in the room communicated a sense of history but left much to the imagination of the visitor. For the writer of a Philadelphia guidebook, this was enough to send "the mind back to the memorable time—to that decisive act, which has consecrated this room to undying fame."[61] An out-of-town visitor in 1851, in contrast, catalogued the contents matter of factly and described the room dispassionately as "a plain substantial chamber, painted of a sober tint but with a ceiling of azure and gilt stars."[62]

16. Nativist politicians, cherishing the memory of the nation's founders and fearing the influence of immigrants, redecorated the Hall of Independence as a shrine after their victories in Philadelphia city elections in 1854. *Interior of Independence Hall, 1856,* by Max Rothermel, shows the return of Charles Willson Peale's portraits to the State House and placement of the Liberty Bell on a pedestal decorated with Revolutionary-era symbols. (Courtesy of the Library Company of Philadelphia)

In redecorating the room in 1854 and 1855, Philadelphia's nativist officeholders defined the room more explicitly as a shrine devoted to worship of the nation's founders. In a time of great turmoil, city officials created a sanctuary for quiet contemplation of past heroes. The chamber received a new coat of paint and oilcloth for the floor. Augmenting the Rush sculpture of George Washington, the City Council appropriated $6,000 to buy portraits of Revolutionary War figures painted by Charles Willson Peale. After an absence of more than twenty-five years, the selection of Peale portraits acquired at auction returned to Independence Hall to become a gallery of heroes.[63]

Reinforcing the room's homage to the founders, the old State House bell with its "Proclaim liberty" inscription was displayed on a new pedestal that perpetuated the bell's purported connection to the Declaration of Independence. The bell, irreparably cracked by the late 1840s and popularized by the fiction of George Lippard, had been a prominent attraction in the Hall of Independence since being brought down from the tower in 1852.[64] With the redecoration project, the bell gained a place atop a tall, octagonal pedestal decorated with liberty caps, American flags, and the names of the signers of the Declaration of Independence. To a visiting woman from Bucks County, Pennsylvania, the pedestal appeared to be "a large monument representing the American flag" with columns "upon which are inscribed all the names of the signers to the Declaration of Independence." Looking up, she observed, "Upon the top of all sits the large bell which sang to proclaim Independence."[65] If visitors were not familiar with George Lippard's story of the bell-ringer on the Fourth of July, they could read on the pedestal that "the ringing of this bell first announced to the citizens who were anxiously waiting the result of the deliberations of Congress . . . that the Declaration of Independence had been decided upon."[66]

The visitor from Bucks County, a thirty-eight-year-old woman named Lettie Smith, noted in her diary that the redecorated Hall of Independence "contained much to attract and interest any patriotic American . . . it may be a pride to the state, to the city and to the council."[67] For the sponsors of the project, patriotic feeling toward the Hall emanated from regard for the founders, especially George Washington. Mayor Conrad rededicated the Hall on Washington's Birthday in 1855, in a ceremony that echoed its historic past, the looming conflicts of the 1850s, and the nativists' claim to the legacy of the founders. The ceremony began as a reception for the visiting volunteer militia of Richmond, Virginia, which prompted allusions to the unifying power of the Hall. Here, said the militia's captain, Northerners and Southerners could come together as friends, "having a common origin and land and history, meeting around a common altar, having a common faith." Mayor Conrad's address then identified the Hall of Independence as a holy place for communing with the great spirits of the past:

> It would be strange, a libel on nature, if we of Philadelphia were not
> proud of this hall and its memories. We recall our fathers as they
> thronged its floor; we knit our hearts to theirs in the tug of the revolution;
> we live on their trials and we share their feelings, fight their battles, and
> swear eternal fidelity to their principles. This is but the reverence of the
> child for the parent; we acknowledge even a profounder feeling of exulta-
> tion over the contacts and deeds that have made this the holiest spot—
> save one—of all the earth; the Sinai of the world, upon which the Ark of
> Liberty rested, when all the earth beside was submerged in oppression and

submission; the fountain source of the principles of freedom, which are
everflowing the world; the starting point of that revolution in human
thought and human action, which will yet redeem the earth, and give us
millions, up to their God, unshackled and free to be good and happy.

Speaking on the birthday of George Washington, Conrad devoted greatest attention to
Washington's achievements in the Revolutionary War and Constitutional Convention
and to his example as a model of virtue. Among all these achievements, Conrad also
found inspiration for the nativists' cause by identifying Washington as an opponent of
unrestricted immigration and officeholding by foreigners.[68]

As a shrine, the Hall of Independence acquired relics associated with the heroes
that it honored. With the passage of time, it seems, rituals alone were insufficient
means of invoking the memory of the founders. During the 1850s, regard for the
founders launched the historic preservation movement, as women in Virginia under-
took restoration of Washington's home at Mount Vernon.[69] At the old Pennsylvania
State House, interest did not yet extend to restoring the building to its eighteenth-century appearance, but artifacts reminiscent of the Colonial and Revolutionary eras
accumulated in the Hall of Independence. By 1859, these included a portion of the pew
that Washington occupied at Christ Church, a bible from 1776, and a desk that
belonged to Benjamin Franklin. Individuals joined in constructing the memory of the
nation's past by contributing such artifacts as a letter by Roger Sherman (nephew of
the signer of the Declaration) describing encounters with George Washington; a dinner invitation from Washington; a portrait of Washington woven in silk; and a piece of
the Charter Oak of Hartford, Connecticut. Demonstrating the industry that some were
willing to devote to preserving material remnants of history, Philadelphian John F.
Watson contributed a chair pieced together from bits of "historical" wood gathered
from sources such as William Penn's city cottage and the U.S. frigate *Constitution*.[70]

In keeping with the intensified interest in the State House, the first book-length
history of the Hall of Independence was published in 1859.[71] Not surprising, given the
events of the mid-nineteenth century, *History of Independence Hall* was the work of
a nativist, David W. Belisle, publisher of an American Party newspaper in Camden, New
Jersey.[72] Rather than a chronicle of events, Belisle's work was a collective biography
and a descriptive catalog, a hymn to the nation's founders and a tribute to the room
that made it possible for nineteenth-century Americans to commune with sacred
memories. After dedicating his book to Millard Fillmore, the American Party's presidential candidate in 1856, Belisle wrote in his preface, "Independence Hall! How

impressive are the associations that cluster around this sacred Temple of our national freedom!" Admiring the shrine opened in 1855, he wrote, "The venerable appearance of the Hall itself has an awe-inspiring sanctity about it that makes us realize we are treading hallowed ground—while the carefully arranged relics and mementoes excite our inquiry and deeply interest our thoughts." Belisle feared, however, that other visitors did not fully appreciate the historic associations that he felt so deeply. He intended his book to provide a more thorough understanding and "to inspire a deeper love for the sacred Temple wherein our nation's infancy was cradled and defended."[73] In the care of nativists who feared for the demise of the republic, the Hall of Independence evolved from civic reception hall into a place of intense, sacred memory. In contrast to African Americans who observed contradictions between Independence Hall and the language of the Declaration of Independence, native-born Americans used the building to ensure that time would not diminish their memory of the achievements of 1776.

Union Stronghold

During the upheavals of the 1850s, Philadelphians attached complex and contradictory meanings to Independence Hall as they contested the memory of the Declaration of Independence, the Constitution, and the heroes of the American Revolution. As with so many other aspects of American life, the Civil War transformed the uses and meanings of Independence Hall in ways that quickly obscured earlier controversies. The first-floor chamber which had been a place for remembering the soldiers and statesmen of the American Revolution came to represent the sacrifice necessary for sustaining the American union forged nearly one hundred years before. Although many Philadelphians had business and family connections with the South, and few white Philadelphians shared the antislavery concerns of local African Americans and other abolitionists, the city mustered support for preserving the Union.[74] The potential collapse of the nation brought new, more widespread attention to the old Pennsylvania State House as the birthplace of both the Declaration of Independence and the United States Constitution.

As the northern city closest to the Mason-Dixon Line, Philadelphia stood to play a significant role in the Civil War as a staging ground, receiver of wounded soldiers, and possible target for the Confederate army. Independence Square, as the seat of city and county government, became a center of activity for preparing defenses, celebrating victories, and mourning the dead. Even before the war, with tensions mounting and Southern states threatening to secede, an estimated fifty thousand Philadelphians thronged around the State House to demonstrate support for the Union. The Protestant Episcopal Bishop of Pennsylvania invoked the historic associations of the State House as he prayed that "a double portion of the wisdom and patriotism of the fathers might descend and rest upon their sons, that from this place there may go forth an influence which will be felt throughout the republic."[75] The opening shots at Fort Sumter in April 1861 began four years in which the State House and its square served practical as well as ceremonial purposes. Independence Square became a drilling ground for soldiers and fife-and-drum teams. Recruiters pitched tents along the walk that extended from Walnut Street to the rear of the State House. The Home Guard, charged with defending the city if the need arose, occupied headquarters in the State House row. Meeting in the State House, the Philadelphia City Councils appropriated money for defense and for the support of families of absent soldiers. Military units paraded on Chestnut Street on their way to war.[76]

In February 1861, Abraham Lincoln helped to unite the State House with the cause of the Union when he stopped in Philadelphia on his way to Washington for inauguration as President of the United States. Presidents had visited the State House in the past, but Lincoln's journey embraced the potent symbolism of returning to the Union's birthplace at a time of national crisis. On February 22, Washington's Birthday, Lincoln raised over the State House an American flag with thirty-four stars—the thirty-fourth star representing Kansas, newly admitted as a free state after years of bloody confrontation. Before the flag-raising, near dawn, Lincoln participated in the ritual welcome in the Hall of Independence. The president-elect had prepared a speech for the crowds waiting outside, but inside he spoke extemporaneously, quietly, to the assembled dignitaries. "I am filled with deep emotion at finding myself standing here in the place where were collected together the wisdom, the patriotism, the devotion to principle, from which sprung the institutions under which we live," Lincoln said. Frequently interrupted by cheering and applause, he reflected on the actions of the Continental Congress and the ideals embodied by the Declaration of Independence: "I have often inquired of myself, what great principle or idea it was that kept this Confederacy so long together. It was not the mere matter of the separation of the colonies from the mother land; but something in that Declaration giving liberty, not alone to the people of this country, but hope to the world for all future time." Could the Union be preserved on the same principle on which it had been founded? Lincoln concluded offhandedly, but prophetically, "If this country cannot be saved without giving up that principle—I was about to say I would rather be assassinated on this spot than to surrender it."[77]

17. Although the sectional controversies of the mid-nineteenth century had echoed in Independence Hall during fugitive slave hearings and the Christiana trial, the Civil War quickly transformed the old State House into a headquarters for defending the Union. Here, in a photograph attributed to Frederick deBourg Richards, a Civil War encampment flanks the central walk of Independence Square during the autumn of 1862. (Courtesy of the Library Company of Philadelphia)

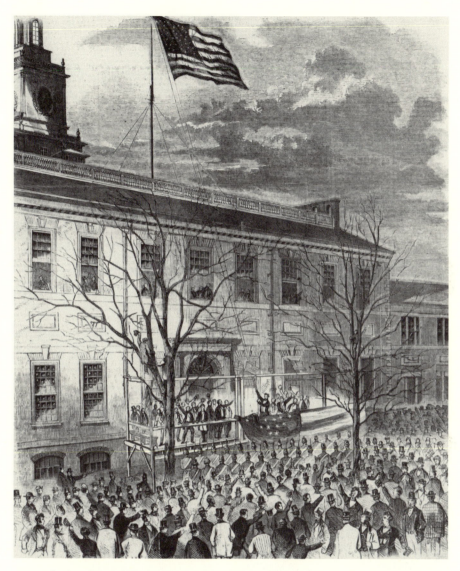

18. Newly elected President Abraham Lincoln affirmed Independence Hall as a symbol of national Union when he visited Philadelphia in 1861 en route to his inauguration. This illustration in *Harper's Weekly Journal of Civilization* shows Lincoln raising a thirty-four-star American flag, the latest star representing the newly admitted state of Kansas. (Courtesy of the Library Company of Philadelphia)

With its portraits, sculpture of Washington, and historical relics, the Hall of Independence had honored famous heroes of the nation. With the Civil War, the room also became a hall of honor for casualties of war. Between 1861 and 1865, seven officers killed in battle lay in state briefly in the Hall of Independence. Four were prominent Philadelphians—Lieutenant John T. Greble, killed at Big Bethel, Virginia, in 1861; Major General Charles F. Smith, killed at Savannah in 1862; Major Thomas Hawksworth, wounded at Fredericksburg in December 1862, dead a month later; and Colonel Ulric Dahlgren, son of an admiral, shot in a raid before the fall of Richmond in 1865.[78] In addition to these local martyrs, the Hall of Independence also received three officers of the Second Rhode Island Regiment whose remains, recovered from battlefield graves at Bull Run, were being transported from Washington to Providence.[79] Whenever military coffins were placed in honor among the images of Revolutionary heroes, streams of mourners came to the Hall of Independence to pay respects. The place identified with the founding of the nation also became associated with sacrifices made to preserve the Union.

In April 1865, short weeks after Philadelphians crowded around the State House to celebrate the Confederacy's surrender at Appomattox, the Hall of Independence once again was pressed into solemn service to the union. The corpse carried into the State House on April 22, 1865, was not that of a soldier but of the commander in chief. The Hall of Independence, which received the body, was not simply a room in an old State House, but a sacred chamber that recalled the nation's founders. The *Evening Bulletin* noted the appropriate association of Abraham Lincoln, the fallen president, with the historic events of nearly a century before:

> Tonight the ashes of the most illustrious Martyr of Freedom will rest in the
> Hall where the great American Charter of equal rights was given to the
> world. They will lie upon the spot where little more than four years ago
> our slaughtered President declared his willingness to make the sacrifice
> that has since been exacted from him. His body will rest at the feet of the
> statue of the most illustrious of the early Apostles of American freedom; it
> will be surrounded with the effigies of the great representative men who
> gave power and glory to the United States during three quarters of a century.

Having united Lincoln with the memory of past heroes, the continuing description also incorporated him into the mythic story of the Liberty Bell: "Most fitting of all, perhaps, at the mangled head of the most illustrious victim of slavery will be found the old bell which first sounded abroad the glad tidings of a people disenthralled, and which bears upon its face the sacred injunction: 'PROCLAIM LIBERTY THROUGHOUT THE LAND AND TO ALL THE INHABITANTS THEREOF.'"[80] An estimated eighty-five thousand people filed by Lincoln's casket in the Hall of Independence, draped in black for the occasion. On those mournful April days, they crossed through a chamber made sacred by forty years of reverence for lost American heroes and fear for imperiled American ideals. Christened by the Revolutionary War's General Lafayette, sustained by civic pride and nativist anxiety, contradicted by slavery, and consecrated by the honored dead, one room in the old Pennsylvania State House had become a permanent shrine.

From the 1830s through the 1860s, Independence Hall and Independence Square echoed with the most vital issues of the day—slavery, immigration, the status of labor in an industrial economy, and the rise and collapse of the second party system. In and around Independence Hall, collective memories of the American Revolution were articulated and contested by African Americans, industrial workers, and native-born opponents of immigration. How is it, then, that so much of this was so long forgotten in the history of Independence Hall? The answer lies in our ability to remember the past selectively and to organize public memory around buildings in ways that obscure conflict, thereby allowing unobstructed appreciation of the heroes and principles so closely associated with American national identity. In the case of Independence Hall, the process of forgetting has been aided by the visual record of this era. In prints and photographs, the old State House appears in a row of brick office buildings on a fashionable commercial street. The images show pedestrians, but never demonstrators. Portrayals of the interior are similarly sedate, showing admirers of the shrine in the Hall of Independence or mourners attending the funeral of a lost hero. The images are not inaccurate, but they are incomplete. They have contributed to a history that has been accurate, but not complete.

The continuing use, remodeling, and later preservation of Independence Hall also has supported a memory of eighteenth-century consensus rather than nineteenth-century conflict. Like the visual record, research into the building's history during this period has been incomplete, uncovering much about the building's structural history and changing use, but lifting those findings out of the social and cultural context of the city and nation.[81] The memory of fugitive slave hearings persisted in Philadelphia until at least the 1880s, when published biographies of lawyers and judges who participated included references to their role in enforcing or challenging the Fugitive

Slave Law.[82] However, material evidence of the federal offices on the second floor of Independence Hall disappeared when city council chambers were installed in 1854. The nativist victories of the 1850s have been recorded in the city's history, but never before connected with the 1855 shrine at the Hall of Independence, which has undergone a series of subsequent renovations. These are layers of history—city, state, and national events of the nineteenth century which overlaid eighteenth-century memories. Building restoration allows such layers to be pulled apart so that a select story can be told.

As a place of memory, Independence Hall during the mid-nineteenth century continued to function as a depository, defined by intense regard for the nation's founders and founding documents. Perpetuating the memory of the American Revolution articulated during the 1824 visit of Lafayette, the room designated as the "Hall of Independence" held portraits and relics of heroes, making the room sacred by association. Nevertheless, these decades constituted an important turning point in the history of Independence Hall as Americans of a new generation marshaled the memory of the American Revolution to new purposes. Bridging past and present, native-born Philadelphians transformed a civic reception room into a sacred space. The old Pennsylvania State House provided a place where local people could erect a shrine to the founding fathers, visit the shrine, and add their valued relics to a place of the nation. Among the relics, the old State House bell acquired increasing status, tethered in memory to the Declaration of Independence.

Surrounded by conflict, Independence Hall served as a sounding board that echoed the principles of the Declaration of Independence—principles treasured and defended by some, but to others still out of reach. Activities in and around the building increasingly engaged the United States Constitution as well, calling attention to perceived gaps between the framework for national government and the ideals expressed in the Declaration. Independence Square provided a place for civic engagement where citizens could participate in the political life of the nation, whether demonstrating for equality, keeping vigil during fugitive slave hearings, staging riots, or assembling to keep the peace. Because this was a place in a city, a great diversity of people converged in acts of citizenship; because this was a place of national significance, their activities resonated beyond local concerns.

By the end of the Civil War, Independence Hall had gained increased standing in public memory of the American Revolution and in the determination to hold the Union together despite the frightening upheavals of the mid-nineteenth century. Emerging from the Civil War, Americans faced the challenge of reuniting North and

South. Forging a shared national identity would be complicated by new circumstances of industrialization, immigration, and the Constitutional recognition of former slaves as full citizens of the United States. In the postwar decades of great social and economic transformation, Philadelphians, as the guardians of Independence Hall, put their historic shrine to work for the reunited nation.

Chapter 5

LEGACY

Staking Claims to the Past Through Preservation

On the Fourth of July in 1866, Pennsylvanians who fought to preserve the Union returned their regimental flags to Independence Hall, the Union's birthplace. Two hundred thirteen regiments, including veterans of Bull Run and Gettysburg, marched in a grand parade through the streets of Philadelphia to Independence Square. In salute to the tattered battle flags, bright new American flags and bunting decked the parade route, up to and including the old Pennsylvania State House. Able-bodied soldiers, wounded veterans, and most poignantly the children orphaned by the Civil War entered Independence Square to cheers, applause, and waving handkerchiefs. In a ceremony of patriotism and thanksgiving, the soldiers returned their flags to the governor of Pennsylvania. A band played "The Star-Spangled Banner" and Handel's "Hallelujah" chorus. Speakers recounted the valor shown in war and thanked God for bringing the conflict to an end. They invoked the memory of Independence Hall. "This is a hallowed place—this is a hallowed day," Governor Andrew Curtin declared. "Here and now in the name of Pennsylvania I accept these colors fitly, for we are assembled upon the birth-day in the birth-place of American liberty." On this Fourth of July, the pageantry in Independence Square echoed with the distant and recent past, the pride of victory, and the confidence that the nation had been saved from disaster.[1]

The ceremony at Independence Hall reflected the extent to which Pennsylvania's old State House was evolving into a place of significance to the nation, tied not only to events of the American Revolution but also to the continuing struggle to sustain the Union. Representing the foundation of a nation that might have been lost, the building acquired a magnified significance, reflecting a civil religion that united religious belief with faith in the nation's progress.[2] In the decades after the Civil War, as Amer-

19. With Independence Hall cloaked in patriotic buntings of American flags, Pennsylvania soldiers marked the end of the Civil War by returning their tattered regimental flags to the birthplace of the Union. "The Boys in Blue," an 1866 commemorative lithograph as well as an advertising device for the King & Baird publishing firm (see lower left), shows the culmination of a grand parade through the streets of Philadelphia. (Courtesy of the Library Company of Philadelphia)

icans searched for ways to reunify and strengthen the nation, Independence Hall gained increasing attention as a historic place. By the end of the nineteenth century, the space considered "historic" grew from the first-floor meeting place of the Second Continental Congress to encompass the entire interior of the old Pennsylvania State House, its exterior appearance, and the surrounding public square. But in a heterogeneous nation, whose legacy did Independence Hall represent? Even as Philadelphians enhanced Independence Hall as a material reminder of the past, they encountered the complications of their patriotic impulses. Issues of class, race, gender, sectional difference, and the growth of the city all entered into the process of restoring an eighteenth-century ambiance in Independence Hall and constructing a history to meet the needs and expectations of nineteenth-century Americans.

Sacred Square

By the late 1860s, Philadelphia's population of more than 600,000 people had spread far beyond the original city boundaries envisioned by William Penn, reaching westward across the Schuylkill River.[3] These Philadelphians of the nineteenth century occupied an urban landscape rich with historic associations. Their streets aligned with the grid of Penn's city plan. Their public squares were legacies of the founder, placed one in each quadrant within the city's original boundaries with a fifth in the center for future public buildings. Philadelphians had layered historic associations onto these squares, naming them Washington, Franklin, Logan, Rittenhouse, and Penn. They had created an additional public square around the first Pennsylvania State House, naming it Independence Square in memory of the momentous events of 1776. With such associations embedded into the urban landscape, the evolution of the nineteenth-century city involved not only population and geography, but also Philadelphians' regard for the past.

Since the 1730s, Independence Square had been the city's civic center. However, the growing city's demands on municipal government had long overwhelmed the eighteenth-century State House, adjacent office buildings, City Hall, and Court House (Congress Hall). Through the middle decades of the nineteenth century, officials had offered plans for new civic buildings, but the projects had been stalled by economic recessions, legal entanglements between the city and county governments, and the Civil War.[4] In 1867, the new County Court House erected on the west side of Independence Square, behind Congress Hall, relieved some of the pressure for courtroom space, but did not fulfill the need for more city government offices.[5] The so-called

"Mills Buildings" or "State House row" of office buildings flanking the old State House were not only crowded, but embarrassingly old-fashioned amid the rising marble and cast-iron structures of the nineteenth-century city.[6]

In the late 1860s, the pressing need for a new, much larger city hall forced Philadelphians to consider the historic associations of their public squares, particularly Independence Square and Penn Square, the centrally located block that William Penn had originally intended for public buildings. Like the selection of a site for the Pennsylvania State House in the 1730s, the location for the new buildings would affect the spatial organization of the city. However, it would also reflect Philadelphians' regard for the past and vision for the future. Should more buildings be placed on Independence Square, the traditional civic center? If so, how should they relate to the historic buildings already there? Would it be better for the municipal offices to move eight blocks west to Penn Square, following the westward movement of the city's population? What consequences might that have for the older neighborhoods left behind? Such questions addressed the practical concerns of the city, but engaged Philadelphians in a process of defining the historical significance of the old State House and its surroundings in the years following the Civil War.

The city's westward growth affected its politics in ways that made the public buildings question especially difficult. The Republican Party controlled the city government, but the two-chamber City Council was divided between the interests of the new western districts of the city and the representatives of the traditional business and civic center near Independence Square. Apart from any consideration of the historical associations of the city's squares, such divided geographic interests left the Councils unable to agree on where to place new public buildings. In 1868, with representatives of the older districts in control, the City Councils passed legislation to place a new city hall on Independence Square just in time for Mayor Morton McMichael to sign it on December 31, his last day in office.[7] However, the new term brought a new impasse. Newly elected councilmen with ties to the city's western growth stymied the plans to build on Independence Square by trying to shift the site to the more western Penn Square.[8]

In ensuing arguments over where to place a new city hall, issues of history and urban geography intertwined. The city's newspapers, many of which had offices near Independence Square and wanted government offices to remain there, propelled the debate with news coverage, editorials, and letters to the editor. "Common sense and propriety both assert that the State House Square is the proper place," argued the *Press*, citing the square's proximity to the federal courts, the post office, and the U.S.

Customs House. Letters published in the *Press* reflected the opposing sides of the debate. Those who favored Penn Square felt that it was a more central location. In addition, Penn Square already was divided into quadrants, allowing buildings to be arranged around the central intersection of Broad and Market Streets. Near the end of one letter, a writer added a note of history, arguing that, "Independence Square, being classic ground, should be occupied only by Independence Hall. That it has been desecrated, is no argument in favor of continuing to desecrate it."[9] As the place designated by William Penn for public buildings, Penn Square had its own powerful historic associations, dating to the earliest settlement of the city.

Supporters of Independence Square also had history in mind, but they viewed new buildings around Independence Hall as an appropriate sign of progress. They agreed that Penn Square's four quadrants offered advantages. However, they argued that the business center of the city was not Penn Square, but in the area of Independence Square, long the neighborhood of the city's leading financial institutions, publishing houses, and light manufacturers. These advocates of Independence Square as a city hall site invoked history, but they gave precedence to the needs of the nineteenth-century city. "Sacred associations connected with a spot in a city should never bar the progress to which the events that created the very association have led," one letter writer said. "If the city needs the Independence Square, she would be false to the sentiment which it inspires if she declined to take it."[10]

Amid the impasse, designs for a new city hall on Independence Square showed a determination to represent Philadelphia architecturally as an up-to-date, nineteenth-century city rather than a place of the past. Although the site question had not been settled, a city-appointed committee conducted a design competition for the Independence Square location. From seventeen plans, the committee chose a design by John McArthur, Jr., an architect who had contributed to the nineteenth-century growth of Philadelphia with a succession of churches, residences, and commercial buildings designed during the 1840s, 1850s, and 1860s.[11] In 1860, McArthur had created a plan for "County Buildings" on Independence Square which incorporated the old State House into a massive complex of office buildings that dwarfed the landmark but echoed its Georgian design.[12] In 1870, his design also filled Independence Square with public buildings, but under heavy direction from the city-appointed committee, McArthur changed the design to the ornate, then-fashionable Second Empire style. It was, the committee decided, "in complete accord with the purposes of the building and the prevailing taste of the age."[13]

More than a statement of architectural taste, McArthur's design embodied deci-

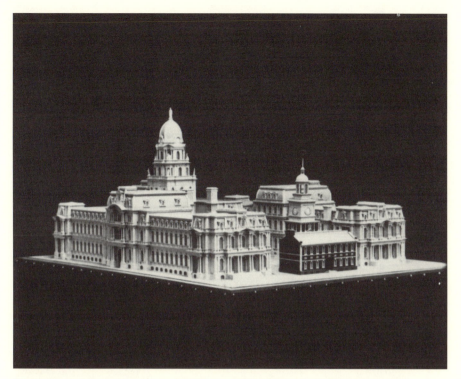

20. Amid controversy over where to build a new Philadelphia City Hall, architect John McArthur, Jr., envisioned this structure, shown in a model photographed by James Cremer. The massive Second Empire design would have enveloped Independence Hall and replaced all other buildings on Independence Square. (Courtesy of the Library Company of Philadelphia)

sions about the relative significance of the new city hall, the existing eighteenth-century buildings, and Independence Square. Of the buildings already on the square, only the old State House would have been spared. Not regarded as worthy of preservation, both Congress Hall and the old City Hall would have been demolished, along with the Mills buildings and the new County Court House. Independence Square would have been largely obliterated by the massive new city hall, which was envisioned as three sides of a square, with an open side facing Chestnut Street. In that space along Chestnut Street, Independence Hall would have been left, dwarfed by the surrounding municipal building. In its size and style, the design for the new city hall called attention to the contrast between the eighteenth-century past and the progress and aspirations of the nineteenth century.[14]

Alarmed by the momentum for the Independence Square site, opponents from the city's western districts seized on the historical associations of Independence Hall to advance their fight to place the new public buildings on Penn Square instead. In doing

119

so, they projected historical significance from the old State House to all of Independence Square. They articulated their strategy in "An Appeal to the Legislature to Prevent the Desecration of Independence Square," adopted on February 25, 1870. Imploring state lawmakers to intercede, the appeal included geographic and aesthetic arguments, stating that Independence Square was no longer the central point of the city and that the narrow streets around the square would not afford a good view of the new building. However, the appeal also invoked history to make its case: "As Independence Square is a scene of the deepest historical interest, connected as it has always been with the Hall and its hallowed memories, it is not well that influences so sacred should be lost to our city, with their power for general good, by concentrating there all crowds, litigations and trials of criminals necessary for the security of human society; but, on the contrary, it should cease to be an arena of human strifes and woe, and become wholly sacred to Liberty, where her Hall shall stand in simple grandeur amid trees and verdure, alone forever."[15] In essence, Independence Square was being defined as an artifact to be appreciated for its association with Independence Hall. Criminal justice activities, which had always been present, were being cast as inherently inconsistent with such a sacred place.

Arguments based on the historical associations of Independence Hall carried added weight with the approaching one hundredth anniversary of the Declaration of Independence. Opponents of the Independence Square site noted that Philadelphia officials had only recently asked Congress to authorize the city to host the 1876 centennial celebration. "They ask that the American people shall come to Philadelphia in 1876 to see how faithfully we have kept the sacred charge entrusted to us by our grandfathers," the opponents wrote. "What will they be able to show the pilgrims who throng from all parts of the country to this 'American Mecca?'"[16] Such arguments exploited the history of Independence Hall, but in doing so, enhanced its reputation as a place important not only in Philadelphia but in the nation at large.

As opponents of the Independence Square site mounted a petition campaign, Philadelphia's newspapers mocked their efforts. The publishers heaped particular scorn upon the idea that Independence Square, not just the Independence Hall building, was somehow sacred. "Independence Square never was sacred ground. A sacred building stands on one edge of it, which the proposed plan will restore to its original unity," wrote the *Evening Bulletin*.[17] A month later, the newspaper took its argument to new extremes: "The trees are not sacred, for they are of comparatively modern growth. The grass is not sacred, for it ceased to exist, long ago. The muddy 'cow-paths' that traverse this Square in all directions are not sacred, for they are the recent inventions of irreverent lawyers, making short cuts to and from the courts. . . . Nothing was ever done upon the 'sacred soil' on which the proposed buildings have been located, to sanctify it."[18] Independence Square had long functioned as a place for civic activism, but none of the public demonstrations that had taken place over the last one hundred years were invoked as historic, let alone "sacred" to the memory of the square.

By early March 1870, two citizens groups were actively campaigning against the Independence Square plan—one based on the geographic argument that Penn Square was the more appropriate site, and the other adding the historical dimension that Independence Square should not be desecrated. Both groups bombarded the Pennsylvania General Assembly with petitions asking the state to intervene, perhaps by calling an election to decide the location for the city hall.[19] In this, they succeeded. In addition to authorizing an election, the General Assembly also eliminated Independence Square from contention. Legislation drafted by state senators from Philadelphia gave voters two choices for their new city hall: Penn Square or Washington Square, the block diagonally southwest of Independence Hall.[20] Like Penn Square and Independence Square, Washington Square carried its own historical associations as the burial place of Revolutionary War soldiers. Given these choices, with greater numbers of voters living in the western sections of the city, in the election held in October 1870, Penn Square prevailed with 51,625 votes over 32,825 for Washington Square.[21]

By choosing to separate the municipal government of Philadelphia from Independence Square, city voters set the stage for a new era in the history of Independence Hall. With the prospect of government activities vacating Independence Square, the old Pennsylvania State House was poised to function solely as a historic place for the first time. The transition, however, proved to be much longer than Philadelphians in the 1870s anticipated. John McArthur adapted his monumental Second Empire city hall for the site on Penn Square, but the projected ten years of construction stretched to thirty. Elaboration of Independence Hall as a historic place proceeded in stages over the next three decades, propelled by the centennial anniversary of the Declaration of Independence and by the efforts of Americans who viewed Independence Hall as the personal legacy of their ancestors.

National Museum

The nation's centennial in 1876 was a twofold commemoration—a remembrance of 1776, to be sure, but even more a celebration of the progress of the United States in the century since.[22] More than Independence Hall—the birthplace of the

Declaration of Independence—the major attraction in Philadelphia in 1876 was the Centennial Exhibition, a grand world's fair staged five miles to the west, in the city's Fairmount Park. The ten million visitors to the Exhibition could easily fill their days strolling over the 236-acre site with its broad avenues and buildings packed with the arts and manufactures of the world. They could marvel at the machinery of progress, including the massive Corliss engine and Alexander Graham Bell's new invention, the telephone. If they desired a taste of the past, they could visit the Colonial kitchen on the Exhibition grounds or view possessions of George Washington on display. If they did not want to travel into Philadelphia's business district to see the Liberty Bell, they might be satisfied by the many replica Liberty Bells in state displays at the Exhibition.[23]

The Centennial was, nevertheless, an important moment for Independence Hall. The celebration placed the old Pennsylvania State House once again on a national stage, where it called Northern and Southern states to reunification, basked in the nation's founding and persistence, and inspired faith in another century of progress. Covering the commemoration, nationally circulated periodicals such as *Harper's* and *Frank Leslie's Illustrated Newspaper* published images of the building. They routinely identified the structure as "Independence Hall," further eroding the distinction that Philadelphians had made between the room in which the Declaration was signed and the building as a whole. Recognition of Independence Hall also spread beyond Philadelphia through portrayals of the building on Centennial souvenirs and in view books. Even if visitors to the Centennial Exhibition did not venture from the fairgrounds to Independence Hall, they likely took home one or more images of the building.[24] In these images, the old State House appeared alone, lifted out of its urban environment, with at most a few passing horses and carriages. Thus separated from the modern city, the building appeared simply as an artifact of the American Revolution. So, too, did the Liberty Bell, which was often portrayed alone, independent of its home in the State House.

Although the anniversary of independence seemed to offer an opportunity for the nation to join in one harmonious celebration, events at Independence Hall demonstrated the tensions inherent in interpreting American history. Looking ahead to 1876, the Philadelphia caretakers of the old State House enlarged and enhanced the space inside the building considered historic, creating a museum of artifacts intended to represent the nation's history. In the process, however, they confronted the difficult questions of how, and by whom, the events and ideals of the past should be communicated to the present. The project to create a national museum at Independence Hall became immersed in the politics of social class, gender, and sectional identity in the wake of the Civil War.

In Philadelphia in the 1870s, the interests of two disparate social classes converged at Independence Hall. The old State House remained the meeting place of the city government, which by the 1870s was controlled not by elite, wealthy families of long standing, but by a new generation of professional politicians. These politicians drew their support from the working class, particularly from members of the city's numerous volunteer fire companies.[25] The City Councils showed their working-class orientation by turning over their chambers in 1870 to a convention of the Iron Moulders' International Cooperative and Protective Union, which took the occasion to pass resolutions against "Coolie labor" by immigrant Chinese.[26] City officials in the mid-1870s also tolerated massive labor demonstrations in Independence Square.[27] Focused on the city's industrial character more than its historic past, the politicians in the City Councils held legal control over the State House and the public funds that could be used to improve the building for the Centennial.

Meanwhile, wealthier individuals with familial ties to early American history had their own visions of the proper ways to commemorate their ancestors' contributions to the founding of the nation. Although new transportation systems had enabled the elite to move out of the older districts of the city, the perimeter around Independence Square remained a commercial and professional district frequented by lawyers, bankers, architects, and others who had business with the city government. The city's oldest learned societies, the American Philosophical Society and the Library Company of Philadelphia, still occupied buildings near Independence Hall, as did the Historical Society of Pennsylvania. While the City Councils remained in session on the second floor of the State House, awaiting their move to the planned new city hall, they acceded to requests to delegate care of the first floor to members of old Philadelphia families who claimed the expertise necessary to re-create the conditions of 1776. Furthermore, in 1872 the Councils ordered the east room on the first floor to be "set apart forever and appropriated exclusively" to displaying original furnishings from 1776 and portraits of men of the American Revolution.[28] The decision perpetuated the associations of the room that had been articulated during the visit of the Marquis de Lafayette in 1824 and sustained in the nineteenth century through the rituals of civic receptions. However, it also triggered a series of events that exacerbated tensions between the old guard and the new.

The driving force behind the transformation of the first floor of the State House during the 1870s was Frank M. Etting, a lawyer, active member of the Historical Society of Pennsylvania, and descendant of a prominent Jewish family whose history extended to the Colonial era in Pennsylvania and Maryland.[29] Etting was on a personal quest that had begun in 1865, when he had inherited a chair which his family believed was used by the Continental Congress in 1776. In possession of this leather-upholstered armchair, he began to search for others. At the state capitol in Harrisburg, he discovered two more, which the governor agreed to send back to Philadelphia for display in Independence Hall. Later investigations determined that Etting's uphol-stered armchairs had belonged to the federal Congress that met in Congress Hall in the 1790s, but he believed they were the original furnishings of the Continental Congress of 1776.[30] Motivated by his success in locating historical artifacts, Etting tried to inter-est the U.S. State Department in establishing a national museum in Washington, D.C. Failing that, he transferred his ambition to Philadelphia.[31] By 1872, when the City Councils appointed Etting chairman of a Committee on Restoration of Independence Hall, he had developed a plan for presenting the Hall of Independence as it appeared in 1776. Furthermore, he envisioned the building as home for a National Museum of historical artifacts from the Colonial era through the War of 1812.[32]

By the time of Etting's appointment, seventeen years had passed since nativist politicians had established the Hall of Independence as a shrine to the nation's founders. In the interim, the room had become crowded with relics accumulated as gifts to the city. Behavior in the Hall was not always reverent, as writer John Savage observed in *Harper's* magazine. Visiting the Hall, Savage noted the "buzz of assem-bling lawyers" preparing for trials in the nearby courtroom. Other visitors who arrived to see the Hall of Independence seemed "forgetful of the solemnity of the place, shuf-fle noisily about, give their tongues full rein, and break with the jargon of vulgar, although it may be well-intentioned and irrepressible curiosity, the serene significance of the place."[33] The chamber had become a tribute not only to 1776, but also to the heroes of the recent Civil War. Portraits of Abraham Lincoln, General Ulysses S. Grant, and local soldiers killed in battle hung among the heroes of the American Revolution. Among the historical relics stood furniture discarded by the City Councils and a block of marble intended for the Washington Monument under construction in the nation's capital.

The conglomeration of artifacts and disrespectful behavior offended Etting's his-torical sensibilities. Like the politicians of the 1850s, he aspired to create a more spe-cific association between the room and the nation's founding, but his goals and methods differed. Still valuing the memory of the founders, Etting emphasized not hero worship, but the educational potential of artifacts that had been touched by his-

21. For the Centennial celebration, elite Philadelphians redecorated the Hall of Independence to create the genteel parlor shown here in *A Century After* (1876). Stripped of many of the relics that had accumulated over the years, the room was dedicated solely to the memory of the events of 1776. (Courtesy of the Library Company of Philadelphia)

torical figures. "So long . . . as we can preserve the material objects left to us which those great men saw, used, or even touched, the thrill of vitality may still be transmitted unbroken," he wrote in the book published in connection with the restoration.[34] Like other museum curators of his time, Etting stressed the practical benefits to be gained by public display of such artifacts, both as "a system of object instruction in history for the masses" and as an attraction to draw visitors to the city.[35]

As it emerged under Etting's direction, the room in which the Declaration of Independence was signed became the "Independence Chamber," a refined parlor for admiring historical artifacts. Etting's family-heirloom chair and twelve identical chairs that he had located were displayed against the north and south walls, protected by ropes from the public. Visitors could admire these as they walked toward the east wall, the centerpiece of the display. On the wall, Etting arranged a hierarchy of portraits, with signers of the Declaration in places of honor near eye level and other presidents of the Continental Congress and Revolutionary War generals hung in a row just above the floor. Portraits that did not fit this historical arrangement were removed, including likenesses of Indians which in Etting's view "absolutely defiled the walls" and "the vilest daub and caricature of Andrew Jackson" which he called "unfit for a tavern sign."[36] He moved the Liberty Bell to the tower stair hall, where it was encased in original timbers brought down from the steeple. To complete the aura of 1776 in the Independence Chamber, a reconstructed dais in front of the east wall exhibited the speaker's chair believed to have been used by the Continental Congress (another misidentification of furnishings, since this chair dated only to 1779). The chair, with its carving of a rising sun, had been returned to Philadelphia from Harrisburg in 1865, when Etting had requested the leather-upholstered armchairs that matched his own. The state also sent a table which was believed to have served for the signing of the Declaration. On it, in 1876, Etting placed the silver inkstand believed to have been used by the signers. It, too, was returned to Philadelphia from Harrisburg after being privately safeguarded by a state employee since 1849.[37] For a time during the centennial year, the original signed Declaration of Independence was returned from Washington and displayed in a specially made, glass-fronted safe.[38]

While changes in the Independence Chamber reinforced its traditional identity as a historic place, Etting's national museum plan required more space within the State House, additional artifacts, and a curatorial staff. For the space, Etting acquired the west room on the first floor, displacing the courts and for the first time expanding the designated historic space inside the State House beyond a single room. He planned to begin the museum in this room with an exhibit on Colonial Pennsylvania and cases of Revolutionary-era relics, but he hoped that the project might later expand to the second floor of the State House and the adjacent office buildings.[39] To collect artifacts and manage the museum, he recruited socially prominent women, including his own wife, to serve as the board of managers of the National Museum. The "Lady Managers," as they came to be known, further separated management of the State House from the politicians who had traditionally dictated its use and injected issues of gender into preparations for the Centennial exhibits of the National Museum.[40]

In accepting Etting's invitation to join the board of managers, Philadelphia women followed a precedent of female involvement in historic preservation. In the 1850s, women in the South had organized the restoration of Washington's Mount Vernon, stepping out of the private, domestic sphere to save a public, but still domestic, representation of the nation's first president. In Philadelphia during the Civil War, women had taken a leading role in organizing Sanitary Fairs, including exhibits of historical relics.[41] In recruiting women to manage the National Museum, Etting also cast his project as an appropriate female activity. He appealed for the women's assistance by quoting John Adams's admonition that the American Revolution would be regarded as a historic milestone, "provided always that the ladies take care to record the circumstances of it, for by the experience I have had of the other sex, they are too lazy or too active to commemorate them."[42] The first president of the board of managers, Lily Macalester Berghmans, defined the work of preserving history as vital to the nation's future and properly within a woman's sphere. The purpose of the National Museum, she pointed out, was to educate future generations and encourage them to follow the example of the founders. "Thus the work before us is not a mere sentimental one, but a practical and serviceable discharge of our duties as wives and mothers," she said at the board's first annual meeting in 1873.[43]

Operating much like the Mount Vernon Ladies Association, the board of managers developed a network of state corresponding secretaries to locate artifacts. Unlike the Mount Vernon group, however, the National Museum managers had been assembled by Etting's all-male committee on restoration. Anxious to fulfill their responsibilities, the managers at times came into conflict with Etting's committee as they asserted independent authority over their project. The women insisted that the boundaries of authority between the two groups be defined, and they protested when the men took actions that seemed to interfere with the women's work. For example, they objected when Etting's committee interpreted the rules of the board of managers in a way that prevented the service of Berghmans, who lived part of the year away from Philadelphia, in Washington, D.C. When the men tried to assuage Berghmans by suggesting that she direct an additional board in the nation's capital, the managers in Philadelphia asserted that any such expansion must remain subject to their control. At the women's behest, Etting's committee confirmed in writing the managers' authority to make rules governing their own membership and activities.[44]

Pursuing artifacts for the museum, the board of managers significantly enlarged the scope of the project beyond artifacts of war, politics, and famous men. In 1875, their published invitation to donors—likely approved by Etting—identified the National Museum as part of the "effort to dedicate Independence Hall as a perpetual monument to the Founders of America" and sought "revolutionary relics and portraits."[45] However, the managers' instructions to their corresponding secretaries suggested an artifact search encompassing a greater sweep of history both in terms of time and in the character of objects. "Endeavor to collect anything that may belong to, or illustrate the early history of the country," the board instructed its secretaries. Portraits

22. The National Museum, an ambitious project to collect Revolutionary-era artifacts for display in the former courtroom of the State House, evolved under the supervision of the board of managers, a women's committee similar in structure to the Mount Vernon Ladies Association. The women expanded the scope of the collection to include domestic as well as military and political artifacts, shown here in a photograph from Frank M. Etting's *Historical Account of the Old State House* (1876). (Courtesy of Independence National Historical Park)

of prominent men were certainly of interest, but so were "relics and curiosities of colonial and revolutionary times; military arms used during the revolution; valuable deeds or manuscripts, and a few articles of apparel, household utensils or furniture, to illustrate the mode of life at that time."[46] The instructions assured that along with politics and war, the National Museum would reflect something of domestic life of the Colonial and Revolutionary eras.

In striving to create a "national" museum at a time when the memory of the Civil War remained fresh, the board of managers confronted challenges similar to those faced by the larger Centennial Exhibition. Materially decimated by the war, deeply mourning the lost cause, and chafing under Reconstruction, Southerners could muster little enthusiasm for a national celebration in 1876. The National Museum managers encountered the open wounds of the South as they sought corresponding secretaries and artifacts from Southern states. A South Carolina man wrote bitterly that the Union army had made sure he would have no relics to contribute. "Almost every building which possessed an historic interest every thing upon which our families could look back with pardonable pride was committed to the flames and those objects which escaped the torch of the incendiary, did not escape the greed of the plunderers," he wrote. The managers found it difficult to recruit secretaries in Southern states, and even when secretaries were willing, they found little enthusiasm among their neighbors for the Centennial.[47]

As it evolved by the centennial year, the "National" Museum projected a very narrow perception of the nation, but an interpretation that corresponded with the views of its organizers and donors. With artifacts collected primarily from the board of managers' socially prominent friends in Pennsylvania, New Jersey, Connecticut, and Massachusetts, the resulting exhibit presented a view of the nation rooted in British tradition via the colonies of New England and the mid-Atlantic. At least 240 individuals sent at least 400 objects to Independence Hall, either as gifts or temporary deposits, demonstrating their material connection with early British America. No artifacts from the Spanish colonization of Florida or the West came to the museum, and representations of France were limited to relics associated with the Marquis de Lafayette or French kings and queens. Although some donors sent American Indian artifacts, they were objects seized in conquest, and the only item related to African Americans was a document recording the sale of a slave. Although the National Museum occupied the building where independence had been declared from Great Britain, its artifacts emphasized the United States' British cultural heritage while marginalizing the rest. Enhancing the British character of the artifacts, portraits of British kings and queens hung on the walls as part of Etting's chronicle of the Colonial history of Pennsylvania. Emphasizing the rule of law over all, the walls also displayed portraits of members of the Constitutional Convention of 1787.[48]

What was the place of Independence Hall in this national history? Although Etting had designated the east room as a memorial specific to 1776, in the hallway between the Independence Chamber and the National Museum, he erected five tablets that placed Independence Hall within a broader narrative of American history. One of the tablets memorialized William Penn, linking Independence Hall with its history as the State House for the province of Pennsylvania. Two tablets traced the union of the colonies, one with quotations from William Penn, the Declaration of Independence, and George Washington, and the other tracing cooperative acts beginning with the plan of union offered by Benjamin Franklin at Albany, New York, in 1754. A fourth tablet, titled "INDEPENDENCE," linked the nonimportation agreements in Philadelphia, Boston, and New York with the later action by the Continental Congress in 1776. Finally, the fifth tablet memorialized the Centennial: "The State House of Pennsylvania Consecrated by the Memories of the Events That Occurred Within and Under the Shadow of Its Walls Is Dedicated by the Citizens of Philadelphia to Their Fellow Countrymen of the United States as a Perpetual Monument to the Founders of American Independence on the National Centenary Anniversary July 4, 1876." In effect, the fifth tablet, written by Etting and approved by the mayor of Philadelphia, memorialized Etting's own work in Independence Hall.[49] It was a reflection of the attitude that led to Etting's dismissal within days of the date inscribed on the tablet.

In the four years leading to the Centennial, Etting had taken personal control of Independence Hall, acquiring and arranging artifacts to suit his taste and interpretation of the nation's history. While the project of "restoring" Independence Hall drew praise, Etting alienated his political sponsors as well as members of the press. Clearly, class antagonism played a part. Newspaper editorials called attention to the extent to which Independence Hall had been given over to the control of elites. "A man named Etting . . . seems to have taken a lease of Independence Hall, and the appurtenances thereto, for his own special glory and benefit, and that of a few high-toned ladies," the *Sunday Times* complained.[50] Etting's offenses against the press included excluding reporters from an organizational meeting of the board of managers. He angered politicians by not obtaining appropriate permits from city departments, and he surprised the president judge of the court of common pleas by beginning renovations for the National Museum before the court was satisfied with its new quarters. He insisted on decorum in the Independence Chamber and restricted admission to the National Museum to the hours between 9 A.M. to 1 P.M., with 1 P.M. to 3 P.M. reserved for school groups whose teachers agreed to come in advance to receive proper instruction about the rooms and their contents.[51]

Secondary to complaints about Etting's personal zeal, his historical displays angered politicians and the public. While intending to celebrate the achievements of the nation's founders, Etting precipitated conflict. His broader narrative went too far for some, who objected to portraits of British kings, and not far enough for others, who protested the absence of heroes of the Civil War. Why were the portraits of such heroes as Lincoln, Jackson, and Grant removed from the Independence Chamber? Worse, why was the Jackson portrait relegated to the cellar? "This gentleman would take advice

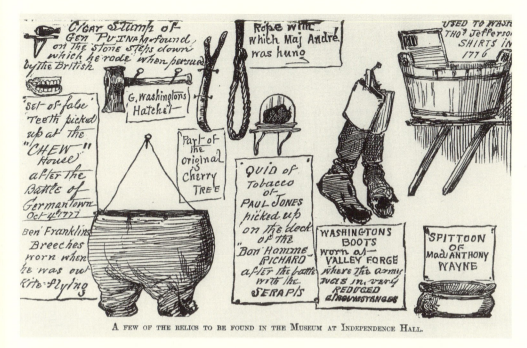

A FEW OF THE RELICS TO BE FOUND IN THE MUSEUM AT INDEPENDENCE HALL.

23. The great abundance of artifacts in the National Museum claiming authentic connections to the American Revolution inspired this lampoon in *Going to the Centennial: A Guy to the Exhibition*, a humorous account of the celebration published in 1876 by Collin & Small of New York. (Courtesy of the Historical Society of Pennsylvania)

from no one," one council member fumed. Why should a portrait of King George III be part of the National Museum's display of the colonial history of Pennsylvania? "That the figure of so disreputable a person is allowed within the sacred precincts of Independence Hall [is] a gross profanation," petitioners wrote to the City Councils. In a lighter vein, a humorous account of the Centennial Exhibition lampooned the genteel ambiance of the Independence Chamber and the numerous artifacts labeled as authentic relics of the American Revolution.[52]

By July 1876, with the Centennial Exhibition fully under way, the City Councils decided to tolerate Etting no longer. Could it be that their aggravation toward Etting stemmed from anti-Semitism? The question may be reasonably asked, but the answer is not explicit in the historical record. If Etting's Jewish heritage was a source of irritation, such objections were masked in complaints about the personal ownership that he appeared to exercise over Independence Hall. His worst offense seems to have involved his attempts to manage city employees, particularly the father of one member of the Common Council.[53] By nearly unanimous votes on July 14, 1876, the City

Councils reorganized the Independence Hall restoration committee to eliminate Etting as chairman and give control back to government officials.[54]

Although Etting lost all influence over the presentation of American history in Independence Hall, his project transformed the interior and function of the building for years to come. The museum remained, with a changing and ever-growing collection of relics, until the next major renovation of the building twenty years later. Although many of the "lady managers" resigned after Etting's dismissal, the board's secretary, Mary Chew, kept her keys to the exhibit cases and maintained watch over the collection.[55] Despite the objections to some of Etting's exhibition choices, even the portraits of the British sovereigns remained hanging in Independence Hall until at least 1915.[56] Whatever objections Philadelphians expressed about the content of the National Museum, their greatest source of irritation was Etting, the man who had stepped into the divide between the old families descended from Philadelphia's past and the new cadre of politicians who controlled the city's present government.

During the centennial year, Independence Hall competed for attention with the grand exposition of technology in Fairmount Park, but took center stage on two occasions: the opening festivities on New Year's Eve and ceremonies for Independence Day. The New Year's Eve that heralded 1876 allowed Philadelphians to announce with pride that they had safeguarded Independence Hall for a century and now welcomed the nation and the world to celebrate the anniversary of the Declaration of Independence. Thousands crowded into the streets around the old building on a misty, rainy night. The State House was decorated for the occasion with an allegorical painting of Washington crowned by the Goddess of Liberty and the arms of the thirteen original states. Calcium lights mounted on the American Hotel across the street lit the scene, including the statue of George Washington that had been placed in front of the State House in 1869. Just before midnight, Mayor William Stokley stepped into the space cleared for him and began to hoist over Independence Hall a large flag, a replica of a battle flag raised by George Washington in 1776. Like the exhibits inside the building, the flag with the Union Jack in one corner represented a link to British ancestors. At midnight, the flag unfurled, thousands of voices united in cheers, and a cornet band struck up "The Star-Spangled Banner." Militia units marched into Independence Square and fired salutes. The bell in the State House steeple pealed for half an hour, echoed by church bells around the city.[57]

Centennial planners envisioned the Fourth of July as a similarly festive event— even more so, since a multitude of visitors would be in town for the Centennial Exhibition. Organizers planned three days of events at Independence Hall, beginning on July 2 with one of Frank Etting's last official acts, a presentation in the National Museum of biographies of the signers of the Declaration of Independence. On July 3, a torchlight procession led the public to the old State House to await the first moments of the Fourth of July. At midnight, the first tones emitted from a new tower bell that had been presented to the State House. In another personal contribution to the public commemoration of the Centennial, Henry Seybert, a Philadelphia scientist whose interest in spiritualism inspired him to honor past deeds of the departed, had ordered the thirteen-thousand-pound bell cast from armaments from both sides in the Revolutionary and Civil Wars, symbolically melding together Great Britain and America, North and South. City officials accepted the gift and arranged for the tower to be reinforced to support the heavier bell.[58]

On Independence Day, the ceremony in the square was to be an emotional, patriotic endorsement of America's past, present, and future. So it was—but not only in the manner that Centennial organizers intended. As planned, a parade led thousands to Independence Square, where dignitaries took reserved seats and others crowded into the streets and up into the trees for a view. President Grant had decided to pass the day in Washington, but Vice President Thomas W. Ferry came to deliver an address. In a gesture of unity between North and South, the grandson of Richard Henry Lee, the Virginian who had proposed the resolution of independence to the Continental Congress of 1776, came to Philadelphia to read aloud from the original, signed Declaration of Independence. The ceremony radiated pride in American achievement, represented by the Declaration and the progress of the nation over one hundred years. In the shadow of the church-like State House tower, speeches gloried in the progress of the nation as a fulfillment of the will of God.

However, Philadelphians who had been reading the newspapers knew that another view of American democracy was present in the city during the early days of July. Advocates of woman suffrage had long pointed to the contradictions between the language of the Declaration of Independence and the experiences of American women. In 1848, the "Declaration of Sentiments" issued in Seneca Falls, New York, adapted the language of the 1776 document to proclaim that "all men and women are created equal." Almost thirty years later, although a Women's Building at the Centennial Exhibition celebrated women's art and industry, suffrage activists expressed dismay at the commemoration's lack of attention to women's political concerns. Acting on their frustration, members of the National Woman Suffrage Association drafted a new document, the "Women's Declaration of Rights and Articles of Impeachment Against the United States," which itemized the nation's failures to extend full legal and political rights to women. Leading suffragists, including Susan B. Anthony, Elizabeth Cady Stanton, and Lucretia Mott, were determined to present their document to the national officials in Independence Square on the Fourth of July.[59]

The suffragists asked permission to present a copy of their document to Vice President Ferry during the Independence Day program, but they were refused. ("We propose to celebrate what we have done the past hundred years; not what we have failed to do," the Centennial's chairman said.)[60] The women asked for tickets to the program for fifty members of their association, but this request also was denied. The organizers of the Independence Square program provided the suffragists with four tickets, and Anthony acquired a press pass in connection with a newspaper published by her brother. It was a sufficient opening wedge. Seated in Independence Square, the five women listened as Richard Henry Lee's grandson read the Declaration of Independence of 1776. Then, as the audience stood for a musical number to honor visiting dignitaries from Brazil, the women stood, too, and made their way to Vice President Ferry. "Mr. President, we present this Declaration of the Rights of the women citizens of the United States," Anthony said, handing a rolled, embossed copy of the document to the vice president. Surprised, Ferry bowed and accepted the document without comment. Triumphant, the women departed from the stage distributing printed copies of their declaration to the audience as the Centennial chairman shouted, "Order, order!"[61]

Because the parade that preceded the ceremony in Independence Square had attracted large crowds that exceeded the capacity of the square, the suffragists found an audience on the Chestnut Street side of Independence Hall. While the official program continued behind the building, the five women climbed onto a bandstand facing Chestnut Street, and Anthony read the women's document. "While the nation is buoyant with patriotism, and all hearts are attuned to praise, it is with sorrow we come to strike the one discordant note," she said. "We cannot forget, even in this glad hour, that while all men of every race, and clime, and condition, have been invested with the full rights of citizenship under our hospitable flag, all women still suffer the degradation of disfranchisement." Anthony presented the women's call for impeachment of the government on the grounds stated in their declaration. "We ask of our rulers, at this hour, no special privileges, no special legislation," she concluded. "We ask justice, we ask equality, we ask that all the civil and political rights that belong to citizens of the United States be guaranteed to us and our daughters forever."[62]

Ancestral Domain

In the decades that followed the Centennial, Independence Hall and the city around it embodied Americans' pride in the national past as well as anxiety about the future. The building was seen increasingly as a Colonial-era gem, in need of rescue from modern encroachments. Its historical significance gained renewed attention not only in 1876, but again in 1887 when Americans marked the centennial of the U.S. Constitution. Looking back on these documents and ahead with faith in economic progress, Americans reached for a shared sense of national identity that bridged the sectional divide of the Civil War.[63] However, to Americans who identified the strength of the nation with a distinctly British heritage and the steady accumulation of wealth, the United States also seemed to be threatened in ways that could be seen in the urban environment around Independence Hall. Labor unrest periodically stopped manufacturing in the vicinity of Independence Square, and the Knights of Labor occupied an office across the street from Independence Hall, at 505 Chestnut Street. To the southeast, toward the Delaware River, a wave of immigration from southern and eastern Europe created a new Jewish quarter teeming with Russian emigres who packed into aging rowhouses and found work in nearby sweatshops. The new Jewish population pressed against the African American neighborhood that had existed south of Independence Hall for nearly a century. Although black Pennsylvanians had regained the vote after the Civil War, the community of African Americans in Philadelphia suffered its own social and economic isolation, chronicled in the 1890s in W. E. B. DuBois's landmark sociological study, *The Philadelphia Negro*.[64]

In this setting, small but determined groups of Philadelphians worked to restore an eighteenth-century ambiance to Independence Hall, the adjacent buildings, and Independence Square. Their work took place within the broad context of the Colonial revival, a popular embrace of early American material culture in the late nineteenth and early twentieth centuries. Interest in the Colonial era of American history had been stirred by the Centennial Exhibition in 1876, particularly displays such as the Colonial kitchen and the exhibit of George Washington relics. In retrospect, however, historians have viewed the Colonial revival as not only a resurgence of interest in the past, but also a reaction to disconcerting conditions of the present. At a time of high immigration, urbanization, and industrialization, the Colonial revival focused attention on the more easily controlled domestic environment. In the decades after the Centennial, Colonial-style housewares, furniture, gardens, and architecture grew in popularity. Images of George and Martha Washington proliferated. Native-born Americans placed high value on the memory of distant ancestors and the seemingly quaint, orderly world that they inhabited.[65] At Independence Hall, the broad currents of the Colonial revival merged with the building's specific associations with the Declaration of Independence and the Constitution. The building became the special project of Philadelphians who could trace their ancestry to the era of British colonization and the American Revolution. To them, Independence Hall and the other eighteenth-century buildings on Independence Square represented a legacy that was simultaneously historical, architectural, and very personal.

Traditionally valued for its association with the Declaration of Independence, during the late nineteenth century Independence Hall became increasingly identified with the U.S. Constitution as well. In earlier years, Americans had done little to celebrate the Constitution; in fact, the history of the document was not widely known.[66] September 17, the date on which the Convention agreed on the Constitution, had been commemorated occasionally in Philadelphia during times of real or perceived national crisis. For example, during the 1850s, when nativists controlled the Philadelphia city government, their opponents in the Democratic Party staged commemorations of the Constitution on September 17.[67] The anniversary also was celebrated with vigor during the Civil War.[68] Associations between Independence Hall and the Constitution grew stronger as a result of the Centennial. In the National Museum, portraits of members of the Constitutional Convention marked Independence Hall as the birthplace of the national government. The "rising sun" chair placed in the Independence Chamber also was an artifact of the Constitutional Convention. George Washington had presided over the convention from the chair, and Benjamin Franklin had remarked that he had often wondered whether the carving on the chair was a rising or a setting sun. At the close of the Constitutional Convention, he concluded that the sun was rising.[69]

Having reaped the benefits of one Centennial, Philadelphians after 1876 were eager to organize another national commemoration for the Constitution in 1887. The Constitution Centennial in 1887 was far less extravagant than the event of 1876, lacking a world exposition and concentrating on a much shorter three-day program of commemoration. However, like the 1876 Centennial, the program celebrated one hundred years of national strength and progress. And like the Declaration of Independence commemoration eleven years earlier, the Constitution Centennial celebrated triumphant aspects of the nation's past while obscuring controversies and complexities. During the 1880s, Americans were still coming to terms with the three constitutional amendments ratified after the Civil War to end slavery, define citizenship to include

African Americans, and extend voting rights to African American men. Southern states enacted laws that disenfranchised black voters, despite the Fifteenth Amendment. In the North, African Americans encountered anger and discrimination as they pursued political and economic opportunity. In Philadelphia, the presence of federal troops had been required in 1870 to ensure black voters' access to the polls on the first election day under the Fifteenth Amendment. The next year, a prominent African American educator and political organizer, Civil War veteran Octavius Catto, was murdered during an election-day riot. For African Americans in the late nineteenth century, civil rights were written into the Constitution, but in practice they were not guaranteed.[70] The Constitution was similarly controversial among women's rights activists, who were dismayed that the Fourteenth Amendment used the phrase "male citizens" in its references to voting for president and vice president of the United States. Women continued to invoke the language of the American Revolution to assert their rights, particularly calling attention to their status as taxpayers despite the Revolutionary-era principle of "no taxation without representation."[71]

Such controversies were mostly silent during the three-day commemoration of the Constitution in Philadelphia in 1887. To the extent that they surfaced, disputes remained distant from Independence Hall. On September 15, a "Civic and Industrial Procession" of merchants and tradesmen paraded up and down Broad Street, passing the rising new City Hall in a display of the economic progress of the nation in the previous century. African Americans created a minor stir by refusing to portray slaves on a float intended to celebrate the end of slavery by displaying contrasts between 1787 and 1887. After a second day of celebrating devoted to a massive military parade of 23,722 marchers from Broad Street to Independence Hall, a second hint of discord emerged on Constitution Day itself, September 17. The day began with President Grover Cleveland greeting citizens in the completed portion of the new City Hall. First in line stood Lillie Devereux Blake of the National Woman Suffrage Association. In an action less dramatic but in the spirit of the women's rights demonstration at Independence Hall in 1876, Blake handed the president a typewritten document signed by Susan B. Anthony and others protesting the Constitution's exclusion of women from voting. According to news reports, the president smiled and passed the document to an aide.[72]

The ceremony that followed at Independence Square infused the building traditionally associated with the Declaration of Independence with renewed memory of its connections to the Constitution. Like the Centennial celebrators of 1876, the thousands who gathered in the square in 1887 had come to heap praise on one of the nation's founding documents, not to call attention to the conflicts of its creation or implementation. In an amphitheater specially constructed in Independence Square, an audience of elected officials, international guests, and the public heard patriotic marches played by the Marine Band under the direction of John Philip Sousa and "Hail Columbia" sung by a boys' choir. The speakers who faced Independence Hall did not recount the bitter conflict that had ensued within the building over Pennsylvania's ratification of the Constitution one hundred years before. Instead, speakers invoked memories of George Washington, Benjamin Franklin, Alexander Hamilton, and other members of the federal convention in 1787. Describing the history of ratification, Supreme Court Justice Samuel F. Miller provided a more abstract discussion of issues raised by the Constitution's opponents, portraying ratification as a resolution of legalities rather than a drama of human conflict. President Cleveland, referring to the "rising sun" chair displayed on the platform, observed, "We stand to-day on the spot where this rising sun emerged from political night and darkness, and in its own bright meridian light we mark its glorious way." As a frame of government, the Constitution had been tested by debate, litigation, and war, but had emerged triumphant. Independence Hall, the document's birthplace, represented a past populated by patriots and uncluttered by dissent.[73]

The Constitution centennial also reflected a fixation on ancestry, defined by race and family connection to the American Revolution, which propelled decisions about Independence Hall through the rest of the nineteenth century. At the Constitution commemoration in Independence Square, Justice Miller invoked the language of ancestry to praise the document's heritage as particularly Anglo-Saxon in its respect for the rule of law.[74] Attention to ancestry also became apparent in decisions about the use of space in the buildings on Independence Square during the 1890s, as government offices gradually relocated to Philadelphia's new City Hall. On the first floor of the old State House, the Independence Chamber and the National Museum room remained set aside for historic purposes. Beyond those two rooms, however, as government gradually vacated the buildings on Independence Square, the space was turned over to patriotic and hereditary societies. More than ever before, Independence Hall and the adjacent buildings became the domains of descendants of Colonial or Revolutionary-era ancestors. The Sons of the Revolution, the Daughters of the American Revolution, the Colonial Dames, and the Society of Colonial Wars all inhabited Independence Square. They shared the buildings with military patriots—the Grand Army of the Republic, the Pennsylvania Reserve Association, and the Naval Veterans Association. With space to spare, the city also allocated offices in Old City Hall to the Pennsylvania Prison Society and the Universal Peace Union, a group that promoted mediation of international conflicts and labor disputes. From 1895 to 1900, the first floor of Congress Hall as well as the "new" county courthouse built on the square in 1867 became home to the Law School of the University of Pennsylvania.[75]

The presence of the patriotic and hereditary societies, coinciding with the departure of city government, opened a new phase of restoration for Independence Hall and the adjacent buildings. Although the historic preservation movement of the nineteenth century had focused primarily on historic homes, there was little danger that a public building as significant as Independence Hall would be left to decay. Elsewhere, non-residential buildings with ties to the Colonial or Revolutionary eras were deemed worthy of preservation. In Massachusetts, by the 1890s preservationists had devoted their efforts to such nondomestic structures as the Old South Church, Faneuil Hall, and the old Massachusetts State House. In Texas, preservationists persuaded the state government to take custody of the Alamo in 1883, and in 1893 an architect drafted plans for its restoration.[76] As part of this thriving and growing historic preservation movement, Philadelphians also were taking steps to save bits of their city's architectural history. In 1883, they moved William Penn's cottage, Letitia, from the crowded neighborhood east of Independence Hall to the safe expanses of Fairmount Park. In the 1890s, Philadelphians saved the reputed home of Betsy Ross, who had been identified by her descendants as the seamstress of the first American flag.[77]

From 1894 through the turn of the century, the space designated as historic in and around Independence Hall grew to encompass the building's second floor, Congress Hall, and the exterior appearance of all the buildings facing Chestnut Street. These restoration projects were acts of patriotism, intended to inspire national unity. However, like the projects that accompanied the Centennial of 1876, restoration efforts in the 1890s revealed contours of American society. Restoring the second floor of Independence Hall to its eighteenth-century appearance would obscure all connection to the Philadelphia City Councils, which by the 1890s were earning a reputation for corruption that spread beyond the city.[78] In addition to the political dimensions of restoration work at Independence Hall, some conflicts related to gender, as men and women who traced their ancestry to the American Revolution vied for control over historical space. The new projects also raised questions of authenticity, pitting enthusiastic amateur preservationists against professional architects.

Hereditary societies, which were organized nationally in the United States in the 1880s and 1890s, took a natural interest in preserving buildings from the Colonial and Revolutionary eras. In Philadelphia, the City Councils declined in 1894 to turn over custody of Independence Hall to the Colonial Dames, who sought to renovate the second floor after the Councils moved to the new City Hall. Although members of the society had been among the women who had cared for the artifacts of the National Museum since 1876, the Councils viewed the proposed restoration as too large a project for the small group. Beyond that, the Councils noted, many of the Dames' ancestors had been Tories during the American Revolution.[79] The Dames contented themselves with the second floor of Congress Hall, while the Councils delegated the second-floor space in Independence Hall to the Pennsylvania Society of the Sons of the Revolution, expecting that the Sons would establish a public museum. Shortly thereafter, the Councils gave the Daughters of the American Revolution equal access to the second floor.[80]

By opening the second floor to both the "Sons" and the "Daughters," the City Councils unwittingly ignited a gendered contest over the use of the second floor of Independence Hall. At the national level, the Sons and Daughters had a history of conflict; the Daughters of the American Revolution had been founded in 1890 after the Sons had declined to accept women into their organization.[81] In Philadelphia in 1895, the Sons were willing to allow the Daughters to meet in Independence Hall, but argued that shared control of the space was not feasible. The Sons also wanted no part of a plan by the Daughters to restore the second floor as the banquet hall that had existed during the eighteenth century.[82] The Daughters envisioned stripping away the nineteenth-century political, male-oriented City Council chambers, which resembled men's club rooms of the time, and replacing them with a more domestic, social environment. Underscoring the gendered character of the dispute, the women's detractors mocked their plan as a plot to install a tearoom, a significant accusation in that tearooms in this era provided an avenue for women to enter into a business world dominated by men.[83] The conflict divided long-time acquaintances within Philadelphia's elite, with Sons' treasurer Charles Henry Jones fighting to retain Independence Hall as a private meeting place and his friend of more than thirty years, Ellen Waln Harrison, leading the women's group. "If only you could see the case in another light we could make the rooms a place that all the world would be glad to visit," Harrison pleaded with Jones. "It could be made most attractive by a refined hand of woman. Yes, more attractive than you dream of." Jones was unswayed.[84]

Faced with the women's determination to turn their meeting rooms into an eighteenth-century banquet hall, the Sons of the Revolution appealed to the City Councils to give them full control of the second floor of Independence Hall. If they could not have this control, the Sons said, they would withdraw entirely.[85] If the offer was a bluff,

24. From 1854 until the late 1890s, the second floor of Independence Hall served as the meeting place for the two-chamber Philadelphia City Council. Members of the Common Council of Philadelphia are shown here in their session of April 11, 1893, prior to the city government's move to a new City Hall. (Courtesy of Independence National Historical Park)

it backfired. On February 5, 1896, before a standing-room only crowd at the new City Hall, the City Councils' Committee on Public Property considered the Sons' request for total control. Harrison testified that when the Daughters had proposed restoration, Jones had replied that they were being "entirely too patriotic." Council members observed that the Sons had not progressed toward the promised public museum. The committee rejected the Son's request for total control, forcing the men to follow through on their promise to withdraw from Independence Hall rather than share authority with the Daughters of the American Revolution. Shortly thereafter, the restoration of the second floor was placed entirely in the hands of the DAR.[86]

The dispute between the men and women of Philadelphia's hereditary societies cooled, but did not disappear. Instead, differing perceptions of "authentic" restoration came into conflict as the DAR supervised re-creation of the eighteenth-century banquet hall. As the nineteenth-century City Council chambers were torn away, the DAR's architect, Thomas Mellon Rogers, attentively identified original features of the second floor. He could see the outlines of the banquet hall, or Long Room, where colonial Philadelphians had celebrated special occasions. He could identify the locations of the smaller rooms on the south side of the building, and he could see the original fireplaces. These features corresponded with Andrew Hamilton's eighteenth-century plans, which Rogers consulted at the Historical Society of Pennsylvania.[87] Apart from the placement of walls and fireplaces, however, Rogers's work took a Colonial-revival turn, creating a nineteenth-century vision of colonial domesticity that was more elaborate than the interior of an eighteenth-century public building. The "restored" second floor of Independence Hall had ornamental mantels and cornices, and a doorway copied from Cliveden, a surviving Colonial mansion in Germantown. The result was beautiful and drew great praise from the city's newspapers when it opened in February 1897. But it did not restore the interior of the eighteenth century.[88]

Criticism of Rogers's work for the DAR came from some of the city's most prominent architects, some of whom happened to be members of the Sons of the Revolution. In 1895, at least fifty architects worked in offices within a block of Independence Hall, most in the next block eastward on Walnut, Chestnut, or Fourth Streets.[89] Unlike Rogers, the critics of the DAR restoration were affiliated with the American Institute of Architects (AIA), a professional association which in 1890 had begun to call attention to endangered public buildings. At the national level, for example, the AIA decried the deterioration of the Massachusetts State House and the demolition of the New York Customs House.[90] The architects were concerned not only with the survival of old buildings, but also with accurate restoration of original architectural details. In Philadelphia, architects affiliated with the AIA were horrified by the inaccurate "exercise of individual fancy" that Rogers had carried out on the second floor of Independence Hall. As a result, the Philadelphia chapter of the AIA aggressively volunteered time and effort to oversee future alterations to Independence Hall, adjacent buildings, and the surrounding square.[91] When the city hired Rogers to oversee restoration of the rest of Independence Hall, the AIA architects injected their advice at every step of the way.

Despite the controversy among the architects, city officials impressed by the DAR project on the second floor decided on a more extensive restoration that would re-create a courtroom setting on the first floor, relocate the National Museum collection begun during the Centennial to other parts of the building, and rebuild arcades and wing buildings similar to the eighteenth-century originals. With Rogers and the AIA both involved, the project became a continuing debate over how to ensure "authentic" restoration. Rogers believed in "reading" the building and developing imaginative solutions to restoration problems. For example, he based his designs for the exterior arcades on the interior archways of the first floor, which he knew to be original. His AIA critics, on the other hand, insisted that the new arcades match drawings of the old Pennsylvania State House that had survived from the late eighteenth and early nineteenth century. They called the city's attention to the Scull and Heap map of Pennsylvania, with its 1752 image of the State House. With this visual evidence, the AIA prevailed.[92] Still, the reconstructed arcades reflected a Colonial-revival aesthetic, as they provided an open view of Independence Square rather than sheltering stairways, as the originals did in the eighteenth century.

The newly restored Independence Hall opened to the public on July 4, 1898. For Philadelphians accustomed to Independence Hall as an aged government building and a crowded museum left over from the Centennial, the restoration projects of the late 1890s were astonishing. Thousands toured the building on the Fourth of July. The city's newspapers praised the beauty of the renovated building and interiors, noting their embodiment of Colonial style. Inside, the greatest change appeared in the west room of the first floor, in which the furnishings of a stately Colonial courtroom had replaced the old National Museum collections ("accumulations that had long disfigured the interior," the *Evening Bulletin* observed). The Independence Chamber had been cleaned and rearranged so that the chairs stood in positions that they might have occupied in 1776. Outside, the building had changed dramatically, with the long-derided Mills Buildings demolished and replaced by arcades and wing buildings reminiscent of the originals. The new arcades afforded a picturesque view from Chestnut Street through to the landscaped Independence Square. In keeping with the spirit of the Colonial revival, accounts of the building's renovation radiated appreciation for the building's aesthetics as well as its historic associations.[93]

As Philadelphians toured their renovated landmark in 1898, the United States once again was at war, and the newly pristine condition of Independence Hall reinforced the intense patriotism that accompanied the Spanish-American conflict. Oratory in Independence Square on the Fourth of July proclaimed faith in the strength of the nation. "On this very classic ground, the nation was born which has grown to be the mightiest and the best that ever nestled in the providence of God," Philadelphia Mayor Charles Warwick declared.[94] And when the war was over, when the United States had prevailed, Philadelphians gathered again at Independence Hall for a Peace Jubilee. In keeping with the westward growth of the city, the greatest celebration took

25. Inspired by the Colonial Revival and made possible by the removal of city government to new quarters, restoration projects in the late 1890s brought a new aura of eighteenth-century authenticity to the second floor of Independence Hall and the building's exterior. In these illustrations from *Harper's Weekly*, July 24, 1897, the long-despised office buildings adjacent to Independence Hall (frame 3, center left) were demolished in favor of re-created arcades similar to the originals (frame 5, bottom). (Courtesy of the Library of Congress)

place on Broad Street, south of the massive new City Hall. But on October 28, President William McKinley joined a civic parade of thousands to Independence Square for a ceremonial rededication of Independence Hall. Pennsylvania Governor Daniel Hastings spoke of the old but preserved building, representative of old and new triumphs accomplished by the grace of God. "In the rededication of this precious temple, as in the attendant celebrations, I believe the true American thought has been embodied in the words 'Peace Jubilee,'" he said. "The mould and rust of time were gradually crumbling these walls. A patriotic city has restored them to their pristine simplicity and beauty. So may the recent, stirring events tend to restore us as a people to that simplicity and beauty of national life which was contemplated by the fathers."[95]

During the last decades of the nineteenth century, Independence Hall was a workshop of memory for elite Philadelphians, who stripped away most material reminders of the building's nineteenth-century history. The building functioned as a place where Philadelphians could construct their idealized vision of the nation, simultaneously preserving memories of national order and consensus while obscuring the complications of local history and conflict. By the turn of the twentieth century, no visitor to the building could discern that it had ever been home to smoke-filled city council chambers, federal courtrooms where accused fugitive slaves had faced the loss of freedom, or the natural history museum of Charles Willson Peale. With the artifacts from the National Museum of 1876 dispersed throughout the building and its newly constructed wings, memory of Frank Etting's project and the relic-filled west room on the first floor quickly faded. Independence Hall was not exactly as it had been in 1776—the new arcades differed from the originals, and clocks remained in the 1828 steeple because of their importance to keeping time in the city. Nevertheless, the building presented an image of the eighteenth century that appeared to have been untouched by the passing of time. Long regarded as important for its association with the Declaration of Independence, the building acquired a broader significance that also encompassed reverence for the Constitution and appreciation for Colonial style.

Independence Hall in these years became more recognizably "historic," but it was a history to be visited rather than lived. For so much of the nineteenth century, the old Pennsylvania State House and Independence Square had been places of active civic engagement, reflecting the ongoing project of constructing a nation from a diverse citizenry. Sustaining national unity remained a contentious task, as the Civil War, the social and political upheavals of the Gilded Age, and even the restoration projects at Independence Hall demonstrated. However, at Independence Hall as in other historic buildings, restoration projects produced a vision of the nation's history that was as refined as a Colonial parlor, as silent as the voices of departed ancestors. The descendants of Colonial and Revolutionary-era families who took such a personal interest in Independence Hall simultaneously enhanced its historic appearance and narrowed recognition of its place in the complexity of national life. Acting on a collective memory of Independence Hall as a place of ancestral legacy, they saved the building for the nation. However, just as they had physically removed themselves from old and congested city neighborhoods, they separated Independence Hall from its history in the city of Philadelphia.[96]

As a national landmark, however, Independence Hall had a significant limitation. Like all buildings, its place in public memory could extend only as far as its public recognition. However revered it became among Philadelphians, and despite publication of its image during events such as the Centennial Exhibition, Independence Hall remained anchored in Philadelphia. Even in its restored ambiance of the eighteenth century, the place most associated with the Declaration of Independence and the U.S. Constitution could be fully appreciated only by those who could visit it in person. In the decades after the Civil War, this limited the experience to local people, dignitaries, and others who had sufficient money and leisure time to travel by rail. The old building on Chestnut Street periodically attracted attention on a national scale and functioned as an important workshop of public memory for Philadelphians, but it remained more a place of historic importance than a symbol of national identity.

Chapter 6

PLACE AND SYMBOL

The Liberty Bell Ascendant

On April 26, 1893, in an oil-boom town 340 miles northwest of Philadelphia, a baby girl was born to Josephine Cooper and her husband, William. They named their new daughter in honor of the major event that day in Oil City, Pennsylvania.[1] So it was that little Liberty Bell Cooper became a living memorial to the day that the Liberty Bell came through Oil City on a train bound for the World's Columbian Exposition in Chicago. Named for the old bell of the Pennsylvania State House, she also was a testament to a symbolic transformation. Although Independence Hall gained increasing attention in the late nineteenth century as a place worthy of preservation, the building was surpassed as a popular patriotic symbol by one of its own artifacts—the bell which had been ordered for the State House in 1751. While Independence Hall stood anchored in Philadelphia, tied by restoration to its eighteenth-century past, the Liberty Bell traveled the nation, acquiring a more timeless, inspirational identity. Like Independence Hall, its reputation grew from association with the American Revolution, but in seven journeys by rail between 1885 and 1915, the bell with its signature crack drew enormous crowds and inspired political oratory, sentimental poetry, and prayerful sermons. Detached from its eighteenth-century home in Philadelphia, the Liberty Bell eclipsed its identity as a relic of the American Revolution. More than an artifact, it resonated with the idea expressed by its inscription: "Proclaim liberty throughout all the land unto all the inhabitants thereof."[2]

While Independence Hall helps us to see the role that buildings can play in the construction of public memory, the Liberty Bell provides a useful counterpoint, calling attention to the potential limitations of buildings as place-bound, time-bound artifacts. During the period of the Liberty Bell's travels, Independence Hall also gained expanded recognition through the visits of travelers, the spread of its image on picture postcards, and the popularity of Georgian-revival architecture, which led to buildings resembling Independence Hall across the country. However, in an age in which structural marvels such as the Brooklyn Bridge and the first skyscrapers captured public attention, an eighteenth-century brick building stood a limited chance of crossing the threshold from historic place to popular symbol. Unlike the Liberty Bell, the building did not transcend its attachment to place (Philadelphia) or to time (the eighteenth century). Independence Hall was the scene of the Declaration of Independence. It was the scene of the Constitutional Convention. It was a prime example of Colonial architecture. But most especially for Americans of the late nineteenth and early twentieth centuries, Independence Hall was the home of its most famous artifact, that symbol of American ideals, the Liberty Bell.

As it traveled to world's fairs and other exhibitions, the Liberty Bell joined the array of American symbols that excited patriotic enthusiasm during this period in United States history, a time marked by regional reconciliation, high immigration, economic transition, and imperial expansion. Other symbols such as the American flag, the Statue of Liberty, and Uncle Sam have attracted greater attention among scholars.[3] However, the Liberty Bell also played an important and underappreciated role in the construction of American nationalism. Taken together, the bell's journeys comprised 376 scheduled stops in thirty states, reaching to every region—the South, the West, the Midwest, and New England. At the center of local receptions, speechmaking, and rituals of bell-touching, the Liberty Bell served as an instrument through which thousands if not millions of Americans could imagine themselves as one nation, despite differences in geography, social status, or heritage.[4]

Venerable Relic

The Liberty Bell embodies a powerful convergence of fact and belief, cloaked in history and shrouded by myth, beginning with its association with the American Revolution. By the late nineteenth century, George Lippard's story of the bell ringing to announce the Declaration of Independence on the Fourth of July had become widely accepted as fact. In actuality, bells had not rung until July 8, when they called Philadelphians together for the first public reading of the Declaration. Even then, the shaky condition of the State House steeple might have prevented ringing the State House bell. But in the late nineteenth century, no one doubted that the bell had rung for the Declaration of Independence, whatever the date, making it a cherished relic of

26. As the Liberty Bell traveled the nation between 1885 and 1915, its display reinforced connections between the bell and the story (popularized by George Lippard in the 1840s) of its ringing for the Declaration of Independence. As shown here during the bell's journey to Boston in 1903, participation by children and photography contributed to the bell's growth as an American symbol. (Courtesy of Independence National Historical Park)

the American Revolution. This association was reinforced as the bell traveled the country on decorated railroad cars bearing the words "Proclaim Liberty" and "1776," escorted by Philadelphia dignitaries and an honor guard of the city's largest policemen. En route, Philadelphians distributed printed histories emphasizing the bell's role as a clarion of the American Revolution.[5] Thus defined and protected as an heirloom with unique significance to the nation's history, the Liberty Bell journeyed to New Orleans for the World's Industrial and Cotton Exposition in 1885; to Chicago for the World's Columbian Exposition in 1893; to Atlanta for the Cotton States and International Exposition in 1895; to Charleston for the South Carolina Interstate and West

Indian Exposition in 1902; to Boston for the Bunker Hill Monument anniversary in 1903; to St. Louis for the Louisiana Purchase International Exposition in 1904; and finally to San Francisco for the Panama-Pacific Exposition in 1915.[6]

In its travels, the Liberty Bell did not lose its identity as a historic relic, but it became something more. While Philadelphians and other visitors to Independence Hall experienced the Liberty Bell primarily as an artifact of the American Revolution, protected for much of this period in a glass case in Independence Hall, other Americans saw the bell at the center of lively hometown festivities. Not confined to a building or separated from the artifact by glass, as they would have been in Philadelphia, people across the country serenaded the bell with patriotic tunes, reached out to touch it, and staged ceremonies that they hoped their children would long remember. In these more emotional, personal engagements with the Liberty Bell, Americans beyond Philadelphia enhanced the relic's reputation.

During its journeys by rail, the Liberty Bell gave Americans throughout the country opportunities to define and merge regional and national identities. Significantly, three of the first four journeys of the Liberty Bell were into the South—to New Orleans in 1885, to Atlanta in 1895, and to Charleston in 1902. These trips into former Confederate states were seen by Philadelphians and their Southern hosts as reunification tours, calling the attention of North and South to their common history. In initiating the first of the Liberty Bell's trips, city officials in New Orleans asked for the relic as a statement of national reunion. Although their states had seceded from the Union, Southerners maintained a strong identification with the legacy of the American Revolution. Indeed, many viewed the Civil War as a fight that honored the original intents of the Declaration of Independence and the Constitution.[7] In addition to affirming that legacy, many Southerners viewed the Liberty Bell's appearances as evidence of the region's trustworthiness and loyalty.[8]

On each of the Southern trips, the theme of sectional reconciliation prevailed in speeches exchanged by local dignitaries and the Philadelphians traveling with the bell.[9] In one of the better-known of these exchanges, Jefferson Davis in 1885 paid tribute to the "harmonizing tendency of this journey of the old bell." However, even as Americans reached toward national unity in the decades after the Civil War, they did so from positions of strong regional identification. While Jefferson Davis's speech at the Liberty Bell paid tribute to a common past, the former president of the Confederacy also defended Southern honor. "I think the time has come when reason should be substituted for passion and when men who have fought in support of their honest convictions shall be able and willing to do justice to each other," he said.[10] Other less prominent individuals in the South expressed similar sentiments, as did local newspaper editorials. Greeting the Liberty Bell in their communities, they spoke of unity, but with an emphasis on regional identity. As a clergyman in Farmville, Virginia, put it in 1895, "No people in this broad land of ours have a better right to share in or more causes to be proud of Liberty Bell than we Virginians."[11] Who offered the resolution for independence? Richard Henry Lee of Virginia. Who wrote the Declaration? Thomas Jefferson of Virginia. Who led the army? George Washington of Virginia. On its journeys into the South, the Liberty Bell was often greeted by bands that played not only "The Star-Spangled Banner," but also "Dixie." Even in Philadelphia, the bell got a "Dixie" sendoff.[12]

The Liberty Bell traveled into the South during a period of sharp racial tension, as white Southerners confronted a social landscape changed by the end of slavery and an emerging generation of African Americans born in freedom. Since the collapse of Reconstruction in 1877, a backlash against African Americans had taken hold in the form of Jim Crow laws, disfranchisement of black voters, and other strategies aimed at maintaining the social structure of the prewar South. At its worst, racial animosity took the form of lynchings, which peaked in the 1890s.[13] There is scant documentation of black reaction to the Liberty Bell traveling through such a racially stratified society, and most of the evidence which does exist is filtered through the perceptions of white observers. In newspaper accounts, white journalists described "picturesque darkeys" and "old black mammies" among the people who greeted the Liberty Bell with enthusiasm.[14] African Americans were present in these accounts, but described in tones of nostalgia for the plantation South.

Surely, "liberty" was a bittersweet promise for African Americans, especially in southern states which explicitly denied them the full rights of American citizenship. On the one hand, they might revel in the presence of a symbol of liberty, as Thomas Nast suggested in a cartoon published in 1885 in *Harper's Weekly*. In Nast's imagination, the Liberty Bell served as an instructional tool used by a Northerner to enlighten a Southern planter about the principle of freedom. Behind the planter, an African American stood smiling, as if to appreciate the irony and the planter's comeuppance.[15] However, the Liberty Bell might also represent unfulfilled promises rather than progress. The bell was on display in 1895 in Atlanta when Booker T. Washington gave his famous "Atlanta Compromise" address, which advised African Americans to pursue economic advancement through manual labor while deferring their pursuit of political equality. An image of the Liberty Bell created during the Atlanta Exposition constructed a correspondingly humble relationship between black Southerners and the

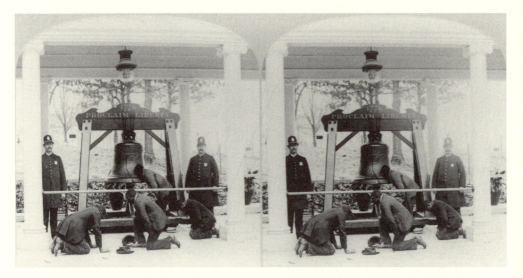

27. "Bowing to the Old Liberty Bell, Atlanta Exposition," a stereoview created by B. W. Kilburn in 1895, purports to show African Americans in the South paying homage to the symbol of American freedom. In its attempt to portray African Americans in subservient positions, the view corresponds with sculptural representations during this period of high racial tension. (Courtesy of the Liberty Bell Virtual Museum)

relic of American history. The stereopticon view labeled "Bowing to the Old Liberty Bell" depicted African American men in kneeling, subservient positions in front of the bell and the white policemen standing guard. On close inspection, however, the African Americans do not seem to be bowing to the bell but rather looking for something lost on the ground. The title constructs a message of African American obedience and loyalty, but the image itself calls the title into question. Like historical monuments of the time, which also tended to portray African Americans as kneeling and subordinate to whites, this image may reveal more about whites' expectations than black perceptions of the Liberty Bell.[16]

By the late nineteenth century, memory of the Liberty Bell's use as a symbol of abolitionism had faded, not to be revived until the twentieth century. But as a relic of the American Revolution, the Liberty Bell called African Americans' attention to what the Revolution did—or did not—achieve for them. This was suggested in an essay published in 1904 in the *Freeman*, the "National Illustrated Colored Newspaper" published in Indianapolis. Writing on the occasion of the bell's stop in Indianapolis on its way to the St. Louis World's Fair, columnist W. Milton Lewis noted, "The people were genuine in their enthusiasm over the relic," and "the expense of the exhibition was worth the while; it was an excellent test of the sentiment of the people." But in recounting the Liberty Bell's association with the American Revolution, he defined the Declaration of Independence as "the first great emancipation on American soil," to be followed only much later by the "sweeter tones" that accompanied the defeat of slavery.[17] For African Americans, the Declaration of Independence embodied a promise of liberty, but not the achievement of the ideal that the Liberty Bell represented.

When the bell traveled into New England—only once, in 1903 for an anniversary of the Bunker Hill Monument—the trip functioned as a reunion among historical cousins of the original thirteen colonies. However, it was a reunion in which cousins competed for attention, reflecting a rivalry between Philadelphia and Boston as cities that made vital contributions to the American Revolution.[18] Crowds surged around the Liberty Bell in Boston, just as in other cities on other tours, but Bostonian orators drew attention to the relative significance of the two cities and their memorials to the American Revolution, the Liberty Bell and the Bunker Hill Monument. "Today 'Liberty' bell kisses the sacred soil of Bunker hill, making it more sacred than ever," the mayor of Boston declared. "Philadelphia and Boston are twin cities. Here the cradle of liberty was made and it was Philadelphia that rocked it." In the *Boston Daily Globe*, a cartoon showed the Bunker Hill Monument and the Liberty Bell as partners in a patriotic dance, with the monument as the leading, male partner. The Liberty Bell was perceived as an "honored guest," but a guest paying fitting tribute to New England's unique place in the nation's history.[19]

Western regional identity infused the Liberty Bell's final and most elaborate trip, to the Panama-Pacific Exposition in San Francisco in 1915. En route, its appearances served as opportunities for regions added to the United States since 1776 to proclaim that they shared in the nation's common principles. These regions had been colonized largely by the Spanish and French, and large portions of the Southwest had been United States territory only since the Mexican War of 1846–48. The nation that grew from the original thirteen British colonies along the eastern seaboard expanded into these western lands with waves of settlement and an ideology of manifest destiny—the belief that the United States had a God-given duty to occupy and civilize the continent. In 1915, speakers and newspaper editorialists identified the West as fulfilling the destiny announced by the Liberty Bell in 1776. In Tacoma, Washington, for example, the local newspaper editorialized: "In welcoming Liberty Bell today, the proudest thing we Americans on the western slope of the most fortunate nation under the sun can say is that we are living in the realization of those ideals for which the bell has stood."[20] As in the South and New England, expressions of national unity were tinged with regional pride. News accounts noted the rugged determination of Westerners traveling great distances to see the bell, including a cowgirl in Wyoming who rode horseback for sixty miles and a Kansas boy who walked five miles in bare feet.[21] In Texas, especially, the newspapers emphasized regional history, for example adding the history of the bells of the Alamo to reports of the visiting Liberty Bell from Philadelphia.[22]

Wherever it traveled, an appearance by the bell presented an opportunity for honoring the past, connecting that past with the present, and envisioning the future.[23] In keeping with the Liberty Bell's association with the American Revolution, ancestor worship played an important role, with welcoming committees frequently assembled from Sons and Daughters of the American Revolution.[24] However, the Liberty Bell also enabled Americans without Revolutionary lineage to share in the national history— whether or not their ancestors had been present in the United States in 1776. The appearance of the bell incorporated nineteenth-century immigrants into a longer narrative of American history. Newspaper reports often described recent immigrants among the crowds of people who greeted the Liberty Bell. Some communities arranged naturalization ceremonies to correspond with the bell's visit.[25] The bell also incorporated local communities into the national narrative. In the published histories of the Liberty Bell that were distributed as souvenirs, the bell's trips to the world's fairs became part of the story, along with the bell's first passage from England to America and its journey to Allentown, Pennsylvania, for safekeeping during the American Revolution. Individuals who met the bell in its later journeys made themselves part of the continuing story. As the *Rocky Mountain News* reported in 1915, "The desire to catch and keep something of the passing moment drew thousands as they filed by to stop a moment by the side of the car, to stretch out to the guards a key, a coin, a bit of jewelry, a picture, any object that they had at hand, so that it might touch the old bell and then be treasured after the bell was gone. . . . Every other man, woman and child had a camera, anxious to get a picture of the occasion."[26] American history became shared, personal history in pockets and family photograph albums across the country. The Liberty Bell made the memory of the American Revolution part of the lived experience of the many thousands of people who viewed and recorded its visit to their towns.

Seeking to transmit the lessons of the past into the future, organizers of Liberty Bell receptions recruited children to join adults in leading roles.[27] Children presented flowers to the bell, sang patriotic songs, and waved American flags. They were given the best places in line, and Philadelphia's giant policemen often hoisted them onto the bell car to have their pictures taken. Adults saw the Liberty Bell rituals as a way of instilling patriotism in future generations. In Indianapolis, for example, where the bell paused on its way to the World's Columbian Exposition in 1893, the event was arranged entirely around the children. Fifteen thousand schoolchildren gathered at the state capitol building, where they waved flags and cheered a speech by former President Benjamin Harrison.[28] On arrival in Chicago, Philadelphia Mayor Edwin Stuart called the Liberty Bell's trip "a wonderful object lesson in patriotism to the people of America. The passage of the bell through the country will mark an era in many children's lives."[29]

For children, the Liberty Bell was the main character of a wonderful story—the story that had been popularized by George Lippard. In the same manner that children of this era were being taught to pledge allegiance to the flag, they were being taught the story of the Liberty Bell when they learned about the Declaration of Independence. These schoolroom lessons made lasting impressions, which were reflected in a 1915 account of the bell's visit to Denver, Colorado. A Denver journalist, clearly recalling personal experience, began his front-page story this way: "Out of the romantic memories of childhood's lessons, the school-bench history surrounded by the mystic spell of a nation's early struggle for life, set forth against a background of great names vaguely associated with stories, traditions, and old cuts in text books—the Liberty bell appeared to 140,000 persons in Denver yesterday like the nucleus of an American idea."[30] The Liberty Bell was part of history; it was a curiosity, with that big crack in the side; and it was exciting, the centerpiece of a major local event in which children shared the stage. While adults viewed the Liberty Bell as an object lesson, a means for securing the nation's future, children could experience it as enormous fun. But the lesson was not lost. The bell was more than an inanimate object; as the journalist in Denver recalled from his schooldays, it was "the nucleus of an American idea."

The Sacred Symbol

As the Liberty Bell traveled the country on its seven trips between 1885 and 1915, the symbolic significance of the artifact grew and changed. Among Americans of this era, the Liberty Bell tapped into the same widespread patriotism that inspired the initiation of Flag Day, the writing of the Pledge of Allegiance, and the groundswell of enthusiasm for the Spanish-American War of 1898. At the center of enormous crowds, the Liberty Bell became a featured attraction for local pageantry.[31] It became elaborated as an icon of civil religion, providing an object and occasion for celebrating the grace of God's goodness to the United States.[32] It was sacred, even magical. But in an era of big business and the rise of modern advertising, the Liberty Bell also became a commodity, promoting Philadelphia as it traveled, luring visitors to exhibition sites, and helping to sell products from Pennsylvania to Wyoming. Both sacred and secular, not to mention wildly popular, the Liberty Bell gained flexibility as a national symbol that far outdistanced its eighteenth-century home in Philadelphia.

As they received the Liberty Bell on its travels, Americans reached for explanations for why an old, cracked bell should be worthy of such great attention. The journey to Chicago in 1893—the bell's second trip and its first with a destination other than the South—appears to have been pivotal in elaborating the bell's symbolic significance. For the World's Columbian Exposition, John Philip Sousa composed the "Liberty Bell March," giving the relic of the American Revolution a patriotic, martial anthem in tune with the times.[33] Just as Americans of the 1890s attached new significance to the American flag, they promoted the Liberty Bell as a symbol rather than merely a thing. Speeches and newspaper editorials during this trip stressed the importance of the symbol. As the *Indianapolis Journal* editorialized: "In reality it is nothing but a rough and cracked old bell, nothing like as large or handsome as hundreds of others throughout the country. Yet to every intelligent and patriotic American it is worth infinitely more than all the rest. They would fight for it. If necessary they would go to war to protect it or to rescue it from an invader. . . . Why? Because it represents a sentiment and an idea that Americans would die for. The American imagination has invested it with a dignity that makes it sacred and with something like a personality that endears it to every man, woman and child who knows its history."[34] In its travels, the bell did become intensely symbolic as well as personified. Press accounts referred to what the bell had heard and seen, to the fact that it could no longer speak. People who viewed the bell often spoke to it, in a ritual confirming their own patriotism.[35]

In the transformation of the Liberty Bell from artifact to symbol, the press played a significant role. Local newspapers across the country vigorously covered such an unusual event as the arrival of the Liberty Bell from Philadelphia. The mechanics of journalism contributed to the changing perception of the Liberty Bell, as reporters searching for synonyms referred to the bell as the "sacred relic," the "precious burden," the "golden symbol," and the "venerable herald of liberty," among many other alternatives. Coverage of the bell's travels also alerted communities to the elaborate receptions that had been staged earlier in the journey, building awe, anticipation, and determination to surpass previous welcomes. Newspapers helped to link Americans in distant communities in a shared experience, thereby contributing to a shared sense of national identity organized around the Liberty Bell.[36]

Every stop of the Liberty Bell provided newspapers with an opportunity to portray a local event of national significance. In doing so, they emphasized the bell's power to unite a heterogeneous population—a population that some native-born Americans viewed as especially worrisome, given the high rate of immigration from southern and eastern Europe that distinguished these years. Reporters who covered the bell's appearances had before them an opportunity to characterize the American nation. Faced with crowds of thousands or tens of thousands, reporters could select from a dizzying variety of anecdotes to portray the spirit of the day. Given such a range of sources, the newspaper stories might have taken infinite form, but they did not. They were strikingly similar, building on a standard array of characters: reporters zeroed in on the giant Philadelphia policemen, mothers with babies, children with flags, weeping senior citizens, and veterans of the Civil War and Spanish-American War. Frequently, the stories included one or two vivid anecdotes of heartfelt enthusiasm displayed by immigrants, former slaves, or American Indians. The reporters counterposed the contrasts in the crowd—old and young, rich and poor, native and immigrant—with the unifying properties of the Liberty Bell.[37] Only rarely did a reporter acknowledge that some people seemed bored rather than reverent, that some boys threw stones instead of waving flags, or that a crowd occasionally objected to an African American child posing with the bell.[38] In the pages of the local press, the United States was one nation, patriotic, with the Liberty Bell at its center.

As it traveled, the Liberty Bell also acquired sacred properties that enveloped and mixed with its association with the American Revolution. Prompted by the biblical inscription on the bell, local clergy made it the subject of sermons and benedictions. The language of religion crept into news accounts, which characterized the bell as a shrine and its trips as pilgrimages. Philadelphia dignitaries who accompanied the bell embraced and promoted its significance in a civil religion uniting love of country with providence of God. Consider, for example, the speech delivered by Philadelphia Mayor Charles Warwick upon the bell's arrival in Atlanta in 1895: "No religious ceremony in the bearing of relics could have produced more reverence than this old bell," he said. "It is not an idol before which we bow—it is not a fetish before which we abase ourselves—It is the sentiment, the memories and the associations of the past that induce our regard and elevate our thoughts in a purer devotion to our country and inspire us to greater efforts for the future."[39] In the same spirit, the *Atlanta Journal* announced in a headline that "Atlanta is Now the Sanctuary of the Nation's Precious Emblem of Liberty," and reported the arrival of the bell "whose brazen tongue in cloister tones rang forth a hymn of liberty that was heard around the world."[40]

Significantly, the symbolic power of the Liberty Bell was being imagined as not only national, but global. For the World's Columbian Exposition in 1893, a New Jersey businessman raised funds to create a large copy of the Liberty Bell to be rung on anniversaries of events important to liberty throughout the world. Although the plan to take the "Columbian Liberty Bell" on a world tour foundered because of financial difficulties, the enlarged copy of the Philadelphia bell was exhibited at the exposition in Chicago, and the fundraising campaign enhanced associations between the Liberty Bell and world affairs.[41] In this period of overseas expansion, the imagined tones of the Liberty Bell echoed into considerations of American principles in the context of events in the Caribbean, in the Pacific, and in Europe. Speakers often mistakenly quoted the Liberty Bell's inscription as proclaiming liberty throughout "all the world" instead of "all the land."[42] The devout Mayor Warwick, in his Atlanta speech in 1895, made a global connection, expressing a hope that "the tones that once issued from its throat be carried across the waters of the Atlantic and give cheer and comfort to that island, the gem of the Antilles, where Cuban patriots are struggling to throw off the yoke and despotism of Spain. May it be heard throughout the world, penetrating every state or section of Europe and Asia, wherever tyranny exerts its power or oppression burdens the people." Although specific to the Liberty Bell, the mayor's remarks reflected the confidence in the superiority of American principles that served as a foundation for American imperial expansion around the turn of the century.[43]

Beyond Americans' self-perception of their national principles and symbols, the Liberty Bell gained a degree of international recognition through the experiences of foreign students and travelers. As early as 1885, the Liberty Bell appeared in a popular Japanese novel written by Shiba Shiro, who studied at the University of Pennsylvania during the 1880s and wrote under the pseudonym Tōkai Sanshi, "The Wanderer of the Eastern Sea." His novel of Japanese nationalism, *Kajin no Kigu (Strange Encounters of Elegant Females),* opens in Independence Hall, where the author as protagonist reflects on the Liberty Bell as a symbol of the struggle of the American colonies against British tyranny. At the Liberty Bell he first encounters two European "elegant females," whom he meets repeatedly as he travels the world. When they meet again, one of the women encourages the hero, "Now that your country has reformed its government and, by taking from America what is useful and rejecting what is only superficial, is increasing month by month in wealth and strength, the eyes and ears of the world are astonished by your success." She predicts that Japan will surpass the achievements of the United States and Europe: "It is your country and no other that can bring the taste of self-government and independence into the life of millions for the first time, and so spread the light of civilization."[44] In this scenario, Japan would bring to fruition the struggle for liberty symbolized by the Liberty Bell in Independence Hall.

In contrast to Shiba Shiro's novel, which presented an Asian view of the Liberty Bell, a literary hoax of the early twentieth century reflected an American's preconceptions of how an Asian might perceive the Liberty Bell. *The Memoirs of Li Hung-chang*, "edited" by William Francis Mannix and published in 1913, purported to be based on the diary of the Chinese statesman who played a prominent role in efforts to modernize China during the late nineteenth century. The book was revealed to be fiction in its 1923 edition, but by then a poem about the Liberty Bell included in the book had become widely reprinted.[45] The poem describes Li as initially unable to grasp the significance of the Liberty Bell, but under the tutelage of his American escorts he learns that the bell represents the United States' "struggles against wrong." Having learned this lesson, he comes to appreciate the depth of the Liberty Bell's significance:

> These good sons of America
> Call the "Liberty Bell" ancient;
> But I who came from the oldest of all lands,
> A student of the philosophy of ages,
> Know what this Bell speaks
> Is of heaven's wisdom,
> Millions of centuries before the earth was born.[46]

Reflecting a prevailing justification for Western imperialism in Asia, the "memoir" positioned the Chinese statesman in the role of student to American teachers, a non-Westerner needing to be schooled by the West. In his reaction to the Liberty Bell, the imagined Li validated the American view of the Liberty Bell as a symbol with meaning not only to the nation, but to the world.

Americans' sense of the global significance of the Liberty Bell intensified with the bell's final journey in 1915. With the Great War under way in Europe, the *Daily Ledger* of Tacoma, Washington, paid tribute to the Liberty Bell as representative of American ideals, saying: "Since the traditional ringing of the bell to announce the signing of the Declaration of Independence, there has never been a time in American history when those ideals were not dominant. The dark days of the Civil War could not dim them. The present international crisis finds them radiating still."[47] The next day, the *Oregon Journal* marveled at the contrast between the condition of the old bell and its power as a global symbol: "All over the world, the liberty bell is ringing still. Its echoes roll on from Maine to the Philippines and from Oregon to Africa and the islands of the sea."[48] In the context of these times, when anti-German sentiment led to

28. The Liberty Bell's travels were front-page news across the country, contributing to its widespread reputation as a symbol of American freedom. (Courtesy of the Library of Congress)

renaming sauerkraut as "liberty cabbage" and hamburgers as "liberty sandwiches," it is not surprising to find the Liberty Bell in a prominent place among the propaganda devices promoting support for World War I. Posters and placards urged Americans to "Ring It Again" by contributing to Liberty Loans.[49]

The Liberty Bell was a flexible symbol, reaching across regions and across generations. In the process of its travels, it also became commodified. In their patriotic enthusiasm, people desired souvenirs of the bell, and civic groups often obliged. Local merchants realized that crowds converging on the Liberty Bell were good for business, and newspaper ad salesmen helped them make the most of the opportunity by using Liberty Bell themes in advertisements. Some ads appeared during the early trips, such as the 1904 advertisement for the Metropolitan Music Company in Minneapolis: "The Liberty Bell played an important part in the growth of the nation, but did you ever stop to think what an influence music has on the mental growth of children?"[50] But the full power of the Liberty Bell as an advertising device emerged in its 1915 tour through the American West, where it appeared in ads for banks, flour, department stores, rail companies, home furnishings, and movie theaters. For example, in Salt Lake City, "The Liberty Bell sounded freedom from a foe. The women of this region have been freed from the worries of poor bread by White Fawn Flour."[51] And in Cheyenne, Wyoming: "As the Liberty Bell announced a people's determination to be politically independent, the first dollar put in the Wyoming Trust and Savings Bank announces an individual's determination to be financially independent."[52] In 1916, the Liberty Bell was adopted as the advertising logo of the Pennzoil Company, which advertised nationally beginning in the 1920s.[53] Moviegoers saw the Liberty Bell at the beginning of every picture made by Siegmund Lubin, a Philadelphia film pioneer.[54] The appearance of the Liberty Bell in such advertising reflected the bell's significance and demonstrated expectations that the bell's message would have wide appeal among consumers. Such commodification may appear to trivialize the bell as a sacred symbol, but it also extended public recognition and placed the relic from the American Revolution into a modern context. The bell could be simultaneously patriotic, spiritual, and commercial, and, therefore, a more powerful symbol bridging past and present.

Representing not only history but also destiny, the Liberty Bell became viewed as an object of good luck. This perception of the bell could be seen during its journeys, as people touched it and pressed pennies against it to keep as good-luck charms. However, an even better view of the Liberty Bell as symbol of good fortune might be gained by venturing into the nation's saloons. There, the Liberty Bell was a constant presence on slot machines, where a nickel might turn up three Liberty Bells—jackpot! The slot machine with three spinning wheels had been invented in 1899 in San Francisco by an immigrant mechanic from Bavaria. For the jackpot alignment of three identical symbols, he chose Liberty Bells. Charles Fey, who had changed his name from the less American-sounding August (Gus), manufactured about one hundred of his Liberty Bell Slot Machines. Major game-machine manufacturers picked up the design, and Liberty Bell slots proliferated across the country. The M. B. Mills Manufacturing Company of Chicago alone put more than one thousand Liberty Bell machines into operation by 1907, with more than thirty thousand manufactured by the start of World War I. Until Prohibition closed saloons during the 1920s, limiting the venue for slot machines, Americans had ample opportunity to fix their hopes on the Liberty Bell as a literal messenger of good fortune. Even when state gaming laws restricted gambling, slot machines remained in operation by dispensing Liberty Bell chewing gum in exchange for deposited nickels.[55]

Adding to its magical qualities and its value as an advertising commodity, the Liberty Bell demonstrated in 1915 that it could transcend time and space. On February 11, 1915, before the bell's cross-country tour to the Panama-Pacific Exposition, the N. W. Ayer advertising agency of Philadelphia arranged for the Bell Telephone Company of Pennsylvania to use the Liberty Bell to demonstrate its new transcontinental telephone service. At 5 P.M. Philadelphia time, Bell Telephone connected Independence Hall with San Francisco. The first sound heard over the first transcontinental telephone transmission was a tap, tap, tap on the Liberty Bell, struck with mallets by Philadelphia's chief of city property. It was believed to be the first official sounding of the Liberty Bell since the death of Chief Justice John Marshall eighty years before. For posterity, the sound was recorded on a Victor Victrola.[56]

While much of the Liberty Bell's symbolic significance reflected a celebratory view of the symbol and the nation, the occasional use of the Liberty Bell to call attention to the limitations of American ideals also attested to its symbolic power and flexibility. The inversion of the more widely accepted view of the bell's significance emerged during American involvement in the Philippines between 1899 and 1902. The United States had gone to war to keep the Philippines after the Spanish-American War, spurring intense debate at home over whether subduing an overseas possession contradicted American principles such as liberty and self-government. During the bell's trip to Charleston in 1902, several South Carolina newspapers made the point that no Filipinos were in the welcoming crowds, nor would they recognize the sentiments being expressed from the speakers' platform. "Had there been one of these new citizens of the United States by adoption present, he would have perhaps wondered why the

Ring Out and Proclaim Trust-Imperialism Throughout the Land.

29. The Liberty Bell's evolution into a symbol of American ideals became apparent during the nation's debate over annexation of the Philippines at the turn of the twentieth century. "The New Anthem at Philadelphia," a cartoon published in the *New York Journal and Advertiser* during the Republican National Convention in 1900, focuses on the irony of American politicians providing instructions in liberty to a people being governed by force by the United States. (Courtesy of the Library of Congress)

people gathered about this historic piece of metal, and scratched his head as he tried to reason out the meaning of the inscription," the *State* in Columbia observed.[57]

In similar fashion, the women's suffrage movement tapped the symbolism of the Liberty Bell to call attention to the limitation of political rights for women. In the campaign for the vote, Pennsylvania women in 1915 commissioned a replica of the Liberty Bell with an additional inscription, "Establish Justice." They hauled their "Justice Bell" throughout the state for suffrage rallies, keeping the clapper of the bell silent until women gained the vote.[58] When the Nineteenth Amendment was ratified in 1920, they freed the clapper and let the bell ring for the first time at a jubilee celebration in Independence Square. While elected officials spoke of the Nineteenth Amendment in patriotic terms, portraying it as a natural next step in a story of American progress, the women emphasized that the success of their movement had corrected earlier wrongs. "Men gave liberty to America and to the world," the organizers of the celebration told the mayor of Philadelphia. "Women will bring to the nation as their gift justice."[59] Nearly a half century after Susan B. Anthony had been prevented from reading a women's rights declaration in Independence Square on July 4, 1876, the replica Liberty Bell symbolized a long struggle to combat inequality and achieve voting rights for women.

The travels of the Liberty Bell and its increasing adaptability as a national symbol raised a significant question for Philadelphians: Who "owned" the Liberty Bell? Who should make decisions regarding its care and safekeeping? City dignitaries who accompanied the bell on its rail journeys repeatedly asserted that the Liberty Bell belonged not only to Philadelphia, but to the nation at large.[60] They facilitated recognition of the Liberty Bell as an icon separate from Independence Hall in Philadelphia. However, the enthusiasm generated by the bell's tours also raised an awareness among Philadelphians that they were guardians of a national treasure—an artifact perhaps too precious to be hauled around the country on railroad cars. Did a proper regard for patriotism require Philadelphians to lend the Liberty Bell, or was it incumbent on other Americans to travel to Philadelphia to see it? Did the separation of the Liberty Bell from Independence Hall diminish the sacredness of both the place and the artifact? What if the Bell fell victim to a train wreck or collapsed into pieces from vibration on the rails? Like decisions regarding the restoration and use of Independence Hall during the late nineteenth and early twentieth centuries, such questions forced Philadelphians to examine their own regard for their city's historic past.

Like the Independence Hall projects of the 1870s and 1890s, the questions about the Liberty Bell pitted Philadelphia elites, many of whom traced their ancestry to the

30. Women also adopted the Liberty Bell as a symbol of their struggle to achieve the vote. As shown here in a photograph from 1916, women created a replica "Justice Bell," which they took on tours to campaign for woman suffrage. (Courtesy of the Historical Society of Pennsylvania)

time of the American Revolution, against the machine politicians who controlled the city's property. In addition to their personal sense of guardianship over surviving relics of the American Revolution, members of the city's hereditary societies and the Historical Society of Pennsylvania questioned whether the Liberty Bell was simply an excuse for expensive cross-country junkets for the politicians who invariably accompanied the bell on its tours. An 1895 lawsuit challenging the city's authority over the Liberty Bell ended with a common pleas court ruling that affirmed public officials' control over city property.[61] The decision cleared a legal path for the Liberty Bell's travels, but the relic's growing reputation and fragility kept the issue alive. By 1915, San Francisco's elaborate invitation to the Liberty Bell, including a three-mile-long petition signed by California schoolchildren, met with a vigorous petition drive against the trip by the Daughters of the American Revolution in Philadelphia. Close examination of the bell showed an additional hairline fracture beyond the more visible signature crack in its side. Would the Liberty Bell be sacrificed for the sake of an expensive cross-country trip? City officials prevailed, but the engineer who identified the additional crack installed a metal brace inside the bell to prevent further damage.[62] Although Philadelphia's mayor, the reformer Rudolph Blankenburg, refused to make the trip, a committee of the City Councils accompanied the bell on its longest and most elaborate journey at a cost of $60,000, most of which paid for the special train to San Francisco and back.[63]

The 1915 journey to San Francisco was the Liberty Bell's last trip outside Philadelphia. In 1922, the state of Illinois invited the bell to Chicago for the Pageant of Progress, hoping that "that great symbol of national life" would address "a regrettable slump in visible and audible patriotism since the close of the war," in the words of the state's superintendent of public instruction.[64] However, even a two-mile-long petition with signatures from 3.5 million children in the Midwest, personally delivered to Philadelphia by three Chicago schoolboys, could not budge Independence Hall's most famous artifact from its home city. Council members approved the trip, but Mayor J. Hampton Moore vetoed the plan. Henceforth, the mayor decided, "the Liberty Bell, the most cherished of our national symbols, shall not be removed from Independence Hall, its historic home."[65]

By the time Philadelphia prepared to commemorate the 150th anniversary of the Declaration of Independence, the celebrity status of the Liberty Bell was clear. The Sesquicentennial International Exposition in 1926 was a dismal failure, owing to late planning and bad weather, but it showed that Philadelphians along with the rest of the nation had developed a regard for the Liberty Bell that was both different and separate from Independence Hall.[66] Billed as the "Liberty Bell Fair," the sesquicentennial featured the bell on official sesquicentennial guidebooks, postcards, and souvenirs. In contrast to the opening of the centennial year in 1876, when crowds had gathered around Independence Hall, the sesquicentennial year of 1926 opened with prominent Philadelphians gathering around the Liberty Bell. Mabel Kendrick, wife of the mayor, struck the bell with a gold, rubber-tipped hammer: one tap, pause; nine taps, pause; two taps, pause; six taps—1926. The mayor stood by her side, silently counting each stroke; a microphone stood beneath the bell to broadcast its sound over the radio. The old bell emitted dull, metallic little tones, but the audience heard music. "People listened almost breathlessly as the dull but proud voice of the cracked old bell welcomed the year of this 150th anniversary of its triumph," the *Evening Bulletin* reported. "It was a spectacle, inspiring. Patriots of today bowed in reverent homage to those of yesterday. . . . Every voice seemed stilled by a momentary surge of emotion, a strange but glorious emotion that seemed to put deeper into the hearts of all a renewed sense of patriotism."[67]

On the Sesquicentennial grounds in South Philadelphia, towering over South Broad Street, Philadelphians constructed an unmistakable monument to the Liberty Bell's reputation. Like a colossus for the 1920s, the largest copy of the Liberty Bell ever constructed spanned the avenue. Standing eighty feet high, leaving sufficient room for automobiles to pass below, it was spectacular. Like a jewel, it sparkled, lit by 26,000 electric light bulbs. In contrast to Independence Hall, this was not just a relic of the American Revolution, but a modern symbol, inflated to absurd proportions, saying as much about the present as its largely imaginary past. The enormous, electric bell over Broad Street demonstrated the rise of the Liberty Bell in national consciousness and its transformation into a symbol that could be manipulated to keep pace with modern times.

Historic Home

The Liberty Bell and Independence Hall had entwined histories, but during the period of the Liberty Bell's travels, they developed diverging identities. Although both were associated with the American Revolution, the Liberty Bell became a national celebrity, transcending time and place to represent the American ideal of liberty. Appreciation for Independence Hall, meanwhile, combined regard for its role in eighteenth-century events with admiration of its architectural character. Independence Hall was a place more than a symbol. It was capable of inspiring reverence for the nation's achievements, but it remained closely tied to its location in Philadelphia and its history as a place of famous eighteenth-century events. While the Liberty Bell stepped out of its moment in history to generate contemporary excitement, Independence Hall permitted visitors to inhabit a distant past. Postcards called attention to the symbolic divergence, frequently portraying the Liberty Bell and Independence Hall on the same card but as separate entities, with the Bell out of proportion, much larger than the building. Independence Hall appeared as a physical landmark, but the Liberty Bell often appeared on postcards with other national symbols, such as the American flag. Sent by Philadelphia residents and visitors to distant friends, postcards reinforced the symbolic divergence developed during the Liberty Bell's journeys around the country.

In contrast to the Liberty Bell, regard for Independence Hall developed not only

Chestnut Street, west from Fifth — Philadelphia.

31. Many postcards at the turn of the twentieth century portrayed images of Independence Hall and the Liberty Bell separate from their urban environment—but this rare view, mailed in 1906, shows the old Pennsylvania State House as it appeared from the street. Notice that passersby are intent on their daily business, showing little interest in the landmark building at left. (Courtesy of Pennsylvania State Archives, Harrisburg)

from patriotism but also in the context of the changing urban environment around the historic landmark. Surrounded by office buildings up to ten stories high, caught in the racket of passing streetcars, Independence Hall by the early twentieth century appeared diminutive and rather dull. Further defining the building as a place of the past, the city government had finished its move to Philadelphia's new City Hall in 1901, leaving behind the buildings on Independence Square. Writing soon after the departure of city government, a journalist pondered, "How many of us pass that way, alas, without a glance, to say nothing of a loving look, to say nothing of a kindling memory?" The government's move westward had produced some benefits, he observed: "The State House pavement, the sidewalks of Fifth and Sixth Street, are no longer peopled with unbecoming leisure and wretched expectancy, with hangers-on, petty litigants, political workers." However, "The vacancy about the old State House borders on the painful. Occasionally one comes near feeling that the old life, such as it was, was better than no life at all."[68]

While the Liberty Bell gained its popularity by traveling the country with few restrictions placed on who could see or touch it, Philadelphians sought to enhance the patriotic character of Independence Hall by exercising increased control over the structure, its contents, and its surroundings. The building had a variety of interested guardians, including professional architects, members of hereditary and historic societies, and city officials. Although the city government was physically separated from Independence Hall, Philadelphia's two landmarks remained connected by politics. As in other American cities in the early twentieth century, machine politics clashed with progressive reform. Independence Hall was a patronage prize in the Fifth Ward, a neighborhood crowded with eastern European immigrants, whose votes were coveted by factions of the city's dominant Republican Party.[69] To reform-minded Philadelphians, political control of Independence Hall in the first years after the removal of the city government had created a shocking display of neglect that would only get worse. The government—"corrupt and contented" in Lincoln Steffens's famous 1903 phrase—appropriated money for guards and maintenance, but far too little to keep up with the demands of such an aging structure.[70] By 1912, patriotic and historical societies complained of exterior cracks, interior walls disfigured by leaks, and vandalism, including holes poked into paintings by the canes and umbrellas of unattended visitors. From time to time, smokers discarded cigars and cigarettes through open cellar windows, igniting small fires. And scandalously, in the view of the societies, souvenirs were sold in close proximity to the table where the Declaration had been signed. Citing a litany of abuses, the patriotic and historical societies tried but failed to force the city to place Independence Hall, Congress Hall, and Old City Hall under the control of a nonpartisan commission.[71]

In this Progressive-era conflict between urban politicians and reform-minded professionals, the competing constituencies of Independence Hall often disagreed on who should manage the building, but they agreed on the mission of protecting it as an authentic, historic, and patriotic place. Although city officials resisted the reform efforts of the patriotic and historical societies, they gradually yielded to local architects' proposals for restoring the buildings on Independence Square. Basing their case on the structural needs of the buildings rather than on the questionable character of city politicians, members of the American Institute for Architects gained permission from the city to undertake new restorations of Congress Hall (1913–15), Old City Hall (1919–22), and finally the second floor of Independence Hall (1924), which they had criticized since its Colonial-revival decoration under the auspices of the Daughters of the American Revolution in the 1890s.[72] In pursuing accurate historic restoration based on structural and documentary research, the architects' work further enhanced the identity of the buildings on Independence Square as places of the past rather than the present. City officials added to the effect—and perhaps rid themselves of annoying critics—by evicting private organizations from offices in Congress Hall, Old City Hall, and the wings of Independence Hall so that all of the space could be devoted to historical exhibits.[73]

Perhaps the most significant break from the nineteenth-century history of Independence Hall came in 1912 when reformers briefly wrested control of the city government away from the Republican organization. During the single term of Democratic Mayor Rudolph Blankenburg, Philadelphians enacted the first city ordinance restricting activities in Independence Square. Since the earliest days of the State House, the square had been a public arena. From Stamp Act protests to labor rallies, from solemn funeral processions to salutes to national anniversaries, Independence Square had been a place of public protest and commemoration, echoing with commentary on the controversies, triumphs, and tragedies of the times. To historically minded Philadelphians of the early twentieth century, protest activities seemed disorderly and inconsistent with the carefully restored, picturesque character of Independence Hall and its square. In particular, they sought to end the long tradition of protest by laborers who embraced the language of the Declaration of Independence to argue for their rights as workers. Informally, city officials began refusing access to the square for groups such labor unions while encouraging patriotic celebrations.[74] In 1912, faced with a request from the Industrial Workers of the World to hold a rally on the square, Philadelphia City Councils took the decisive step of voting to ban all meetings from Independence Square except for city-sponsored "patriotic meetings to celebrate some event in the history of the Nation, State, or City."[75]

The new ordinance left wide latitude for city officials to decide whose meetings were "patriotic" and thus permitted. With the city's approval, women suffragists used Independence Square and the Liberty Bell to promote their inclusion in the right to vote both before and after the ordinance passed.[76] In 1912, prior to the ordinance, the National Woman Suffrage Association assembled in Independence Square, placing speakers on five platforms to argue that women had been unjustly blocked from participating in the republic created on the same square. Within earshot of the place where the Declaration of Independence was enacted, the suffragists read the Declaration of the Rights of Women that Susan B. Anthony had delivered to the vice president of the United States in 1876. In the shadow of Independence Hall, the women of 1912 denounced the limitations placed on women's citizenship.[77]

Subsequent suffrage parades in Philadelphia respected the ban on meetings in the square, but after ratification of the Nineteenth Amendment, city officials cooperated with suffragists to stage a celebration jubilee on Independence Square. The women brought to the square their "Justice Bell," the copy of the Liberty Bell they had commissioned which bore the additional inscription "Establish Justice." While the suffragists, supported in their cause by the mayor of Philadelphia and his wife, were welcomed onto Independence Square, the Justice Bell's position on the square precipitated conflict over control of the public space around Independence Hall. The Justice Bell remained for five months on a wooden platform outside the hall, within yards of the Liberty Bell on display inside. Women in the suffrage movement hoped to secure permission to keep their bell in a permanent enclosure on the square, but city officials wanted the bell removed. The replica of the Liberty Bell was confusing to people who came to see the real thing, they said. Most alarmingly, a group of soldiers passing through the square had been seen cheering and waving their caps at the Justice Bell—surely mistaking it for the Liberty Bell inside, the chief of city property complained.[78]

In February 1921, city employees hoisted the Justice Bell from its platform onto a truck and drove it to a stable in League Island Park in far South Philadelphia. The women who had placed the bell in Independence Square objected, arguing that the Liberty Bell stood only for the freedom of one sex, while their bell stood for justice for all. "It would be a valuable addition to Independence Hall instead of a rival to the Liberty Bell as some seem to think," said Katherine Wentworth Ruschenberger, who had commissioned the bell. She spoke of raising money to build a "Tower of Justice" or "Tower of Citizenship" as a home for the Justice Bell on Independence Square.[79] The tower was never built, however. Ruschenberger finally provided a home for the Justice Bell in her will, bequeathing it to the Washington Memorial Chapel at Valley Forge.[80]

Through increasing regulation and attention to architectural authenticity, Philadelphians divorced Independence Hall and its surroundings from their histories as places of active civic engagement. Instead, the buildings on Independence Square—especially Independence Hall—became defined solely as places to be visited for the special purpose of paying homage to the past. They represented a distinctly eighteenth-century past, transmitted to the present as if the intervening years had never occurred. Increasingly, tourism was a guiding consideration. Beginning in 1914, the city sold postcards in the Supreme Court Room and provided visitors with descriptive leaflets. Guards patrolled inside and out, and cleaning crews attended to housekeeping. City workers installed mahogany benches, a checkroom to handle coats and umbrellas, and a first-aid box. They converted a closet into an office for the chief guard, to get his unsightly desk out of the Supreme Court Room. To the extent that city appropriations would allow, they performed the endless maintenance duties of painting, cleaning, and fixing the aging structures that had been battered by the last century of day-to-day city business.[81]

Even in the midst of a declining commercial neighborhood, abandoned by city government and packed with once-proud industrial structures falling into decline, Independence Hall attracted several hundred thousand visitors each year. A metal turnstile installed inside the Chestnut Street entrance in 1916 yielded what was probably the first accurate visitor count: 321,480 tourists, an average of 936 a day. What were they coming to see? Inside Independence Hall and its east and west wings, visitors could examine case after case of colonial and Revolutionary War relics—books and broadsides, weapons and wearing apparel, maps, medals, and musical instruments. Many of the objects had been in Independence Hall since Frank M. Etting established his National Museum in 1876; others had been donated to the city since then. In addition to viewing relics, visitors could pause before portraits painted by Charles Willson Peale, Rembrandt Peale, and Thomas Sully. At times, the city arranged for historical lectures (for which folding chairs were set up in Congress Hall) or special exhibits of historical paintings or old firefighting equipment. On occasion, thousands of people were drawn by more somber events, such as the viewing of the bodies of two sailors from Philadelphia, Charles Allen Smith and George Poinsett, who were killed in the April 1914 U.S. invasion of Vera Cruz, Mexico. Sixty thousand passed by their caskets in the Supreme Court Room in Independence Hall.[82]

Most of all, people came to Independence Hall to see the Liberty Bell. Philadelphians responded to public interest in the bell by changing its method of display inside the building. At the time of the bell's first journey outside Philadelphia, in 1885, the relic had been suspended over the heads of visitors, hanging from a thirteen-link chain in the tower stair hall. In 1894, following the bell's triumphal tour to Chicago for the World's Columbian Exposition, the Liberty Bell was moved to eye level in Independence Hall, but it was enclosed in a glass case, separated from the public.[83] In 1915, after the bell's long journey west, the glass case was abandoned. But like other aspects of Independence Hall, the Liberty Bell was subject to regulation. In 1923, in an attempt to control commercial exploitation of Independence Hall's celebrity artifact, city officials restricted photography. "I am getting tired of taking pictures of chorus girls, chewing-gum promoters and the like standing beside the bell," the chief of city property complained. To preserve the dignity of the bell, henceforth all picture-taking would require a permit. Regulation of behavior both outside and inside Independence Hall was complete, extending even to well-intentioned Boy Scouts who could find themselves scolded for snapping unauthorized pictures of the famous artifact they had come to see.[84]

Echoes of History, Near and Far

Philadelphians saw in Independence Hall some of the same qualities that others attached to the Liberty Bell—the power to inspire patriotic feeling, for example, and to unite diverse people into a single nation. Philadelphia newspapers marveled at the numerous nationalities recorded in the visitors' register at Independence Hall.[85] But what place did Independence Hall hold in public memory, especially in contrast to the intensified national regard for its most famous artifact? Early twentieth-century events and trends in American architecture reflected continuing recognition of the old Pennsylvania State House but also demonstrated the symbolic limitations of an eighteenth-century structure in an eastern American city.

The First World War, involving an intense propaganda campaign at home as well as military campaigns abroad, revealed Independence Hall as place retaining local significance but losing symbolic ground to the Liberty Bell as well as the Statue of Liberty in New York Harbor. For Philadelphians, Independence Hall served as an important gathering place for homefront activities, much as it had during times of crisis reaching back to the American Revolution. The old State House served as a center for recruiting and building support on the home front from the time the United States entered the war in 1917. The Navy Department and the War Department set up recruiting stations, the local American Red Cross Society moved in to collect money for the war effort, and the YMCA solicited funds from a facsimile of a battlefront hut outside on Chestnut Street.[86] The city's Home Defense Committee organized its first patriotic rally on Independence and Washington Squares on March 31, 1917, a week before the United States' declaration of war. Throughout the war, servicemen stationed in Philadelphia were led about town on Sunday afternoon "Historical Hikes," pausing at Independence Hall for commemorative photographs.[87]

The hoopla over the war rode on a current of anxiety. In April 1917, Philadelphia police received a report that "strangers" had been heard making threats against Independence Hall. Attempts to arrest the suspects failed, so extra guards were posted inside and outside the building for the duration of the war.[88] Over the next year, Philadelphians concerned with the preservation of Independence Hall eyed the destruction of landmark buildings in Europe and worried. German submarines were known to patrol American waters in the Atlantic, and Rear Admiral Robert Peary himself had said that

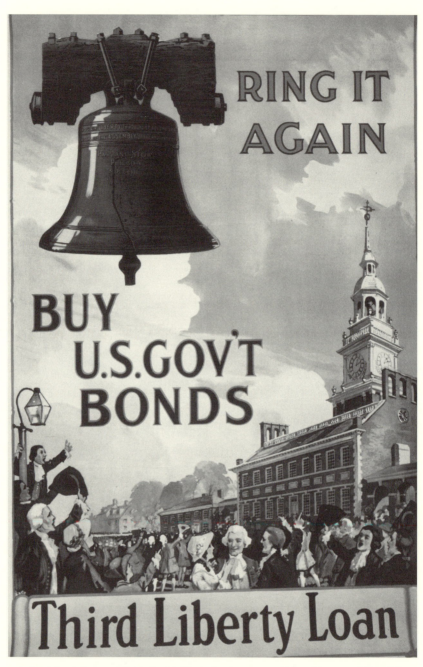

RING IT
AGAIN

BUY
U.S.GOV'T
BONDS

Third Liberty Loan

32. This propaganda poster from World War I shows the divergent symbolism of the Liberty Bell and Independence Hall that evolved during the period of the bell's journeys around the country. The Liberty Bell appears disproportionately large in comparison to the building, and Independence Hall is tied firmly to its eighteenth-century past. (Courtesy of Pennsylvania State Archives, Harrisburg)

Philadelphia was vulnerable to air attack. Emotional newspaper advertisements warned of the potential consequences. "Picture a burly German soldier marching down Broad Street at the head of a squad, a baby impaled on his bayonet," said an ad sponsored by the Cadillac-Automobile Sales Corporation. "Picture the defiling of the State House, the burning of the flags of the Revolution and the Rebellion; the destruction of the Liberty Bell."[89] If such danger appeared imminent, Philadelphia city officials thought one way to protect Independence Hall might be to pack the inside solidly with sand and disguise the outside.[90] Architects mobilized to safeguard the building for posterity by producing precise architectural drawings of the structure, assuring that it could be replaced if the worst were to occur.[91]

In a war waged by Americans "to make the world safe for democracy," Independence Hall acquired an aura of international significance, particularly when supporters of democracy movements in Europe gathered at the landmark in October 1918 to issue a "Declaration of Independence" for Czechoslovakia. In fact, the declaration had been announced by Czechoslovak President Thomas G. Masaryk a week before. The meeting was not evidence of the international significance of Independence Hall, but a media event arranged to garner maximum publicity in the American press. An American translated and edited Masaryk's document so that it would produce a familiar ring to American ears.[92] On October 26, delegates from the Mid-European Union met in the Assembly Room of Independence Hall to sit in John Hancock's chair and sign Masaryk's declaration. In Independence Square, the Europeans received and rang a replica of the American Liberty Bell, reported to be a gift of the schoolchildren of Philadelphia. On this day, "A new Democracy spread its wings over the cradle of American Liberty," the *Philadelphia Inquirer* reported the next day.[93]

Even in Philadelphia, however, Independence Hall and the Liberty Bell did not serve alone as symbols of American patriotism during the First World War. To whip up enthusiasm for the Third Liberty Loan in 1918, Philadelphians also erected a twenty-nine-foot facsimile of the Statue of Liberty, crafted of plaster and concrete, on the south plaza of Philadelphia's City Hall. With special appeal for American immigrants, the statue, facing toward heavily Italian South Philadelphia, drew patriotic demonstrations away from the neighborhood of Independence Hall.[94] When the war ended, on November 11, Philadelphians sought out not one shrine, but two, the *Inquirer* reported: "one at Independence Hall, where their fathers, many of them, had prayed and sung, had wept or made merry, as the great news of the hour might be; and the other at the great golden Statue of Liberty at the South Plaza of the City Hall, where so many of them had dedicated their own lives and their own resources to a mightier labor than the mere enfranchisement of their country and their own people—the enfranchisement of the living, breathing, suffering and enduring world of all mankind."[95] To celebrate the end of the war, organized groups paraded to Independence Hall, and thousands came to touch the Liberty Bell. Meanwhile, on South Broad Street near the "Statue of Liberty" at City Hall, streamers and confetti rained from the tall buildings. A French woman climbed onto the Statue of Liberty to lead the throng of nearly 25,000 people in singing "The Marseillaise." Spontaneous parades arrived from the city's industrial districts. With each arriving band, the crowd would pick up whatever new tune carried into the celebration. At Independence Hall, Philadelphians paid tribute to historic principles successfully defended; at City Hall, they crowded at the feet of the Statue of Liberty to revel in the happy present.[96]

Beyond Philadelphia, international exhibitions staged in the United States also provided evidence that Independence Hall lacked popular appeal. Despite the enthusiasm for early American architecture that accompanied the Colonial revival, the Pennsylvania buildings at world's fairs showed a determination to adapt Independence Hall to suit contemporary expectations. For the World's Columbian Exposition in Chicago in 1893, for example, Philadelphia architect John Notman grafted an Independence Hall-like tower onto a building in the style of a Victorian manse.[97] For the Jamestown Tercentenary Exposition in 1907, Pennsylvania constructed a reduced-scale Independence Hall accurate in most details, but with the flanking piazzas transformed into verandas on both ends of the building.[98] The Pennsylvania building at the Panama-Pacific Exposition in 1915 was a copy of Independence Hall stretched to greater height with an open passageway through the center for displaying the Liberty Bell. Finally, in 1939, an enlarged copy of Independence Hall housed Pennsylvania's exhibits at the New York World's Fair, but the building also provided a restaurant and a view over a reflecting pool.[99] The exposition buildings presented images of Independence Hall to audiences beyond Philadelphia, but they were altered images, adapted to modern tastes and removed from an urban environment.

Like the world's fair pavilions, public and commercial buildings designed in the popular Georgian-revival style projected an impression of Independence Hall while adapting its architectural characteristics to the needs and tastes of the late nineteenth and early twentieth centuries. American architects trained in the method of the highly regarded Ecole des Beaux-Arts in Paris had been schooled to master the principles of classical architecture, then apply that knowledge to the architectural needs of the present. As a result, the United States from the late nineteenth century through the first decades of the twentieth century burgeoned with new buildings that echoed classical

33. The popularity of Georgian Revival architecture led to numerous buildings incorporating architectural features similar to Independence Hall. The Baker Memorial Library at Dartmouth College, shown here, features a similar tower and steeple but differs from Independence Hall in scale and floor plan. (Courtesy of Dartmouth College Library)

designs, from railroad stations to world's fair pavilions to new federal office buildings. The goal was not to create exact copies of past structures, but to learn from their example and apply their architectural vocabulary. In this way, the United States gained skyscrapers clad in Gothic ornament and railroad stations with Greek columns, as well as buildings faced with Georgian-style red brick, with symmetrical floor plans, Palladian windows, and bell towers. Especially through designs incorporating Georgian-style towers and steeples, by the late 1930s the nation abounded with buildings strongly reminiscent of Independence Hall.[100] Architects were striving not to duplicate the exact structure in Philadelphia, which an architectural reference work briefly dismissed as "perhaps" important "from a sentimental point of view," but to embrace its example of Georgian principles. Lavishing special attention on Georgian-style steeples, the same reference work included three photographs of the Independence Hall tower.[101]

Because of its association with colonial America, Georgian-revival architecture was viewed by architects and educators as especially appropriate for school buildings, where it would imbue scholars with an appropriate appreciation for their nation's past. Writing in *Architectural Forum* in 1929, a New York state education official praised the aesthetic and educational effects of Georgian-revival school buildings. Singling out a new high school building in Lake George, New York, he observed, "It embodies the spirit of the forefathers, a fit expression of the Colonial period through which the village gained its first fame, a beauty in a spot in an attractive modern village, and a fit companion piece to the famous lake."[102] In such pastoral settings, particularly on college campuses that embraced Georgian-revival design, buildings whose architectural elements resembled Independence Hall were stylistic echoes of the historic landmark more than tributes to its specific historical significance.[103]

While architects focused on applying and adapting architectural elements of the past, eschewing exact copies of buildings, a precise replica of Independence Hall did rise in Dearborn, Michigan, where automobile manufacturer Henry Ford created Greenfield Village. The project, dedicated to portraying American history through objects with meaning to everyday life and work, gave this "Independence Hall" the prominent role of museum to house Ford's vast collection of artifacts. The idea for re-creating Independence Hall for the museum has been attributed to Robert O. Derrick, a Detroit architect who met Ford aboard an ocean liner in 1928. As Derrick recalled the meeting, Ford asked him if he had any ideas for design of a museum to house his collection. "The first thing I could think of would be if you could get permission for me to make a copy of Independence Hall in Philadelphia," Derrick recalled telling Ford.

"It is a wonderful building and beautiful architecture and it certainly would be appropriate for a collection of Americana."[104] Ford's architects duplicated Independence Hall in exact detail. Like many other buildings that incorporated Georgian-style towers similar to the tower on Independence Hall, the Henry Ford Museum reversed the orientation of the building, making the tower the front entrance. Far too small to accommodate Ford's collection of Americana, the "Independence Hall" dedicated at Dearborn in 1929 was extended on both sides with long brick wings that culminated in reproductions of Congress Hall and Old City Hall.

In Philadelphia, Georgian-revival architecture also contributed to the growing sense of controlled, historic ambiance around Independence Hall. Around the eighteenth-century landmark, new Georgian-revival buildings replaced older structures, projecting a more sedate, colonial atmosphere but on a scale suited to the twentieth century. The commercial district north of Independence Hall remained untouched, and the landmark's nearest neighbor to the east was the Italianate headquarters of the Drexel Company. However, south and west of the square, new buildings for the first time were designed to harmonize with the historic buildings on the square. On Sixth Street facing Independence Square, Cyrus H. K. Curtis, publisher of the *Saturday Evening Post* and the *Ladies' Home Journal*, built two Georgian-revival headquarters for the Curtis Publishing Company (1910) and the *Public Ledger* newspaper (1924).[105] In 1925, the Independence Companies, an insurance firm founded just three years before, also tied its corporate identity to Independence Hall by building a Georgian-revival headquarters at Fifth and Walnut Streets.[106]

The publishing and insurance companies facing Independence Square constructed corporate identities that took advantage of their location and reinforced perceptions of Independence Hall in the early twentieth century. In addition to serving the companies' commercial interests, advertising by these Philadelphia firms reinforced recognition of Independence Hall as a historic place. The Curtis Publishing Company advertised its address as "Independence Square" and displayed its Georgian-revival headquarters in magazine promotions. In the perception of one long-time employee, "The new Curtis Building [became] a Philadelphia landmark almost as familiar as Independence Hall itself. In marble and steel solidity it said big business success and stability. It proclaimed publishing genius, editorial acumen, the power of the mass magazine, and the power of mass advertising—and it did not lie."[107] Along Walnut Street directly south of the square, the Penn Mutual Insurance Company occupied a ten-story tower of granite rather than Georgian-revival brick, but it tied its corporate advertising to its location: "Back of Your Independence Stands the Penn Mutual."[108]

The Liberty Bell could stir patriotic enthusiasm, but Independence Hall as an advertising device evoked honesty, order, and stability. Carefully restored and regulated, it was as reassuring and reliable as a paid-up life insurance policy or the weekly appearance of the *Saturday Evening Post*.

From common origins, Independence Hall and the Liberty Bell grew apart during the late nineteenth and early twentieth centuries. In some ways, these two artifacts of the American Revolution embodied the precarious balance of American national life. The Liberty Bell was free-ranging and unregulated, purveying the ideal of individual liberty. It had the resonance of a church bell, a school bell, or an alarm bell, calling people together in a shared community that seemed to obscure differences of race, class, and ethnicity. It was unique, it was fun, and it seemed to belong to everyone who reached to touch it. Striking a balance against such unfettered liberty, Independence Hall was stationary, orderly, and carefully regulated. While the Liberty Bell transcended its largely fictional history to achieve present-day celebrity, Independence Hall was history incarnate. Restoration and regulation preserved the structure's ties to the Declaration of Independence and the Constitution, but in the process increased the distance between the eighteenth-century building and modern life.

Buildings do not translate easily into national symbols. There are exceptions, to be sure—the United States Capitol, which was self-consciously constructed to be symbolic of the United States; the White House, the seat of national political power; and perhaps the Empire State Building, a soaring symbol of technological progress. Not only were these buildings created as symbols of national strength, they have remained actively used in ways that reinforce their meaning for the present as well as the past. Independence Hall has a different history. In common with other buildings from the colonial era, it became tethered in time and place, and its architectural characteristics were widely copied and manipulated in the creation of new structures. Independence Hall, tied to Philadelphia and its eighteenth-century history, had a host of Georgian-revival cousins born in the late nineteenth and early twentieth century. They adopted its most distinctive feature, the brick tower with its white steeple, projecting a diffused sense of the colonial past rather than specific reference to the building in Philadelphia. In contrast to the Liberty Bell, a unique artifact with its distinctive inscription and crack in its side, Independence Hall represented a highly valued but widely emulated architectural style. Although a historically significant place, as a distinctive symbol it paled in comparison to its most famous artifact.

The contrast between the Liberty Bell and Independence Hall highlights a significant function of buildings in the construction of public memory. Although perhaps limited in symbolic power, buildings provide a means of constructing appearances of order and stability, despite conflict and change that might have occurred in the course of history. Left to their natural processes of deterioration, buildings would communicate a sense of history through age and decay. But when buildings become objects of restoration and preservation, they present opportunities for constructing more pristine, orderly representations of the past. Whether they are the structures of everyday life or historic landmarks, buildings allow people to exercise control over public memory as it is represented in the built environment. In the buildings that constitute the scenery of everyday life, restoration and preservation provide reassurance of the steady persistence of the past. A national landmark as significant as Independence Hall provides similar assurance that the nation can be managed and sustained.

Even as the Liberty Bell rose to prominence, Independence Hall remained a workshop of public memory for Philadelphians who wrestled for control of the building and protected its historic character through increasing regulation of the structure and its public square. The Liberty Bell could reach the American historical consciousness by traveling the country, but the condition and reputation of Independence Hall depended on the efforts of Philadelphians. During the Liberty Bell's journeys, Philadelphians had been made aware of the symbolic significance that their old State House bell held for the nation. In the case of Independence Hall, it would be up to Philadelphians to convince Americans that the home of the Liberty Bell also merited the nation's attention. In the years that spanned two world wars and the Great Depression, Philadelphians mobilized to protect Independence Hall, enhance its reputation as a historic treasure, and make it the center of one of the nation's first urban national parks.

Chapter 7

TREASURE

Eighteenth-Century Building, Twentieth-Century City

As it happened, on the afternoon of June 21, 1937, George Washington and Benjamin Franklin were enjoying tea in Independence Hall with some lady friends just when the smoke appeared. "Fire!" cried a passerby. "Man the pumps! Man the pumps!" Benjamin Franklin commanded. Fire apparatus, some dating back to 1765, rumbled to the scene, guided by men wearing protective capes and top hats. The father of our country leapt to the aid of the ladies, scooping the distressed Anne Willing Bingham into his arms and carrying her to safety. Outside, a crowd roared its approval. But there was no fire. It was a stunt, staged with actors and smoke bombs for the benefit of the annual convention of the National Association of Insurance Commissioners. This fire drill, and others like it, dramatically demonstrated the anxious local guardianship exercised over Independence Hall during the first half of the twentieth century. Here was fear cloaked in historic costume—a real fear that in these years when the nation itself seemed threatened, an errant spark or enemy bomb might claim the nation's birthplace. Through theatrical "firefighting" and frequent tests of the modern Fire Department's response time to Alarm Box 1776 in Independence Hall, Philadelphians prepared for the worst. They proved that in the face of great danger, American men would leap into action to preserve the nation and rescue their damsels in distress.[1]

Fires were a great concern in large cities in the nineteenth and early twentieth centuries, but the fire drills at Independence Hall reflected broader concerns.[2] Reacting to conditions in the modern city, the uncertainty of changing times, and the threat of global war, Philadelphians developed an intensified regard for Independence Hall as a national treasure whose survival rested in their hands. Increasingly, they viewed the two-century-old building not only as a reminder of the past, but also as a symbol of patriotism that bridged past and present. In the modern city, however, Independence Hall also seemed small—too small for the expansive ideas it symbolized. Liberty? Democracy? How could these be properly commemorated on a single square? And if a fire should start in one of the nineteenth-century buildings that stood shoulder-to-shoulder across the street, what would save Independence Hall from disaster? Philadelphians raised such questions as they observed the decay of the older districts of the city, weathered the Great Depression, and worried about the threat of war. The fate of the nation seemed especially precarious, the city seemed especially dangerous, and as a result, Independence Hall seemed especially precious. In the spirit of a rescue from dire circumstances, elite Philadelphians for the first time sought support from the state and federal governments to protect Independence Hall from its urban environment and enhance its stature as a national shrine.

The creation of Independence National Historical Park has been understood as the achievement of the Independence Hall Association, a group of patriotic-minded, prosperous Philadelphians organized in 1942.[3] Indeed, this group put together the legislation and public financing that made the park possible. In addition to being a catalyst, however, the Independence Hall Association represented a culmination of a series of events leading up to the 1940s. Creating a national park around Independence Hall was not only a matter of legislation and appropriations, but also the extension of earlier ideas and changes in the urban environment. The founders of the Independence Hall Association were united in a collective memory of the events that had shaped their lives.[4] They had seen immigration, the growth of cities, the threat of wars, economic depression, and the modernization of manufacturing, communication, and travel. Sharing in a patriotism fueled by concern for democracy's future, the celebration of national anniversaries of the Declaration of Independence and the Constitution, and their personal sense of guardianship over a local landmark, the founders of the Independence Hall Association looked at a building and envisioned an American symbol. Their perception of Independence Hall prevailed, leading to the creation of an urban park commemorating the birth and progress of the nation. However, theirs was not the only view of Independence Hall developing in the first half of the twentieth century as a diverse population viewed the eighteenth-century building in relation to varying life experiences and differing perceptions of the nation's past.

Visions and Venues

Cities experienced enormous change during the late nineteenth and early twentieth centuries. Structural steel and elevators made skyscrapers possible, transforming

183

urban skylines. New transportation systems allowed city dwellers with sufficient time and money to move away from the urban core to the ends of the streetcar lines or to suburban estates reached by commuter rail. In northern cities like Philadelphia, especially, the neighborhoods they left behind were carved into multiple-family dwellings for European immigrants or African American migrants from the South. Southeast of Independence Hall, Russian Jews created a Jewish quarter in the city's Fifth Ward, which became notorious as a political battleground for machine politicians seeking immigrant votes. Directly south of Independence Hall, the African American neighborhood around Mother Bethel A.M.E. Church spread westward with the arrival of migrants seeking economic opportunity and relief from racial oppression in the South. The newcomers made their living in factories and sweatshops in the oldest part of the city, including the blocks stretching north of Independence Hall. There, they found work in shoe factories, machine shops, or sewing shops that produced goods that were shipped around the world.[5]

This was the city that surrounded Independence Hall during the years in which the building was being restored and regulated by Philadelphia city officials, professional architects, and concerned descendants of the American Revolution. Given the care bestowed on the building between 1890 and the sesquicentennial year in 1926, it should not come as a surprise that some of these concerned Philadelphians began to look at the neighborhood around Independence Hall and wonder, what if? What if something could be done about the unsettling contrast between their carefully restored landmark and the surrounding city? What if the area around Independence Hall could be made to be just as orderly and dignified as the buildings on the square?

Beginning around the turn of the twentieth century, Philadelphians conceived one scheme after another to preserve and protect Independence Hall by creating an enlarged park around it. In doing so, they once again expanded the perception of the historic space associated with the Declaration of Independence and U.S. Constitution. Philadelphians of the 1820s had revered the Assembly Room where the Continental Congress and Constitutional Convention met, and they changed the name of the State House Yard to Independence Square. For the Centennial of 1876, the historic space inside Independence Hall extended to a first-floor museum. In the 1890s, restoration efforts extended to the second floor of Independence Hall, then to the adjacent buildings on the square. Now, by the twentieth century, the square behind Independence Hall began to strike some as an insufficient setting for the nation's birthplace.

One by one, civic-minded Philadelphians began to suggest ways of cushioning Independence Hall from the city that had grown up around it. Among the first was a

34. In the blocks north of Independence Hall, the construction of the Delaware River Bridge (later renamed the Benjamin Franklin Bridge, upper right) called attention to the aging factories, warehouses, and narrow streets in the older districts of the city. The need to accommodate increased traffic over the bridge breathed new life into proposals to create an enlarged park around Independence Hall. (Courtesy of the Library Company of Philadelphia)

young man who had attended the University of Pennsylvania law school in the 1890s when its classes were held in Congress Hall. Feeling a strong personal attachment to the buildings on the square, George Erasmus Nitzsche began in 1900 to talk of an idea to create a landscaped park in place of the blocks of buildings north of Independence Hall.[6] By 1915, two architects who shared an aversion to Philadelphia's crowded business district had drawn plans for a smaller, half-block park across from the Hall. The plan by David Knickerbacker Boyd and Albert Kelsey included a reviewing square for ceremonial occasions, fountains, statues of Thomas Jefferson and Alexander Hamilton, and a red-brick colonnade with thirteen arches, symbolizing the thirteen original colonies.[7] The park idea surfaced again while Philadelphians bickered about what to do for the sesquicentennial of the Declaration of Independence. In 1922, Eva Stotes-bury, the wife of a wealthy banker, proposed that a park across from Independence Hall be created as a tribute to the Declaration's birthplace, which in her view "continues to exist as it has for many years, overshadowed and crowded in the very heart of the financial district" even though "the whole nation loves and venerates that modest building as America's sacred shrine." During the mid-1920s, prominent architects Jacques Greber and Paul Philippe Cret both drew plans for landscaping the first block north of Independence Hall.[8]

While nothing resulted immediately from these first proposals, by the 1920s, the idea of demolishing buildings to make way for a park across from Independence Hall seemed less far-fetched to Philadelphians than it had in previous decades. The City Beautiful Movement, inspired by the grand buildings and spacious courts of the World's Columbian Exposition in Chicago in 1893, had taken hold in American cities.[9] In Philadelphia, for example, the city demolished a wide swath of nineteenth-century buildings northwest of City Hall to create the Benjamin Franklin Parkway, a broad avenue in the City Beautiful tradition. Like the White City of the Chicago world's fair, the parkway was designed as a majestic civic space to be flanked by monumental Beaux Arts buildings.[10] If a parkway could be created through the densely developed region northwest of City Hall, why not a park across from Independence Hall? Between 1922 and 1926, Philadelphians also demonstrated a willingness to demolish eigh-teenth-century buildings to allow for modernization of the city. Just four blocks north of Independence Hall, buildings were cleared to make way for the Delaware River Bridge (later renamed the Benjamin Franklin Bridge), which briefly was the longest suspension bridge in the world. To accommodate the bridge approach, the Delaware River Joint Bridge Commission demolished thirty waterfront buildings—"some of the city's worst," according to the newspapers. They included a 1796 tavern reputed to be the former haunt of smugglers and pirates who plundered the ships of Stephen Girard.[11]

The new bridge approach and the resulting onrush of traffic into Philadelphia's narrowest streets drew renewed attention to the neighborhood north of Independence Hall. New plans were proposed, and old ideas were revived. A physician, whose hospi-tal had been demolished for the Benjamin Franklin Parkway, began promoting a new idea for a park connecting Independence Hall with the bridge plaza. Between widened streets to accommodate the increased traffic, Dr. Seneca Egbert proposed a "Colonial concourse" with Independence Hall at the south end and a new Pennsylvania Build-ing for state government at the north end, adjacent to the bridge plaza. Facing the concourse, he envisioned twelve harmoniously designed office buildings representing the original colonies other than Pennsylvania. Arched arcades fronting the office buildings would accommodate memorials and three sculptural pylons in the middle of the concourse would commemorate the founding of the nation, reunion after the Civil War, and American participation in the First World War.[12] In addition to Egbert's proposal, the opening of the Delaware River Bridge prompted both George Nitzsche and David Knickerbacker Boyd to revive their earlier plans for parks opposite Independence Hall and present their ideas to receptive business groups.[13] The city government endorsed a revised park plan by Jacques Greber and drafted (but later abandoned) plans for "Randolph Boulevard," a wide street for bridge traffic that would have terminated at Market Street, just one block from Independence Hall.[14]

The Great Depression stalled plans for new approaches to the Delaware River Bridge and plunged the neighborhood around Independence Hall into further decay. Vacancy and for-rent signs became increasingly common in the commercial buildings north of the Hall.[15] East of Independence Hall, interspersed with historic buildings such as Carpenters' Hall and the Second Bank of the United States, poor Philadelphians lived in slum conditions in dilapidated houses without indoor plumbing. Since 1917, the district east and south of Independence Hall had been known as the "Bloody Fifth Ward," recalling the day that a gang imported from New York by one political faction attacked and beat a rival candidate, killing a policeman who tried to intervene.[16] Votes could be purchased from the drunk or the desperate, who would accept the torn half of a dollar bill, go into the polling place to cast the desired vote, then emerge to collect the other half.[17] Like the area that had been cleared for the Delaware River Bridge, the Fifth Ward was part of the original fabric of Philadelphia, but by the 1930s it had reached a state of extreme neglect.

In this neighborhood, the New Deal and the ambition of a Philadelphia real estate agent combined to create a new vantage point for considering the future environment for Independence Hall. Among many projects aimed at creating jobs during the Depression, the Public Works Administration allocated $4 million to build a new U.S. Customs House in Philadelphia. Among the real estate agents hoping to profit from the project was Emerson C. Custis, whose office in the Merchant's Exchange Building at Third and Walnut Streets sat in the midst of the Fifth Ward. Custis, forty-six years old in 1931, was not a member of Philadelphia's college-educated, professional elite, but a former steel plant employee and son of a postal clerk.[18] Within sight of his real estate office, he had a site for the new Customs House: Second and Chestnut Street, three blocks east of Independence Hall. Representing fifty-four property owners,

Custis put together a million-dollar deal and prevailed over other sites favored by the Philadelphia business establishment.[19]

The building that rose on Custis's site between 1932 and 1934 was a seventeen-story tower which the designers, the Philadelphia architectural firm Ritter and Shay, hoped would inspire other "modernized Colonial" skyscrapers. The predominant Colonial characteristic was the red brick of the tower, which rose 295 feet above ground to a beacon that would shine over the Delaware River. The interior decor also created an early American aura with such elements as doorways topped by carved spread-eagles and flanked by Corinthian pilasters.[20] By design and location, the new Customs House defined a corridor for change in the three blocks westward toward Independence Hall. Even before construction began, Mayor Harry A. Mackey proposed a "Customs House Park" that would be created by demolishing additional structures in the interior of the block just west of the new building. The proposed park would leave office buildings facing Chestnut and Walnut Streets, but in the space between them create a landscaped link between the Merchant's Exchange (an 1832–33 building designed by William Strickland), the First and Second Banks of the United States, and Carpenters' Hall.[21] Seeing new development opportunities, Emerson Custis conceived his own plan for a shaded walkway that would extend from Independence Square to the Delaware River between Walnut and Chestnut Streets. He promoted his plan for a "Curtis Mall" (named for the publisher Cyrus Curtis) for the next fifteen years.[22]

By the mid-1930s, Philadelphians had many ideas for change and two new axes from which to consider Independence Hall. Three blocks to the east stood the new Customs House, in tall contrast to the rundown neighborhood around it. Three blocks to the north stood the approach to the Delaware River Bridge, with automobile traffic presenting a modern technological challenge to Philadelphia's narrow streets. Combined, these new features of the urban landscape focused attention on a previously unimagined L-shaped territory, with Independence Hall at the corner, the bridge at the top, and the Customs House on the right. Over time, this became the footprint for a national park.

The Nation's Birthplace in the Great Depression

During the 1920s and 1930s, responding to modernism and embracing nostalgia for a simpler past, Americans became increasingly interested in perpetuating American traditions. In an age of skyscrapers, art deco, and automobiles, they pursued connections with early American culture. On a local and national scale, they became collectors, commemorators, and preservationists.[23] Henry Ford created Greenfield Village, his collection of historic buildings in Dearborn, Michigan, with a museum housed in a replica of Independence Hall. John D. Rockefeller financed Colonial Williamsburg, an idealized re-creation of the eighteenth-century provincial capital of Virginia. In Philadelphia, in addition to restoration projects at Independence Hall, concerned citizens organized the Society for the Preservation of Landmarks to save the home of eighteenth-century mayor Samuel Powel and worked to preserve country mansions that survived in Fairmount Park.[24] At the federal level, meanwhile, the National Park Service took on new responsibility for managing and interpreting historic places.[25] With the upheavals of the Great Depression and the corresponding growth of the federal government, interest in the past fused with concern for the nation's stability and belief in federal solutions to national crises. The economic crisis, combined with festivities to commemorate the 150th anniversary of the Constitution, forged connections between individual citizens and the nation.

Focusing new attention on the famous documents associated with Independence Hall, the Great Depression caused Americans to reexamine the national principles articulated in the Declaration of Independence and the Constitution. In the 1932 presidential campaign, the Enlightenment-era ideals expressed by the Declaration of Independence became a focus for debate over the role of government. Campaigning in San Francisco, Franklin Delano Roosevelt sounded the themes of the Declaration, casting the rights to "life, liberty, and the pursuit of happiness" in economic terms and arguing for an activist federal government to assure that such ideals were accessible for all American citizens.[26] Herbert Hoover, meanwhile, argued that American liberty rested on individual freedom, unfettered by government intervention.[27] With the election of Roosevelt, the Depression-fighting programs of the New Deal raised Constitutional questions about executive power even as they brought relief to the nation's unemployed. In Roosevelt's second term, his proposal to pack the federal courts with new justices sympathetic to the New Deal once again made the Constitution a center of public debate just as the nation prepared to commemorate the document's 150th anniversary.[28]

In the crisis of the Great Depression, the federal government had a clear interest in promoting symbols of national stability, among them Independence Hall. New Deal programs helped to disseminate the image of the building, and in the process contributed to the separation of that image from the urban environment of Philadelphia. Continuing in the Georgian-revival architectural tradition, architects commissioned by the Public Works Administration added school buildings, university libraries, and

35. As a public works project during the Great Depression, WPA workers in Pittsburgh create plaster models of Independence Hall, built precisely to scale. The models were distributed to schools and public officials, perpetuating a symbol of historic stability at a time of economic uncertainty. (Courtesy of Pennsylvania State Archives, Harrisburg)

town halls reminiscent of Independence Hall to the American landscape.[29] In Pittsburgh, meanwhile, the Museum Extension Project of the Works Progress Administration hired 575 men and women to produce 2,600 plaster models of Independence Hall, each standing eighteen inches high, forty-one inches long, and weighing fifty-five pounds. The models were distributed to high schools, public officials (including President Roosevelt), and other citizens who requested them for public display.[30]

In promoting Independence Hall as a symbol of national strength, New Deal projects also demonstrated the extent to which contrasting perceptions of the landmark could be constructed. Like the plaster models manufactured in Pittsburgh, the *Story of Independence Hall* produced by the same Museum Extension Project portrayed the building apart from its urban environment in Philadelphia. Distributed to libraries from coast to coast, the booklet emphasized eighteenth-century events at the State House and the building's architectural history, mentioning its location in Philadelphia only in passing.[31] In contradiction, the Federal Writers Project's *Philadelphia: A Guide to the Nation's Birthplace* incorporated Independence Hall into a study in contrast between Philadelphia's image as a historic place and the reality of the Depression-era city. The elements of the book selected by editors—the title and the many photographs of eighteenth-century buildings—presented a tourist vision of Philadelphia as a place to revisit the past. However, the text portrayed Independence Hall and other remnants of the eighteenth century as integral, but not dominant, in the fabric of the modern city. Besides touring historic sites, the writers walked the slums along the Delaware River waterfront, observed the diverse population of immigrants who had arrived in Philadelphia in recent decades, and explored businesses, factories, and hospitals. In the neighborhood around Independence Hall, they noted the incongruity between old and new, especially the "grotesque architecture of the nineteenth century" that intruded into an area rich with pre-Revolutionary buildings. They were more tolerant of later changes: "The twentieth century, too, has thrust its bulk and ultra-modernism upon the city, without effacing the Philadelphia of yesteryear," the writers observed. "Though the shadow of skyscrapers may fall across such hallowed shrines as Independence Hall and Christ Church, the heavy hand of commerce leaves them unscathed."[32]

Publication of the WPA guide coincided with the 150th anniversary of the Constitution, a commemoration that engaged communities and federal, state, and local officials in devising ways to honor the 1787 framework of government. Amid the continuing economic crisis, American attention turned to the Constitution at a time when stability seemed crucial. The controversy over Franklin Roosevelt's court-packing plan, which consumed much of the spring and summer of 1937, also placed the Constitution at the center of public debate. Just as the federal government had assumed a greater role in American life through the New Deal, federal officials took charge of the Constitution commemoration, planning activities throughout the nation rather than organizing a single, Philadelphia-based exposition similar to the 1926 or 1876 anniversaries of the Declaration of Independence. With programs organized by a U.S. Constitution Sesquicentennial Commission headed by Congressman Sol Bloom as well as state and local commissions, the Constitution's 150th anniversary affords an opportunity to view perceptions of the relationship between Independence Hall and the Constitution from multiple perspectives.

At the national level, Congressman Bloom directed a commemoration focused not on the place where the document was drafted, but on the history and meaning of the document itself. From the view of the national commission, the Constitution anniversary was centered on Washington, not Philadelphia, with events dispersed around the United States. Americans listened to speeches about the Constitution, attended Constitution commemoration dinners, staged historical pageants, and read informative booklets about the Constitution.[33] The national poster promoting the commemoration did not feature Independence Hall, the meeting place of the Constitutional Convention, but Harold Chandler Christy's depiction of a Christy-girl Miss Liberty hovering over the signers. Bloom encouraged Americans to observe the anniversary in Washington by viewing the Constitution at the Library of Congress. Only when Philadelphians intervened was the recommended pilgrimage amended to include Independence Hall.[34]

The national commission's disinterest in Philadelphia struck not only at the city's sense of its historic importance, but also at its hopes of attracting convention business during the Constitution sesquicentennial year. As a destination for early twentieth-century conventioneers, Philadelphia pursued a dual and sometimes contradictory strategy, capitalizing on its historic attractions but also seeking to project itself as a modern city offering exciting entertainment and excellent business opportunities. The Constitution commemoration of 1937 was similarly bifurcated between a focus on Independence Hall and celebratory events elsewhere in the city. Emphasizing its historical appeal and contrasting with the national commission's publicity materials, Philadelphia's posters and programs bore images of Independence Hall and, more frequently, the popular Liberty Bell.[35] To Bloom's dismay, Philadelphia disregarded the national commission's plan to honor the Constitution beginning on September 17, 1937, the anniversary of the Constitutional Convention's agreement on the document.[36] Instead, Philadelphians started celebrating four months early, staging events throughout the period when the Constitutional Convention met in the city.

Some of Philadelphia's events, such as opening ceremonies and patriotic band concerts, took place in the confined space around Independence Hall. The local pride in Philadelphia's place in the nation's history was evident as the anniversary events began on May 14 at Independence Hall. In its coverage of the opening event, the *Philadelphia Inquirer* noted the connections between past and present as well as a dash of modern theatricality: "Mingling freely with such periwigged notables as Washington, Franklin, and James Wilson, Philadelphians yesterday lived again the stirring days of 150 years ago, when delegates from 12 seaboard colonies were gathering here to draw up rules by which a Nation might live." School teachers in costume portrayed the delegates as Mayor S. Davis Wilson struck the Liberty Bell thirteen times with a gavel cut from a Valley Forge dogwood. The Library of Congress had the Constitution itself, but Philadelphia had the first draft, framed under glass and on loan from the Historical Society of Pennsylvania for display in Independence Hall.[37]

The oratory on that rainy opening day in Philadelphia honored the Constitution, but the speakers also projected anxiety about its survival in the future and hope for extending its influence in the world. Mayor Wilson, for example, described "a world held in the grip of doubt and confusion, where new forms of Government rise and others go down, where liberties once dearly won are swept away." He encouraged Americans to rededicate themselves to the Constitution, "which fastens us securely to our moorings." The chief justice of the Pennsylvania Supreme Court, John W. Kephart, called the Constitution "a living instrument, growing with time and extending its beneficent influences into a changing world so that we, who live under it, may partake of its blessings."[38]

Despite the solemn beginning of Philadelphia's observance of the Constitution, the next four months featured far more festive and highly attended activities staged not at Independence Hall, but elsewhere around the city. In May, for example, Philadelphians attended a Historic and Patriotic Festival at Convention Hall in West Philadelphia, where they were entertained by a "historic dance presentation" and costumed reenactment of the Constitutional Convention.[39] In September, 12,000 members of the city's Mummers clubs marched up the Benjamin Franklin Parkway in historic theme costumes, and 300,000 people gathered on the banks of the Schuylkill River for a water carnival featuring speedboat races, aquatic stunts, fireworks—and a floating reenactment of the signing of the Constitution at Independence Hall.[40]

In addition to the city of Philadelphia's events, activities coordinated by a Pennsylvania Constitution Commemoration Committee injected additional perceptions of the relationship between Independence Hall and the Constitution. Like the national commission, leaders of the state commemoration promoted educational projects, such as school programs and essay contests. However, the state also had an interest in Independence Hall, which was still the Pennsylvania State House at the time of the Constitutional Convention. The state commission placed its office in Philadelphia, and its chairman was a Philadelphian, real estate developer Albert M. Greenfield. Greenfield's committee coordinated distribution of the Independence Hall models turned out by the WPA in Pittsburgh. The committee's active publicity campaign also issued a press release explaining Independence Hall's importance to the past, the present, and the Constitution: "It suggests almost mystically, that the Fathers of the Republic must

36. With the 150th anniversary commemoration of the Constitution organized in Washington, D.C., Pennsylvanians organized their own festive events at Independence Hall. Here, the building takes a back seat to the pageantry of American flags, including the large floral flag at right. The Pennsylvania state symbol for the commemoration, shown on the arch on stage, featured another symbol with resonance for new immigrants—the torch of the Statue of Liberty. (Courtesy of Pennsylvania State Archives, Harrisburg)

unhesitatingly have accepted this environment for the due expression of their epochal principles. The structure itself, noble, yet intrinsically unpretending, explicit in outline, spacious in effect, gave strength and inspiration to the patriots within its walls, as the Cradle of Liberty derived its own spiritual meaning through the splendor of human resolution."[41] The press release is notable in several respects, not least among them the apparent necessity of explaining the connection between the Constitution and the building better known for its association with the Declaration of Independence. The writer cloaks the building with mystical power, suggesting that the architectural characteristics so admired by twentieth-century Americans had inspired the

194

drafters of the Constitution, which in turn gave new meaning to the building. It was a rewriting of history as well as a reimagination of the significance of Independence Hall, made available to newspapers throughout Pennsylvania.

Although the state commission praised the noble simplicity of Independence Hall in its press release, it turned to other American symbols to promote its commemorative activities. Rather than feature the signers, as in the national Christy poster, or Independence Hall and the Liberty Bell, as in the city's literature, the state commission chose an altogether different emblem—the Statue of Liberty holding aloft a Pennsylvania keystone. Featuring a symbol with great appeal to immigrants, the state emblem perhaps had special resonance for chairman Greenfield, who had immigrated to the United States from Russia as a young child. On June 20, 1938, when Pennsylvania commemorated the day of its ratification of the Constitution, the emblem was placed on an arch over the speaker's platform behind Independence Hall. The decorations and events that day reflected a perception that the simple Georgian building of the eighteenth century was not nearly sufficient as a setting for twentieth-century celebration. For the commemoration of 1938, the platform was draped with red, white, and blue bunting, with clusters of flags and ornamental shields posted at intervals, blocking the first floor of Independence Hall from view. In an elaborate ceremony, accompanied by trumpet fanfare, women representing the thirteen original states added further decoration by constructing a ten-by-twenty-foot floral flag made from more than 25,000 red and white carnations and 15,000 blue cornflowers.[42] Like those who were thinking of creating a more spacious, more elaborate park around Independence Hall, the state program organizers seem to have found the building too small, too plain to represent such an important event as the ratification of the Constitution.

Patriots and Preservation

When Philadelphia's mayor opened the Constitution observance on May 14, 1937, by referring to a "world gripped by doubt and confusion," he had in mind events in Europe, where German advances on its European neighbors were watched closely by Philadelphians. Local businesses had commercial ties abroad. Many Philadelphians were just one or two generations removed from European homelands. Some wealthy Philadelphians whose families had been in the United States for generations frequently traveled abroad, encountering the devastating remains of the previous world war and indications that another might lie ahead.

Firsthand observation of the effects of war in Europe was a motivating factor in the founding of the Independence Hall Association, the group which ultimately achieved national park status for Independence Hall. The first president of the association, Edwin Owen Lewis, was among the Philadelphians who traveled in Europe in the years between the wars. Lewis had lived in Philadelphia since the 1890s, when he arrived to attend law school at the University of Pennsylvania during its years on Independence Square. Since that time, he had risen to social prominence as a judge in the city court of common pleas and a leader in the Sons of the American Revolution. Touring Europe in the 1920s, he saw the damage inflicted on historic buildings by the bombs of the Great War, and he thought about Philadelphia's historic landmarks. In 1937, driving in Germany, he encountered the German army moving toward Belgium. The convoy of buses, motorcycles, and bicycles forced him off the Autobahn. He watched guns and other paraphernalia of war moving west. Sitting there, watching, he became convinced he was witnessing the mobilization for the next war. Lewis returned to Philadelphia determined to do something to safeguard Philadelphia's historic buildings, including Independence Hall.[43]

At home in Philadelphia, still another plan for creating a park around Independence Hall was emerging. Roy F. Larson, a Chicago native who had moved to Philadelphia in the early 1920s to study architecture at the University of Pennsylvania, had heard about the various schemes for clearing buildings away from the doorstep of Independence Hall. He thought about them as he roamed through old Philadelphia, noticing deteriorating houses, rundown shops, and fire hazards. By the mid-1930s, he noticed that hot dog shops and hamburger joints occupied the first floor of buildings directly across from Independence Hall. At home, he began playing with ideas of his own. By 1937, he had a drawing that joined a park east of Independence Hall to the new Customs House with a mall extending north from Independence Hall to the Delaware River Bridge. For the first time, the two axes from Independence Hall joined in a plan for the future.[44]

While Larson tinkered with sketches and Lewis traveled through Europe, the changing political winds of the nation blew briefly through the neighborhood around Independence Hall. Long a Republican stronghold, in 1936 the Fifth Ward joined in popular support for Franklin Roosevelt and elected a Democrat to the state legislature. Isidor Ostroff, a young, energetic lawyer and a son of immigrants, marveled that he had been elected to represent the district that gave birth to the nation. Independence Hall was a "symbol of everything that's decent in humanity and civic life," he recalled in later years. "It was to me quite an honor that the son of an immigrant in this great

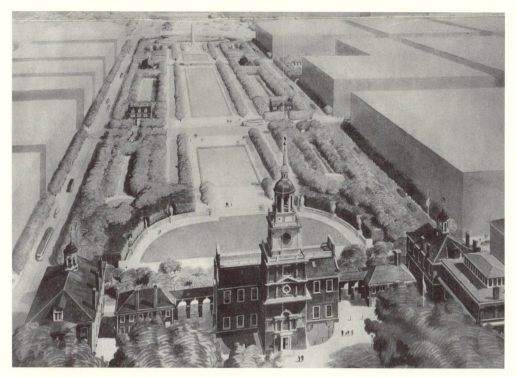

37. While World War II enhanced patriotic regard for Independence Hall, architect Roy F. Larson produced this new vision for a park reaching north from the landmark. Creation of a national park with Independence Hall at its center gained momentum during the war, promoted especially by Philadelphians with Revolutionary-era ancestors and by professional architects and city planners. (Courtesy of the Urban Archives, Temple University, Philadelphia)

country could be elected to represent what to me was the holiest district in all the United States."[45] He had a standing bet of ten dollars with anyone who could catch him walking by the shrine without tipping his hat in respect.[46]

Awed by the historic landmark, Ostroff also was dismayed by the neglect of the rest of the Fifth Ward. Something had to be done to improve housing conditions, he felt, to attract new people into the neighborhood and in the process break the Republican machine's traditional lock on the district. Ostroff served just one term in the state legislature, but he remained active in Democratic politics. In 1940, he sent Democratic committeemen door to door with petitions and an idea: a national park to encompass the historic buildings east of Independence Hall. A plan so grand as a mall north of Independence Hall seemed beyond his power, but Ostroff thought that a smaller-scale park to the east could be the opening wedge for rejuvenating the neighborhood:

It's like the farmer who found a box of shoe polish and figured that he couldn't waste the shoe polish, so he got himself a pair of shoes to shine. He put on the shoes, and those shiny shoes didn't look good unless he had a clean pair of socks, so he bought himself socks. With the shoes and socks he decided that he ought to have nice pants. Well, if he was getting pants, he might as well get a suit. He found himself a well-dressed man because he had started with a box of shoe polish. This is the way we envisioned the project would take place.[47]

Ostroff sent Congress petitions with 1,200 signatures from Fifth Ward residents who wanted a national park in their neighborhood. As a result, Congressman Leon Sachs introduced legislation calling for a national park adjacent to Independence Hall. With war looming, the legislation stalled.

The uncertainties of the Great Depression and the prospects of war produced an intensity of feeling toward Independence Hall that exceeded its identity as a historic building. The perception was evident in *Walk Proudly Here, Americans*, a guidebook published in Philadelphia in 1940.[48] The cover illustration floated Independence Hall out of its urban environment, removing from the object of veneration such distractions as economic calamity, war, and decay. Separated from the city, the Hall appeared not constructed but organic, connected by texture and composition with natural surroundings. Only the perspective of the composition gave it away. Because tall buildings stood directly across the street, the only view of Independence Hall available to the artist was diagonal and elevated, as if from a second-floor window on an opposite corner. The cover of *Walk Proudly Here, Americans* displayed two of the elements contributing to Philadelphians' view of Independence Hall's symbolic significance: patriotism and a perception of the landmark as alien in the city around it.

Walk Proudly Here, Americans was created by Raymond Pitcairn, a multimillionaire of inherited wealth, builder and benefactor of the monumental Bryn Athyn Cathedral in suburban Philadelphia.[49] The text he composed for his guide to Independence Hall spoke of the building with a fervor that went far beyond memory of the American Revolution. The building was not only the birthplace of the nation, Pitcairn wrote, not only the home of the Liberty Bell, not even simply a shrine of American patriotism. "This is the noblest most eloquent, most venerated monument to Free Government on Earth today," he wrote. "Walk proudly here, Americans, amid the symbols of your birthright! Greece in its glory, Rome in its grandeur, left no such heritage to the human spirit. The Pyramids of the Pharaohs, the Capitoline Hill of the Caesars, had no such noble significance." Independence Hall, together with Congress Hall and Old City Hall, stood for "all humanity as Earth's noblest monument to the spirit and achievements of Government by the People."[50] Communicating this perception beyond Philadelphia, Pitcairn distributed more than 90,000 copies of the sixteen-page booklet, at his own expense, to Independence Hall visitors, schools, military posts, and libraries. With satisfaction, he learned from hall guards that when Independence Hall visitors received the booklet, they often straightened their shoulders and looked around the building with pride. "Of course, that was our idea," Pitcairn commented.[51]

World War II came brutally alive for Americans with the bombing of Pearl Harbor on December 7, 1941. In swift reaction, the United States mobilized not only to fight in the Pacific and in Europe, but also to defend the home front. Within a month after Pearl Harbor, Washington issued orders for protecting the nation's cultural resources. "War may mean bombing of our coastal cities and other military objectives, with the damage to or destruction of libraries, museums, art galleries, archives, and historic buildings and monuments," the National Resources Planning Board warned.[52] Orders to plan for the worst passed quickly from Washington to Pennsylvania's Committee on Conservation of Cultural Resources, then to Philadelphia, reawakening the fears of the last world war. "The impartial explosives that rocked the stones of Buckingham Palace and the Alcazar will care no more for the red colonial bricks of Congress Hall and the Betsy Ross House should enemy planes come over the city," the *Evening Bulletin* warned. Philadelphians took action, strategically placing fire-fighting equipment in Colonial buildings. Buckets of sand stood among the fireplace accessories at the Betsy Ross House, and hoses snaked through the aisles of Christ Church. The city posted extra guards at Independence Hall, every one of them armed. "We've got to watch for cranks who might have the idea they can break down morale by pulling some stunt around Independence Square," a captain of the guards explained.[53]

Even if Independence Hall were destroyed, Philadelphians were determined to save the Liberty Bell. Although not readily apparent to visitors, the bell stood on a wheeled platform, and the guards practiced pushing the bell to safety. While some Philadelphians favored moving the bell to Fort Knox for the duration of the war, others vigorously pursued a plan to create an elevator-like shaft below the bell to serve as a bomb shelter. The Insurance Company of North America donated $30,000 to build the shelter.[54] To the dismay of Philadelphians, however, the War Production Board refused to allocate steel for the vault for more than a year. (If a cracked bell was such a treasured symbol, asked a federal official, wouldn't further damage in war enhance

38. City employees demonstrate their ability to save the Liberty Bell in the event of an attack on Independence Hall. During the war, Philadelphians also developed plans for a bomb shelter that would have allowed the Liberty Bell to be lowered into the ground to protect it from harm. (Courtesy of the Urban Archives, Temple University, Philadelphia)

its value?) Although the steel was finally approved in 1943, city officials decided that building the shelter posed too much of a risk to the structural integrity of Independence Hall. In 1944, the bomb shelter plan was abandoned.[55]

Even before the 1941 attack on Pearl Harbor, Edwin Lewis formed a committee of the Sons of the American Revolution to consider ways to safeguard landmark structures not only against the threat of war, but also against fire hazard. As chair of the committee, he appointed architect David Knickerbacker Boyd, the long-time promoter of a park across from Independence Hall. Throwing himself energetically into the task, in May 1942 Boyd invited a strategically selected assembly of government, political, business, and cultural leaders—and, of course, architects—to a meeting to consider ways to protect Philadelphia's historic buildings. By August, the group had evolved into the Independence Hall Association. Lewis was elected president, and Boyd became executive secretary. At a time of intense patriotism brought on by war, an organization with the influence and determination to make major changes around Independence Hall was born.[56]

The twenty-six incorporators of the Independence Hall Association were united in the collective memory of the events that had touched their lives.[57] They were born between 1865 and 1910, years in which America industrialized, modernized, and diversified. Most had lived in Philadelphia all of their lives; if not, they moved to Philadelphia as young adults to attend college. They shared experiences as members of the city's elite; of the twenty-four incorporators who were men, most were college-educated professionals or business executives. Most worked in professions dedicated to establishing order; they practiced law, designed buildings, worked as engineers, or managed companies. More than half of them were associated in some way with the University of Pennsylvania, as alumni, professors, or recipients of honorary degrees. Along with the two women in the group, at least five of the men traced their ancestry to the American Revolution. Within this largely homogeneous group, a vision of Independence Hall exceeding its architectural dimensions and urban environment could be formulated, validated, and promoted.[58] Competitors outside the association were coopted or cast aside. Isidor Ostroff, the Fifth Ward politician, was summoned to the judicial chambers of Edwin Lewis and persuaded that the best way to achieve a park around Independence Hall was to join the association, not fight it. George E. Nitzsche of the University of Pennsylvania, who had pondered the neighborhood across the street from Independence Hall for nearly a half century, read about the new organization in the newspaper and was pleased.[59] The real estate developer Emerson C. Custis battled for years to preserve his "Curtis Mall" idea, angry that his project was dashed by the more influential members of the Independence Hall Association.

In the year after Pearl Harbor, when the Independence Hall Association was formed, it would have been difficult to find anyone who would have objected to any means of protecting Independence Hall and the Liberty Bell. The war was uppermost in the association's concerns. Lewis, recalling his experience in Europe, declared, "It is entirely probable that some of Philadelphia's most hallowed and historically significant buildings may not exist after the war."[60] Demonstrating their view of the city as well as the dangers of war, the association also argued that an enlarged park around Independence Hall would remove fire hazards, especially in the area north of the building. The association and its supporters promoted their idea with a 1943 exhibit that recounted Independence Hall's history, they commissioned a model of Roy F. Larson's L-shaped park plan, and they lobbied city, state, and federal officials for support.

As the war progressed, ideas for the Independence Hall neighborhood grew. The park promoters envisioned not only an improved historic site, but a reinvigorated residential and business district.[61]

While fear for the building's survival provided a strong argument for preservation, especially in the midst of war, it only partly explains the association's motives for an enlarged park around Independence Hall. Increased open space would not safeguard the building from bombing; in fact, would not a large park in an otherwise urban setting make Independence Hall a more visible target? As for fire hazards, the association was justifiably worried about the risk of aging, partially occupied buildings. But while flames might leap to Independence Hall from a burning building across the street, it was not necessary to demolish three blocks of buildings to remove the hazard. Warnings about war and fire dangers helped make an enlarged park around Independence Hall a reality, but the project echoed years of desire among Philadelphians who disliked the character of the neighborhood that had grown up around the landmark during the nineteenth century—the commercial buildings, the slum dwellings, the for-rent signs that announced the abandonment of old Philadelphia. Decades of rapid change had made the past seem more precious.

During the next decade, the Independence Hall Association achieved what earlier visionaries could not: legislation to create parks extending three blocks north and three blocks east of Independence Hall. The association succeeded on two fronts.[62] At the state level, the association appealed for funding to create the long-envisioned mall stretching north from Independence Hall to the Delaware River Bridge. The proposal stalled during the war, but three months after the atomic bomb ended the war with Japan, Governor Edward M. Martin agreed to the project. His announcement reflected the enhanced status that war had conferred on Independence Hall: "It is the intention of this Administration to give the greatest historical shrine in the western hemisphere the attention and the development it so richly deserves," he said.

> The old red brick hall where the Declaration of Independence, the Articles of Confederation and the Constitution of the United States were signed, is a national shrine dear to the hearts of all Americans and to lovers of Liberty everywhere in the world.
>
> Facing Independence Hall and its adjacent buildings on the North are the ugliness and dilapidation of Old Philadelphia, with its rundown and obsolescent buildings and its fire hazards.

There has been a growing concern in Philadelphia and elsewhere for the safety and proper preservation of these priceless and irreplaceable historic buildings on Independence Square and of this hallowed ground.[63]

Martin promised $4 million for the demolition and construction necessary to create Independence Mall. According to Edwin Lewis, a deciding factor for the governor had been a visit to Philadelphia to escort a dignitary to the historic landmarks. Riding down Chestnut Street in a motorcade, in densely packed old Philadelphia, the governor had been unable to recognize Independence Hall.[64]

At the federal level, even before the end of the war, the Independence Hall Association secured a "national historic site" designation from Congress for Independence Hall. While leaving ownership of the building with the city of Philadelphia, the new designation in 1943 meant that the National Park Service would assist with preserving and interpreting the building as a historic site.[65] The designation was a step toward creation of Independence National Historical Park. In 1948, enabling legislation defined the boundaries of a national park consisting predominantly of the three blocks extending east from Independence Square to the new Customs House, including Carpenters' Hall, the First and Second Banks of the United States, and numerous other buildings.[66] In language that guided preservation and interpretation in and around Independence Hall for decades to come, Congress defined the purpose of the park as "preserving historic structures and properties associated with the American Revolution and the founding and growth of the United States."[67] Rather than a place with two centuries of history in a city or a site of conflict as well as consensus, Independence Hall was envisioned as the centerpiece of a park that would commemorate the nation's origins and steady progress.

Contours and Boundaries

By midcentury, the work of the Independence Hall Association had defined Independence Hall and the surrounding area as places for patriotic commemoration of the American Revolution. However, the efforts to create a controlled environment dedicated to past events coexisted in Philadelphia with activities that suggested a wider range of perceptions attached to Independence Hall. The building was associated with the nation's founding documents, but it also occupied a public square in an urban area where diverse people and interests existed in close proximity.[68] People with life experiences that differed from the founders of the Independence Hall Association also turned to the historic building to articulate their views of the ideals expressed in the Declaration of Independence and the Constitution. Through commemorations and demonstrations, they showed that Independence Hall was not simply a mirror of the past, but a place where the nation could be challenged and redefined. In the years after World War II, Philadelphians also learned that the meanings that they ascribed to Independence Hall had boundaries. While they imagined their eighteenth-century landmark to be an inspiration for the world, they found that the world did not always respond with expected reverence to a place representative of American ideals.

For European ethnic groups, Independence Hall was not only a place of the American Revolution, but also a stage for demonstrating that loyalty and ethnic identity could coexist. John Barry, the Irish-American naval commodore, had been honored at Independence Square since 1907, when a statue of Barry was presented to the city by the Friendly Sons of Saint Patrick.[69] Sailors regularly laid wreaths at the statue on Memorial Day. In 1937, the sesquicentennial year of the Constitution, commemoration of Barry shifted to the September anniversary of his death and Irish-Americans initiated an annual parade and program at Independence Square.[70] Similarly, Lafayette Day, long celebrated as a tribute to the Revolutionary War hero, by midcentury became a commemoration of French heritage.[71] The nationalities of Revolutionary War heroes provided European ethnic groups with an avenue for expressing loyalty as well as celebrating ethnic identity.

Although activities in Independence Square were governed by the city's ordinance limiting events to city-sponsored "patriotic meetings to celebrate some event in the history of the Nation, State, or City," city officials interpreted the ordinance as permitting ethnic commemorations related to the American Revolution.[72] During World War II, the so-called "new immigrants" from southern and eastern Europe established their own commemorations of loyalty and ethnicity at Independence Hall. For these newcomers and their children, especially, world wars and nativism called their loyalty into question, confronting them with choices between Americanization and sustaining the traditions of their homelands. Both dynamics became clear in their annual Independence Hall events, which emphasized their inclusion—but not submersion—in American society. Philadelphians of Polish descent were welcomed onto Independence Square in 1945 for the first annual Pulaski Day parade and program, celebrating Polish heritage while also commemorating the Revolutionary War hero Casimir Pulaski.[73] The annual celebration of Columbus Day, long a project of Italian-Americans, also moved to Independence Square during the 1940s.[74]

Through commemorations, ethnic Philadelphians attached new meanings to Independence Hall. On Barry Day, Pulaski Day, and Columbus Day, the landmark became not only a repository of the past, but a monument of a constantly changing present. Ethnic commemorations provided Philadelphians born outside the United States with ways of joining in the national commemorations of George Washington, the Declaration of Independence, and the Constitution, and in the patriotic fervor generated by the first and second world wars. By marching to Independence Hall, they demonstrated allegiance to the United States. However, the costumes and music of their parades also showed that Poles, Italians, and the Irish were determined to maintain and transmit ethnic customs to future generations. In later years, other groups initiated similar commemorations, following the same parade route leading to Independence Hall.[75]

During the 1940s, African Americans also instituted an annual event at Independence Hall that demonstrated patriotism while also calling attention to the still-limited civil rights of blacks. Like other African Americans, among them the labor leader A. Philip Randolph, black Philadelphians perceived a war on two fronts, for democracy at home as well as abroad. In 1942, the year that prominent white Philadelphians formed the Independence Hall Association, a leader of the city's growing African American population organized a commemoration to recognize the contradictory history of American ideals. Richard Robert Wright, Sr., nearly ninety years old, had been born in slavery and in a remarkable lifetime had gone to college in the South, presided for thirty years over a black college in Georgia, and become nationally known in education circles and Republican politics. Known to all as Major Wright, his rank as a paymaster during the Spanish-American War, he moved in 1921 to Philadelphia, where his children had already joined in the Great Migration north. In Philadelphia, he began a new career as cofounder of the Citizens and Southern Bank and Trust Company, created to serve African Americans newly arrived from the South.[76]

Like the men of the Independence Hall Association, Wright's thoughts in 1942 turned to Independence Hall, but for different reasons. While the association was interested in protecting the building, Wright was interested in preserving an idea—the idea of freedom, especially as it applied to the realities of black life in the United States. To remind Americans, black and white, of the value of freedom, he organized a movement for a national holiday to commemorate Abraham Lincoln's signing of the legislation for the Thirteenth Amendment, which ended slavery in the United States. African Americans had long commemorated emancipation on days associated with the Emancipation Proclamation or state ratifications of the Thirteenth Amendment.[77] Wright proposed a National Freedom Day on February 1, the date of Lincoln's signature. With the support of African American religious leaders and funding from the city of Philadelphia, the first Freedom Day commemoration took place in Philadelphia on February 1, 1942. That year and every year thereafter, the Freedom Day program included a wreath-laying at the Liberty Bell.[78]

Freedom Day promoted patriotism and interracial cooperation, but it also carried an implicit critique of the contradictions between American ideals and realities. President Roosevelt talked of the Four Freedoms, but in Wright's view, no American was free until all were free, including African Americans. The true Bill of Rights was not in the first ten amendments to the Constitution, he argued, but in the Emancipation Proclamation and the Reconstruction amendments that extended to African Americans the full rights of citizenship.[79] Philadelphia's African American newspaper, the *Tribune*, concurred, observing that "the Constitution itself was meaningless until the addition of the 13th Amendment."[80] As the newspaper noted, slavery had ended, but the Constitutional promise of full citizenship for African Americans was far from being implemented.

National Freedom Day reflected a collective memory different from that shared by organizers of the Independence Hall Association. Wright, the organizer, was an older man with memories extending to before the Civil War; he was an African American from the South with experiences of slavery and Jim Crow. He was prominent among a growing population of black newcomers who migrated to Philadelphia during the early decades of the twentieth century. Wright's Freedom Day commemoration recognized Independence Hall and the Liberty Bell as symbols of freedom, but shifted the origins of freedom away from the founding documents adopted in Independence Hall. Every year on February 1, beginning in 1942, Freedom Day participants gathered around the Liberty Bell to commemorate not the Declaration of Independence or the Constitution, but the Thirteenth Amendment. In the early years, a speakers' program attended by delegates from around the United States took place in Congress Hall or another building on Independence Square.[81] Launched with great fanfare in 1942 with a parade and delegates sent by governors from around the United States, the commemoration grew quieter over time. Nevertheless, the commemoration far outlived Major Wright, who died in 1947. In 1948, President Harry S. Truman fulfilled Wright's dying wish by proclaiming February 1 National Freedom Day.[82]

During the late 1940s, public debate over the legacy of the Declaration of Independence and the Constitution also provoked legal challenges to the city's restrictions on activities in Independence Square. In 1947, the Progressive Citizens of America

(PCA) obtained a court order to hold a rally in Independence Square to protest congressional investigations into suspected Communism in Hollywood. To the PCA, Independence Hall, the home of the Declaration of Independence and the Constitution, was the most fitting place in the country to defend civil liberties.[83] The city of Philadelphia denied permission for the rally, but a federal judge ruled that the demonstration did not pose a clear and present danger, and, therefore, had to be allowed. The judge commented, "It seems to me that if there is one principle that America stands for, it is that people shall have the right of freedom of speech, and that is true whether there is to be a meeting held for the thing we cherish and love or the thing we hate and despise."[84]

As a result of the judge's ruling, on a Saturday afternoon in September 1947, Joseph Myerson, the president of the Eastern Pennsylvania Chapter of the PCA, stepped onto a wooden platform behind Independence Hall. He could see 1,500 people gathered in Independence Square. Among them, World War I veterans in front of the speaker's platform shouted, "Go back to Russia!" and "Shut up, you Communist bums!" Fist-fights broke out in the crowd. Two hundred fifty police officers and detectives stood by in case of riot. Myerson tried to calm the crowd by announcing, "We will start by singing the Star Spangled Banner," but the song did not quiet the din. He began to speak. "I address you as patriotic Americans," he said. A spectator climbed onto the platform, shouting, "Stop it! Stop it! Back to Russia!" Police took the man away, but he soon returned. "These Communists won't make me shut up," the spectator declared.[85]

For that Saturday, Independence Square was once again contested ground. A month later, when opponents of military conscription similarly challenged the city's right to prohibit a public demonstration, another federal judge ruled the city's ordinance unconstitutional.[86] In response, the city adhered to the ruling that restricting the use of Independence Hall to patriotic activities was unconstitutional, but achieved nearly the same effect with a new ordinance that allowed activities on the square only on sixteen specified days of the year. The list of days included an unsurprising series of national holidays and anniversaries of wartime victories—among them Independence Day, Washington's Birthday, Lincoln's Birthday, Memorial Day, Flag Day, Armistice Day, I Am an American Day, Constitution Day, V-E Day, and V-J Day. However, the city also officially recognized the ethnic commemorations of Revolutionary War heroes and the African American observance of Freedom Day.[87]

While activities in and around Independence Hall attached a variety of meanings associated with the historic landmark, in the years after World War II, Philadelphians learned that perceptions of the building had geographic dimensions as well. During

39. A scuffle breaks out in Independence Square during a rally by the Progressive Citizens of America, an event in 1947 which challenged the city's longstanding ordinance restricting use of the square to patriotic events approved by local officials. (Associated Press photograph, courtesy of the Urban Archives, Temple University, Philadelphia)

the years of war and economic hardship, Philadelphians had developed an intensified sense of Independence Hall as a symbol of American ideals to be protected at all costs. They had persuaded the state and federal governments to endorse this perception and embed it in both the law and landscape by providing funds to create Independence Mall and the Independence National Historical Park. But how widespread was their view of Independence Hall? Was it shared by the world? Was it even shared within the nation? Between 1945 and 1947, Philadelphians encountered the boundaries of their perceptions of Independence Hall as they competed with other American cities to become the permanent headquarters of the new United Nations.

On March 5, 1945, Philadelphians who picked up the *Philadelphia Record* saw a front-page headline: "Philadelphia—Home of the United Nations." Next to a picture of the tower of Independence Hall, in a crisp editorial, publisher J. David Stern argued: "The City of Brotherly Love should be the permanent home of the United Nations. Independence Hall, recognized throughout the world as the birthplace of political liberty and democracy, is the shrine around which the United Nations buildings should be grouped." Stern harbored no great love for Philadelphia, which seemed to him to be a monotonous collection of little red-brick houses, "repeated over and over again until it got on one's nerves like a stuck phonograph."[88] But Stern thought Independence Hall was beautiful.[89] The birthplace of the United States, he argued, would be an inspiration for the new international peace organization of the postwar world.[90] He was so pleased with the idea that he fired it off in a letter to President Roosevelt.[91]

Every day for two weeks after Stern's initial editorial about the U.N., and frequently thereafter, the *Record* carried front-page stories announcing new and powerful supporters for the idea that Philadelphia should be the "Peace Capital of the World." A *Record* reporter solicited the favorable opinions of the governor of Pennsylvania, U.S. congressmen, and the leaders of the project to create a mall in front of Independence Hall. Business and labor groups voiced their support, and the state legislature passed a resolution saying that "Philadelphia, the first capital of the United States, is ideologically and historically suited to become the World Capital of Peace." Philadelphia Mayor Bernard Samuel appointed a committee of prominent citizens to get the job done. Although other Philadelphia newspapers ignored their rival's campaign, Mayor Samuel promoted Philadelphia on the CBS radio network, whose local affiliate was owned by Stern. "We Philadelphians contend that there is no other spot on earth which would be so widely recognized and so readily accepted by men of good will throughout the world as Independence Hall in the City of Brotherly Love," Samuel said during a CBS news program.[92]

Even in Philadelphia, enthusiasm for the *Record*'s proposal was not universal, however. In the *Record*'s own letters to the editor, a few citizens questioned whether Philadelphia was a suitable "Capital of the World." Aside from Independence Hall, the city had few advantages, the letter writers said. "Had you thought of the drawbacks?" one writer asked. "We have bad water, a smelly river, dirty streets, no airport, badly run liquor stores, a wage tax, no snow clearance, inadequate police and a very poor climate. What have you against peace?" Another asked, "How do you reconcile your audacious bid for 'World Capital, Pa.' with the hundreds of pictures The Record has run of the unbelievably filthy slums in Philadelphia, pictures of broken water mains, broken fire hydrants and trash piled high?"[93]

Nevertheless, when the United Nations gathered in San Francisco in May 1945 to draft its charter, delegates were greeted by proclamations from Philadelphia illustrated by a drawing of Independence Hall and extolling the city's heritage as the "City of Brotherly Love" and the "Cradle of Liberty."[94] The proclamations were followed by formal engraved invitations and a promotional booklet featuring a glossy photograph of the Liberty Bell on its cover and inside photographs of Colonial buildings as well as cultural and recreational attractions. Repeatedly, the booklet built upon the phrase "We the People," extending it to encompass not just Philadelphia, not just the United States, but all the citizens of the world. Twenty-one pages in the back of the booklet displayed endorsements of Philadelphia from prominent citizens around the country, including governors of other states.[95]

As the Philadelphians soon learned, the inspiration that might be derived from Independence Hall or the heritage of "Brotherly Love" was not a priority for U.N. delegates. In September 1945, meeting in London, the U.N. Preparatory Commission established its criteria for the headquarters site. The Commission wanted a place with good worldwide communications, accessibility for delegates traveling from around the world, sufficient printing facilities, and favorable public opinion toward the U.N. The organization needed a hall that would accommodate six hundred delegates, plus committee rooms and accommodations for the press and support staff. The priorities did not include seeking an inspirational setting.[96]

Philadelphians persisted in their campaign to attract the United Nations for nearly two years, and came close to winning the headquarters in 1946 with an offer of an enlarged site on the outskirts of the city.[97] In the process, they learned that Independence Hall was not a sufficient lure for other countries. Even delegates who desired a location associated with freedom and democracy did not necessarily think first of Philadelphia. For some, these were ideals associated more generally with the United States rather than with such a specific location as Independence Hall. Others felt that freedom was embodied more by newer cities. "San Francisco is a city which breathes the very spirit of freedom," a delegate from Australia said. "It is a city of progress, it looks with courage and confidence to the future."[98] The presence of Independence Hall did not win automatic support from other regions of the United States, many of which offered their own proposals for the headquarters.[99] Even within the state of Pennsylvania, when it seemed that Philadelphia would not be selected, other communities were ready with bids of their own.[100] Such responses suggest that Independence Hall as a symbol with worldwide significance was a Philadelphia-based conception in these years after World War II, communicated to others but not necessarily shared.

Buildings may be perceived as treasures in any number of ways—for their association with historic events, for their architectural characteristics, or for their connection to individual experience. All of these played a part in attitudes toward Independence Hall during the first half of the twentieth century. Independence Hall was a place associat-ed with the Declaration of Independence and the Constitution, a Georgian building surviving in the modern city, and a tie to individual experience for Philadelphians who participated in commemorative events, worked in nearby offices, or perhaps attended law school when the University of Pennsylvania held classes in Congress Hall. While the building survived from the eighteenth century, it played a part in the lives of twen-tieth-century Americans, particularly Philadelphians who lived or worked in close proximity.

Such multiple meanings suggest that we proceed cautiously when considering buildings designated as historic for very specific reasons, even when those reasons seem as self-evident as the relationship between Independence Hall and the founding of the United States. The sociological concept of collective memory—that is, the idea that memories are constructed among groups of people living at the same time, in the same place—helps in identifying the origins and motivations that lead to a building's official recognition as historic.[101] Because of the work of the Independence Hall Asso-ciation, Independence Hall became identified in federal law as significant for its asso-ciation with the American Revolution. The national park that would grow around the building was dedicated to the birth and growth of the nation, suggesting collective progress and achievement. These views of Independence Hall are best understood as the perceptions of a group of like-minded, homogeneous Philadelphians. If we look beyond this group—to events such as National Freedom Day, ethnic parades, the protest of the Progressive Citizens of America, or the response to Philadelphia's cam-paign to host the United Nations—we see contours and boundaries in the dominant perception. This is not to suggest that the association between Independence Hall and the American Revolution should be downplayed or ignored, but to caution that per-ceptions of the building were more complex than the federal legislation of 1948 or subsequent restorations and interpretations reveal.

The relation between collective memory and buildings is important, because structures tend to have longer life spans than people. From a sociological perspective, collective memory persists only as long as the individuals in the group survive. How-ever, buildings allow that group's collective memory to be encapsulated and commu-nicated to the future.[102] The Independence Hall Association's perception of their treasured landmark, translated into federal law and applied in the future management of the building, long outlived the original members of the group. In effect, buildings can function as conduits between collective memory (bounded by group experience) and public memory (the more widely shared perception of the past). The choices made by interest groups or preservationists dictate the versions of history that future visitors to buildings will absorb. For decades after the incorporation of the Independence Hall Association, visitors to Independence Hall would learn about the national, political, late eighteenth-century history that Edwin Lewis and his colleagues regarded with great reverence.

Regard for buildings also develops in relation to the surrounding environment. Certainly, Independence Hall had associations with eighteenth-century events and individuals highly significant in the nation's history. However, if we view the building in the broad context of its history in an American city, interacting with the twentieth century as well as representing the years that had gone before, we see other factors contributing to its evolution as a historic place. The built environment surrounding the historic structure played a role, presenting a sharp contrast between the modern city and the building that survived from a distant but treasured past.[103] The contrast led individuals to imagine a mall and a park in the midst of an urban environment that resembled neither. New features in the urban landscape, such as the Benjamin Franklin Bridge and the U.S. Customs House, created new vantage points from which to consider Independence Hall and other older buildings. By midcentury, Independence Hall was officially designated as historic because of its role in the American Revolution and the growth of the nation, but the designation had much to do with the city of Philadelphia as it grew in the twentieth century.

Philadelphians had devoted enormous effort to the care of Independence Hall, from the time of its construction in the 1730s through the twentieth century. It had been a place of the city as well as a place of the nation. During the 1940s, the Independence Hall Association made sure that the building's place in the nation's history would be secured by recognition as an official national historic site and as the anchor of a national park. Ironically, this effort by local citizens to protect their cherished landmark set the stage for separating Independence Hall from the city as never before. During the second half of the twentieth century, demolition of nineteenth-century buildings to create Independence Mall and Independence National Historical Park separated Independence Hall from the urban fabric of Philadelphia, as the individuals who had envisioned these projects intended. In the process, though, Independence Hall became a protectorate of the federal government rather than local citizens. With its historical significance fixed by federal law, the city's treasure became the nation's treasure, a time capsule of the American Revolution and the growth of the United States.

Chapter 8

ANCHOR

A Secure Past for Cold War America

Here is a tableau of 1950s America: The Powell family of Clinton, Missouri, has come to Philadelphia on a tour of historic sites of the eastern seaboard. In this summer of 1954—a time of Cold War tension and the quest for suburban security, in a year when television broadcast Senator Joseph McCarthy's hunt for Communist spies as well as *The Adventures of Ozzie and Harriet*—the Powells have dedicated their vacation to American history. For the benefit of their three boys' education, they have come to Independence Hall to see the Liberty Bell and to stand in the chamber that resonates with the timeless, bedrock principles of the United States. But their vacation also has taken an unexpected turn. In Independence Square, a Philadelphia newspaper has singled them out as typical of the tourists who in 1954 were pushing sightseeing at Independence Hall to an all-time record of more than one million visitors per year. And so the Powells stand, posed behind Independence Hall while eleven-year-old Rex Powell takes his own snapshot of the family visiting the historic landmark. Like so many of the families pictured in popular magazines of the decade, the Powells appeared the next day in the *Philadelphia Evening Bulletin* as an image of the wholesome, nuclear family which seemed to epitomize the American way of life during these potentially dangerous times.[1]

The tableau created for the *Evening Bulletin* also introduces Independence Hall as it was being redefined by and for the Cold War era. The building behind the Powell family shows no evidence of being anything other than an eighteenth-century treasure transmitted whole from the nation's founders to the tourists of the twentieth century. Like the school textbooks and histories being written by scholars of the 1950s, the park around Independence Hall represented a firm consensus that the nation's principles

40. During the 1950s, Independence Hall became a magnet for tourism, as shown here in a photograph created in 1954 for the *Philadelphia Evening Bulletin*. Parents passing the lessons of American history on to their children and patriotic pageantry converged at Independence Hall in a powerful expression of pride in the American past during the Cold War era. (Associated Press photograph, courtesy of the Urban Archives, Temple University, Philadelphia)

enunciated in 1776 and 1787 could be counted upon to shape and sustain the American national character.[2] In the Cold War era, these principles formed a vital line of defense against the spread of Communism. At historic sites such as Independence Hall, crucial memories of the nation's past could be presented for mass consumption, offering a patriotic parallel to Americans' postwar appetites for changing fashions or the latest-model automobiles. A brief visit to a historic place allowed Americans to make the nation's history part of their own experience, bolstering their patriotism in a merger of historical and individual memory. The memory was not ephemeral or illusory, but experienced as a material reality which could be possessed and perpetuated in the form of a snapshot, a postcard, or a souvenir.[3]

The photograph of the Powell family is also notable for what it does not show: the enormous effort required to create the tourist experience and the greater variety of activities that enveloped Independence Hall in the concerns of Americans during the height of the Cold War. In the photograph, we do not see bulldozers clearing away nineteenth-century buildings from blocks adjacent to Independence Hall in order to present an unobstructed view of the eighteenth-century past. We do not see the teams of National Park Service historians and restoration architects toiling to rehabilitate Independence Hall and present it to the public as a national shrine. Nor, in this carefully posed photograph, do we see the nearly daily ebb and flow of commemorative activity that reflected the tensions of the Cold War era. For all the effort devoted to creating a place where a clarified narrative of the American past could be consumed, Independence Hall during the 1950s became a place where tourism, preservation, and pageantry converged in a powerful expression of patriotism and defense against contemporary enemies.[4]

Consensus Landscape: Obscuring the Nineteenth Century

We should pause at the start of the 1950s and survey an urban landscape about to disappear. In 1950, the three blocks north of Independence Hall are crowded with five- and six-story warehouses, factories, stores, and office buildings, most of them constructed during the commercial expansion of the nineteenth century and now showing their age. The three blocks east of Independence Hall are dotted with remarkable structures from the nation's history, such as Carpenters' Hall and the First and Second Banks of the United States, surrounded by later landmarks of commercial enterprise as well as ramshackle dwellings lurking in shadowed alleys. We should look closely because history is about to be rewritten by bulldozers. In these blocks radiating from

Independence Hall, some buildings will be viewed as historic and, therefore, spared. The rest will be treated as buildings without history, deserving demolition. A predominantly eighteenth-century history will be protected, while a predominantly nineteenth-century history will be swept away. Buildings with a clear association with national history will survive while the architectural fabric of city life will be eliminated. The result? An architectural impression that the significant events of the nation's history occurred during the era of the American Revolution, a time defined by crisply maintained, stately buildings, ornamental plazas, and carefully tended lawns.

If an artifact could be put on display to represent this era of changing landscape around Independence Hall, perhaps it would be the ceremonial crowbar wielded by Edwin O. Lewis, the Philadelphia judge who had led the movement to create expanded parks around Independence Hall. On May 5, 1951, Lewis applied the first ceremonial crowbar to the row of nineteenth-century commercial buildings across Chestnut Street from Independence Hall.[5] For the next eight years, stalled periodically to wait for state funding or to resolve design issues, wrecking machinery tore into nineteenth-century buildings and gradually revealed Independence Hall to more distant vistas. The result was Independence Mall State Park, reaching from Chestnut Street northward for three blocks to the Benjamin Franklin Bridge. On April 27, 1954, in the block directly east of Independence Hall, Lewis raised a ceremonial crowbar once again to start razing the ten-story Drexel Building, a relic of the city's nineteenth-century financiers. In its place, the American Philosophical Society would build a reconstruction of a 1790 landmark, Library Hall.[6] To the east, in the blocks designated as Independence National Historical Park, the federal government began clearing away "nonhistoric" buildings as if they were weeds in an ornamental garden.

By starting the demolition process with ceremony, the promoters of expanded parks around Independence Hall defined the destruction of the nineteenth-century urban landscape as an act of triumph. Viewed in retrospect, the sorting of "historic" from "nonhistoric" buildings also shows the significance of destruction as well as preservation in constructing perceptions of the past.[7] The buildings in the blocks north and east of Independence Hall were not buildings without history—they were buildings where people had worked, lived, interacted, and contributed to the "growth of the nation" that was to be commemorated by Independence National Historical Park. Even at the time of their destruction, some of the buildings were defended as architectural landmarks, and a later generation surely would have regarded others as significant to the social or industrial history of a nineteenth-century city. But their destruction made sense in the context of postwar America. Reflecting the tension of the early Cold War years, acting Secretary of the Interior Oscar L. Chapman supported a national park adjoining Independence Hall as "particularly appropriate for the Nation . . . at the present time when the ideals of our democratic government and way of life are being tested in a world theater."[8] In agreement, a congressional committee in 1948 had noted that the deteriorating, nineteenth-century neighborhood around Independence Hall detracted from its effectiveness as a symbol of American ideals: "The blanket of urbanization which covers this part of the old city of Philadelphia and the expansion of the city have so crowded the area with unsightly or large buildings that they have obscured the early history surrounding the writing of the Declaration of Independence and the Constitution and have diluted the richest historical association it is possible for an American citizen to experience."[9] Like the "consensus school" of American history-writing that emerged in the years after the Second World War, the envisioned parks would emphasize consensus and continuity over conflict and change. When the nineteenth-century buildings were in place, the varying states of structural deterioration in the blocks near Independence Hall offered unmistakable evidence that the nation had changed considerably since 1776, not necessarily for the better. Without the nineteenth-century buildings, an illusion of eighteenth-century stability and continuity could be sustained. "It should be possible for the future visitor to approach Independence Hall through harmonious surroundings which would provide a fresh appreciation for its central place in history," the congressional report predicted.[10]

The creation of enlarged parks around Independence Hall also corresponded with the city of Philadelphia's program of urban renewal during the 1950s. Led by reform mayors who overthrew the Republican organization beginning in 1951 and an energetic team of young city planners, Philadelphia like other older American cities embarked on a widespread remaking of its urban core.[11] New high-rise office buildings replaced a "Chinese Wall" of elevated railroad tracks west of City Hall. Public housing towers replaced acres of deteriorated rowhouses. While not as ideologically driven as the government officials involved in authorizing parks around Independence Hall, Philadelphia's professional city planners advocated a philosophy of urban redevelopment that melded in some ways with the prevailing mood of the nation. Led by Edmund N. Bacon, executive director of the City Planning Commission from 1949 to 1970, the planners sought sweeping change in the city's landscape, but they also strived to create environments of "harmony" and "continuity." Furthermore, Bacon advocated a planning process based on democratic exchange between planners and citizens—a process that might invite disagreement but would ultimately lead to consensus.[12]

In a decade in which the federal government was funding wholesale demolition of residential areas in the name of urban renewal, demolishing the predominantly commercial area north of Independence Hall made eminent sense as a method for improving the city as well as protecting a national landmark. Philadelphia's city planners also viewed the expanded parks as an opening wedge for wider redevelopment, especially in the residential blocks south of Independence Hall where African Americans and Eastern European Jews lived in crowded courtyards and deteriorating rowhouses, interspersed among warehouses and factories. Planners envisioned an urban renewal project that would combine demolition, renovation, and historically sensitive new construction, creating a museum-like community recalling earlier days. "Handled in a sensible way, this area could give Philadelphia something that would far outshine Williamsburg and would be much more significant historically," Bacon predicted in 1955.[13]

Demolition associated with Independence Hall began with the blocks north of the landmark. Prior to plans for an expanded park, there would have been little reason to regard the three blocks that became Independence Mall as a district with a historical or geographic character distinct from the rest of old Philadelphia. For that reason, they were not treated as a defined historical district in the early chapters of this book. Like the other blocks of the original city grid, these blocks developed within the steady tide of construction and population growth that had swept across Philadelphia from east to west since the days of William Penn. The planned Independence Mall, extending south to north, would run crosscurrent to the city's historical development. In making such an extreme change in the urban environment, local park boosters and state officials perceived little of historic value. But the blocks that became Independence Mall did have a history. It was a history submerged in the workaday life of one of the nation's oldest cities, never written down or commemorated but representing a cross-section of the city's economic development from neighborhoods of artisans in the eighteenth century, to the light manufacturing district of the nineteenth century, to the emerging tourist landscape of the 1950s.

Many of the buildings that faced demolition for Independence Mall were from the generation of nineteenth-century construction that replaced earlier buildings destroyed by fire in 1851 and 1855.[14] For twentieth-century proponents of the mall, these buildings were eyesores, described in 1951 by Professor William E. Lingelbach of the University of Pennsylvania as an "incongruous mixture of cheap buildings on the one hand, and heavy pseudo-Roman architecture on the other, all so strikingly out of accord with the beauty and simplicity of the Colonial group of buildings across the street on Independence Square."[15] But in the second half of the nineteenth century, the buildings later razed for the mall represented the city's commercial success. The blocks north of Independence Hall constituted a busy retail and manufacturing district, attracting out-of-town merchants who filled the city's hotels and exporting products around the world. *The Industries of Pennsylvania*, a directory published in 1881, described with pride a wide range of light manufacturing within the boundaries of the future Independence Mall. Exemplifying the manufacturing diversity of late nineteenth-century cities, there were makers and wholesalers of goods ranging from undertakers' supplies, hardware, and window shades to fishing tackle, shoes, and false teeth. The enterprises included individual proprietors, such as a wig and toupee-maker across the street from Independence Hall who advertised herself as a "Premier Artiste in Hair," as well as factories with hundreds of employees, among them the shirt manufacturer L & S Sternberger, which employed six hundred people in a five-story building at 503 Market Street, with piece-work sent out to four hundred more. Sternberger's also operated as a retailer on Market Street, which remained a prime shopping thoroughfare.[16]

This was the district that fell into decline through the early decades of the twentieth century, particularly during the Great Depression. As demolition plans emerged during the late 1940s, retailers fronting on Market Street resisted, arguing that the three-block mall that would consume their businesses was out of scale with the comparatively diminutive landmark at its south end. However, their protests found little sympathy in a hearings process presided over by Edwin Lewis, then chair of the federally created Philadelphia National Shrines Park Commission.[17] By 1959, when the state of Pennsylvania's bulldozers finished work on Independence Mall, only one building remained—the Free Quaker Meeting House, built in 1783 by Quakers who had been read out of the Society of Friends for participating in the American Revolution. Clearly supporting the goal of creating an environment harmonious with Independence Hall, the meeting house had to be moved slightly westward to accommodate a widening of Fifth Street, but it was preserved. Since 1836, when it ceased to be a weekly meeting house, the building had changed with its surroundings, housing an apprentice's library in the mid-nineteenth century and later being put to commercial use. With the creation of Independence Mall, like other buildings that had stood in Philadelphia since the time of the American Revolution, the Free Quaker Meeting House shed the remnants of its nineteenth-century history and functioned anew as a patriotic museum.[18]

The prominent Philadelphia promoters of Independence Mall had envisioned a

41. With buildings cleared from the blocks north of Independence Hall, the *Philadelphia Evening Bulletin* found it necessary to insert an arrow into this photograph to help readers find the landmark building in its new, unfamiliar surroundings. (Courtesy of the Urban Archives, Temple University, Philadelphia)

dignified, regulated environment that would guard the city's jewel, Independence Hall. But as the new park developed with lawns, plazas, and ornamental fountains, it presented an unanticipated challenge that called attention to the continuing relationship between the mall and the city around it. The open space created an avenue between Independence Hall and Philadelphia's tenderloin district, a skid row of taverns, brothels, and single-room-occupancy hotels that bordered the northernmost reaches of the mall. The new walkways, benches, and fountains invited migration from the tenderloin. "For nearly a generation, Philadelphia civic leaders and patriotic groups worked diligently to have Independence Hall enshrined in a setting worthy of the nation's birthplace . . . So what happens?" the *Philadelphia Inquirer* asked rhetorically in 1955. "Even before the finishing touches have been put on the project, the Square and the Mall have become a haven for vagabonds and drunks."[19]

In the summer of 1955, Philadelphia police began sweeps through the mall area to collar "undesirables," arresting thirty-five "vagrants, drunks, and panhandlers." A city magistrate warned the offenders that he was going to "break up this bottle gang if it takes all year," and sentenced five of the men to three months in the House of Correction for public intoxication.[20] It took a letter writer to the *Evening Bulletin* to point out the irony of police sweeps through the new front lawn of Independence Hall: "I realize that the privileged classes who leave their summer and winter resorts to visit the Shrine of Liberty are very much annoyed by these underprivileged begging for a handout. They certainly have my sympathy. Yet I cannot help but feel with those 'evil-breathed' disreputables, whose freedom is being taken away from them by a short-sighted magistrate for no commission of crime, except squatting on a park bench instead of a beach chair somewhere at a summer resort."[21] Independence Mall had created a buffer between Independence Hall and the urban environment, but the new park remained embedded in a city that would continue to be part of its history.

In the blocks east of Independence Hall, the National Park Service faced challenges that differed from the state's Independence Mall project to the north. The new national park was created not just to provide a vista toward Independence Hall, but to safeguard historic structures and make them accessible to the public. The Park Service representatives who arrived in Philadelphia during the late 1940s and early 1950s faced the challenge of creating a visitor experience in a park that did not yet exist. For the new federal administrators, it was essential to create a distinction between the unruly, unregulated urban environment and the historic sites that tourists wanted to see. "The Independence National Historical Park Project lies in the center of a highly congested district of Downtown Philadelphia," the project's chief historian observed in 1952. "All the intrusions, distractions, and noise inherent in such a district are present here, militating against a 'historic atmosphere.' "[22] In 1954, park administrators noted that there was still no identifiable "park," leaving visitors confused. "The average visitor . . . comes simply to 'Independence Hall to see the Liberty Bell.' . . . He arrives in the area without knowing it; there are no controlled entry stations or points to inform him; there are no markers or other facilities to direct him."[23] For the benefit of tourists, the Park Service installed an information center and sales shop in the west wing of Independence Hall.

The members of the Independence Hall Association who secured state and federal support for an enlarged park around Independence Hall valued the building for its Revolutionary-era history, and through their influence, that period in history had been designated by federal law as the reason for creating Independence National Historical Park.[24] Acting under that law, the National Park Service defined the historic significance that would be communicated to the public in and around Independence Hall: "The general theme of development is to interpret the story of independence and the establishment and early development of the United States in the period from 1774 to

1800, and to restore, reconstruct and preserve structures and landscape features necessary and appropriate for this interpretation. Any other factors shall be incidental to and should not conflict or intrude upon this basic theme."[25] This statement of interpretation guided the history that would be remembered and, by omission, the history that would be forgotten at Independence Hall and within the adjacent national park. The selected periodization, 1774 to 1800, beginning with the First Continental Congress and ending with the removal of the nation's capital from Philadelphia, defined the park as a place for communicating the early political history of the nation. "Other factors"—which might have encompassed social history, state and local history, or the longer life of Independence Hall as a place of civic engagement —were subordinated to the story of establishing and developing the nation. The selected period for interpretation encompassed the Declaration of Independence, the drafting of the Constitution, and the years when federal officeholders occupied Congress Hall. They were singular, significant events in United States history and natural choices for defining the significance of Independence Hall. Furthermore, the national mood of the country during the 1940s and 1950s and the building's appearance supported the Park Service's interpretive choices. In the aftermath of World War II and with the emergence of the Cold War, Americans were concerned with preserving such national ideals as freedom and democracy. Surviving in Philadelphia over the centuries, Independence Hall was a material reminder of the nation's endurance.

The interpretive plan guided the remaking of the urban landscape in the three blocks east of Independence Hall. While these blocks included such notable structures as Carpenters' Hall, where the First Continental Congress met in 1774, a much longer and broader history remained visible in the streets and structures between Chestnut and Walnut Streets, from Second to Fifth Streets. Chestnut Street had been the banking center of the United States before losing prominence to Wall Street in the early nineteenth century; by the mid-twentieth century it remained fronted by substantial banks and insurance company buildings.[26] Walnut Street had homes associated with notable individuals, such as Bishop William White and Dolley Todd (later Dolley Madison), but these were interspersed with buildings of later vintage or little historical pedigree. In these densely developed blocks, some preservation choices were obvious and indeed dictated by the park's enabling legislation. But while the state's demolition proceeded north of Independence Hall during the early 1950s, a prolonged debate ensued among Park Service professionals over what should be preserved and what should be demolished in the creation of Independence National Historical Park.

Particularly at issue in the blocks east of Independence Hall were nineteenth-century buildings regarded by architects, both inside and outside the National Park Service, as historically significant innovations in architecture. No one argued for demolition of the Second Bank of the United States (1818–24) or the Merchant's Exchange (1832–33), both neoclassical buildings designed by the notable architect William Strickland, even though they lay beyond the park's interpretive emphasis on the eighteenth century. The Second Bank, focus of the Andrew Jackson–Nicholas Biddle bank war of the 1820s and 1830s, had long been in federal hands, serving as a U.S. Customs House until the 1930s, when it was placed under protection of the Department of the Interior. The Merchant's Exchange, located at the east end of the designated park space, seemed a logical possibility for a visitors' center. However, other structures vigorously defended by architects, including Charles E. Peterson of the National Park Service, were lost to the quest for a park-like ambiance dedicated to the political history of the eighteenth century. Federal demolition claimed the 1875 Guarantee Trust Building by Frank Furness; the Jayne Building, a prototypical skyscraper designed by William Johnston in 1849; and the first home of the Penn Mutual Insurance Company, one of the country's first cast-iron buildings, designed by G. P. Cummings in 1850.[27] In the Cold War climate of the 1950s, presenting an unobstructed view of the nation's origins prevailed over arguments to preserve reminders of intervening years.

Beyond the limits of the new state and federal parks, the influence of Independence Hall extended into the city of Philadelphia's efforts at urban redevelopment. In the blocks south of the new Independence National Historical Park, where deteriorating eighteenth- and nineteenth-century rowhouses had been converted into warehouses and carved into apartments for the poor, planners envisioned a restored, historic ambiance that would attract affluent professionals to the central city. Like the other sections of Philadelphia so radically transformed during the 1950s, these blocks had a history as old as the city. William Penn originally granted the land to a merchants group, the Free Society of Traders. Although the society failed, its association with the area was revived and embedded in the landscape by the 1950s city planners who renamed the redevelopment area "Society Hill." Long-time Philadelphians knew the district better as the city's notorious Fifth Ward, impoverished and exploited by corrupt politicians. By the 1950s, the area retained a remnant of the city's oldest African American neighborhood near the Mother Bethel A.M.E. Church as well as a significant population of Jewish residents, many of them aged Eastern European immigrants who had created a new Jewish quarter in Philadelphia at the turn of the century. The district boasted some of the city's most historic eighteenth-century and nineteenth-century churches, but these contrasted sharply with numerous small factories and the city's odorous and outmoded Food Distribution Center.[28]

While the state and federal governments concerned themselves with clearing away an urban landscape in order to isolate historic buildings of the eighteenth century, Philadelphia city planners sought to revise and revive Society Hill as a viable city neighborhood. Although motivated by desires to clean up the city and counteract the flight of affluent residents to the suburbs, the Society Hill plan, like the park projects, reflected Cold War era concerns. Restoring a historic, residential ambiance in Society Hill would benefit not only the city but also the nation, Philadelphia architect G. Edwin Brumbaugh argued in 1957 in the *Journal of the American Institute of Architects*:

> Not all history is military history, and old houses are pre-eminently qualified to tell the rest of the story of America, a story that desperately needs to be told—a story of courage and fortitude, of industry and resourcefulness, faith in God and love of liberty. These are things we dare not forget. They are as important in the fabric of the nation today as they were when our forefathers cleared the wilderness. And if our history is worth recalling, because of the lessons it can teach, never forget that old houses are graphic history, like the illustrations in a book, sometimes more readable than the text.[29]

In a decade when many Americans sought security by embracing domesticity, the Society Hill project imagined a domestic landscape linked to the nation's history by surviving rowhouses and proximity to Independence Hall. It would be a neighborhood offering the tranquility and homogeneity of the suburbs, but a cache of quaintness adjacent to a national park. It might be perceived as a "text," as Brumbaugh suggested, but it would be an edited text that emphasized domestic tranquility.

Urban redevelopment raised questions that the nation's founders would have recognized—issues such as property rights and balance between individual liberty and the collective needs of community. Society Hill houses targeted for renovation were purchased by the city's Redevelopment Authority, then sold to private owners who were required to rehabilitate the buildings to standards set by the authority. The original owners were offered the opportunity to repurchase their property, but few could afford the renovation costs. Many gladly accepted the prices paid by the Redevelopment Authority. However, some who faced displacement from Society Hill resisted, invoking

American principles as well as family history as they resisted the city's plans. Tekla Waneliska, a Polish immigrant who had lived at 410 Addison Street for thirty-one years, tearfully but futilely pleaded with the Redevelopment Authority to allow her to stay. A neighbor, Mildred Sobel, said that she and her husband had just finished paying off their mortgage, but the redevelopment project was forcing them to give up their home. "I think it is unconstitutional that we have to put our children in a project and have them live like sardines," she said.[30]

Although the Society Hill project involved preservation more than demolition, the resulting upscale, homogeneous neighborhood obscured the area's nineteenth-century social history. More than the state and national park projects, the area retained an architectural history spanning from the eighteenth century to the twentieth, from Georgian survivals to newly constructed, modern twentieth-century townhouses. Luxury high-rise apartment towers sprouted on the former site of the Food Distribution Center, towering over neat streets of rehabilitated rowhouses and new gated communities. Society Hill became, as its planners intended, a residential haven for prosperous Philadelphians. Factories and warehouses disappeared from the neighborhood, and evidence of Philadelphia's historic ethnic, racial, and class diversity literally faded from the woodwork. Between 1960 and 1970, the neighborhood's population increased from 3,378 to 4,841 people, but the nonwhite population decreased from 20.4 to 7.4 percent of the total. By 1970, Society Hill had fewer children and senior citizens and more young professionals.[31] The neighborhood became newly perceived as historic, but it was in fact a new place transformed from a diverse but run-down slum into a showcase occupied primarily by affluent whites and attractive to tourists strolling south from Independence Hall.[32]

With redevelopment of Society Hill under way, in the 1960s the city of Philadelphia also expanded upon the demolition north of Independence Hall by defining a 115-acre Independence Mall Urban Renewal Area adjacent to the new mall.[33] More than the mall itself, the new redevelopment area met opposition from merchants who would be displaced. Like some of the residents of Society Hill, businesses adjacent to the new Independence Mall invoked the language of the Declaration of Independence and the Constitution to resist the additional demolition envisioned by the city's urban renewal plans. For example, the owner of the Square Deal Furniture Company tried to resist demolition of his store to make way for a modern, $7.5 million headquarters for the Rohm & Haas chemical company. Harry Schaffer, president of the business, protested that he had spent more than $2 million over twenty years to promote his store's address, 606 Market Street. Mustering the ideals represented by Independence

Hall in his own defense, Schaffer argued, "This is an unfair use of the power of the government to favor one citizen over another." He offered to remodel his building in Colonial style, but failed to win his case.[34]

During the 1960s and 1970s, a new canyon of modern office buildings grew around the perimeter of the mall north of Independence Hall. Unlike the structures built facing Independence Square earlier in the century, few of the new buildings tried to mimic the Georgian features of Independence Hall. Some were brick, however, and none exceeded the roof-line height established by the Curtis and Public Ledger Buildings on Independence Square. On Fifth Street facing the mall, the Lafayette Building (1908) and the Philadelphia Bourse (1893–95) remained closest to Independence Hall, but these were joined to the north by modern structures housing a radio and television station, a bank headquarters, a new synagogue for Temple Mikveh Israel, and the U.S. Mint. On Sixth Street facing the mall, a faux-colonial bank stood closest to Independence Hall, but to the north rose modern buildings for the Rohm & Haas company, a federal courthouse, the Federal Reserve Bank of Philadelphia, and a Bicentennial museum later transformed into a public television studio. The newspapers approvingly noted the construction boom, and a marketing consultant hired by the Old City Development Corporation, an agency created to handle redevelopment transactions, traveled the country to recruit new business. He carried with him another new view of Independence Hall: a miniature model of the park, transported inside a suitcase.[35]

In the second half of the twentieth century, the remaking of the landscape for Independence Mall, Independence National Historical Park, and Society Hill had once again expanded the historic space associated with Independence Hall. For Americans in the 1950s, one room was not a sufficient memorial to the nation's founders and their principles, as it had been a century before. Nor was Independence Hall alone adequate to the task, as it had been for the centennial anniversaries of the founding documents. Through selective destruction and preservation of buildings, the patriotic consensus of the 1950s combined with urban renewal to produce a new commemorative landscape, anchored by an eighteenth-century building but serving contemporary desires for an unobstructed view of the nation's past.

Bulwark of Freedom

At the highest levels of the U.S. government during the Cold War, strategies for combating the Soviet Union were cultural as well as military and diplomatic. To contain

42. A cartoon in the *Philadelphia Inquirer*, published on July 4, 1947, makes an early connection between the Liberty Bell and American resistance to Communism. The cartoon projects awareness of a potential threat, but also faith in the strength of the bell and its patriotic message. (Courtesy of the *Philadelphia Inquirer*)

Communism, strategists argued, Americans needed to be strong in their commitment to the American way of life. They needed to understand their country's history and educate the rising generation of new Americans in the nation's time-honored principles.[36] In many ways, Independence Hall facilitated this mission. As a tourist destination, it provided a place to envision the nation's founding and to hear a clearly articulated message about the nation's principles. At this traditional center for commemorative activities in Philadelphia, tourists often found themselves in the midst of Cold War pageantry or ceremony—parades for Loyalty Day or Armed Forces Day, for example, or wreath-layings at the Liberty Bell to call attention to the captive nations of Europe.[37] In these intensely patriotic times, Independence Hall and the Liberty Bell acquired renewed strength as symbols of American freedom.

From the time that the National Park Service assumed responsibility for Independence Hall in 1951, two goals were paramount: preserving the building and making it accessible to visitors.[38] These often conflicting goals were especially challenging at Independence Hall during the 1950s. As the Park Service began its work at the building now nearly 220 years old, a surge in automobile vacationing was under way, fueled by the end of gas rationing and other constraints of World War II.[39] Still, the immensity of visitation to Independence Hall surprised the new federal caretakers, who counted more than 606,153 visitors during 1951 and watched the number increase every year through 1957, when the total exceeded one million. During the 1950s, as the Cold War intensified American patriotism, as the first children of the baby boom began crowding elementary school classrooms, more than 7.2 million visitors passed through Independence Hall on family vacations, convention excursions, or school field trips. Visitation declined in the late 1950s during a period of economic recession and demolition for Independence Mall, but increased again during the 1960s, reaching more than 1.5 million annually in 1964 and 1965, years when tourists passed through Pennsylvania on the way to or from the New York World's Fair.[40]

In a process reminiscent of the construction of nationalism around the Liberty Bell's travels at the turn of the century, Americans during the 1950s pursued direct experience with places and things representing national ideals. Interest in Independence Hall may have been primed by the 1947–49 journeys of the "Freedom Train," a traveling exhibit that allowed more than 3.5 million people to view historical documents including Thomas Jefferson's draft of the Declaration of Independence and George Washington's annotated Constitution. In 1952, the National Archives enshrined the "Charters of Freedom"—the Declaration, the Constitution, and the Bill of Rights—in hermetically sealed cases that allowed tourists to file by during their visits to Washington, D.C. Like tourism to the nation's capital, the flow of visitors to Philadelphia was part of a wider phenomenon of pilgrimage to sites that bolstered faith in American exceptionalism—politically, historically, and environmentally. At historic places such as Colonial Williamsburg, Mount Vernon, and Monticello, at monuments such as Mount Rushmore, and at natural wonders such as Yellowstone National Park, increasing numbers of tourists arrived during the 1950s to express their patriotism and directly experience the nation's shared heritage.[41]

For more than two centuries, Independence Hall had stood surrounded by the conflicts that tested the nation, the commemorations that bolstered founding principles, and an urban environment that changed with the passage of time. The building had a complex history, encompassing conflict as well as consensus, city and state as well as nation, and generations of American life before and after the American Revolution. Independence Hall had echoed with disputes over independence, the political battles of the 1790s, and fugitive slave hearings. Independence Square had been the scene of labor rallies, nativist demonstrations, and women's rights actions. As much as celebrations of the Fourth of July or the laying of wreaths at the Liberty Bell, these were events that defined the building and the nation. But in Cold War America, this was not a story that would or could be told. In a world armed with nuclear weapons and divided by an Iron Curtain, Americans sought security in consensus, patriotism, and a history of national strength. At Independence Hall, they found just such reassurances.

During the 1950s, National Park Service historians, architects, and archaeologists embarked on the most thorough study of Independence Hall that had ever been undertaken.[42] Historians launched a massive research effort to uncover every retrievable detail about Independence Hall during the eighteenth century and structural changes since that time. They combed through the records of the Pennsylvania Assembly, extracting data about the construction and early use of the State House. They moved systematically through Philadelphia archives and libraries, reading newspapers, diaries, letters, and travel accounts, and they extended the search to New York, Washington, D.C., London, and other locations as time and budgets permitted. They convinced the city of Philadelphia to allow access to the basement of City Hall, which held the records of restorations performed during the late nineteenth and early twentieth centuries. The historians' typewritten notes on eighteenth-century life within the boundaries of the new Independence National Historical Park filled thousands of five-by-seven-inch notecards.[43] Drawing upon the continuing research, the park's chief historian, Edward M. Riley, produced a historical handbook that for the first time presented a history of the building that included not only its most famous events, but also the restorations of the nineteenth and twentieth centuries.[44]

For visitors to Independence Hall, the most visible outcome of the National Park Service's research into the building's history appeared gradually from the 1950s through the early 1970s in the walls, floors, ceilings, and furnishings of the building. With historians examining documents and architects minutely inspecting the building, the Park Service solved mysteries about the original interior that had evaded all previous restorations. Before the eyes of tourists, the restorations of earlier decades were peeled away, exposing the architectural clues of the brick walls that had stood since 1732. While restorers dating back to John Haviland in the 1830s had claimed success in re-creating the 1776 appearance of the Assembly Room, the Park Service reached a new understanding of the chamber by removing the paneling that Haviland had installed and inspecting the original brick beneath. There, they found architectural details that corresponded with a painting at the Historical Society of Pennsylvania, the Robert Edge Pine/Edward Savage painting, *Congress Voting Independence*. While less well-known than John Trumbull's portrayal of the Declaration in the U.S. Capitol, the accuracy of the Pine/Savage image from the 1790s was confirmed by the newly revealed architectural evidence and, on that basis, served as a model for restoring and furnishing the room.[45] Details of the room's west wall, not pictured in the painting, were discovered in a private owner's previously unknown sketch from the early nineteenth century.[46] Independence Hall's history as a center of arts and sciences during the late eighteenth and early nineteenth century would not be directly visible to tourists, but the products of that period guided the twentieth-century restorers.

The research of the 1950s also led to refurnishing the Assembly Room in keeping with its eighteenth-century origins. The Pine/Savage painting and documentary research into records of the Pennsylvania Assembly demolished one especially long-standing belief about the furniture used by the Second Continental Congress. National Park Service historians determined that the upholstered leather armchairs, so ardently collected by Frank M. Etting for display during the Centennial, had not been used during July 1776. In fact, the historians found that the Pennsylvania Assembly had ordered Windsor chairs for the room, as shown in the Pine/Savage painting. Etting's chairs were produced somewhat later, during the 1790s to furnish Congress Hall.[47] With funding from the General Federation of Women's Clubs, the Park Service acquired Windsor chairs from the Revolutionary period, including two by the maker who filled the original order for the Pennsylvania Assembly, as well as reproductions to complete the furnishing of the Assembly Room as it existed between 1775 and 1787. With the chairs arranged around tables covered with green baize, curators completed the eighteenth-century aura with period artifacts such as andirons, books, newspapers, and parchment. The Assembly Room project, launched with the fund-raising offer by the Women's Clubs in 1954, continued through 1965. Similar work on the first-floor courtroom and the frequently remodeled second floor continued through 1972.[48]

Although abundant research undergirded the restoration of Independence Hall, for tourist consumption, the park historians advised guards and guides to present the building's history with sensitivity to vacation travelers' interests and attention spans. In keeping with National Park Service guidelines for historic interpretation, "Simplicity, brevity, and informality should be your watchwords," the first guides' manual, issued in 1952, advised.[49] While organized groups could arrange for escorted tours, most visitors during the 1950s moved on their own through Independence Hall and other buildings designated for the national park. Seeing the heavy traffic through

43. The meticulous research program of the 1950s facilitated a restoration of the Assembly Room which allowed visitors to imagine themselves in the surroundings of the Second Continental Congress and the Constitutional Convention. Completed in 1965 and shown here in 1974, the room features the "rising sun" chair occupied by George Washington during the convention of 1787 (background, center). (Courtesy of Independence National Historical Park)

Independence Hall, the historians concluded that the building was best presented as a shrine to be entered, admired, and exited in relatively short order. "Those who have considerable knowledge know that the history of Independence is tremendously complicated," a Park Service study noted in 1959. "But not many visitors are interested in the complications—nor should they be. . . . The concept of Independence Hall as a Shrine simplifies the interpretive problem. It places emphasis where it is needed—on the central theme of Independence National Historical Park."[50] Park administrators hoped that a future museum would provide a more elaborate interpretation of events between 1774 and 1800.[51]

By 1961, when four women joined Independence National Historical Park as the first full-time historical interpreters of Independence Hall, a standard narrative of the building's historic events had evolved. The National Park Service viewed on-site interpretation as an art distinct from classroom history because of its emphasis on engaging visitor attention with stories of people and encounters with artifacts.[52] Nevertheless, the narration of the Independence Hall story corresponded with trends in academic history writing during the 1950s. Like the "consensus historians" of the time, on-site interpreters presented Independence Hall not as a place of ideological struggle, but rather as a setting for inspiring events that offered a reassuring sense of connectedness between twentieth-century visitors and the nation's past. Except for acknowledging that the courtroom on the first floor had been occupied by the Pennsylvania Supreme Court, the narrative focused on national history. The interpreters, all college graduates with majors in history, informed visitors that in the Assembly Room, the Second Continental Congress convened and appointed George Washington commander in chief of the Continental Army. Here they approved the Declaration of Independence, which was read in the State House Square and later signed. The United States entered into an alliance with France and defeated the British, after which twenty-four stands of colors captured at Yorktown were brought to Philadelphia and laid before Congress. When the first plan of government, the Articles of Confederation, proved unsatisfactory, the Constitutional Convention of 1787 met in the Assembly Room and drafted the new federal Constitution. Visitors left Independence Hall with a clear, concise message about its history and significance.

Independence Hall was no longer the cluttered museum of Revolutionary-era artifacts that it had been in the late nineteenth and early twentieth century, but selected artifacts helped to support a narrative of achievement for events in the Assembly Room. When speaking of the Declaration of Independence, interpreters could turn to the silver inkstand crafted by Philip Syng, Jr., in 1752 for the Pennsylvania Assembly and believed to have been used for the signing of the Declaration. Visitors could imagine the brave patriots of 1776 dipping quills into ink and inscribing their names on the founding document.[53] As the narrative continued to the writing of the Constitution of 1787, the carved mahogany armchair used by George Washington as he presided over the Constitutional Convention helped to end the story on a triumphant note. The chair, made by John Folwell for the Speaker of the Pennsylvania Assembly in 1779, featured the sun-on-the-horizon carving that had caused Benjamin Franklin to ponder whether it was a rising or setting sun. With the new federal Constitution, Franklin concluded that the carving was, indeed, a rising sun.[54] Imagining themselves in the place of Franklin, pondering that same chair, twentieth-century visitors knew that he was right—that they were the proof that the nation conceived in the eighteenth century had endured through time.

Like the reception rituals that had taken place in the Assembly Room during the nineteenth century, the interpreters' presentation of the Independence Hall story to appreciative visitors in the 1960s continually renewed recognition of Independence Hall, particularly the east room on its first floor, as a historic place. One interpreter routinely opened her talk by saying, "I would like to welcome you to Independence Hall, the most important historic building in the United States." In the spirit of international concerns during the Cold War, others attributed larger significance to the building. "Today it symbolizes freedom and liberty to all people," one interpreter said. And the Liberty Bell, said another interpreter, "is the most venerated symbol of patriotism in the United States; its fame as a symbol of liberty is worldwide. Through both fact and folklore, it has become firmly established as an image of political freedom." With "Proclaim Liberty" as its inscription, the Liberty Bell added a timeless resonance to the story that visitors heard in the Assembly Room.[55]

The interpretation of Independence Hall for visitors corresponded with the National Park Service's intention to communicate the political history of the nation from 1774 through 1800. At the same time, however, the standard narrative of events obscured the building's more complex history. Even during the selected "historic" period, Independence Hall accommodated a more complicated past, as Chapter 1 of this book demonstrates. During the 1950s, historians had not yet investigated the role of lower-ranking Americans in the resistance that led to revolution, so the emphasis on more elite founders at Independence Hall corresponded with history-writing trends of the time. However, the privileging of national over state history at Independence Hall concealed the complexity of declaring and creating an independent nation. While the public learned about the Second Continental Congress, they heard little or nothing about the conservative Pennsylvania Assembly that balked at independence or the radically democratic constitution of the new state of Pennsylvania. They learned about the federal Constitutional Convention, but they heard little or nothing about the controversies over ratification that also permeated the building. Aided by artifacts such as the Syng inkstand and the "rising sun" chair—both created for the Pennsylvania government—historical interpreters at Independence Hall could conclude their narratives with triumphant flourishes that emphasized the completion of a national act, not the beginning of a series of national struggles. The Liberty Bell, another Pennsylvania artifact that had acquired national significance, helped to enlarge the message that the founding principles reverberated across time.

The message of Independence Hall and the Liberty Bell resonated beyond Philadelphia through the new medium of television, which projected the building and the artifact into American living rooms as symbols of patriotism. With the entertainment industry eager to overcome the suspicions aroused by the anti-Communist crusades of the late 1940s and early 1950s, Independence Hall served as a suitably patriotic stage. Programs presented Independence Hall with emotional appreciation for the nation's founding events, renewing and intensifying awareness of the building and its most famous artifact, the Liberty Bell, as patriotic symbols. In 1952, the husband-and-wife team of Mike Wallace and Buff Cobb toured Independence Hall on their CBS program, *All Around the Town.* "We are at this moment standing before a great national symbol, a monument to freedom," Mike Wallace told the national audience. "It's just a small building, very old, but exceedingly precious to men who value liberty everywhere."[56] On July 5, 1954, Charles Collingwood of *The Morning Show* on CBS and Dave Garroway of NBC's *Today* show both broadcast from Independence Hall in connection with the Fourth of July. NBC and Dave Garroway returned in 1956; while on location, NBC also produced pickups from Independence Hall for *Howdy Doody.*[57]

Programs emanating from Independence Hall could be highly patriotic and soaringly sentimental, as in the *Home* show starring Arlene Francis, which came to Philadelphia for a week in October 1956 under an arrangement with the Convention and Visitors Bureau of the Philadelphia Chamber of Commerce. After leading a televised tour through Independence Hall, Francis turned to the "rising sun" chair in the Assembly Room and marveled at the progress of America since the Declaration of Independence. "Four score and seven years later [the rising sun] shined on a man at Gettysburg who preserved the Constitution that was born here," Francis said.

> It shined on the rivers and the valleys and the mountains . . . on the cities and the towns which made up its domain . . . the United States of America.
>
> From this single room came the sunlight of liberty, not only for one people, but for the whole world to see.
>
> From this room came the inscription, "Give me your tired, your poor, your huddled masses yearning to breathe free."
>
> From this room came the riverboat of Mark Twain and the steamboat of Robert Fulton . . . the covered wagons, the railroads to the west and the buildings to the sky . . .
>
> From this sweet room came the songs of Walt Whitman and the songs of an immigrant's son named Gershwin who sang "Swonderful, Smarvelous" . . .

From this room came Alexander Bell and Samuel Morse who asked "What Hath God Wrought?"

From this blessed room came Helen Keller, and Al Jolson, Ernest Hemingway and Dr. Jonas Salk . . .

From this room came the corn husking bee, the fox-trot and the perfect no-hit game in a World Series . . .

From this wonderful room came thirty-seven Presidents and eighty-three Congresses . . . and the greatest nation on earth.[58]

Linking Independence Hall to every heart-tugging emblem of American pride, television helped to define Independence Hall as a place of pilgrimage for patriotic Americans. As the national park's filmstrip for schoolchildren pointed out, preserving and visiting Independence Hall was a way to sustain the American way of life. "Why does America and her 160 million people want to keep such an old building in a modern city?" asked the script accompanying the filmstrip. "Here is the answer. All Americans, from our president to our young people . . . want Independence Hall to stand as a symbol of freedom, showing all the world that personal freedom builds a strong country, a happy country."[59]

As symbols of freedom during the Cold War, Independence Hall and the Liberty Bell played central roles in demonstrations of support for the American way and opposition to the spread of Communism. Commemorative celebrations such as Flag Day, the Fourth of July, Memorial Day, the National Freedom Day remembrance of the end of slavery, and the parades honoring heroes of the American Revolution continued from earlier years. But during the 1950s, the calendar of patriotic rituals at Independence Hall became crowded with events such as Loyalty Day, a commemoration created by the Veterans of Foreign Wars to be celebrated each spring as a patriotic counterpoint to the May Day demonstrations of the Communist Party. Passing in review every year at Independence Hall, Philadelphia's Loyalty Day parade dramatized "one nation, under God" by uniting veterans groups such as the Catholic War Veterans, Jewish War Veterans, the American Legion, and the VFW in a common show of patriotism with European ethnic groups, schoolchildren, and high school bands. For two to four hours each year, the Loyalty Day parade passed cheering throngs of people waving American flags. Philadelphians also gathered along the parade route leading to Independence Hall to cheer the nation's military strength on Armed Forces Day. Members of the legal profession encouraged respect for authority with annual Law Day events. These shows of patriotic unity became contested in later years, during the Vietnam controversy, but during the 1950s they constituted a calendar of consensus.[60]

As symbols of American freedom, Independence Hall and the Liberty Bell both acquired enhanced international significance for Eastern European immigrants to the United States and other critics of the Soviet Union or the spread of Communism. Independence Hall frequently accommodated wreath-layings at the Liberty Bell in protest of Soviet control over the Baltic states. By the 1960s, Philadelphians participated in an annual "Captive Nations Week" to call attention to continuing Soviet control. Jewish Philadelphians turned to Independence Hall and the Liberty Bell as places to call attention to the plight of Soviet Jewry as well as to commemorate the independence of the State of Israel.[61]

Independence Hall and the Liberty Bell also became part of a broader, state-sponsored promotion of American ideals as a defense against the spread of Communism. Located conveniently between New York City and Washington, D.C., Philadelphia served as a handy venue for giving foreign visitors a firsthand look at American history and, it was hoped, an appreciation for the American way. International visitors constituted a small percentage of visitors to Independence Hall, but travelers from thirty to forty countries visited each month, often on trips escorted by the U.S. State Department, Commerce Department, or other federal agencies. Especially after the Soviet Union successfully launched the Sputnik satellite into space in 1957, the federal government turned to historic sites as means for communicating the United States' accomplishments to international visitors. Between 1957 and 1959, groups of Filipinos, Mexicans, Portuguese, and Russians came to Independence Hall with escorts by the State Department; leaders of the South East Asia Treaty Organization visited with the Governmental Affairs Institute of Washington, D.C.; and students from the British Commonwealth came on a tour arranged by the U.S. Information Agency. As the United States and the Soviet Union competed for control of the postwar world, dignitaries from newly independent nations in Africa and Asia increasingly appeared among the escorted guests at Independence Hall.[62]

During these years of intense regard for the nation's principles, the Liberty Bell in particular gained a new aura of significance as an international beacon of American ideals. The National Park Service lifted earlier restrictions on photography at the Liberty Bell, which became a popular prop not only for vacation snapshots but also for publicity photos of movie stars and group portraits of employees for the covers of company magazines. In the years following World War II, a new generation of replicas expanded international recognition of the American symbol. After the war, the Free

44. The Liberty Bell gets a new mission during the Cold War, as a symbol encouraging Americans to buy U.S. Savings Bonds. Launched with a costumed Miss Liberty, the bond drive provided each U.S. state and territory with a full-scale replica of the Liberty Bell. (Associated Press photograph, courtesy of the Urban Archives, Temple University, Philadelphia)

Asia Committee in San Francisco sent a replica Liberty Bell to Hiroshima, to be installed near the site where the first atomic bomb had ended World War II. An American general presented one to West Germany, where it was installed in the tower of the city hall of West Berlin.[63] European countries recognized the United States role in World War II by presenting replica Liberty Bells as gifts. Italians sent a replica Liberty Bell to Philadelphia in 1948; the French sent a replica to Independence, Missouri, the hometown of Harry Truman, in 1950.[64]

Although the Liberty Bell had not traveled outside Philadelphia since 1915, it found new significance during the 1950s as a symbol of individual and national security. In 1951, in a campaign to promote U.S. Savings Bonds, each American state and territory received its own replica Liberty Bell.[65] Even Pennsylvania, home of the actual bell, received a replica, which was displayed at the State Museum at Harrisburg and taken on a tour around the state. In 1962, the replica was permanently enshrined in Allentown, Pennsylvania, where the real Liberty Bell had been hidden during the British occupation of Philadelphia in 1777.[66] Installed around the country, the Savings Bond Liberty Bells acquired their own symbolic lives. Hawaii's bell came back to Independence Hall in 1958 on the back of a truck in a demonstration seeking admission of Hawaii as the fiftieth state in the union.[67] Wisconsin's bell was placed in the Wisconsin Girls Detention Center, a location later protested by a state senator who felt the bell might inspire the inmates to proclaim liberty, literally, by trying to escape.[68] Reflecting changing times, Oregon's bell was attacked and destroyed in 1970 by an explosion in Portland City Hall.[69]

Like the Liberty Bell replicas for the Savings Bond drive, a building inspired by Independence Hall during the 1950s linked individual action with national security, economically and politically. In 1954, banker Sidney L. DeLove opened the "Independence Hall of Chicago," a building for the Cook County Federal Savings and Loan Association that housed a patriotic museum and headquarters for DeLove's "Independence Hall Association" on the second floor. DeLove, a World War II veteran who had immigrated to the United States from France in 1921, devoted patriotic energy to promoting American strength and calling attention to the evils of Communism. At his building on Chicago's Devon Avenue, in press releases, in books, and on radio programs, DeLove's business and civic activities were mutually reinforcing, uniting financial and moral fortitude to defend the United States against Communism. "From within Independence Hall, built by a people of free men, America began its destiny to become the greatest country on God's earth," DeLove declared. "But more important, Independence Hall stands as testimony of your right to own your own Independence

Hall—your right to the challenge of achievement, your right to the pride of posses-sion, your right to the honor of responsibility, your right to the security of your person and property, your right to freedom and expression and worship, and your right to the primacy and privacy of your God-given individuality." In fact, DeLove's "Independence Hall" bore limited resemblance to the original, despite its brick construction and white clock tower. But for DeLove, the building honored the legacy of Independence Hall, "a symbol of our national origin; the American Flag waving above its room, symbol of our land; the Liberty Bell ensconced in its tower, symbol of individual freedom. Togeth-er they reign, expressing in the thunder of their silence that which mere words cannot possibly say." In this constellation of American symbols—Independence Hall, the Lib-erty Bell, and the American flag—DeLove perceived a convergence of past with pres-ent, and individual with nation, that would secure the United States against the threat of Communism.[70]

During the 1950s and 1960s, Independence Hall became a time capsule of the eighteenth century, carefully restored and interpreted as significant to the birth and growth of the nation from 1774 to 1800. Ironically enough, this determined effort to return Independence Hall to its past coincided with an intensified connection between the eighteenth-century landmark and present-day concerns. It was a place anchored in the American Revolution, but also very much a place of the Cold War. President John F. Kennedy made the point on July 4, 1962, in a speech at Independence Hall that attached Cold War resonance to the Declaration of Independence. Looking out over thousands of people gathered on the newly created Independence Mall, he declared:

> If there is a single issue that divides the world today, it is independence—
> the independence of Berlin or Laos or Viet-Nam; the longing for independ-
> ence behind the Iron Curtain; the peaceful transition to independence in
> those newly emerging areas whose troubles some hope to exploit. . . .
> Today this Nation—conceived in revolution, nurtured in liberty, maturing
> in independence—has no intention of abdicating its leadership in that
> worldwide movement for independence to any nation or society committed
> to systematic human oppression.[71]

In his speech, Kennedy joined the declaring of American independence in 1776 with American concerns for the world in 1962, from the recently constructed Berlin Wall to the impending perils of Southeast Asia. In its material representation in Philadelphia, independence was an event of the past, neatly encased in a Georgian building and

45. With crowds filling the new expanse of Independence Mall, President John F. Kennedy (lower right) addressed the nation from Independence Hall on July 4, 1962. His speech built upon the lessons of American independence to argue for resistance against Communism. (Courtesy of the Urban Archives, Temple University, Philadelphia)

landscaped parks. But for an American president determined that the United States should prevail in the Cold War against Soviet Communism, the building presented a place to grasp the idea of independence and unfurl it for the postwar world.

During the 1950s, the powerful consensus that the United States must stand strong in its principles converged at Independence Hall in the forms of tourism, preservation, and pageantry, creating for the future a time capsule anchored by eighteenth-century architecture, artifacts, and the story of the American Revolution. For this period in its history, Independence Hall was a not place of contested memory, but a place that drew Americans together in agreement. The official projects of government harmonized with the vernacular expressions of Cold War culture.[72] The 1950s consensus, promoting the American way as an antidote to the spread of Communism, provided a supportive foundation for restoring and promoting Independence Hall as a national shrine. The expanded parks, the influence of television, and the Liberty Bell, standing like a sentinel in the building's tower stair hall, amplified regard for Independence Hall as a place for savoring American freedom. The building and its most famous artifact allowed visitors to connect their personal experience to the nation's past during a period when Americans looked to their history for reassurance of the strength and endurance of the United States.[73]

This intense period of attention to Independence Hall and its surroundings, beginning in the 1950s and extending into the 1970s, anchored the building's appearance and interpretation for decades to come. In the service of public memory, a re-creation of the late eighteenth century stood in a twentieth-century city, protected from deterioration and the encroachments of urban life. Buildings translate readily (if not easily or inexpensively) into such time capsules, defined by architectural style and filled with period furnishings. They provide a concentrated engagement with a selected moment in time, an opportunity to imagine a past that predates personal experience. But if history is the study of change over time, then history is belied by the very precision of such re-created environments. They stop time. They eliminate the clatter, the dust, and changing experiences. They are inanimate, providing a reassuring sense of stability and obscuring any hint of conflict. Like exquisite corpses, they seem lifelike, but they are not quite like life.

Life comes into such places through use and interpretation, but the time capsule exerts influence over both. At Independence Hall, the building, the artifacts, and the interpretation focused attention on political events between 1774 and 1800, emphasizing national history, consensus, and a simplified narrative over the complexity of eighteenth-century life. From a history of more than two centuries, a twenty-six year period prevailed. These interpretative choices were validated by the use of the building as a place of heritage tourism, where visitors could express their patriotism and renew their dedication to the nation's founding principles. During the 1950s, the interests of visitors corresponded with the interpretation of Independence Hall as a place to bask in American triumph and distinctiveness. But times would change, even if Independence Hall created an impression that they never had. The consensus mood that had prevailed in the United States since World War II shattered in the 1960s, bringing the controversies of the nation to the doorstep of Independence Hall.

Chapter 9

PRISM

Redefining Independence for a Third Century

FBI agents circulated among the three thousand people gathered at Independence Hall for the Independence Day celebration of 1965. The summer had been packed with patriotic festivities, including a naturalization ceremony for new American citizens, a reunion of the Fourth Division of the U.S. Marines, a ceremony for World Freedom Day, and an announcement of the winners of a national Yankee Doodle Dandy essay contest. On June 28, with eight hundred people in attendance, the National Park Service dedicated the restored, refurnished Assembly Room of Independence Hall. But the United States in 1965 was a nation taut with tension. During the spring, the United States escalated its military involvement in Vietnam, igniting a surge of protest at home. In Selma, Alabama, local authorities resorted to violence against voting-rights demonstrators. In New York, bullets ended the life of Malcolm X. For the guardians of Independence Hall, the nation's anniversary in 1965 called for special precautions. The National Park Service set up a control center and coordinated security with the Philadelphia police and the FBI, whose agents shadowed potential troublemakers. In the heat and humidity of the Philadelphia summer, the FBI removed one individual regarded as a "lone picket of former prominence" from Independence Square before the featured address by the nation's chief law enforcement officer, Attorney General Nicholas Katzenbach.[1]

Katzenbach took the podium at Independence Hall just three years after President John F. Kennedy embraced the building's history as a symbol of American leadership in the Cold War. But by 1965, the youthful president was dead, memorialized at Independence Hall by a bronze plaque set into the Chestnut Street sidewalk, near the statue of George Washington and a similar plaque commemorating Abraham Lincoln.

The consensus of tourism, preservation, and public commemoration that had defined Independence Hall during the 1950s had shattered into multifaceted conflict. While commemorations continued to validate Independence Hall as a place for demonstrating patriotism and loyalty to the nation, protests during the 1960s placed the building at the center of debate over whether the nation was living up to its founding principles. The preservation work of the National Park Service continued through the decade, enhancing the aura of eighteenth-century authenticity for the benefit of visitors, but tourists came in such great numbers that they undercut the effect. While the National Park Service worked to safeguard the building and regulate the tourist traffic, the city of Philadelphia viewed tourism as a potential economic windfall. Countering the National Park Service's efforts to turn back time at Independence Hall, Philadelphians devised events and promotions to make the historic building a place of lively, modern entertainments.

If the Independence Hall of the 1950s had seemed to be a beacon of American patriotism, the building during the 1960s operated more like a prism, a place of not one but many meanings. It was a historic place for remembering the famous events of 1776 and 1787, but Americans in the 1960s disagreed about whether the promises of the Declaration of Independence and the Constitution were being fulfilled. Some saw Independence Hall as a place of achievement, but others saw it as a symbol of their exclusion from the full benefits of American citizenship. Some embraced the specific language of the founding documents, while others invoked associated principles such as liberty, equality, and justice. From the 1960s through the Bicentennial of 1976, Independence Hall and the adjacent public parks were places of conflict between dissenters and authorities, young and old, liberals and conservatives, and federal caretakers and vocal Philadelphians. Despite the attention lavished on Independence Hall to make it a place for envisioning the culminating acts of creating a nation, events in and around the building served as reminders that the nation remained a work in progress.

Contested Ground

As conceived in the patriotic fervor of World War II and created during the 1950s, the expanded parks around Independence Hall had been imagined as dignified settings for the nation's birthplace. Viewed only as physical entities, they appeared to be exactly that: across the street from the honored landmark, Independence Mall began with a block-long lawn flanked by raised plazas offering shaded benches enclosed by red-

46. An aerial view in 1959 shows the newly cleared parks radiating from Independence Hall. Independence National Historical Park extends from left to right in this photograph, connecting Independence Hall with the Colonial revival skyscraper of the U.S. Customs House. Independence Mall extends north of Independence Hall toward the terminus of the Benjamin Franklin Bridge, visible in the distance. (Associated Press photograph, courtesy of the Urban Archives, Temple University, Philadelphia)

brick walls. In the second block, a magnificent fountain stood in the foreground of a terraced plaza, which was bordered by arched colonnades that mimicked the piazzas of Independence Hall. In the third block, landscape architects created a park that echoed Philadelphia history with brick pavement and fountains placed in rectangular spaces reminiscent of the grid of the original city plan. The three-block expanse offered an unobstructed vista toward Independence Hall. To the east of the building, Independence National Historical Park retained more historic structures, but they occupied a neat urban park with old, narrow streets transformed into walkways across green lawns. The new landscape retained a hint of the old, with a visible depression in the ground at the site of Dock Creek, which in Colonial times had accommodated vessels from the Delaware River.

While the design of these public spaces paid homage to eighteenth-century events, their use during the 1960s spoke to the nation's longer history of conflict. Like the National Mall in Washington, D.C., the Lincoln Memorial, and the Pentagon, Independence Hall and its surroundings became sites for challenging authority and demonstrating the power of dissent in American society.[2] Events in and around Independence Hall often involved national organizations, but more than that, the building and public space functioned as places where Philadelphians responded to national crises and controversies. These were the places where Philadelphians gathered to debate civil rights and the Vietnam War, launch campaigns against poverty and environmental destruction, and mourn the deaths of President John F. Kennedy, the Reverend Dr. Martin Luther King, Jr., and the students killed at Kent State and Jackson State Universities. Their activities echoed a history of Independence Hall long obscured—the history of the nineteenth century, when conflict surrounded the building even as it was being remodeled into a shrine to the nation's founders. That history had faded from memory, but the survival of Independence Hall helped to trigger a similar range of public activities that seized upon the historical associations of the Declaration of Independence and the Constitution. With picket signs and banners, chants, speeches, and hand-lettered fliers, demonstrators at Independence Hall constructed alternative interpretations of Independence Hall focusing on the nation's continuing controversies as well as the triumph of American ideals.

More than the city officials who had controlled Independence Hall prior to 1951, federal officials tolerated dissent as well as celebration, reasoning that the exercise of First Amendment rights was a suitable activity at the birthplace of the U.S. Constitution. In keeping with the National Park Service's mission to both safeguard and provide public access to national treasures, the federal administrators banned meetings from Independence Hall itself, in order to preserve the structure, but they readily allowed a variety of activities in the public space around the building. For students at Philadelphia's many colleges and universities, Independence Hall became the best place in the city to stage a demonstration. Perhaps reflecting the shifting understanding of the American Revolution among their history professors, students viewed their protests at Independence Hall as honoring a founding legacy of ideological conflict and resistance. "In the last few years, the spirit of political controversy enshrined here in 1776 has been revived by picketers and protesters," noted a guidebook published by college students in 1968. "Police grumble and tourists look on amazed, but nothing could be more appropriate at the place where the hot-headed Founding Fathers declared their independence."[3] Energized by the youth movements of their time, college students who had come to Philadelphia from around the country formed an important constituency among demonstrators who turned to Independence Hall as a local connection to the nation.

Advocates of justice for African Americans came to Independence Hall to demonstrate support for the civil rights movement in the South and to criticize the federal government's inaction toward Southern racial conflict. Occasional gatherings of African Americans occurred during the 1950s, including the continuation of National Freedom Day to commemorate the end of slavery and new anniversary celebrations of *Brown v. Board of Education*, the 1954 Supreme Court decision ordering desegregation of public schools.[4] However, the greatest concentration of activity for African American civil rights at Independence Hall came between 1963 and 1965 as civil rights activity in the South met with increasing violence, attracting widespread public attention. In response to events such as the murders of civil rights workers, the blocking of schoolhouse doors, and the turning of fire hoses on marching children, Independence Hall became a place where Northerners—black and white—could demonstrate their support for the movement and their sympathy for its martyrs.

Like the annual National Freedom Day program, which by the 1960s had attracted such notable guests as Thurgood Marshall and the Reverend Dr. Martin Luther King, Jr., civil rights demonstrations identified Independence Hall and the Liberty Bell as symbols of freedom, but a freedom not fully shared by all Americans. King made the point in his famous "I Have a Dream" speech in Washington on August 28, 1963, when he cited the United States' failure to live up to the promises of the Declaration of Independence and the Constitution. In Independence Square, birthplace of both documents, the NAACP staged a freedom rally for 5,000 people in 1963, students from the NAACP and the Student Nonviolent Coordinating Committee picketed for civil rights later that year, and 250 people attended an Inter-Religious Witness for Civil Rights in 1964.[5] While these programs featured speakers outside Independence Hall, sit-ins in 1963 and 1965 took protest inside the building to the base of the Liberty Bell. In 1963, members of the Congress of Racial Equality spent a night at the Liberty Bell to criticize race conflict in Birmingham, Alabama.[6] In 1965, another sit-in at the bell by students from the University of Pennsylvania and Cheyney State College lasted fifty-two hours. "The Liberty Bell again serves as a national focal point in the struggle for freedom, which today is taking place in Selma, Alabama," stated the students' mimeographed handbill, referring to the voting-rights march from Selma to Birmingham.[7] One of the student leaders further explained, "We feel that this is a definite place that people look to when they think of freedom, and when they think of what our government stands for and what our Constitution means." In this view, Independence Hall

47. Continuing a tradition begun during World War II, African Americans gather on February 1, 1964, for National Freedom Day, an annual commemoration of the end of slavery and reminder of the continuing struggle for freedom. (Courtesy of the Urban Archives, Temple University, Philadelphia)

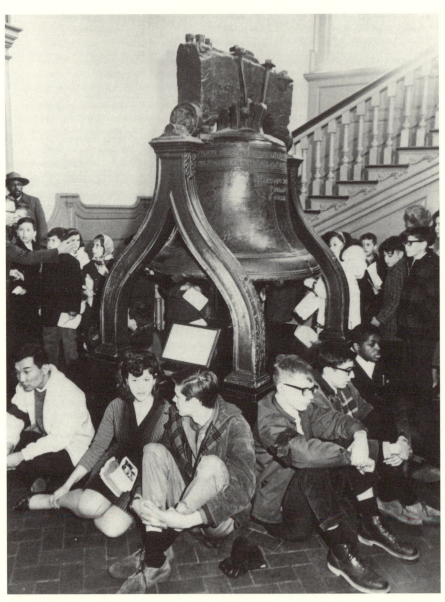

48. In 1965, protest meets tourism as college students stage a civil rights sit-in at the Liberty Bell inside Independence Hall. Tours for schoolchildren continue in the background during this demonstration, which drew irate responses from Philadelphians. (Courtesy of the Urban Archives, Temple University, Philadelphia)

and the Liberty Bell served as reminders of promises that were being denied to African Americans in Alabama.[8]

Sit-ins at the Liberty Bell directly challenged perceptions of Independence Hall as a place reserved for reverent appreciation of the nation's history, placing the National Park Service in the role of mediator between the young demonstrators and angry Philadelphians. While Park Service officials often took the precaution of notifying the Philadelphia police about demonstrations on park property, they did not interfere with the sit-ins at the Liberty Bell. The park's assistant superintendent explained to the press, "We are doing this because the Liberty Bell is a symbol for the people of the United States, and because we do not believe American citizens should be forcibly removed from the Liberty Bell while they are giving peaceful expressions to their beliefs."[9] However, the 1965 sit-in came just seven months after poverty and racial tension exploded in Philadelphia's worst twentieth-century riot, which left two people dead, more than three hundred injured, and an estimated $3 million in property damage in north-central Philadelphia.[10] Furthermore, one month prior to the sit-in, New York City police had uncovered a plan by members of the Black Liberation Front to bomb prominent American symbols, especially the Statue of Liberty but secondarily the Liberty Bell and the Washington Monument. The foiled plot prompted the posting of additional guards around the Liberty Bell and focused local press attention on the security of Philadelphia's treasured relic.[11]

Strained race relations in Philadelphia and the generational conflict that characterized the 1960s combined in an angry backlash against the Liberty Bell demonstrators. The Park Service received more than 150 telephone calls, only one of which praised the park's tolerance of the students. The callers included two veterans who threatened to come down to the hall and "throw the s.o.b.'s out."[12] Letters to Philadelphia newspapers denounced the demonstrators as publicity seekers who were being given special treatment by the Park Service. Writers called attention to the Liberty Bell as a symbol defended by the World War II generation, but now desecrated by young protesters. "If our cradle of liberty is to be periodically used as a flophouse to further the cause of liberty, please close it," one writer said. "Too many men have bled and died in forthright demonstrations of defense of freedom, and this defense did not include the license of disobedient juveniles to make their own rules."[13]

The civil rights movement for African Americans was the vanguard of a rights revolution in the United States in the 1960s as other minority groups asserted their own claims to equal treatment under the law. Several months after the 1965 civil rights sit-in, homosexual rights groups gathered at Independence Hall on the Fourth of July for the first in an annual series of demonstrations calling attention to the contradictions between the United States' founding documents and their experience in American society. Each year from 1965 until 1969, members of the Mattachine Societies and the East Coast Homophile Organizations and their supporters marched in a large circle in front of Independence Hall, injecting their pursuit of civil rights into the gatherings of tourists and locals for the Fourth of July. Dressed conservatively as a matter of strategy, the demonstrators carried picket signs with such messages as "Equality for Homosexuals," "Homosexuals, Our Last Oppressed Minority," and "Anti-Sodomy Laws Violate the Constitution." The number of demonstrators grew from between thirty and fifty in 1965 to more than 150 in 1969.[14] A columnist for the *Philadelphia Inquirer* captured the reactions of passersby in 1967: "They stop . . . peer at the signs. They look like they can't believe what they are reading. They inch across the street. Yep, that's what those signs say, all right. The bolder ones stand around and stare. And you can hear the mumbling. 'Are those people all . . . I mean, they look okay . . . do you think they are really . . . that is, both the men and women, too?' A couple of the marchers walk through the crowd giving out mimeographed handbills explaining the protest. The handbills are accepted . . . but not with anything resembling a friendly smile" (ellipses in original).[15]

In the literature they distributed, the activists contrasted their experiences with the ideals expressed in the Declaration of Independence and the Constitution. They called attention to contradictions with the Declaration's statement that "All men are created equal," saying that homosexual citizens were unfailingly regarded as second-class citizens. They argued that sodomy laws robbed them of individual rights and, having been enacted without their consent, the laws contradicted the principle of government by consent of the governed. When public officials refused to hear their grievances, the activists said, they were no better than the British government that had refused to address the grievances of the American colonies. "The homosexual American citizen finds himself denied many of those unique and special features of American life whose initial affirmation we both solemnly and joyously celebrate at Independence Hall on July 4," the demonstrators said. "That we do not now have these basic essentials to a life lived in the American tradition is the reason for which homosexual American citizens, and other enlightened citizens who support them, are picketing in front of Independence Hall."[16]

During the 1960s, Independence Hall and its surroundings attracted both conservatives and liberals, often drawing these two currents of American political activism into direct contact.[17] With Independence Hall as a rallying point, Cold War pageantry

49. Calling attention to conservative views, in 1966 the Young Americans for Freedom stage a rally replete with American symbolism. Arriving in Independence Square, the president of Boys Nation carries a torch lit at the Statue of Liberty and escorts the reigning Miss USA (Courtesy of the Urban Archives, Temple University, Philadelphia)

such as the Loyalty Day and Armed Forces Day parades continued with enthusiastic support in Philadelphia longer than in many other American cities.[18] Such events helped to define Independence Hall as a place for supporting the American government and especially the military, making it a keenly contested place during the Vietnam War. In the public space around Independence Hall, antiwar demonstrators and counterdemonstrators both demanded to be heard. While antiwar protests took place at various places around Philadelphia, Independence Hall was the favored staging ground for rallies to defend the war effort or support American troops. In 1965, three thousand members of the American Legion and Veterans of Foreign Wars paraded to Independence Hall for a Dedication Day program "to affirm our dedication to the principles of democracy and freedom, and to express our appreciation to our fighting men for their defense of those principles in Viet Nam."[19] Early in 1966, the veterans joined with the conservative Young Americans for Freedom at Independence Hall for a

50. In the shadow of Independence Hall in 1966, both sides of the debate over the Vietnam War demand to be heard. Philadelphia police maintain distance between demonstrators for and against U.S. involvement in Vietnam. (Courtesy of the Urban Archives, Temple University, Philadelphia)

"freedom rally in support of U.S. policy in Vietnam." The gathering brought the full force of patriotic symbolism to bear: the president of Boys Nation arrived bearing a torch that had been lit at the Statue of Liberty, and he escorted Miss USA, who had just returned from touring South Vietnam with the Bob Hope troupe. A line of pompon-waving cheerleaders welcomed them to Independence Square.[20]

The potential for another battle of Independence Hall, reminiscent of the 1947 confrontation between World War I veterans and the Progressive Citizens of America, presented itself on a Saturday afternoon in August 1966. On the anniversary of the atomic bombing of Hiroshima, about five hundred peace demonstrators marched to Independence Hall to the beat of muffled drums, led by twenty-five people dressed in white masks and white gowns, representing the dead of Hiroshima and Vietnam. When they arrived at Independence Hall, a rally of about two hundred members of the Young Americans for Freedom, the American Legion, and the Veterans of Foreign Wars was already in progress. The rally broke up as the parade passed. "Go home, you creeps," one person shouted. "Remember Pearl Harbor!" shouted another. As the volume of taunts increased, about seventy-five police officers deployed along Chestnut Street in front of Independence Hall, separating the groups. When the antiwar demonstrators assembled on the mall and began a program of speeches and antiwar songs, they were joined by some of the demonstrators from the other side. When a speaker called the Vietnam conflict "a war which the American people have never been permitted to vote against," he was met with calls of "Kill the Red pigs!" and "Get the Commies out of here!" Police escorted the loudest hecklers away; plain-clothes officers mingled in the crowd. By the end of the afternoon, demonstrators from both sides dispersed without serious incident.[21]

In the conflict over Vietnam, as with civil rights activities, the Liberty Bell became a contested symbol. For supporters of the U.S. government's Vietnam policy, any commemorative activity at the Liberty Bell that suggested sympathy with the Communist government of North Vietnam seemed to be subversive and a desecration of a patriotic symbol. On September 10, 1969, ten members of the antiwar organization Resist placed flowers in a bowl of rice under the Liberty Bell. This act, which the group described as a way to "honor the rights of all people to independence," triggered a reaction among Philadelphians who observed that the flowers were placed on the day of burial for Ho Chi Minh, the nationalist and Communist leader of North Vietnam. The Liberty Bell had been "used to glorify a man whose lifelong actions promoted totalitarianism," said Bruce Underwood, a Temple University professor who emerged as a spokesman for Philadelphians who objected to the act. The next week, 225 people gathered for a symbolic cleansing of the Liberty Bell, with eight members of the Philadelphia Police Civil Disobedience Squad on hand to guard against conflict. "In our symbolic cleansing of the bell, we will be remembering our dedication to the ideals of liberty, justice, and equality which the bell represents," Underwood said. Two secretaries who worked for another of the event's organizers wiped the Liberty Bell "clean" of the stain of Communist sympathy.[22]

Together, Independence Hall and the Liberty Bell cast a spectrum of meanings across the controversies of the United States during the 1960s. The expanded public parks around Independence Hall provided space for a variety of events, including countercultural activities that sometimes mocked, inverted, or redefined the traditional historic symbolism of the place. Independence Square served as a stage for political and social activism, but in 1967 it also was overrun by a "be-in" of 2,500 young people who gathered for an "unbirthday party" in the manner of Alice in Wonderland. They exchanged flowers, candy, and, according to police, marijuana cigarettes.[23] Twenty people were arrested after surrounding a police car on Chestnut Street and shouting "Flower power!" while showering the car with flowers and food. Similarly communal in spirit, but more serious in intent, thousands filled Independence Mall in April 1970 for the first Earth Day. With environmental activist Ralph Nader presiding, demonstrators signed a "Declaration of Interdependence," which appropriated the memory of the document of 1776 to proclaim unity among the people of the earth against environmental degradation. At a place associated with creating a nation, with entertainment provided by the Native American rock group Red Bone and the Broadway cast of the musical *Hair,* the Earth Day demonstration called attention to issues that transcended national boundaries.[24]

In many ways, the events of the 1960s at Independence Hall revived the building's earlier history as a place of conflict as well as commemoration. As shown in Chapter 4, a similar dynamic was present during the mid-nineteenth century, when Philadelphians reserved the "Hall of Independence" for civic ceremonies but tolerated public demonstrations in Independence Square. As in the nineteenth century, the commemorative uses of Independence Hall during the 1960s reflected only part of its significance to the American people. The building's caretakers guarded it as a place to commemorate the past, but public activities sustained Independence Hall as a place for contemporary debate over the nation's past, present, and future.

"Philadelphia Fling"

Although the turmoil of the 1960s somewhat diminished the postwar surge in tourism, the United States remained locked in a Cold War with the Soviet Union, and Independence Hall and the Liberty Bell continued to be magnets for vacationers. The appeal of Independence Hall as a tourist attraction could be seen not only in Philadelphia, but also in two replica buildings constructed during the 1960s. Reinforcing identification of Independence Hall as a tourist site, the Knott's Berry Farm amusement park in Orange County, California, created its own replica complete with a Liberty Bell ("authentically" cracked) and dedicated the new attraction on July 4, 1966.[25] Americans of the 1960s could also express patriotism by shopping at "Independence Mall" near Wilmington, Delaware, a strip shopping center with an imitation Independence Hall as its focal point, built between 1963 and 1965.[26] Occupying landscapes of consumption, such replica buildings made it possible for patriotic Americans to make their pilgrimages to the bulwark of democracy and have their souvenirs, too—all within the secure environment of a theme park or shopping center and without traveling to the city of Philadelphia.

In Philadelphia, although the city had given up management of Independence Hall in 1951, city boosters retained an active interest in historic sites as lures for tourist dollars. Philadelphia's association with its historic buildings seemed as much a burden as a benefit, however. Tourism promoters were eager to profit from out-of-town visitors, but reluctant to tie the city's image to an eighteenth-century building. Where was the excitement? The sophistication? The night life? Even Philadelphians exhibited ambivalence toward their national landmark. (In 1959, when WRCV Radio launched a contest to encourage Philadelphians to visit Independence Hall, where they could drop postcards in a box to be eligible to win, the prize was a week's vacation *away* from Philadelphia, to the new state of Hawaii.)[27] While the National Park Service worked to restore the city's historic buildings, tourism promotions during the 1950s and 1960s emphasized the fun that visitors would find in Philadelphia, apart from the historic sites. The city invited travelers to enjoy "Philadelphia in Spring" (1958), to discover that "Summer Time Is Fun Time in Philadelphia" (1967), to explore "Surprising Philadelphia" (1968), and to have a "Philadelphia Fling" (1969).[28] When the Convention and Visitors Bureau built a new headquarters in the late 1950s, the "hospitality center" was not a brick building in the historic district but a glass-walled, flying saucer-like cylinder on a plaza near City Hall.[29] When promoters wanted to inject more excitement into tourism promotions during the 1960s, they sent "Miss Welcome to Philadelphia Girls"—women aged twenty to forty, nominated by their employers—to visit governors throughout the United States.[30]

The quest to position Philadelphia as a modern, entertaining destination extended to Independence Hall, especially on the Fourth of July. In the view of tourism promoters, visitors to Philadelphia could demonstrate their patriotism, but in festive ways that would enhance their family vacations. Beginning in 1958 and continuing through the 1960s, July Fourth became the central event of an annual, city-sponsored "Freedom Week" festival. The first year, activities around Independence Hall included band music, folk dancing, and a swearing-in ceremony for new citizens. As the festival evolved, it retained a solemn "Pageant of Flags" in front of Independence Hall on Independence Day, but added such entertainment elements as fashion shows, musical plays, and the crowning of a "Miss Liberty Belle." Children from each of the original thirteen states, who also had the good fortune of being born on July 4, were invited to enter the "Yankee Doodle Dandy Essay Contest," with the winner to be announced in Philadelphia on the Fourth of July.[31] In their drive to attract tourists, Philadelphians defined Independence Hall not only as a historic place, but a destination for fun and recreation.

Philadelphia's interest in promoting tourism, coexisting at Independence Hall with attention to historic preservation and the frequent unrest of the 1960s, contributed to the rise and fall of an especially elaborate attempt to add pizzazz to the city's historic landscape—the "Lumadrama," a nighttime sound-and-light spectacle that premiered in Independence Square in 1962. At the urging of city boosters, the National Park Service agreed to allow Lumadrama Inc. of New York, backed by start-up money from a private foundation and local donations, to create a show in the style of similar attractions at the Palace of Versailles, the Parthenon, and the Pyramids. For the Independence Hall show, the audience sat on folding chairs in Independence Square, surrounded by trees in which lights and speakers had been hidden, watching lights highlight various rooms in the building and points around the square while listening to a recording of Fredric March and other actors performing a drama written by the Pulitzer Prize–winning poet Archibald MacLeish.

With taped music, sound effects, and light, the show titled "The American Bell" appealed to popular sentiment toward the Liberty Bell by weaving together the early history of the State House bell with events leading to independence from Great Britain. In contrast to the simplified narrative ordinarily presented to visitors touring Independence Hall, MacLeish's script integrated contrasts between the modern city and earlier times, direct quotations from historical figures, and thematic attention to the meaning of freedom. In MacLeish's view, Independence Hall's size and plain exterior belied the significance of events that occurred within. "The essence of this building is its simplicity, contrasted with the monumental events that took place here," MacLeish explained to a reporter. "A simple, modest building, but so powerful in its impact on men's minds." In the production, the poet said, he wanted to create "a positive statement of freedom." Each night, the show ended with a chorus of bell-ringing (on tape) and voices shouting, "Let it ring!"[32]

Whatever its literary merits, "The American Bell" flopped as a tourist attraction. Although some viewers found the program so inspirational that they knelt in prayer at the conclusion or started singing "America the Beautiful," the show routinely filled fewer than one-fourth of the one thousand seats available in Independence Square. Neither tourists nor Philadelphians could be persuaded to stay in the historic district after dark, and the spectacle of lights shining on a building was no match for the action of television or the movies, especially for younger viewers. A notable exception to the usually dismal attendance occurred in 1968—a year of protest over the Vietnam War, violence at the Democratic National Convention, the rise of the Black Power movement, and the assassinations of Robert F. Kennedy and Martin Luther King, Jr. During that summer of discontent, a record 12,425 people attended "The American Bell."[33] Even so, the show contributed to the ongoing conflict around Independence Hall during the 1960s. Some audience members praised its patriotism. "This program makes you proud to be an American," one viewer wrote in an audience survey. "In times such as these, when indifference spreads like a cancer throughout our land, it brings a lump to my throat and tears to my eyes to be so graphically reminded of our American Heritage," wrote another. For others, the show revived a long history of Independence Hall as a place representing contradictions between the nation's founding principles and American society, particularly for African Americans. In the audience survey, one African American wrote, "The program is for whites only. Negroes and other minorities (and foreign visitors) must be embarrassed at the gulf between our noble words and actual deeds." Some African Americans left the show before its conclusion. The Lumadrama illuminated aspects of Independence Hall that the show's creators had not intended.[34]

Like the Lumadrama, the National Park Service interpretive programs by the late 1960s acknowledged Independence Hall as the park's centerpiece but at the same time demonstrated an interest in broadening the park's message to the public. Beginning in 1968, the Park Service extended its interpretive reach beyond political events to pursue three themes for interpretation: the American Revolution, Benjamin Franklin—Man of Ideas, and Philadelphia—Capital City.[35] Without breaking the boundaries of the eighteenth-century period considered "historic," the themes reflected park officials' interest in presenting not only the history of Independence Hall but also other structures and stories within the park's boundaries. Within the Franklin theme, the Park Service looked forward to establishing a museum at the site of Franklin's former home, an objective accomplished in 1976. The Capital City theme provided a framework for interpreting Congress Hall and Old City Hall as places of significance during the 1790s, when Philadelphia served as the nation's capital. While still the center of attention, Independence Hall stood as one of several historic sites presented to visitors.

Within Independence Hall, tourism and social conflict during the 1960s converged to challenge and redefine perceptions of the building's historic significance. Contemporary conflict intruded on the historic space physically, as on those occasions when college students demonstrated for civil rights around the Liberty Bell or when

Vietnam War opponents and supporters clashed on Independence Square. While park administrators did not change the basic narrative of events presented to visitors at Independence Hall, chants and picket signs awakened an awareness of the building as a place of the present as well as the past. A park master plan in 1971 interpreted the rooms of Independence Hall as places not only of famous events but also powerful ideas. Here, the plan acknowledged, "each generation by turn can, through review of the past, discover new meaning in the present." After a decade of sharp conflict, however, park officials did not view this process as a contentious expression of views about the past and present. Rather, they proposed that the experience of visiting Independence Hall should provide a "rational basis for the life to be led today and tomorrow." Ironically, but fully in keeping with the building's history, the language of the planning document reflected a continuing interest in maintaining order at a place firmly associated with the American Revolution.[36]

Lock Down

Often in its history, Independence Hall had been a place of dual character—a place of conflict and commemoration, both local and national, both past and present. With the Liberty Bell situated inside Independence Hall, the building and its most famous artifact operated together as reminders of the nation's history and magnets for its continuing controversies. Through the 1960s and into the 1970s, Independence Hall was a place where diverse citizens from Philadelphia and elsewhere contested the issues of the times, but it was also a tourist attraction and a carefully restored time capsule of the eighteenth century. Could Independence Hall be all of these things? Preservation demanded that the structure be protected, but this mission was continually challenged by tourists, demonstrators, and everyday movement through a building whose doors were open to the city. With the Bicentennial of the Declaration of Independence approaching, the federal caretakers of Independence Hall considered this dilemma as they braced for a new surge of tourism and the likelihood that protest and commemoration would battle for attention on the nation's 200th anniversary. Their solutions, guided by the requirements of preservation and the demands of tourism, erected a new and long-lasting barrier between Independence Hall and the city around it, locking the building in its eighteenth-century past.

As transformed by the National Park Service, by 1972 Independence Hall offered four venues for historical interpretation: the Assembly Room, where the story of the Declaration of Independence and the Constitution could be told; the Court Room, where visitors could learn about the eighteenth-century judicial system; the tower stair hall, where the Liberty Bell stood; and the second floor, which was restored to its appearance prior to 1777, creating a space that would tell the story of British rule and the social life of Philadelphia before the American Revolution. Each room was a period piece as perfectly re-created as possible, including appropriate furnishings and paint colors scientifically determined by analyzing the many layers of paint that had been applied to the walls over more than two centuries.[37] By 1972, with completion of restoration on the second floor, Independence Hall had been fully transformed from a container of miscellaneous historic artifacts to an assemblage of meticulous re-creations of the past. More than one million people visited each year.

The volume of visitation was a paramount concern for the National Park Service, charged with preserving Independence Hall as well as making it accessible to the public. The ultimate response, in 1973, created a new degree of separation between the building and its home city. For the first time, the National Park Service banned individuals from wandering through Independence Hall in favor of a continuous flow of orderly tours. For visitors, the tours were intended to provide a more satisfying encounter with the building's history. For Philadelphians, there would be no more casual short-cutting through the building or stopping for brief touches of the Liberty Bell. However, for most Philadelphians, Independence Hall had long been a distant place in a section of the city they seldom visited. Some people complained, but not loudly or in great numbers.[38] The number of people passing through Independence Hall plummeted from 1,284,954 in 1972 to a more manageable 851,275 in 1973, the first year of restricting access to organized tours. Demonstrations and the activity of everyday life continued outside its doors, but as the nation approached its Bicentennial, Independence Hall stood safeguarded as a place of the nation rather than the city, managed for the appreciation of tourists and in the interest of preservation.

The National Park Service recognized that despite the effort expended on historic preservation, the primary attraction for many tourists was not Independence Hall itself, but the Liberty Bell. A Park Service plan for Independence Hall interpretation in 1959 had illustrated the needs of visitors with a dashing tourist leaping the hurdles of visitor center, rest rooms, souvenirs, signs and markers, historic buildings, and museums to get to the Liberty Bell—"The Finish Line."[39] Positioned in the tower stair hall, its home base since the 1870s, the bell presented problems for interpretation as well as traffic flow. At most, fifty people at a time could be accommodated in the space around the bell, creating a bottleneck that slowed movement of visitors through the other, larger rooms in the building. As the interior of Independence Hall was restored to its

51. Tourist interest in Independence Hall builds in the years leading to the Bicentennial. Lines in Independence Square, shown here in 1975, became common after the National Park Service instituted access only by guided tours in 1973. (Courtesy of the Urban Archives, Temple University, Philadelphia)

eighteenth-century appearance, the Liberty Bell stood out as an anachronism.[40] The bell had been in the Pennsylvania State House since 1752, but during the late eighteenth century it had been up in the tower, not sitting in the hallway, cracked and silent. To satisfy the interests of tourists and to complete the aura of eighteenth-century authenticity inside Independence Hall, the Liberty Bell would have to be moved.

Prospects for moving the Liberty Bell remained within the pages of Park Service documents until the park and the city of Philadelphia began looking toward the Bicentennial. City boosters hoped that as many as forty million tourists would flock to Philadelphia during 1976 to visit the nation's birthplace, perhaps to see another grand world's fair like the Centennial Exhibition of a century before. For 1976, the world's fair never advanced beyond wishful thinking. Philadelphia was slow to organize and unable to agree on a plan for celebration, and city officials' highly publicized fears of urban unrest dampened the potential for tourism.[41] Furthermore, the city found that it could no longer lay claim to the nation's birthdays, as it had done successfully in 1876 and less successfully in 1926. By 1976, the nation encompassed many assertive constituencies identified by region, age, gender, race, and ethnicity, and the Northeast had declined in population and political influence. Instead of a centralized commemoration, the American Revolution Bicentennial Commission decided in 1972 that the anniversary would be celebrated with locally organized events around the nation. Further diminishing Philadelphia's role, the commemoration was viewed as a celebration of "200 years—not 200 years ago." Emerging from the turbulence of the 1960s, the United States would focus more on its endurance than on its origins. Even in Pennsylvania, the state emblem for the Bicentennial showed not Independence Hall or the Liberty Bell, but a family of three holding hands, walking through a planet-like sphere over the slogan, "So your children can tell their children."[42]

Despite the decentralized plan for the Bicentennial, administrators at Independence National Historical Park expected a surge of visitors. By the time planning began in the late 1960s, an identifiable park existed. Most buildings that fell outside the interpretive period of the park had been demolished, leaving the First and Second Banks of the United States, Carpenters' Hall, and the homes of Bishop William White and Dolley Todd in the three blocks east of Independence Hall. Two eighteenth-century buildings had been reconstructed in front of Carpenters' Hall to house military museums, and park curators were looking forward to installing the Independence Hall portrait collection in a new gallery in the Second Bank. Before the Bicentennial, a final push of development would place exhibits at the site of the home of Benjamin Franklin, reconstruct the eighteenth-century City Tavern and the house where Thomas

Jefferson wrote the Declaration of Independence, and—to serve the needs of tourists during the Bicentennial and beyond—provide a new, modern visitors' center at the eastern end of the park.[43]

Tourism was so closely associated with the Liberty Bell by the 1970s that the new visitors' center seemed to park planners and architects to be a natural new home for the bell. The architectural firm Cambridge Seven Associates of Cambridge, Massachusetts, designed a modern, modular brick structure with a 105-foot tower for displaying the Liberty Bell. The plan combined reverence for the bell with efficient traffic flow and a 1970s concern for its safety. From the top of the tower, the bell was to be suspended to eye level by steel cables. Tourists would have easy access through the lobby of the visitors' center or through sliding doors of bullet-proof glass on two sides of the tower. Inside, shafts of sunlight from massive windows high in the tower would create a cathedral-like aura for the Liberty Bell and its visitors, heightening the symbolic power of the bell. Planners estimated that as many as 1,200 people an hour would be able to move through the visitors' center to watch a new film produced by Twentieth-Century Fox, view exhibits, buy souvenirs, and see the Liberty Bell before moving on to the park's other attractions, including Independence Hall.[44]

More than restricted access to Independence Hall, the announcement of the visitors' center plan in 1972 reawakened Philadelphians' sense of guardianship over the Liberty Bell. Although Independence Hall and the Liberty Bell were part of the national park, the city retained ownership of both. Park Service employees would come and go, tourists would take pictures and get back in the car, but Philadelphians had been going to Independence Hall to see the Liberty Bell for generations. Locally, Independence Hall and the Liberty Bell *together* defined a historic place. Invoking the same reasoning that had stopped the Liberty Bell's out-of-town journeys earlier in the century, Philadelphians argued that separating the building and its most famous artifact would diminish both. Park officials were at first successful in persuading Mayor Frank Rizzo to endorse moving the bell to the new visitors' center, but public opinion soon intervened. The center was too far away from Independence Hall, Philadelphians complained. If the bell must go there, couldn't the building have a nice Colonial design? The writer of one letter to the editor said the planned tower looked like a prison turret; another said that if tourist traffic was the main concern, the Liberty Bell might as well be set up in a drive-through window. The debate was carried on largely in the city newspapers and within the citizens' advisory commission of the park, but lawyer Isidor Ostroff, who in the 1930s had been one of the first Philadelphians to envision a national park at Independence Hall, filed a federal lawsuit to try to stop the move. As construction of the new visitors' center, including the tower, began in 1973, the Liberty Bell question remained undecided.[45]

The solution to the Liberty Bell dilemma was found not within the boundaries of Independence National Historical Park, but north of Independence Hall, on the three-block mall created during the 1950s by the state of Pennsylvania. On the block closest to Independence Hall, the Liberty Bell could be separated from its eighteenth-century confines but kept within sight of its original home. Tourists would have to walk only one block, not three, to see both the hall and the bell. With the state agreeable—even eager—to turn over the expense of maintaining the mall, politicians at all levels of government, park administrators, and the Philadelphians who served on the park's advisory commission agreed to the new site. By the end of 1973, the three-block expanse of lawns and plazas north of Independence Hall became part of the national park. In 1975, in the space where nineteenth-century buildings had been demolished to create a less urban environment for Independence Hall, construction began for the twentieth-century building to house the Liberty Bell.[46]

By providing a home for the Liberty Bell separate from its eighteenth-century confines in Independence Hall, the new Liberty Bell Pavilion opened a new era in the long and entwined history of the building and its renowned artifact. The pavilion, designed by Mitchell/Giurgola Associates of Philadelphia, enclosed the bell in a modern design of glass, copper, steel, and white granite, reinforcing recognition of the bell as a timeless American symbol. A sloping roof swept up toward Independence Hall, visually linking the new building with the old. While some Philadelphians criticized the pavilion, saying they disliked the modern design or that it was a mistake to place a building on the mall, the new structure fulfilled the needs of tourists. Greater numbers of people would be able to see the Liberty Bell. They would assemble in a waiting area, proceed through a corridor of white oak, and gather closely around the bell, which would be mounted on steel supports in front of a large window facing Independence Hall. Passersby would be able to see the bell through the window, and they could listen to a tape-recorded message about the Liberty Bell by pressing a button outside the pavilion.[47]

With the Liberty Bell Pavilion completed just in time for the Bicentennial, Park Superintendent Hobart G. Cawood diverted attention from controversy to celebration by turning the moving of the Liberty Bell into the first grand event of 1976.[48] Although rain washed out planned fireworks and choral performances, at midnight on December 31, 1975, the Centennial Bell in the tower of Independence Hall struck thirteen times, once for each of the original states. Bells in church steeples around the city

52. With the Liberty Bell installed in a new, modern pavilion in 1976, Independence Hall fades into the background. With this separation of the bell from its historic home, interpretation of the famous artifact could focus on its timeless, symbolic qualities, while information presented in the building emphasized events of the eighteenth century. (Courtesy of the Urban Archives, Temple University, Philadelphia)

replied. The Liberty Bell, mounted on a four-wheeled cart and shielded by plastic from the rain, moved out of Independence Hall down a ramp, under the guidance of uniformed construction workers. A fife and drum corps led the one hundred-yard procession, followed by city dignitaries, clergymen, and Philadelphia police. As many as 40,000 people watched from beneath umbrellas, and WCAU-TV interrupted Guy Lombardo's televised New Year's Eve concert with four live cut-ins from the Liberty Bell. Inside the new pavilion, workers hoisted the bell onto its new steel supports, in front of the new picture window. The crowd cheered, and several hundred people stayed to be among the first to pass through the pavilion and touch the Liberty Bell in its new home.[49]

A century before, on the New Year's Eve that opened the nation's centennial year, Independence Hall had been bathed in light and celebrated for its significance to

American history and national unity. In 1976, Independence Hall stood in darkness while lights focused on the Liberty Bell moving away from the old building to its modern home. The building that had stood in Philadelphia since 1732 was, by the late twentieth century, thoroughly defined, restored, and preserved as a historic place. But "independence" was an event that occurred in the past, something to learn about on the tours that moved through Independence Hall every ten minutes. "Liberty" was an enduring idea, represented by the old bell with its distinctive crack, an icon to contemplate and touch. Preservation and tourism demanded that the bell hang separately, not together with a building yoked to the past. On the first day of the bicentennial year, 11,500 people filed through the Liberty Bell Pavilion.[50] While more than 1.3 million people toured Independence Hall during the 200th anniversary year of the Declaration of Independence, viewing a re-creation of the eighteenth century more precise than any previous restoration had achieved, more than 3.6 million people visited the Liberty Bell.[51] Bathed in light and the flashes from thousands of cameras, the bell received its visitors in the foreground of Independence Hall, which seemed distant and small through the glass of the pavilion and across a gulf of time.

By the time of the Bicentennial, Independence Hall appeared to be a solid, stable bridge between the eighteenth-century past and the twentieth-century present.[52] However, activities in and around the structure reflected a much more complex relationship between history and memory. The building operated more like a prism—solid, but refracting a spectrum of meanings. Independence Hall communicated the memory of the Declaration of Independence and the Constitution across two centuries, to be seized and contested by twentieth-century Americans. In and around Independence Hall, public memory refracted across a spectrum of allegiance and dissent. From the perspectives of varied constituents, Independence Hall stood as a reminder of the language contained in the Declaration of Independence and the Constitution, the principles associated with those founding documents, or the extent to which the nation had succeeded or failed to realize its potential.

Managed by the federal government, Independence Hall functioned as a place for constructing an official version of the past as well as a multitude of other views.[53] However, the spectrum of meanings attached to Independence Hall did not fall into a neat dichotomy of a government version of history contested by the vernacular activities of interest groups. Rather, Independence Hall stood at the center of complex interactions between authorities and the public. The public both validated and contested the National Park Service's interpretation and management of Independence Hall as a place to honor the eighteenth-century acts that culminated in the Declaration of Independence and the U.S. Constitution. In validation, tourism and patriotic commemorations reinforced the celebration of the hallmark events of 1776 and 1787. However, even these corroborating activities operated in contemporary contexts that challenged the interpretation of Independence Hall as strictly a place of the eighteenth century. Vacationers were both citizens and consumers. In addition to validating Independence Hall as an important place in the nation's history, they contributed to its significance in the modern economy of tourism. Patriotic commemorations expressed love of country associated with the nation's founding ideals, but at the same time they operated as defensive acts to safeguard the nation against a perceived decline in respect for American principles.

Activities that overtly challenged the National Park Service's control over Independence Hall were similarly complex. While many of the demonstrations staged in and around the building criticized the federal government in some way, others sought to support government policies and embrace Independence Hall and the Liberty Bell as symbols of national endurance. Local responses to the Park Service's decision-making constituted an additional layer of complexity. Philadelphians sought to capitalize on the presence of a national landmark but also to criticize management decisions that seemed to alter the place of Independence Hall and the Liberty Bell as local treasures. Rather than dividing into categories of official memory promoted by the government and vernacular memory forged by the general public, the public memory constructed at Independence Hall during the 1960s and 1970s constituted an array of perspectives that crossed boundaries between the official and the vernacular, past and present, and local and national.

Interestingly, Americans during the 1960s and 1970s were reenacting a history of Independence Hall that had been mostly forgotten. In its appearance and interpretation, Independence Hall was a place of famous eighteenth-century events that culminated in the Declaration of Independence and the Constitution. As a historic site, it was quiet, controlled, and reverently presented for the public's appreciation. With the interpretation focused on national history in the eighteenth century, visitors did not hear of the conflicts that had animated Independence Hall and its surroundings, especially in the contentious years of nation-building that followed the American Revolution. However, in the public space around Independence Hall and sometimes inside the building at the base of the Liberty Bell, the public demonstrated that the nation remained a work in progress, continually constructed and reconstructed around its founding principles. The building, a site of memory, triggered associations with the past and engaged the public in the long tradition of dissent that had enveloped Independence Hall for much of its history.[54]

Would this latest spectrum of activity at Independence Hall be remembered? Guards at Independence Hall kept careful notes of every event and often collected handbills and programs, but their reports were filed away among the administrative records of Independence National Historical Park. Newspapers published articles and photographs, but these went into the newspapers' morgues and onto microfilm, not into the public interpretation of Independence Hall. Tourists who happened upon demonstrations took their memories and snapshots home with them. The college students moved on. When the dust settled, the contests over issues such as civil rights and the Vietnam War faded from view, leaving no trace on the landscape. Independence Hall, the building-turned-time capsule of the eighteenth century, communicated little of its history as a place of nineteenth- or twentieth-century conflict. The forces of tourism and preservation prevailed, ensuring that future generations would be able to visit Independence Hall, where they would learn much about the founding of the United States of America but very little about the lengthy struggles that tested and defined the nation as it grew and changed.

Chapter 10

MEMORY

The Truths We Hold to Be Self-Evident

On an autumn evening in 1995, a man riding an eastbound bus on Market Street in Philadelphia called his companion's attention to Independence Hall, which they could see from the bus window. "You know the difference between Independence Hall and City Hall?" he asked. "There's where they gave us freedom," he said, motioning at Independence Hall. "And there," he said, indicating the Philadelphia City Hall at a distance behind them, "is where they take it away." Glimpsing Independence Hall from a one-block distance had reminded him of the joke, had triggered an association with the history of Independence Hall, and had affirmed his sense of contrast between past and present. Although the nation's founding had taken place more than two hundred years before, the building tapped the joker's memory of what had happened—not a living memory of his own experience, but a public memory of the meaning of the American Revolution, absorbed perhaps from schoolbooks, popular culture, or a trip or two to Independence Hall. Sitting in its spacious park in twentieth-century Philadelphia, Independence Hall was a depository of memory, preserving the perceptions of the past of many generations, as well as a conduit of memory, communicating with present observers like the man on the bus and his companion.

Surviving from the eighteenth century, Independence Hall seems to be a direct bridge between past and present for the millions of people who experience it every year as tourists or in the course of daily life in Philadelphia. There it is: the architecture of Colonial America, the story of the American Revolution, the creation of the nation. As with so many other historic buildings, preservation and interpretation seem to stop time. However, as a twentieth-century German philosopher, Hans-Georg Gadamer, has observed, "Works of architecture do not stand motionless on the shore of the stream of history, but are borne along by it."[1] Independence Hall has been carried from the eighteenth century to the present by the currents of American life. The building originated as a cultural statement of British gentility at a time when Americans valued their ties to a distant homeland. As the Pennsylvania State House, it was immersed in the Enlightenment, in the American Revolution, and in the politics of creating a nation. The place became known as Independence Hall, dedicated to remembering the nation's founders, but it echoed with the conflicts of slavery and nativism. From the nineteenth century into the twentieth, citizens gathered not only to honor the nation's founding but also to demand full inclusion in the promises of the Declaration of Independence and the Constitution. From the American Revolution to the turn of the millennium, Independence Hall has been a place for celebrating the nation's triumphs and mourning its tragedies, but it also has been a place in a large American city, surrounded by a diverse population engaged with contemporary issues and the business of everyday life.

If we look at Independence Hall today, how much of this history do we see? Only a snapshot, carefully framed but closely cropped. Instead of seeming to move with the currents of time, Independence Hall appears more like a stepping stone in the stream of history, a place to gain a sense of stability when all around seems to be in motion. It is a meticulously restored eighteenth-century building, protected and interpreted by the federal government for the benefit of visitors. It is a remarkable survival from a time that is increasingly slipping away. Independence Hall educates, it inspires, and it sustains a material connection to the Declaration of Independence and the Constitution. This is work that bolsters public memory of the nation's founders, its earliest official documents, and ideals that resonate across time. Supporting this memory has meant letting go of much of the rest—not in a conscious betrayal of history, but in a quest to preserve the history at Independence Hall that has seemed most self-evidently significant to those who exercised political or cultural authority over the building.

The quest continues.

The previous chapter of this book ended in 1976, with Independence Hall fully restored to an eighteenth-century appearance, presented to the public on guided tours, and distanced from its popular artifact, the Liberty Bell. In the years between the Bicentennial and the publication of this book, Independence Hall has been more static and unchanging than at any comparable period of time in its history. Important events have come and gone, notably a session of Congress in Independence Hall in 1987, during the commemoration of the Bicentennial of the U.S. Constitution. Significant work has been done to upgrade and stabilize the building's infrastructure. But in its outward appearance and interpretation, Independence Hall has remained largely the same for the past quarter-century. With time fully reversed to the eighteenth century, the building has become a finished product of historic restoration. Still, as the central feature of a national park, Independence Hall has been surrounded by continuing efforts to engage visitors with history and to bolster Philadelphia's tourist economy. If not for Independence Hall, there would likely be no historical park in Philadelphia to sustain the memory of the nation's founding and lure visitors from across the country and around the world. So, while 1976 is a logical end to this study, more recent developments also warrant mention to explain the changing environment at Independence National Historical Park.

At the turn of the twenty-first century, bulldozers went to work again on the landscape adjacent to Independence Hall. Independence Mall, which opened a vista north of Independence Hall during the 1950s, began to be converted from a Cold War landscape of ceremonial plazas to a more park-like campus for tourism and civic education. Plans envisioned a new, larger pavilion for the Liberty Bell and exhibits to explain its history and significance. On the second block of the mall, the new Independence Visitor Center opened in November 2001 to promote tourist attractions throughout the region as well as dispense information about the national park. Fundraising began for an Independence Park Insititute to serve as headquarters for educational programs. Finally, in the third block of the mall, builders broke ground for a National Constitution Center, which Congress had authorized during the Constitution's 200th anniversary. Clearly, more than two hundred years after the famous events of 1776 and 1787, Independence Hall no longer speaks for itself. The historic space associated with the building is becoming ever more elaborate, with new venues for telling visitors what is important about this place and why. If these changes were not already occurring, they might have been predicted given the history of Independence Hall. Over time, ever since the Marquis de Lafayette visited the old Pennsylvania State House in 1824, ever-increasing spaces in and around the building have been dedicated to the memory of the nation's founding.

In its new configuration, Independence Mall represents something of a reintegration of Independence National Historical Park with the city of Philadelphia. A lengthy and sometimes contentious process of planning and public hearings preceded the remaking of the mall. At this juncture in the history of the park, the discussion had little to do with Independence Hall. Instead, the decision-making process focused on ways to remodel the blocks north of the building to serve the needs of the national park, its visitors, and the city's economy. Furthermore, supporters of the planned

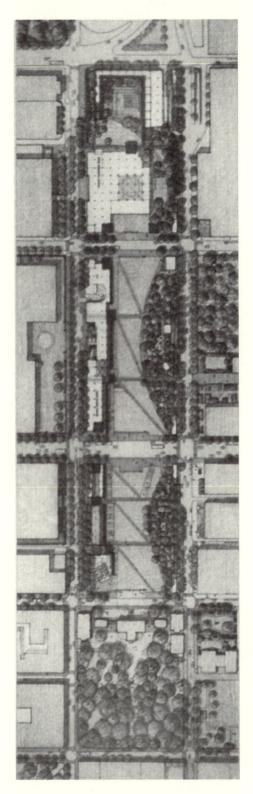

53. Fulfilling a new master plan for Independence National Historical Park adopted in 1997, a landscaped campus devoted to tourism and civic education replaces the ceremonial plazas of the Cold War era. Extending north from Independence Hall, this design by the Olin Partnership of Philadelphia shows a park bordered by a new Liberty Bell pavilion, Independence Visitor Center, Independence Park Institute education center, and National Constitution Center. (Courtesy of Independence National Historical Park)

54. The opening of the Independence Visitor Center (right) in November 2001 began the transformation of Independence Mall into a campus devoted to tourism and civic education. Landscaping remains under way and the Liberty Bell Pavilion of 1976 still stands in the foreground of Independence Hall. (Photo by the author)

National Constitution Center, mandated by Congress to be located in or near the park, sought a prime location. The open vista reaching northward from Independence Hall had its defenders, but the plazas of earlier decades were viewed primarily as opportunities for solving problems related to tourism. The National Park Service saw an opportunity to construct a new visitors center to replace the center built in 1976, which had never fully succeeded in drawing tourists three blocks eastward from Independence Hall and the Liberty Bell. Tourism boosters saw opportunities to create a more lively historic district with multiple attractions that would entice visitors to stay overnight in Philadelphia and explore city sites beyond Independence Hall. The resulting new structures on the mall would not be solely the domain of the National Park Service, but rather joint efforts with organizational partners and private donors.

Recent developments at Independence National Historical Park demonstrate that while restored buildings and landscapes may obscure aspects of history, these material remnants of the past also make it possible to recover histories long dismissed as marginal. Since its founding, the park has emphasized national history. A new park master plan adopted in 1997 signalled a change, with interpretive themes also addressing the history of Philadelphia and its diverse inhabitants. Instead of focusing on Philadelphia only in relationship to the American Revolution or as the capital city during the 1790s, the plan extended the park's interpretive reach to the eighteenth-century city more generally, including the "diverse population that contributed to its dynamic and cosmopolitan character."[2] In the renovation of Independence Mall, reminders of the diverse population of Philadelphia literally sprang from the ground as archaeologists uncovered evidence of eighteenth- and nineteenth-century inhabitants, including African Americans. Furthermore, in connection with a National Park Service initiative to present the history of the Underground Railroad, historians at Independence amended the park's documentation for the National Register of Historic Places to include a broad sweep of African American experience within the boundaries of the park. In October 2000, Park Superintendent Martha B. Aikens, herself African American, welcomed participants in the Underground Railroad initiative to Independence Square, where she noted that Frederick Douglass had once spoken against slavery in the shadow of Independence Hall. Such events suggest that Independence Hall and other buildings and spaces within the park are primed for more pluralistic interpretations than at any time in their history.

At the center of all of this activity, where does Independence Hall stand in the public mind? Today, it is more difficult than ever to say. The building is securely managed by the National Park Service, which controls nearly all of the aspects of buildings and public memory identified at the start of this book—its architectural characteristics, its environment, its preservation, and its use. While the Park Service cannot dictate the building's cultural significance, it has a strong hand in shaping it through the process of presenting the building to the public on guided tours. To a large degree, Independence Hall itself is no longer a site where everyday people construct public memory, but rather a place where memory is constructed for them, through the re-created ambiance of the eighteenth century and the officially sanctioned stories of the Declaration of Independence and the Constitution. As a physical record of public memory, Independence Hall has come to reveal more about the federal government's commitment to perpetuating the memory of the nation's founding than the public's attitudes toward the building and its famous events.

Tourism represents one measure of public attitudes toward Independence Hall. The lines of visitors who wait to tour the building affirm its importance in the minds of many. Significantly, 800,000 or more people tour Independence Hall each year. But are visitors drawn to this place by reverence for the building and the events that it recalls? Or are they delivered there by the prescribed itineraries of commercial tour operators, by the requirements of school field trips, or in quests to conquer checklists of important sites to see? Routinely, visitors to Philadelphia bypass Independence Hall rather than wait in the sometimes lengthy line to take a guided tour. Each year, approximately twice as many people visit the Liberty Bell, where the lines are shorter and the brief interpretive talks allow more people to pass by the artifact within the hours of the park's operation. The visitation of 822,070 people to Independence Hall in 2000 paled in comparison to the 5.5 million people who visited the Statue of Liberty, the 2.5 million who viewed Mount Rushmore in South Dakota, the 1.4 million who visited the U.S.S. *Arizona* Memorial at Pearl Harbor, or the 1.17 million who toured the White House.[3]

Does this mean that travelers are less interested in Independence Hall or consider it less important than other places of significance to American history? Perhaps, but tourism is driven by many factors, not only the pursuit of history. The Statue of Liberty benefits from its location at the tip of Manhattan as well as its powerful symbolism. The White House draws upon the massive flow of visitors to the nation's capital, where they can visit not only the White House but also the U.S. Capitol, the national memorials to American presidents, and cultural attractions such as the Smithsonian Institution. Factors such as these, combined with the limited capacity of Independence Hall, complicate the interpretation of visitor statistics as evidence of the significance of the building. The statistics show, however, that fewer people experience Independence Hall than some of the nation's other historic places. Because fewer people visit, the building has less opportunity to function as a bridge between personal experience and historical memory.

Even as tourism affirms the historic significance of Independence Hall, the building's appeal to contemporary travelers continues to be called into question by local efforts to infuse Philadelphia's historic district with lively entertainment. Visitors to Independence National Historical Park during 2001 could tour Independence Hall, visit the park's other historic structures, or join walking tours to learn more of the park's story. However, efforts by tourism promoters ensured that visitors also encountered actors in eighteenth-century costumes strolling through the park and performing skits or songs at scheduled intervals. Tourists who stayed into the evening could don multimedia headsets to listen to the voices of the Revolution while on a walking tour sponsored by a local energy company. With the historic buildings functioning as giant screens, flashing images brought historic figures and emotional conflict to life. In the grand finale, participants in this "Lights of Liberty" tour gazed at Independence

Hall while the text of the Declaration of Independence scrolled up the tower and a recorded chorus sang "God Bless America." The scene echoed the Lumadrama spectacle of the 1960s, but with the added admonition (in the words of the tour staff) to "Enjoy the Revolution!" Independence Hall was a historic landmark cloaked as evening entertainment. Price of admission: $17.76.

Like tourism, recognition of Independence Hall as a World Heritage Site both affirms the significance of the building and to some extent calls it into question. Named to the United Nations list in 1979, Independence Hall by 2000 was one of 690 sites in the world (twenty-two in the United States) to be designated for their cultural or natural significance. Does this reflect a shift in international perception since the 1940s, when Independence Hall failed to lure the U.N. to Philadelphia as a site for its permanent headquarters? Perhaps. The U.N.'s recognition of Independence Hall resulted from a vote by the International World Heritage Committee of UNESCO (United Nations Educational, Scientific, and Cultural Organization). However, sites are placed on the World Heritage list by nomination of their home countries. Furthermore, the nomination of Independence Hall appealed less to international recognition of the building itself than to regard for the global impact of the U.S. Declaration of Independence and the Constitution. As a World Heritage Site, the building serves as a stand-in for less tangible characteristics of U.S. history, such as commitment to freedom and representative government.[4]

Beyond the World Heritage Site designation and tourism, we might also look to public activities of commemoration and dissent as indications of the place of Independence Hall in public memory. However, as a treasured historic resource, Independence Hall is safeguarded by National Park Service regulations that have become far more stringent since the days when the building stood at the center of 1960s protest. The building is scrupulously protected and, therefore, strictly separated from all but the most orderly conduct. As a result, it is impossible to know how Americans of the early twenty-first century might freely express their attitudes toward the birthplace of the Declaration of Independence and the Constitution. Park officials firmly uphold the right to free speech, but they have authority to designate where "special events" are permitted within a national park. With an expanse of public space within the park's boundaries, park managers have many options in making decisions about what may take place and where. The perception of place as it pertains to Independence Hall extends to the boundaries of the park, so that public activities may be accommodated but also positioned in ways that do not disrupt the ambiance of the building or threaten its preservation.

Park regulations reserve Independence Square for commemorative activities. New American citizens are naturalized in the square. Every Fourth of July, Philadelphia awards its Liberty Medal to an international champion of freedom. Such activities are allowed by the park's regulations, which are based on Title 36 of the Federal Code of Regulations. While exercising careful stewardship over the spaces closest to Independence Hall, the regulations also invoke a selective history. Independence Square, so often in its history the scene of public demonstrations, is defined as a place that "historically . . . always included walks and greens for public enjoyment." The language brings to mind the Birch prints of the 1790s, which portrayed the State House Yard as a pastoral garden—an accurate portrayal, but an incomplete image of a decade punctuated by political activities in the square. To preserve the surviving "historic landscape," consisting of a 1915 redesign of the square, the regulations reason that "special events are [to be] minimized to preserve the atmosphere of peace and tranquility and to avoid unreasonable interference with interpretation, visitor services, or other program activities."[5] To be considered for permits, events must be sponsored by government agencies or be directly associated with historic events that occurred in the square. The regulations echo an earlier era of control over Independence Square—the Philadelphia city ordinance approved in 1912 to eliminate all but patriotic, city-sponsored events from the square. The 1915 landscaping, an artifact from that time, indeed communicates a sense of order, but it represents only part of the square's history. The regulations protect aspects of the square's history that serve preservation and management goals, but they displace a long tradition of conflict and dissent from Independence Square.

Interestingly, the regulations governing Independence National Historical Park have transferred the tradition of dissent from Independence Hall to the Liberty Bell, displayed in a separate pavilion across the street since 1976. The divergent symbolism of the building and its most famous artifact, which emerged during the Liberty Bell's cross-country travels between 1885 and 1915, remains evident in on-site interpretation. The Liberty Bell is presented to visitors as an artifact with a long history of significance in the pursuit of civil rights, from the abolitionists of the 1830s to today's demonstrations, while Independence Hall is presented as a place noted solely for the historic events of the late eighteenth century. The park's regulations further the distinction between Independence Hall and the Liberty Bell by identifying the bell as a symbol that "encourages the guaranteed exercise of free speech and assembly." In contrast to the controls exercised over Independence Square, park officials designate space near the Liberty Bell pavilion for "the exercise of First Amendment rights includ-

55. Conforming to park regulations, peace activists in the summer of 2000 stage an orderly demonstration outside the Liberty Bell pavilion, where "special events" are permitted at a safe distance from Independence Hall. The mounted police patrol indicates increased security during the 2000 Republican National Convention. (Photo by the author)

ing freedom of assembly, speech, religion, or press."[6] The regulations may indeed reflect the public's perception of the Liberty Bell, but they also dictate a connection between the Liberty Bell and public assembly by positioning demonstrations at this location. If not for the regulations, would demonstrators choose this site near the Liberty Bell but a block from Independence Hall? It is impossible to know. Clearly, in addition to allowing free speech, the regulations keep potentially unruly behavior a safe distance from Independence Hall. Although the latest park redesign moves the Liberty Bell to a new pavilion closer to Independence Hall, the designated "First Amendment Area" of Independence Mall will remain at the same safe distance—a block away.

Although such regulation of dissent seems a far cry from the spirit of the American Revolution, a spectrum of protest activity has continued within the bounds determined by the National Park Service. Periodically, organizations have tested the boundaries. Twice during Independence Day festivities, capitalizing on public and media attention trained on the nation's birthplace, groups have staged takeovers of the Liberty Bell. On the Fourth of July in 1992, seventeen of approximately two hundred abortion-rights demonstrators occupied the pavilion while the rest surrounded the building and chanted, "No choice, no liberty." Another occupation occurred on July 3, 1999, when the Liberty Bell pavilion was taken over for three hours by supporters of Pennsylvania death-row inmate Mumia Abu-Jamal, who they believed had been unfairly convicted for the murder of a city police officer. In addition to the Independence Day occupations, in 1995 an advocacy group for the homeless camped overnight near the Liberty Bell Pavilion to call attention to needs for affordable housing. Although the campers moved on after one night, their leader stayed in protest and was charged with "residing in a park area"—that is, violating the park's regulations against camping.[7] Despite regulatory control in and around Independence Hall during the last quarter of the twentieth century—perhaps in reaction against it—Americans have continued to turn to the surrounding national park as a place to test the limits of government tolerance for free speech. Within this park devoted to the memory of the American Revolution, the boundaries between liberty and order have remained contested.

As one of the longest-standing public buildings in the United States, Independence Hall provides one of the most extensive material records of perceptions of the nation, its ideals, and its controversies. Viewing this record as it has developed over time, rather than focusing exclusively on events of the eighteenth century, adds to our understanding of Independence Hall as a place where Americans have put great effort into implementing, sustaining, and challenging the ideals expressed in the nation's founding documents. When we look at changes made to the building not just to understand the structure for preservation purposes but also to understand public memory, we can see not only how changes were made but also why. We can see that the survival of Independence Hall depended on its history, but also on human imagination, as successive generations remodeled the building to create a satisfying ambiance of the past. From the early nineteenth century until the beginning of federal management of Independence Hall in 1951, physical alterations of the building often represented the collective memory of like-minded Philadelphians of high social standing. In recent times, stewardship of the building demonstrates the federal government's commitment to preserving a material reminder of the nation's founding. Beyond this, however, Independence Hall has been a site of contested memory, with meanings defined by public activities in and around the building from the time of its construction to the present. In the shadow of Independence Hall, Americans have both celebrated and debated the memory of the Declaration of Independence and the Constitution.

In addition to its significance in American history, Independence Hall demonstrates that buildings play an important role in constructing and perpetuating public memory. In particular, historic buildings like Independence Hall function as depositories and conduits for public memory; as a result, they provide a rich historical record of the processes of remembering aspects the nation's past. Furthermore, such buildings operate as filters, allowing some traits or time periods to be preserved while others are obscured. Without taking the full record of remembering and forgetting into account, we cannot fully understand the meaning of historic places; nor can we fully understand public memory without incorporating buildings into the rich variety of sources that preserve perceptions of the past. Works of art, literature, monuments, traditions, and commemorative events have all been examined by scholars seeking to understand public memory. Buildings, as long-lasting, substantial elements of public life, deserve similar attention. Decisions about the construction, use, renovation, and preservation of a building, together with its social, environmental, and cultural histories, reveal the extent to which people have valued the past that the building represents. As these decisions are made, they communicate versions of the past to a wide public; this is especially true when buildings are associated with prominent historic events. Over time, as new perceptions of the past emerge, the use and appearance of a building may change repeatedly, each time offering a new insight into public memory.

Independence Hall has a powerful story to tell. Certainly, it is a story of the Declaration of Independence and the Constitution. But it is also a story of a place where Americans have participated for more than two centuries in the construction of a nation through the memory-work of commemoration, preservation, and dissent. When viewed as more than a time capsule of the eighteenth century, Independence Hall demonstrates that historic buildings and associated public spaces have much to tell us—if we let them. They are places of history, but also places of memory where we continually interact with the past and sustain our ideas of what it means to be a nation.

NOTES

The following abbreviations are used in the notes.

AHR	*American Historical Review*
AIA	American Institute of Architects
AQ	*American Quarterly*
DAB	*Dictionary of American Biography*
GPO	Government Printing Office
HABS	Historic American Buildings Survey
HSP	Historical Society of Pennsylvania
INHP	Independence National Historical Park
JAH	*Journal of American History*
JAIA	*Journal of the American Institute of Architects*
JSAH	*Journal of the Society of Architectural Historians*
LC	Library of Congress
LCP	Library Company of Philadelphia
MG	Manuscript Group
NA	National Archives
NPS	National Park Service
PCA	Philadelphia City Archives
PH	*Pennsylvania History*
PMHB	*Pennsylvania Magazine of History and Biography*
PSA	Pennsylvania State Archives, Harrisburg, Pa.
RG	Record Group
UA	Urban Archives, Temple University
WMQ	*William and Mary Quarterly*
WP	*Winterthur Portfolio*

Introduction

1. Roy Rosenzweig and David Thelen, *The Presence of the Past: Popular Uses of History in American Life* (New York: Columbia University Press, 1998), 105–8.

2. For discussion of these and other controversies, see Mike Wallace, *Mickey Mouse History and Other Essays on American Memory* (Philadelphia: Temple University Press, 1996); Edward T. Linenthal and Tom Engelhardt, eds., *History Wars: The Enola Gay and Other Battles for the American Past* (New York: Metropolitan Books, 1996); and Gary B. Nash, Charlotte Crabtree, and Ross E. Dunn, *History on Trial: Culture Wars and the Teaching of the Past* (New York: Random House, 1997).

3. The problem of decontextualized memory is delineated in James Fentress and Chris Wickham, eds., *Social Memory* (Oxford: Blackwell Publishers, 1992), 201; see also Peter Carrier, "Places, Politics, and the Archiving of Contemporary Memory in Pierre Nora's *Les Lieux de Mémoire*," in Susannah Radstone, ed., *Memory and Methodology* (Oxford: Berg, 2000), 40–42.

4. This linkage among buildings, a nation, and memory has been demonstrated in a different national context by Rudy Koshar, *Germany's Transient Pasts: Preservation and National Memory in the Twentieth Century* (Chapel Hill: University of North Carolina Press, 1998).

5. The significance of remembering and forgetting is developed most fully in David Gross, *Lost Time: On Remembering and Forgetting in Late Modern Culture* (Amherst: University of Massachusetts Press, 2000). The need for greater attention to forgetting is argued in Adrian Forty and Susanne Küchler, eds., *The Art of Forgetting* (Oxford: Berg, 1999).

6. Ernest Renan, "What Is a Nation?" in Geoff Eley and Ronald Grigor Suny, eds., *Becoming National: A Reader* (Oxford: Oxford University Press, 1996), 42–55.

7. Benedict Anderson, *Imagined Communities: Reflections on the Origins and Spread of Nationalism,* revised edition (1983; London: Verso, 1991), 5–7.

8. The relationship between architecture and memory dates to ancient Greece and Rome, where orators visualized structures as mnemonic devices for recalling the sequence of speeches. See Frances Yates, *The Art of Memory* (Chicago: University of Chicago Press, 1966).

9. James W. Loewen, *Lies Across America: What Our Historic Sites Get Wrong* (New York: New Press, 1999).

10. Norman Tyler, *Historic Preservation: An Introduction to Its History, Principles, and Practice* (New York: W. W. Norton, 2000), 44–50; U.S. Department of Interior, *National Register Bulletin 15: How to Apply the National Register Criteria for Evaluation* <http://www.cr.nps.gov/nr/publications/bulletins/nr15_toc.htm>, April 10, 2002.

11. John Bodnar, *Remaking America: Public Memory, Commemoration, and Patriotism in the Twentieth Century* (Princeton, N.J.: Princeton University Press, 1992), 15.

12. Scholarly attention to public memory has surged since the 1980s in a variety of disciplines, including anthropology, sociology, history, and communication studies. Groundbreaking scholarship appears in Fentress and Wickham, eds., *Social Memory*; Forty and Küchler, eds., *The Art of Forgetting;* Radstone, ed., *Memory and Methodology*; Paul Connerton, *How Societies Remember* (Cambridge: Cambridge University Press, 1989); David Middleton and Derek Edwards, *Collective Remembering* (London: Sage Publications, 1990); Jacques Le Goff, *History and Memory*, trans. Steven Randall and Elizabeth Claman (New York: Columbia University Press, 1992); Geneviève Fabre and Robert O'Meally, *History and Memory in African-American Culture* (New York: Oxford University Press, 1994); W. Fitzhugh Brundage, ed., *Where These Memories Grow: History, Memory, and Southern Identity* (Chapel Hill: University of North Carolina Press, 2000); David Thelen, ed., *Memory and American History* (Bloomington: Indiana University Press, 1990). The Thelen volume contains articles from the March 1989 issue of *JAH*, which marked an emergence of interest in public memory among historians of the United States.

Among works investigating public memory related to historical figures and events, Michael Kammen's *A Machine That Would Go of Itself: The Constitution in American Culture* (New York: Alfred A. Knopf, 1986) and *A Season of Youth: The American Revolution and the Historical Imagination* (New York: Alfred A. Knopf, 1978) are especially relevant to the history of Independence Hall, although they do not deal extensively with the structure.

13. While not focused specifically on buildings, relations among relics, memory, and history are explored in David Lowenthal, *The Past Is a Foreign Country* (Cambridge: Cambridge University Press, 1985). Buildings are also included among the "sites of memory" analyzed in Pierre Nora, *Realms of Memory: The Construction of the French Past,* ed. Lawrence D. Kritzman, trans. Arthur Goldhammer, 3 vols. (New York: Columbia University Press, 1996–98).

The often-cited works of Charles B. Hosmer, Jr., establish a periodization of historic preservation and show how the preservation movement reflected currents in American social thought. See *Presence of the Past: A History of the Preservation Movement in the United States Before Williamsburg* (New York: G. P. Putnam's Sons, 1965) and *Preservation Comes of Age: From Williamsburg to the National Trust, 1926–1949* (Charlottesville: University Press of Virginia, 1981). Among recent studies of historic preservation addressing issues of memory are Diane Barthel, *Historic Preservation: Collective Memory and Historical Identity* (New Brunswick, N.J.: Rutgers University Press, 1996); James M. Lindgren, *Preserving the Old Dominion: Historic Preservation and Virginia Traditionalism* (Charlottesville: University Press of Virginia, 1993) and *Preserving Historic New England: Preservation, Progressivism, and the Remaking of Memory* (New York: Oxford University Press, 1995); and Martha K. Norkunas, *The Politics of Public Memory: Tourism, History, and Ethnicity in Monterey, California* (Albany: State University of New York Press, 1993). On the activism of women in historic preservation, see Patricia West, *Domesticating History: The Political Origins of America's House Museums* (Washington, D.C.: Smithsonian Institution Press, 1999). Koshar, *Germany's Transient Pasts*, significantly extends the analysis of historic preservation and memory by considering relationships with national identity.

14. The interdisciplinary study of buildings is a growing pursuit, including considerations of religion and architecture, as in Jeffrey F. Meyer, *Myths in Stone: Religious Dimensions of Washington, D.C.* (Berkeley: University of California Press, 2001), and Margaret Visser, *The Geometry of Love: Space, Time, Mystery and Meaning in an Ordinary Church* (New York: Viking, 2000). Charles T. Goodsell, *The American Statehouse: Interpreting Democracy's Temples* (Lawrence: University Press of Kansas, 2001), combines political and social analysis in a study of state capitol buildings. Angus Kress Gillespie applies folklore methodology in *Twin Towers: The Life of New York City's World Trade Center* (New Brunswick, N.J.: Rutgers University Press, 1999).

15. Approaches to building history by architectural historians are exemplified by the *Buildings of the United States* series coordinated by the Society of Architectural Historians and published by Oxford University Press: David Gebhard, *Buildings of Iowa* (1993); Alison K. Hoagland, *Buildings of Alaska* (1993); Julie Nicoletta, *Buildings of Nevada* (2000); Thomas J. Noel, *Buildings of Colorado* (1997); and Pamela Scott, *Buildings of the District of Columbia* (1993). Also see Carl R. Lounsbury, *From Statehouse to Courthouse: An Architectural History of South Carolina's Colonial Capitol and Charleston County Courthouse* (Columbia: University of South Carolina Press, 2001); John M. Bryan, *Creating the South Carolina State House* (Columbia: University of South Carolina Press, 1999).

Although not concerned with public memory, Mary P. Ryan demonstrates analysis of public buildings beyond their architectural characteristics in "'A Laudable Pride in the Whole of Us': City Halls and Civic Materialism," *AHR* 105 (October 2000): 1131–1170.

16. As a material culture study, this history of Independence Hall extends the usual parameters for studying artifacts. Like other recent work, this study views artifacts as sources for understanding human behavior. The significance of artifacts as evidence in the study of social and cultural history is argued in Thomas Schlereth, ed., *Material Culture: A Research Guide* (Lawrence: University Press of Kansas, 1985). For example, the social relationships of colonial Virginia are examined through study of the Governor's Palace in Williamsburg, its artifacts, and its inhabitants in Graham Hood, *The Governor's Palace in Williamsburg* (Williamsburg, Va.: Colonial Williamsburg Foundation, 1991). Artifacts are examined as evidence of Victorian culture in the United States by Kenneth Ames, *Death in the Dining Room and Other Tales of Victorian Culture* (Philadelphia: Temple University Press, 1992). This study of Independence Hall differs from studies such as these by following a group of artifacts—a building and its contents—over an extended period of time rather than viewing the artifacts as evidence of one particular moment in the past.

17. Landscape studies were pioneered by J. B. Jackson, whose essays are collected in Ervin H. Zube, ed., *Landscapes: Selected Writings of J. B. Jackson* (Amherst: University of Massachusetts Press, 1970). Yi-Fu Tuan identified connections between place and time in *Topophilia: A Study of Environmental Perception, Attitudes, and Values* (Englewood Cliffs, N.J.: Prentice-Hall, 1974) and *Space and Place: The Perspective of Experience* (Minneapolis: University of Minnesota Press, 1977). On the symbolic significance of landscape in society, see Denis E. Cosgrove, *Social Formation and Symbolic Landscape* (London: Croom Helm, 1984). Recent contributions to the field include Simon Schama, *Landscape and Memory* (New York: Alfred A. Knopf, 1995), and essays in Arnold R. Alanen and Robert Z. Melnick, eds., *Preserving Cultural Landscapes in America* (Baltimore: Johns Hopkins University Press, 2000). On urban landscapes, see Christine Boyer, *The City of Collective Memory: Its Historical Imagery and Architectural Entertainments* (Cambridge, Mass.: MIT Press, 1994); Dolores Hayden, *The Power of Place: Urban Landscapes As Public History* (Cambridge, Mass.: MIT Press, 1995); David Hamer, *History in Urban Places: The Historic Districts of the United States* (Columbus: Ohio State University Press, 1998); and Kevin Lynch, *The Image of the City* (Cambridge, Mass.: MIT Press, 1960) and *What Time Is This Place?* (Cambridge, Mass.: MIT Press, 1972).

On the evolution of meanings of historic landscapes, see Edward Tabor Linenthal, *Sacred Ground: Americans and Their Battlefields* (Urbana: University of Illinois Press, 1991); John F. Sears, *Sacred Places: American Tourist Attractions in the Nineteenth Century* (New York: Oxford University Press, 1989); Lorett Treese, *Valley Forge: Making and Remaking a National Symbol* (University Park: Pennsylvania State University Press, 1995); and Chris Wilson, *The Myth of Santa Fe: Creating a Modern Regional Tradition* (Albuquerque: University of New Mexico Press, 1997).

18. See especially Koshar, *Germany's Transient Pasts*; Lindgren, *Preserving the Old Dominion* and *Preserving Historic New England*; Norkunas, *The Politics of Public Memory*. On constructed images of the past, also see Peter Borsay, *The Image of Georgian Bath, 1700–2000: Towns, Heritage, and History* (Oxford: Oxford University Press, 2000).

19. Lewis F. Fisher, *Saving San Antonio: The Precarious Preservation of a Heritage* (Lubbock: Texas Tech University Press, 1996); Michael Holleran, *Boston's Changeful Times: Origins of Preservation and Planning in America* (Baltimore: Johns Hopkins University Press, 1998); Lawrence Kreisman, *Made to Last: Historic Preservation in Seattle and King County* (Seattle: University of Washington Press, 1999); Robert R. Weyeneth, *Historic Preser-*

vation for a Living City: Historic Charleston Foundation, 1947–1997 (Columbia: University of South Carolina Press, 2000).

20. Such biographical works include Eric Darton, *Divided We Stand: A Biography of New York's World Trade Center* (New York: Basic Books, 1999); Marc Leepson, *Saving Monticello: The Levy Family's Epic Quest to Rescue the House that Jefferson Built* (New York: Free Press, 2001); Jack McLaughlin, *Jefferson and Monticello: The Biography of a Builder* (New York: Henry Holt, 1985); John Tauranac, *The Empire State Building: The Making of a Landmark* (New York: Scribner, 1995); William Seale, *The President's House*, 2 vols. (Washington, D.C.: White House Historical Association, 1986). An approach to building biography through "rites of passage" such as dedication ceremonies is developed in Neil Harris, *Building Lives: Constructing Rites and Passages* (New Haven: Yale University Press, 1999).

21. As focal points for such public rituals, buildings contribute to the construction of the public sphere, the modern interaction between citizens and the state described in Jürgen Habermas, *The Structural Transformation of the Public Sphere: An Inquiry into a Category of Bourgeois Society*, trans. Thomas Burger (Cambridge, Mass.: MIT Press, 1989). The significance of "invented" traditions as engagements with the past is argued in Eric Hobsbawm and Terence Ranger, eds., *The Invention of Tradition* (Cambridge: Cambridge University Press, 1983). The major work on the history of tradition in the United States is Michael Kammen, *Mystic Chords of Memory: The Transformation of Tradition in American Culture* (New York: Alfred A. Knopf, 1991). Also see David Glassberg, *American Historical Pageantry: The Uses of Tradition in the Early Twentieth Century* (Chapel Hill: University of North Carolina Press, 1990), and Len Travers, *Celebrating the Fourth: Independence Day and the Rites of Nationalism in the Early Republic* (Amherst: University of Massachusetts Press, 1997).

22. Nora, *Realms of Memory*, vol. 1, 1–20.

23. Bodnar, *Remaking America*, 13–20; Scott A. Sandage, "A Marble House Divided: The Lincoln Memorial, the Civil Rights Movement, and the Politics of Memory," *JAH* 80 (June 1993): 135–67. Contested views of the past in relationship to a historic building are examined from an anthropological perspective by Holly Beachley Brear, *Inherit the Alamo: Myth and Ritual at an American Shrine* (Austin: University of Texas Press, 1995).

24. Maurice Halbwachs, *The Collective Memory* (1950; New York: Harper & Row, 1980).

25. A similar case could be made for the Palace of the Governors, Santa Fe, New Mexico, built in the 1610s. While Independence Hall provides a record of public memory of the nation founded in 1776 by the British colonies in North America, the Palace of the Governors represents the different but also rich story of Spanish colonization and collective memory exercised through historic preservation. See Wilson, *Myth of Santa Fe*, 124–28.

26. Thelen, *Memory and American History*, vii-xix.

27. *Philadelphia Inquirer*, June 12, 1991, August 26, 1992, February 28, 1993; *New York Times*, July 3, 1992.

28. Most books about Independence Hall have focused extensively on events of the eighteenth century, treating later events lightly, if at all. These works include David W. Belisle, *History of Independence Hall: From the Earliest Period to the Present Time* (Philadelphia: James Challen & Son, 1859); Harold Donaldson Eberlein and Cortlandt Van Dyke Hubbard, *Diary of Independence Hall* (Philadelphia: J. B. Lippincott Co., 1948); Frank M. Etting, *An Historical Account of the Old State House of Pennsylvania Now Known as the Hall of Independence* (Boston: James R. Osgood and Company, 1876).

Since assuming administration of Independence Hall in the 1950s, the National Park Service has completed extensive research on the structural history of the building. This research is contained in internal reports located in the Independence National Historical Park library as well as in Lee H. Nelson, "Independence Hall: Its Fabric Reinforced," and Penelope Hartshorne Batcheler, "Independence Hall: Its Appearance Restored," in Charles E. Peterson, ed., *Building Early America* (Mendham, N.J.: Astragal Press, 1976), 277–318. Other publications emanating from NPS research include Edward M. Riley, "The Independence Hall Group," *Transactions of the American Philosophical Society* 43 Part 1 (March 1953): 7–42 and "Philadelphia: The Nation's Capital, 1790–1800," *PH* 20 (October 1953): 357–79; Dennis C. Kurjack, "Evolution of a Shrine," *PH* 21 (June 1954): 193–200; James M. Mulcahy, "*Congress Voting Independence:* The Trumbull and Pine-Savage Paintings," *PMHB* 80 (January 1956): 74–91; Doris Devine Fanelli, "The Assembly Room: All Those Reinterpretations and It's Still Not Right?" *CRM Bulletin* 8 (June-August 1985): 21–24; and Anna Coxe Toogood, "Philadelphia As the Nation's Capital, 1790–1800," in Kenneth R. Bowling and Donald R. Kennon, eds., *Neither Separate Nor Equal: Congress in the 1790s* (Athens: Ohio University Press, 2000), 34–57.

The collections catalogs are John C. Milley, ed., *Treasures of Independence: Independence National Historical Park and Its Collections* (New York: Mayflower Books, 1980); and Doris Devine Fanelli and Karie Diethorn, *History of the Portrait Collection, Independence National Historical Park* (Philadelphia: American Philosophical Society, forthcoming).

29. Constance M. Greiff, *Independence: The Creation of a National Park* (Philadelphia: University of Pennsylvania Press, 1987). The guidebook, Edward M. Riley, *The Story of Independence Hall* (Washington, D.C.: National Park Service, 1954; reprint Gettysburg, Pa.: Thomas Publications, 1990), is adapted from Riley, "The Independence Hall Group," noted above. More than other works, this guide and the article upon which it is based presented Independence Hall as a building that has changed over time. However, in their brevity, these works did not explore how or why changes occurred.

30. Limited reference to place in many of these works has contributed to the detachment of Independence Hall from important aspects of its history. Scholars would contribute significantly to public understanding of historic places if they would give greater attention to locations in their texts and indexes.

Non-NPS articles about Independence Hall include Charles H. Browning, "The State House Yard, and Who Owned It First After William Penn," *PMHB* 40, no. 1 (1916): 85–103; Arthur H. Frazier, "Henry Seybert and the Centennial Clock and Bell at Independence Hall," *PMHB* 102 (January 1978): 40–58; John Maass, "Architecture and Americanism, or Pastiches of Independence Hall," *Historic Preservation* 11 (April–June 1970): 17–25. Independence Hall is one of the buildings treated in Max Page, "From 'Miserable Dens' to the 'Marble Monster': Historical Memory and the Design of Courthouses in Nineteenth-Century Philadelphia," *PMHB* 119 (October 1995): 317–19. See also Charlene Mires, "The Difference This Day Makes," *Pennsylvania Heritage* (Winter 1998): 4–11; "In the Shadow of Independence Hall: Vernacular Activities and the Meanings of Historic Places," *The Public Historian* 21 (Spring 1999): 49–61; and "Slavery, Nativism, and the Forgotten History of Independence Hall," *PH* 67 (Autumn 2000): 481–502.

31. Kammen, *A Machine That Would Go of Itself* and *A Season of Youth*; Philip F. Detweiler, "The Changing Reputation of the Declaration of Independence: The First Fifty Years," *WMQ*, 3rd ser., 19 (October 1962): 557–74.

Chapter 1. Landmark

1. Adolph B. Benson, ed., *Peter Kalm's Travels in North America* (New York: Wilson-Erickson, 1937), 25.

2. Martin P. Snyder, *City of Independence: Views of Philadelphia Before 1800* (New York: Praeger, 1975), 36–41.

3. Mary Maples Dunn and Richard S. Dunn, "The Founding, 1681–1701," in Russell F. Weigley, ed., *Philadelphia: A 300-Year History* (New York: W. W. Norton, 1982), 1–32; Edwin B. Bronner, "Village into Town, 1701–1746," in Weigley, ed., *Philadelphia*, 36–37, 60.

4. Craig W. Horle et al., eds., *Lawmakers and Legislators in Pennsylvania: A Biographical Dictionary*, vol. 2 (Philadelphia: University of Pennsylvania Press, 1997), 15–19, 42–56.

5. *Votes and Proceedings of the House of Representatives of the Province of Pennsylvania*, in *Pennsylvania Archives*, 8th ser., vol. III, 1950 (hereafter cited as *Votes of Assembly*).

6. Jon Butler, *Becoming America: The Revolution Before 1776* (Cambridge, Mass.: Harvard University Press, 2000), 96–107.

7. *Votes of Assembly,* 8th ser., vol. III, 1950; Horle, *Lawmakers and Legislators,* 42–47.

8. *Votes of Assembly,* 8th ser., vol. III, 1732.

9. On British nationalism, see Linda Colley, *Britons: Forging the Nation, 1707–1837* (New Haven, Conn.: Yale University Press, 1992), 2–6.

10. Colley, *Britons*, 129–30.

11. Burton Alva Konkle, *The Life of Andrew Hamilton, 1676–1741* (Philadelphia: National Publishing Company, 1941), 4–5, 9, 16, 21, 51–59.

12. *Votes of Assembly,* 8th ser., vol. III, 1869, 1875, 1877, 1951, 1956; Horle, *Lawmakers and Legislators*, 49–50. Although the legislation passed, it was repealed less than a year later after appeals by German and Scots-Irish Pennsylvanians.

13. Sylvia Doughty Fries, *The Urban Idea in Colonial America* (Philadelphia: Temple University Press, 1977), 79–89; Bronner, "Village into Town," 57–59. For population estimates, see Gary B. Nash and Billy G. Smith, "The Population of Eighteenth-Century Philadelphia," *PMHB* 99 (July 1975): 362–68.

14. Benjamin Franklin, *Autobiography* (New York: W. W. Norton, 1986), 20–22.

15. John Andrew Gallery, ed., *Philadelphia Architecture: A Guide to the City* (Philadelphia: Foundation for Architecture, 1994), 22.

16. *Votes of Assembly,* 8th ser., vol. III, 2144; Horle, *Lawmakers and Legislators*, 13.

17. John L. Cotter, Daniel G. Roberts, and Michael Parrington, *The Buried Past: An Archaeological History of Philadelphia* (Philadelphia: University of Pennsylvania Press, 1993), 114.

18. John Fanning Watson, *Annals of Philadelphia and Pennsylvania, in the Olden Time*, vol. 1 (Philadelphia: John Fanning Watson, 1850), 396; J. Thomas Scharf and Thompson Westcott, *History of Philadelphia, 1609–1884* (Philadelphia: L. L. Evarts, 1884), 97–98; Charles H. Browning, "The State House Yard, and Who Owned It First After William Penn," *PMHB* 40, no. 1 (1916): 85–103.

19. James S. Ackerman, *Palladio* (Middlesex, England: Penguin Books, 1966), 160–74; Frederick Doveton Nichols, "Palladio in America," in Walter Muir Whitehill, *Palladio in America* (Milan: Electra Editrice, 1976), 101; Adolf K. Placzek, introduction to Andrea Palladio, *The*

Four Books of Architecture (New York: Dover Publications, 1965), v–vii; Gallery, *Philadelphia Architecture,* 14.

20. James Gibbs, *A Book of Architecture Containing Designs of Buildings and Ornaments* (1728; reprint New York: Benjamin Blom, 1968).

21. Dana Arnold, "The Country House: Form, Function and Meaning," in Dana Arnold, ed., *The Georgian Country House: Architecture, Landscape, and Society* (Phoenix Mill, England: Sutton Publishing, 1998), 16–18.

22. Alan Gowans, *Images of American Living: Four Centuries of Architecture and Furniture as Cultural Expression* (Philadelphia: J. B. Lippincott, 1964), 115–119. The exact dimensions of the State House are 106 feet, 10½ inches by 44 feet, 7¼ inches. See Photogrammetric Documentation Project (1985–90), Addendum to HABS, PA 1430, Sheet 9.

23. Lee H. Nelson, "Independence Hall: Its Fabric Reinforced," in Charles E. Peterson, ed., *Building Early America: Contributions Toward the History of a Great Industry* (Mendham, N.J.: Astragal Press, 1976), 279–85; Richard Webster, *Philadelphia Preserved: Catalog of the Historic American Buildings Survey* (Philadelphia: Temple University Press, 1976), 77.

24. Nelson, "Independence Hall," 279–80.

25. *Votes of Assembly,* 8th ser., vol. IV, 3316.

26. Staff, Independence National Historical Park, *Historic Structures Report Part I on Independence Hall* (March 1959), INHP. The tower structure is 34 feet, 2⅛ inches on its south side; 30 feet, 11¾ inches on the east side; and 31 feet, ¼ inch on the west. See Photogrammetric Documentation Project (1985–90), Addendum to HABS, PA 1430, Sheet 9.

27. Nelson, "Independence Hall," 279–85; John C. Paige, *The Liberty Bell: A Special History Study* (Washington, D.C.: U.S. Department of the Interior, n.d.), 4–5. On Philadelphia's building boom, see Gary B. Nash, *The Urban Crucible: Social Change, Political Consciousness, and the Origins of the American Revolution* (Cambridge, Mass.: Harvard University Press, 1979). While attempts were made to recast the State House bell, the Assembly ordered a duplicate from England. The second bell, which became known in the twentieth century as the "Sister Bell," functioned as a clock bell at the State House until a new steeple and clock were constructed in 1828. The bell then served as the church bell at St. Augustine Roman Catholic Church until destruction of the church during nativist riots in 1844. Recast from fragments surviving the riot, the bell was moved to Villanova University, where it was displayed in Falvey Library. See Louis A. Rongione, *The Liberty Bell's Sister* (Villanova, Pa.: Villanova University, 1976).

28. Newton D. Mereness, ed., *Travels in the American Colonies* (New York: Macmillan, 1916), 410–11.

29. G. Taylor, *A Voyage to North America* (Nottingham: S. Creswell, 1771), 174–75.

30. Watson, *Annals,* 396–97.

31. *Pa. Gazette,* September 16, 1736, March 7, 1738; Peter Thompson, *Rum Punch and Revolution: Taverngoing and Public Life in Eighteenth-Century Philadelphia* (Philadelphia: University of Pennsylvania Press, 1999), 79; Hannah Benner Roach, "The Independence Mall, Work No. 610 for the Philadelphia City Planning Commission, Preliminary Report, Historic Sites—First Block," INHP.

32. On the intellectual climate in America, see Robert A. Ferguson, *The American Enlightenment, 1750–1820* (Cambridge, Mass.: Harvard University Press, 1997).

33. *Votes of Assembly,* 8th ser., vol. IV, 3618; Harold Donaldson Eberlein and Cortlandt Van Dyke Hubbard, *Diary of Independence Hall* (Philadelphia: J. B. Lippincott, 1948),

45–107; Jacob Cox Parsons, ed., *Extracts from the Diary of Jacob Hiltzheimer* (Philadelphia: William F. Fell, 1893), April 13, 1769; Henry Simpson, *The Lives of Eminent Philadelphians Now Deceased* (Philadelphia: W. Brotherhead, 1859), 800–804.

34. Margaret C. Jacob, *The Cultural Meaning of the Scientific Revolution* (Philadelphia: Temple University Press, 1988); Bernard A. Cohen, *Science and the Founding Fathers: Science in the Political Thought of Jefferson, Franklin, Adams, and Madison* (New York: W. W. Norton, 1995); Brooke Hindle, *The Pursuit of Science in Revolutionary America, 1735–1789* (Chapel Hill: University of North Carolina Press, 1956); Lisa Jardine, *Ingenious Pursuits: Building the Scientific Revolution* (New York: Doubleday, 1999).

35. Gary F. Frick, "The Library Company of Philadelphia: America's First Philosophical Society," in Catherine E. Hutchins, ed., *Shaping a National Culture: The Philadelphia Experience, 1750–1800* (Winterthur, Del.: Henry Francis DuPont Winterthur Museum, 1994), 181–200; Edwin Wolf 2nd, *"At the Instance of Benjamin Franklin": A Brief History of The Library Company of Philadephia, 1731–1976* (Philadelphia: Library Company of Philadelphia, 1976), 6–12; *Early Proceedings of the American Philosophical Society for the Promotion of Useful Knowledge* (Philadelphia: McCalla & Stavely, 1884), 8–20.

36. Jacob, *Cultural Meaning of the Scientific Revolution*, 152–60.

37. *Pa. Gazette*, September 14, 1752.

38. *Pa. Gazette*, November 11, 1762; Eberlein and Hubbard, *Diary,* 106.

39. Hindle, *Pursuit of Science,* 65.

40. Ibid., 146–65; Jardine, *Ingenious Pursuits,* 140–41.

41. Horle, *Lawmakers and Legislators,* 70–78; Frederick B. Tolles, *Quakers and the Atlantic Culture* (New York: Octagon Books, 1980), 36–54; Jack D. Marietta, *The Reformation of American Quakerism, 1748–1783* (Philadelphia: University of Pennsylvania Press, 1984), 150–168; Alan Tully, *Forming American Politics: Ideals, Interests, and Institutions in Colonial New York and Pennsylvania* (Baltimore: Johns Hopkins University Press, 1994), 257–303.

42. James H. Hutson, "The Campaign to Make Pennsylvania a Royal Province, 1764–1770, Part I," *PMHB* 94 (October 1970): 427–63.

43. Ibid.; Bernard Bailyn, *The Ideological Origins of the American Revolution* (Cambridge, Mass.: Harvard University Press, 1967), 232–33.

44. Ferguson, *American Enlightenment,* 150–91.

45. John L. Cotter et al., *The Walnut Street Prison Workshop* (Philadelphia: Athenaeum of Philadelphia, 1988), 15–17; Ellis P. Oberholtzer, *Philadelphia: A History of the City and Its People* (Philadelphia: S. J. Clarke, 1911), 228.

46. Horle, *Lawmakers and Legislators*, 55. According to this study, one-third of representatives elected to the Assembly between 1703 and 1756 had at some time owned at least one slave.

47. *Pa. Gazette*, March 7, 1738, September 3, 1761, March 18, 1762.

48. Quoted in Joseph J. Ellis, *American Sphinx: The Character of Thomas Jefferson* (1996; New York: Random House, 1998), 64.

49. Ellis, *American Sphinx,* 54–70; Pauline Maier, *American Scripture: Making the Declaration of Independence* (New York: Alfred A. Knopf, 1997), 97–153; Philip F. Detweiler, "The Changing Reputation of the Declaration of Independence: The First Fifty Years," *WMQ* 3rd ser., 19 (October 1962): 557–74.

50. During the 1970s and 1980s, historians of the American Revolution produced a body of work on the social aspects of this era paying particular attention to Pennsylvania, which experienced the greatest upheaval. The major works include Pauline Maier, *From Resistance to Revolution: Colonial Radicals and the Development of American Opposition to Britain, 1765–1776* (New York: W. W. Norton, 1972); Nash, *Urban Crucible*; Charles S. Olton, *Artisans for Independence: Philadelphia Mechanics and the American Revolution* (Syracuse, N.Y.: Syracuse University Press, 1975); Steven Rosswurm, *Arms, Country, and Class: The Philadelphia Militia and "Lower Sort" During the American Revolution, 1775–1783* (New Brunswick, N.J.: Rutgers University Press, 1987); Richard A. Ryerson, *The Revolution Is Now Begun: The Radical Committees of Philadelphia, 1765–1776* (Philadelphia: University of Pennsylvania Press, 1978).

51. Nash, *Urban Crucible*, 374–82; Rosswurm, *Arms, Country, and Class,* 45–48.

52. Harry M. Tinkcom, "The Revolutionary City," in Weigley, ed., *Philadelphia*, 112–99.

53. Eberlein and Hubbard, *Diary,* 113, 128–29.

54. Sylvester K. Stevens, *Pennsylvania: Birthplace of a Nation* (New York: Random House, 1964), 107–8.

55. "Continental Association of 20 October 1774," in Julian P. Boyd, ed., *The Papers of Thomas Jefferson*, vol. 1 (Princeton, N.J.: Princeton University Press, 1950), 153–54; Sydney George Fisher, *The True Story of the American Revolution* (1902; Boston: Gregg Press, 1972), 182–84.

56. Silas Deane to Mrs. Deane, September 1–3, 1774 and September 5–6, 1774; John Adams, Diary, September 5, 1774; James Duane, Notes of Proceedings, September 5, 1774; Joseph Galloway to the Governor of New Jersey, September 5, 1774, in Edmund C. Burnett, ed., *Letters of Members of the Continental Congress*, vol. 1 (Washington, D.C.: Carnegie Institution of Washington, 1921), 4–11.

57. John C. Fitzpatrick, ed., *The Diaries of George Washington*, vol. 2 (Boston: Houghton Mifflin, 1925), 164; Tinkcom, "The Revolutionary City," 119; *Pa. Journal*, September 21, 1774, in Eberlein and Hubbard, *Diary*, 139.

58. *Pa. Gazette*, April 26, 1775.

59. Eberlein and Hubbard, *Diary*, 141–42.

60. In June 1776, Thomas Jefferson observed that the Pennsylvania Assembly was "sitting above stairs" on the second floor of the State House. See Worthington Chauncey Ford, ed., *Journals of the Continental Congress, 1774–1789*, vol. 6 (Washington, D.C.: GPO, 1906), 1088.

61. Allen French, *The First Year of the American Revolution* (Boston: Houghton Mifflin, 1934), 274–93.

62. *Votes of Assembly*, 8th ser., vol. VIII, 7241, 7447, 7467.

63. The history of the Liberty Bell is treated more fully in Chapters 4 and 6. The State House steeple had grown dangerously unstable by 1774, when the Pennsylvania Assembly discussed removing the steeple, but took no action. See Paige, *The Liberty Bell: A Special History Study*, 15–16. Two additional published references to the steeple describe it as too unstable to permit the ringing of the bell: Samuel L. Wharton, "A Description of the State House," *The Universal Magazine and Literary Museum* (1774) in *PMHB* 23, no. 4 (1899), 417–19; and "Postscript to the Pennsylvania Gazette No. 3424, List of the Numbers That Came Up Prizes in the Fourth Class of the Pettie Island and Cash Lottery, for the Benefit of St. Paul Church," *Pa. Gazette*, July 7, 1773. The latter source announces a lottery to raise money for a cupola and bell

for St. Paul's Church, explaining that "the Honourable Assembly of the Province having been pleased to let the State House Bell be rung until now, when the Condition of the Tower will not admit of it any longer."

64. See Gordon S. Wood, *The Creation of the American Republic, 1776–1787* (Chapel Hill: University of North Carolina Press, 1969).

65. See, for example, Richard Henry Lee to Charles Lee, May 11, 1776, in Burnett, *Letters,* 442.

66. *Votes of Assembly*, 8th ser., vol. VIII, 7233.

67. Ibid., 7353.

68. John Adams to James Warren, May 15, 1776, in Burnett, *Letters,* 445.

69. J. Paul Selsam, *The Pennsylvania Constitution of 1776: A Study in Revolutionary Democracy* (1936; New York: Da Capo Press, 1971), 112–13.

70. *Votes of Assembly*, 8th ser., vol. VIII, 7542–43.

71. Selsam, *Pennsylvania Constitution*, 155–56; Thomas McKean to Caesar A. Rodney, August [September?] 22, 1813, in Burnett, *Letters*, 535.

72. *Minutes of the Proceedings of the Convention of the State of Pennsylvania, Held at Philadelphia, July 15th, 1776*, RG 5, PSA, 35–36.

73. Stevens, *Pennsylvania*, 108–9; *Votes of Assembly,* 8th ser., vol. VIII, 7548–90; Diary of James Allen, in *PMHB* 9, no. 2 (1885): 188.

74. *Minutes of the . . . Convention*, 9.

75. Ibid., 65–67.

76. Stevens, *Pennsylvania,* 111–12.

77. Gary B. Nash, *Forging Freedom: The Formation of Philadelphia's Black Community, 1720–1840* (Cambridge, Mass.: Harvard University Press, 1988), 60–63.

78. John W. Jackson, *With the British Army in Philadelphia, 1777–1778* (San Rafael, Calif.: Presidio Press, 1979); David G. Martin, *The Philadelphia Campaign, June 1777–July 1778* (Conshohocken, Pa.: Combined Books, 1993), 77–98.

79. John Maxwell Nesbitt to Aleck (?), July 4, 1778, quoted in Jackson, *With the British Army*, 276.

80. Jackson, *With the British Army,* 265–73.

81. Tinkcom, "The Revolutionary City," 144–63.

82. Bailyn, *Ideological Origins*, 55–93.

83. Cotter, *Buried Past*, 105–6.

84. Watson, *Annals*, 397.

85. Webster, *Philadelphia Preserved,* 78–79, 92.

86. Oberholtzer, *Philadelphia,* 323.

87. Gallery, *Philadelphia Architecture*, 30–31.

88. Robert N. C. Nix, Jr., and Mary M. Schweitzer, "Pennsylvania's Contributions to the Writing and the Ratification of the Constitution," *PMHB* 112 (January 1988): 3–24; Robert F. Williams, "The Influence of Pennsylvania's 1776 Constitution on American Constitutionalism During the Founding Decade," *PMHB* 112 (January 1988): 25–48.

89. See Jack N. Rakove, *Original Meanings: Politics and Ideas in the Making of the Constitution* (New York: Random House, 1996). For a narrative of the meeting in the State House, see Catherine Drinker Bowen, *Miracle at Philadelphia: The Story of the Constitutional Convention, May to September 1787* (Boston: Little, Brown, 1966).

90. Owen S. Ireland, *Religion, Ethnicity, and Politics: Ratifying the Constitution in Pennsylvania* (University Park: Pennsylvania State University Press, 1995), xvii.

91. Eberlein and Hubbard, *Diary*, 308–9.

92. Ireland, *Religion, Ethnicity, and Politics*, 72; John Bach McMaster and Frederick D. Stone, eds., *Pennsylvania and the Federal Constitution, 1787–88*, vol. 1 (1888; New York: Da Capo Press, 1970), 204–11.

93. McMaster and Stone, *Pennsylvania and the Federal Constitution*, 418–31; Stevens, *Pennsylvania*, 121.

94. For analyses of the Grand Federal Procession, see Laura Rigal, *The American Manufactory: Art, Labor, and the World of Things in the Early Republic* (Princeton, N.J.: Princeton University Press, 1998), 21–54; Len Travers, *Celebrating the Fourth: Independence Day and the Rites of Nationalism in the Early Republic* (Amherst: University of Massachusetts Press, 1997), 70–106.

95. Stevens, *Pennsylvania*, 118.

96. On construction of memory and the invisibility of the process, see James Fentress and Chris Wickham, *Social Memory* (Oxford: Blackwell, 1992), 49–58.

Chapter 2. Workshop

1. On the public culture of politics, see Simon P. Newman, *Parades and the Politics of the Street: Festive Culture in the Early American Republic* (Philadelphia: University of Pennsylvania Press, 1997); David Waldstreicher, *In the Midst of Perpetual Fetes: The Making of American Nationalism, 1776–1820* (Chapel Hill: University of North Carolina Press, 1997); Saul Cornell, *The Other Founders: Anti-Federalism and the Dissenting Tradition in America, 1788–1828* (Chapel Hill: University of North Carolina Press, 1999). On individual experience of the post-Revolution generation, see Joyce Appleby, *Inheriting the Revolution: The First Generation of Americans* (Cambridge, Mass.: Harvard University Press, 2000).

2. *Pa. Gazette*, February 24, 1790.

3. For national politics of this period, see Stanley Elkins and Eric McKittrick, *The Age of Federalism: The Early American Republic, 1788–1800* (Oxford: Oxford University Press, 1993); James Roger Sharp, *American Politics in the Early Republic: The New Nation in Crisis* (New Haven, Conn.: Yale University Press, 1993); and John R. Howe, Jr., "Republican Thought and the Political Violence of the 1790s," *AQ* 19 (Summer 1967): 147–65. For Pennsylvania, see Harry M. Tinkcom, *The Republicans and Federalists in Pennsylvania, 1790–1801* (Harrisburg: Pennsylvania Historical and Museum Commission, 1950). For Philadelphia, see Richard G. Miller, *Philadelphia—The Federalist City: A Study of Urban Politics, 1789–1801* (Port Washington, N.Y.: Kennikat Press, 1976).

4. Kenneth R. Bowling, *The Creation of Washington, D.C.: The Idea and Location of the American Capital* (Fairfax, Va.: George Mason University Press, 1991).

5. Ellis P. Oberholtzer, *Philadelphia: A History of the City and Its People* (Philadelphia: S. J. Clarke Publishing Co., 1911), 382–411; Anna Coxe Toogood, "Philadelphia as the Nation's Capital, 1790–1800," in Kenneth R. Bowling and Donald R. Kennon, eds., *Neither Separate Nor Equal: Congress in the 1790s* (Athens: Ohio University Press, 2000), 34–57. The population figure includes people within the city limits as well as those in the adjoining districts of Northern Liberties and Southwark. See Gary B. Nash and Billy G. Smith, "The Population of Eighteenth-Century Philadelphia," *PMHB* 99 (July 1975): 362–68.

6. J. M. Powell, *Bring Out Your Dead: The Great Plague of Yellow Fever in Philadelphia in 1793* (Philadelphia: University of Pennsylvania Press, 1949).

7. Beatrice B. Garvin, *Federal Philadephia, 1785–1825: The Athens of the Western World* (Philadelphia: University of Pennsylvania Press, 1987), 22–26.

8. Kenneth R. Bowling and Helen E. Veit, eds., *The Diary of William Maclay and Other Notes on Senate Debates,* in *Documentary History of the First Federal Congress, 1789–1791,* vol. IX (Baltimore: Johns Hopkins University Press, 1988), 355–81.

9. Jacob Cox Parsons, ed., *Extracts from the Diary of Jacob Hiltzheimer* (Philadelphia: William F. Fell, 1893), 158–257.

10. On the Birch prints, see Martin P. Snyder, "William Birch: His Philadelphia Views," *PMHB* 73 (July 1949): 271–315.

11. James Hutchinson to Albert Gallatin, August 19, 1792, quoted in Tinkcom, *Republicans and Federalists,* 58.

12. Tinkcom, *Republicans and Federalists,* 55–58; Miller, *Philadelphia,* 44–48.

13. *Diary of William Maclay,* 367.

14. *Pa. Gazette,* May 14, 1794.

15. *Pa. Gazette,* July 29, 1795.

16. Abigail Adams letter, May 10, 1798, in Stewart Mitchell, ed., *New Letters of Abigail Adams, 1788–1801* (Boston: Houghton Mifflin, 1947), 171–72; Miller, *Philadelphia,* 103–9.

17. Philip S. Foner, ed., *The Democratic-Republican Societies, 1790–1800: A Documentary Sourcebook of Constitutions, Declarations, Addresses, Resolutions, and Toasts* (Westport, Conn.: Greenwood Press, 1976).

18. Newman, *Parades and the Politics of the Street,* 83–119.

19. Miller, *Philadelphia,* 145–49.

20. Ibid., 32–33, 136.

21. Rosemarie Zagarri, "Representation and the Removal of State Capitals, 1776–1812," *JAH* 74 (March 1988): 1239–56.

22. Richard G. Miller, "The Federal City, 1783–1800," in Russell F. Weigley, ed., *Philadephia: A 300-Year History* (New York: W. W. Norton, 1982), 203–5.

23. Donald R. Kennon, ed., *A Republic for the Ages: The United States Capitol and the Political Culture of the Early Republic* (Charlottesville: University Press of Virginia, 1999); Pamela Scott, *Temple of Liberty: Building the Capitol for a New Nation* (New York: Oxford University Press, 1995).

24. John Andrew Gallery, *Philadelphia Architecture: A Guide to the City* (Philadelphia: Foundation for Architecture, 1994), 31.

25. On cultural nationalism, see Lillian B. Miller, *Patrons and Patriotism: The Encouragement of the Fine Arts in the United States, 1790–1860* (Chicago: University of Chicago Press, 1966); Neil Harris, *The Artist in American Society: The Formative Years, 1790–1860* (New York: George Braziller, 1966). On artists in Philadelphia, see J. Thomas Scharf and Thompson Westcott, *History of Philadelphia, 1609–1884,* vol. 2, 1042–45; Edgar P. Richardson, "The Athens of America, 1800–1825," in Weigley, ed., *Philadelphia,* 208.

26. Charles Willson Peale's life and work has been chronicled by a descendant, Charles Coleman Sellers, in *Charles Willson Peale* (New York: W. W. Norton, 1969) and *Mr. Peale's Museum: Charles Willson Peale and the First Popular Museum of Natural Science and Art* (New York: W. W. Norton, 1980). Documentation of Peale's life and work is available in Lillian B. Miller, ed., *The Collected Papers of Charles Willson Peale and His Family* (Millwood, N.Y.:

Kraus Microform, 1980), and in Lillian B. Miller, ed., *The Selected Papers of Charles Willson Peale and His Family,* 5 vols. (New Haven, Conn.: Yale University Press, 1983–88). Scholarship that follows publication of the papers includes David R. Brigham, *Public Culture in the Early Republic: Peale's Museum and Its Audience* (Washington, D.C.: Smithsonian Institution Press, 1995); Lillian B. Miller and David C. Ward, eds., *New Perspectives on Charles Willson Peale: A 250th Anniversary Celebration* (Pittsburgh: University of Pittsburgh Press, 1991); Lillian B. Miller, ed., *The Peale Family: Creation of a Legacy, 1770–1870* (New York: Abbeville Press, 1996); Edgar P. Richardson, Brooke Hindle, and Lillian B. Miller, eds., *Charles Willson Peale and His World* (New York: Harry N. Abrams, 1982).

27. *DAB*, vol. 7, part 2 (New York: Charles Scribner's Sons, 1964), 344–45.

28. Resolve of the Supreme Executive Council to Commission a Portrait of Washington, January 18, 1779, in Miller, *Selected Papers*, vol. 1, 302–3; Sellers, *Mr. Peale's Museum*, 58.

29. "Peale's Museum," Broadside, 1790, in Miller, *Selected Papers*, vol. 1, 580–82.

30. Charles Willson Peale, *Autobiography*, in Miller, *Selected Papers*, vol. 2, part 1, 95–96, note 2; Sellers, *Charles Willson Peale*, 264, 278, 333, 438–39. Peale paid property tax as a slaveowner until 1802; see Brigham, *Public Culture,* 70–71.

31. Brigham, *Public Culture,* 152–63.

32. Sidney Hart and David C. Ward, "The Waning of an Enlightenment Ideal: Charles Willson Peale's Philadelphia Museum, 1790–1820," in Miller and Ward, *New Perspectives*, 219–35.

33. Sellers, *Mr. Peale's Museum*, 152; Miller, *Selected Papers,* vol. 2, part 2, 412, note 1; Select Council of Philadelphia Minutes, November 13, 1805, and Charles Willson Peale to Nathan Sellers, December 4, 1805, in Miller, *Selected Papers,* vol. 2, part 2, 910, 913–14.

34. *Journal of the House of Representatives of the Commonwealth of Pennsylvania*, February 8, 1802, and *Journal of the Senate of the Commonwealth of Pennsylvania*, February 9 and 10, 1802, in Miller, *Selected Papers*, vol. 2, part 1, 394–95.

35. Lillian B. Miller, "Charles Willson Peale: A Life of Harmony and Repose," in Richardson et al., *Charles Willson Peale and His World*, 171–235.

36. Broadside, 1792, in Miller, *Selected Papers,* vol. 2, part 1, 16–18.

37. Miller, *Selected Papers,* vol. 2, part 1, 308–13.

38. Sellers, *Mr. Peale's Museum*, 154.

39. Charles Willson Peale to Philip DePeyster, July 29, 1804, in Miller, *Selected Papers,* vol. 2, part 2, 744; Lillian B. Miller, *In Pursuit of Fame: Rembrandt Peale, 1778–1860* (Seattle: University of Washington Press, 1992), 24.

40. Charles Willson Peale to Nathaniel Ramsay, April 3, 1805, and Charles Willson Peale to Thomas Jefferson, November 3–4, 1805, in Miller, *Selected Papers,* vol. 2, part 2, 821, 909; Sellers, *Mr. Peale's Museum*, 148.

41. David Steinberg, "The Characters of Charles Willson Peale: Portraiture and Social Identity, 1769–1776" (Ph.D. diss., University of Pennsylvania, 1993), 63, 278.

42. Charles Willson Peale, *Guide to the Museum*, in Miller, *Selected Papers,* vol. 2, part 2, 763.

43. Brigham, *Public Culture,* 26–27.

44. Peale, *Guide to the Museum*, 759–66.

45. Ibid.; Brigham, *Public Culture,* 68–82; Sellers, *Mr. Peale's Museum*, 197–98.

46. Peale, *Guide to the Museum*, 764–65.

47. Letters and diary in the Joseph Downs Collection, Henry Francis du Pont Winterthur Museum and Library; biographical information in *DAB*, vol. 4, 270.

48. John F. Sears, *Sacred Places: American Tourist Attractions in the Nineteenth Century* (New York: Oxford University Press, 1989), 87–121.

49. Frances Wright, *Views of Society and Manners in America*, ed. Paul R. Baker (1821; Cambridge, Mass.: Belknap Press, 1963), ix–xii, 48–49.

50. *DAB*, vol. 9, part 2, 202–5; Monroe H. Fabian, *Mr. Sully, Portrait Painter* (Washington, D.C.: Smithsonian Institution Press, 1983), 6–11.

51. Anneliese Harding, *John Lewis Krimmel: Genre Artist of the Early Republic* (Winterthur, Del.: Winterthur Publications, 1994), 33–34.

52. John Lewis Krimmel, *Election Scene. State House in Philadelphia*, oil on canvas, Henry Francis du Pont Winterthur Museum; *DAB*, vol. 5, part 2, 506.

53. Gary B. Nash, "Reverberations of Haiti in the American North: Black Saint Dominguans in Philadelphia," *PH* 65 (Supplement 1998): 44–73.

54. The major works on African Americans in Philadelphia during this period are Gary B. Nash, *Forging Freedom: The Formation of Philadelphia's Black Community, 1720–1840* (Cambridge, Mass.: Harvard University Press, 1988), and Julie Winch, *Philadelphia's Black Elite: Activism, Accommodation, and the Struggle for Autonomy, 1787–1848* (Philadelphia: Temple University Press, 1988). On African churches, see Carol V. R. George, *Segregated Sabbaths: Richard Allen and the Rise of Independent Black Churches, 1760–1840* (New York: Oxford University Press, 1973).

55. Nash, *Forging Freedom*, 38.

56. "Sketch of the Reverend Absalom Jones," in William Douglass, *Annals of the First African Church in the United States of America, Now Styled the African Episcopal Church of St. Thomas* (Philadelphia: King & Baird, 1862), 121.

57. Articles of the Free African Society, May 17, 1787, in Douglass, *Annals*, 15–16.

58. Constitution of St. Thomas's, August 12, 1794, in Douglass, *Annals*, 96–99.

59. Constitution of the Pennsylvania Augustine Society, 1818, in Dorothy Porter, ed., *Early Negro Writing, 1760–1837* (Boston: Beacon Press, 1971), 92–93.

60. Charges against black relief workers appear in Matthew Carey, *A Short Account of the Malignant Fever Lately Prevalent in Philadelphia* (Philadelphia: Mathew Carey, 1793). The refutation appears in A. J. [Absalom Jones] and R. A. [Richard Allen], *A Narrative of the Proceedings of the Black People, During the Late Awful Calamity in Philadelphia in the Year 1793* (Philadelphia: William W. Woodward, 1794). See also Nash, *Forging Freedom*, 121–25; and Powell, *Bring Out Your Dead*, 94–101.

61. Richard Allen, *The Life Experience and Gospel Labors of the Rt. Rev. Richard Allen* (New York: Abington Press, 1960), 25–26. Although the walkout from St. George's often is dated as occurring in 1787, researchers examining church construction and membership records have identified 1792 as the more likely date. See Nash, *Forging Freedom*, 118–19 and 310, note 62.

62. Douglass, *Annals*, 11.

63. The exact dimensions of the City Hall are 50 feet, 7 inches by 65 feet, 11 inches. See Lee H. Nelson, *Historic Structures Report, Part I, Supplement I, on Old City Hall* (May 1961), 20, INHP.

64. David Kennedy and William Lucas, "A Sunday Morning View of the African Episcopal

Church of St. Thomas in Philadelphia," lithograph, 1829, HSP; "Outline Sketch of the Building," in Douglass, *Annals*, 135–36; Samuel Magaw, *A Discourse Delivered July 17th, 1794, in the African Church,* in Douglass, *Annals*, 64–84; Allen, *Life Experience,* 28.

65. Allen, *Life Experience,* 80–81; Nash, *Forging Freedom,* 164–65.

66. Nash, *Forging Freedom,* 64–65, 108.

67. Letter from Benjamin Banneker to the Secretary of State, With His Answer (Philadelphia: Daniel Lawrence, 1792) in Porter, *Early Negro Writing*, 324–29; Herbert Aptheker, ed., *A Documentary History of the Negro People of the United States* (New York: Citadel Press, 1951), 39–44.

68. James Forten, *Series of Letters of a Man of Color*, 1813, in Aptheker, *Documentary History*, 59–66.

69. Ibid.; Nash, *Forging Freedom,* 177.

70. Absalom Jones, *A Thanksgiving Sermon Preached January 1, 1808* (1808; Philadelphia: Rhistoric Publications, 1969); Russell Parrott, *An Oration on the Abolition of the Slave Trade,* January 1, 1812, and *Address on the Abolition of the Slave Trade*, January 1, 1816, LCP.

71. William Lloyd Garrison, *Thoughts on African Colonization: or an impartial exhibition of the Doctrines, Principles & Purposes of the American Colonization Society. Together with the Resolutions, Addresses & Remonstrances of the Free People of Color*, 1832, in Aptheker, ed., *Documentary History*, 71–72; James Forten, *To the Humane and Benevolent Inhabitants of the City and County of Philadelphia*, 1818, in Porter, ed., *Early Negro Writing,* 267–68.

72. Edward M. Riley, "Philadelphia: The Nation's Capital, 1790–1800," *PH* 20 (October 1953): 357–79.

Chapter 3. Relic

1. Fred Somkin, *Unquiet Eagle: Memory and Desire in the Idea of American Freedom, 1815–1860* (Ithaca, N.Y.: Cornell University Press, 1967), 55–90; Michael Kammen, *A Season of Youth: The American Revolution and the Historical Imagination* (Ithaca, N.Y.: Cornell University Press, 1978), 37–47.

2. *Saturday Evening Post*, July 17, 1824.

3. Records of the Supreme Court, Eastern District, Courts of Oyer and Terminer and General Gaol Delivery, 1778–1786 and 1787–1800, RG 33, PSA.

4. On the symbolism of principles over place, see John Higham, "America in Person: The Evolution of National Symbols," *Amerikastudien/American Studies* 36 (4): 473–93.

5. Ibid.; Alfred F. Young and Terry J. Fife, with Mary E. Janzen, *We the People: Voices and Images of the New Nation* (Philadelphia: Temple University Press, 1993), 192–99.

6. Barry Schwartz, *George Washington: The Making of an American Symbol* (New York: Free Press, 1987); Kammen, *Season of Youth*, 41–42.

7. Len Travers, *Celebrating the Fourth: Independence Day and the Rites of Nationalism in the Early Republic* (Amherst: University of Massachusetts Press, 1997).

8. J. Thomas Scharf and Thompson Westcott, *History of Philadelphia, 1609–1884*, vol. 2 (Philadelphia: L.H. Evarts, 1884), 991; John L. Cotter, Daniel G. Roberts, and Michael Parrington, *The Buried Past: An Archaeological History of Philadelphia* (Philadelphia: University of Pennsylvania Press, 1993), 90–93.

9. Henry Wiencek, *The Smithsonian Guide to Historic America*, vol. 2 (New York: Stewart, Tabori & Chang, 1989), 35–38, 40–41.

10. *DAB*, vol. 7, part 1 (New York: Charles Scribner's Sons, 1964), 9–13.

11. John Andrew Gallery, *Philadelphia Architecture: A Guide to the City* (Philadelphia: Foundation for Architecture, 1994), 32.

12. John M. Bryan, ed., *Robert Mills* (Washington, D.C.: American Institute of Architects Press, 1989), 41–42; Kenneth Ames, "Robert Mills and the Philadelphia Row House," *JSAH* 27 (June 1968): 140–46.

13. Robert Mills, *Elevation on Chestnut Street of the Court Houses, State House, and Fireproof Offices contemplated to be erected as Wings to the State House*, April 1812, Athenaeum of Philadelphia Architectural Archive.

14. Robert G. Stewart, *Robert Edge Pine: A British Portrait Painter in America, 1784–1788* (Washington, D.C.: Smithsonian Institution Press, 1979), 13–39.

15. Scholars disagree on the origins of the Savage work. Charles Henry Hart, who discovered the Savage painting in the Boston Museum in the 1890s, believed that the painting he found was Pine's work, finished by Savage. During the 1950s, historians for the National Park Service concluded that Savage did not finish Pine's earlier painting, but created the work himself. See James M. Mulcahy, "*Congress Voting Independence*: The Trumbull and Pine-Savage Paintings," *PMHB* 80 (January 1956): 74–91. Stewart (see above, note 14) states that Pine's *Congress Voting Independence* "does not survive but is known from the copy made by Edward Savage" (p. 29).

16. Mulcahy, "*Congress Voting Independence*," 89–90.

17. John Trumbull, *Autobiography, Reminiscences and Letters from 1756 to 1841* (New York: Wiley and Putnam, 1841), 158.

18. Ibid., 95.

19. Stewart, *Robert Edge Pine*, 28–29.

20. Trumbull, *Autobiography*, 416–18.

21. Irma B. Jaffe, *Trumbull: The Declaration of Independence* (London: Penguin Books, 1976), 59–92.

22. *Portfolio*, April 1824, in Staff, INHP, *Historic Structures Report Part I on Independence Hall* (March 1959), appendix F.

23. Michael Kammen, *A Machine That Would Go of Itself: The Constitution in American Culture* (New York: St. Martin's Press, 1994), 91–92.

24. Scharf and Westcott, *History of Philadelphia*, vol. 2, 984, 1034–35.

25. Scharf and Westcott, *History of Philadelphia*, vol. 3, 1788.

26. Manuscript Minutes of the Philadelphia Select Council, March 10, 1813, PCA. "City Councils" refers to Philadelphia's bicameral governing body, consisting of the Select Council and Common Council.

27. Norman Tyler, *Historic Preservation: An Introduction to Its History, Principles, and Practice* (New York: W. W. Norton, 2000), 33; William J. Murtagh, *Keeping Time: The History and Theory of Preservation in America* (New York: Sterling Publishing, 1993), 26–27; Charles B. Hosmer, Jr., *Presence of the Past: A History of the Preservation Movement in the United States Before Williamsburg* (New York: G. P. Putnam's Sons, 1965), 29–30.

28. *U.S. Gazette*, March 9, 1813, March 10, 1813.

29. *Journal of the Senate of the Commonwealth of Pennsylvania*, vol. 23 (Harrisburg, Pa.: William Green, 1812–1813), 362, 452, 455, 458, 469, 482, 497–98.

30. *Journal of the Senate of the Commonwealth of Pennsylvania*, vol. 21 (Harrisburg, Pa.: Christian Gleim, 1815–1816), 174; *Journal of the Twenty-Sixth House of Representatives of the Commonwealth of Pennsylvania* (Harrisburg, Pa.: James Peacock, 1815–1816), 498.

31. *U.S. Gazette*, February 14, 1816; John Read to Nicholas Biddle, February 21, 1816, Nicholas Biddle Papers, Manuscript Div., LC.

32. *Aurora*, February 28, 1816; on Duane's politics, see Samuel W. Higginbotham, *The Keystone in the Democratic Arch: Pennsylvania Politics, 1800–1816* (Harrisburg: Pennsylvania Historical and Museum Commission, 1952), 16–18.

33. *Aurora*, February 10, 1816.

34. *U.S. Gazette*, April 13, 1816. The dynamics of the Council's decision to buy the land are unknown. The ordinance authorizing the purchase was published in the *Gazette* without elaboration. The manuscript minutes for this period have not survived.

35. Somkin, *Unquiet Eagle,* 131–74.

36. Stanley J. Idzerda, Anne C. Loveland, and Marc H. Miller, *Lafayette, Hero of Two Worlds: The Art and Pageantry of His Farewell Tour of America, 1824–1825* (Hanover, N.H.: University Press of New England, 1989), 106–45.

37. Germantown Print Works, *General La Fayette's arrival at Independence Hall, Philad. Sep. 28, 1824*, engraved linen handkerchief, Henry Francis du Pont Winterthur Museum.

38. *Philadelphia in 1824* (H. C. Carey & L. Lea, August 1824), 8, 132.

39. *Saturday Evening Post*, March 27, 1824. The four arson suspects were also charged with conspiring to assassinate Philadelphia mayor Robert Wharton. Ultimately, one of the suspects testified against the other three, who were convicted of arson and conspiracy. Each was sentenced to nine years in the penitentiary for arson and three years for conspiracy. *Saturday Evening Post,* May 15 and May 29, 1824.

40. Minutes of the Committee of Arrangement, August 19, 1824, Marquis de Lafayette Reception Papers, HSP.

41. Agnes Addison Gilchrist, *William Strickland, Architect and Engineer, 1788–1854* (New York: DaCapo Press, 1969), 1–8; Sandra L. Tatman and Roger W. Moss, Athenaeum of Philadelphia, *Biographical Dictionary of Philadelphia Architects: 1700–1930* (Boston: G. K. Hall, 1985), 767–68.

42. Auguste Lavasseur, *Lafayette in America in 1824 and 1825*, translated by John D. Godman, vol. 1 (Philadelphia: Carey and Lea, 1829), 142.

43. Account of expenses, Lafayette Reception Papers, HSP.

44. *Poulson's American Daily Advertiser*, September 30, 1824; Lavasseur, *Lafayette in America,* vol. 1, 142–43; Andrew Burstein, *Sentimental Democracy: The Evolution of America's Romantic Self-Image* (New York: Hill and Wang, 1999).

45. *Saturday Evening Post,* October 2, 1824.

46. *Poulson's American Daily Advertiser*, September 30, 1824; *Saturday Evening Post*, October 2, 1824; Ellis P. Oberholtzer, *Philadelphia: A History of the City and Its People*, vol. 2 (Philadelphia: S. J. Clark Publishing Co., 1911), 137.

47. For example, see *Saturday Evening Post*, August 21, 1824, and *U.S. Gazette*, August 21, 1824.

48. Minutes of Committee of Arrangement, August 19, 1824, to September 9, 1824, Lafayette Reception Papers, HSP.

49. Notice to Councils, September 23, 1824, Lafayette Reception Papers, HSP; *Poulson's American Daily Advertiser*, September 30, 1824; *U.S. Gazette*, September 30, 1824; *Saturday Evening Post*, October 2, 1824.

50. Lavasseur, *Lafayette in America*, vol. 1, 143; Oberholtzer, *Philadelphia,* vol. 2, 139.

51. Oberholtzer, *Philadelphia*, vol. 2, 87.

52. Scharf and Westcott, *History of Philadelphia*, vol. 1, 619; Andrew Burstein, *America's Jubilee: How in 1826 a Generation Remembered Fifty Years of Independence* (New York: Alfred A. Knopf, 2001).

53. On Mount Vernon, see Hosmer, *Presence of the Past*, 41–75.

54. *Register of Pennsylvania*, March 8, 1828.

55. Ibid., Oberholtzer, *Philadelphia,* vol. 2, 133; occupational information on City Council members from Thomas Wilson, ed., *The Philadelphia Directory and Stranger's Guide for 1825* (Philadelphia: John Bioren, 1825).

56. *Register of Pennsylvania*, March 8, 1828.

57. On Strickland as a restoration architect, see Lee H. Nelson, "Independence Hall: Its Fabric Reinforced," in Charles E. Peterson, ed., *Building Early America: Contributions Toward the History of a Great Industry* (Mendham, N.J.: Astragal Press, 1976), 288; Tatman and Moss, *Biographical Dictionary of Philadelphia Architects*, 768; Murtagh, *Keeping Time*, 27.

58. Frank M. Etting, *An Historical Account of the Old State House of Pennsylvania Now Known as the Hall of Independence* (Boston: James R. Osgood and Company, 1876), 162; *Register of Pennsylvania*, March 8, 1828, September 18, 1828; David Kimball, *Venerable Relic: The Story of the Liberty Bell* (Philadelphia: Eastern National Park and Monument Association, 1989), 39.

59. On copies of Independence Hall, see John Maass, "Architecture and Americanism, or Pastiches of Independence Hall," *Historic Preservation* 11 (April-June 1970), 17–25.

60. *Register of Pennsylvania*, April 23, 1831.

61. *Register of Pennsylvania*, November 5, 1831, November 19, 1831.

62. *Register of Pennsylvania*, January 9, 1830.

63. John F. Sears, *Sacred Places: American Tourist Attractions in the Nineteenth Century* (New York: Oxford University Press, 1989), 87–121; Philip Stevick, *Imagining Philadelphia: Travelers' Views of the City from 1800 to the Present* (Philadelphia: University of Pennsylvania Press, 1996), 55–71.

64. To the tip of the spire, the steeple reaches 168 feet, 7 ¼ inches in height. The observation level, with a railing installed, is at 95 feet, 2 ½ inches from the ground; the bell hangs at 118 feet, 4 inches; and the structural portion of the steeple reaches 129 feet, 9 ⅛ inches in height. See Photogrammetric Documentation Project (1985–90), HABS, PA 1430, Sheet 22.

65. *Register of Pennsylvania*, September 26, 1829.

66. On relics as bridges between past and present, see David Lowenthal, *The Past Is a Foreign Country* (Cambridge: Cambridge University Press, 1985).

67. Maurice Halbwachs, *The Collective Memory* (1950; New York: Harper & Row, 1980).

68. Ernest Renan, "What Is a Nation?" in Geoff Eley and Ronald Grigor Suny, eds., *Becoming National: A Reader* (Oxford: Oxford University Press, 1996), 42–55; Benedict Anderson, *Imagined Communities*, revised edition (New York: Verso, 1991), 5–7.

Chapter 4. Shrine

1. George Lippard, "Legends of the Revolution—New Series, Legend Twenty-Seventh, Fourth of July, 1776," *Saturday Courier*, January 2, 1847. The story is reprinted in Victor Rosewater, *The Liberty Bell: Its History and Significance* (New York: D. Appleton and Co., 1926), 113–18.

2. George Lippard, *The Quaker City: or, the Monks of Monks Hall*, edited with an introduction by David S. Reynolds (Amherst: University of Massachusetts Press, 1995), 375.

3. Reynolds, introduction to Lippard, *Quaker City*, i.

4. Although Lippard popularized the story of the Liberty Bell ringing on the Fourth of July, his story reflected a belief that persisted earlier among Philadelphians. On April 5, 1828, the *Register of Pennsylvania* published documents related to the bell and noted that it "was at first used in the steeple and perhaps also on the 4th of July 1776, but of this we are not certain." The association of the bell with the Declaration of Independence also appeared prior to Lippard's story in Sherman Day, *Historical Collections of the State of Pennsylvania* (Philadelphia: George W. Gorton, 1843). Shortly after publication of Lippard's story, it was represented as fact in Benson J. Lossing, *Seventeen Hundred and Seventy-Six, or the War of Independence; A History of the Anglo-Americans, From the Period of Union of the Colonies Against the French, to the Inauguration of Washington, the First President of the United States of America* (New York: Edward Walker, 1847).

5. John Bodnar, *Remaking America: Public Memory, Commemoration, and Patriotism in the Twentieth Century* (Princeton, N.J.: Princeton University Press, 1992), 26–27; Susan G. Davis, *Parades and Power: Street Theatre in Nineteenth-Century Philadelphia* (Berkeley: University of California Press, 1986); on commemorations, politics, and public space, see Mary P. Ryan, *Civic Wars: Democracy and Public Life in the American City During the Nineteenth Century* (Berkeley: University of California Press, 1997).

6. On the market revolution, see Charles Sellers, *The Market Revolution: Jacksonian America, 1815–1846* (New York: Oxford University Press, 1991). The transformation of blocks north of the State House is evident in maps of the period. See William Allen, *Plan of the City of Philadelphia and Adjoining Districts, Philadelphia* (Philadelphia: H. S. Tanner, 1828); S. J. Sidney, *Map of the City of Philadelphia Together With All the Surrounding Districts, Including Camden, N.J.* (Philadelphia: Smith & Wistar, 1849). Also see Bruce Laurie, *Working People of Philadelphia, 1800–1850* (Philadelphia: Temple University Press, 1980), 10–13.

7. Harry L. Watson, *Liberty and Power: The Politics of Jacksonian America* (New York: Farrar, Straus & Giroux, 1990), 132–60; Davis, *Parades and Power*, 130–32; Robert Remini, *Andrew Jackson and the Course of American Democracy, 1833–1845*, vol. 3 (New York: Harper & Row, 1984), 69–71.

8. Davis, *Parades and Power*, 132–34; Philip S. Foner, *We the Other People: Alternative Declarations of Independence by Labor Groups, Farmers, Woman's Rights Advocates, Socialists, and Blacks, 1829–1975* (Urbana: University of Illinois Press, 1976), 1–14, 47–76.

9. Laurie, *Working People*, 85–99.

10. *Public Ledger*, August 23, 25, 1836.

11. Laurie, *Working People*, 181; *Public Ledger*, November 13, 1857.

12. J. Thomas Scharf and Thompson Westcott, *History of Philadelphia, 1609–1884*, vol. 2 (Philadelphia: L. H. Evarts, 1884), 678, 682, 686.

13. *Public Ledger*, April 25, 1848.

14. Scharf and Westcott, *History of Philadelphia,* vol. 2, 636–37, 657–58, 687, 702–3, 704–5, 708, 748; Edward M. Riley, "The Independence Hall Group," *Transactions of the American Philosophical Society* (March 1953): 35.

15. *Journal of the Select Council Beginning Friday, October 14, 1836, Ending Thursday, October 5, 1837* (Philadelphia: Charles Alexander, 1837), 14, 19; Appendix, 4–5.

16. Glenn C. Altschuler and Stuart M. Blumin, *Rude Republic: Americans and Their Politics in the Nineteenth Century* (Princeton, N.J.: Princeton University Press, 2000); *Public Ledger*, July 5, 1848, July 6, 1852.

17. *Journal of the Select Council of the City of Philadelphia for 1844–45* (Philadelphia: J. Crissy, 1845), 91, 97, 106; *Journal of the Select Council for 1847–48* (Philadelphia: Crissy & Markley, 1848), 91, 104; *Journal of the Common Council of the City of Philadelphia for 1847–48* (Philadelphia: King & Baird, 1848), 114–15; R. Craig Sautter, *Philadelphia Presidential Conventions* (Highland Park, Ill.: December Press, 2000).

18. *Evening Bulletin,* March 3, 1848, March 7, 1848; *Public Ledger*, March 7, 1848, March 8, 1848; Leonard L. Richards, *The Life and Times of Congressman John Quincy Adams* (New York: Oxford University Press, 1986), 202–3; Josiah Quincy, *Memoir of the Life of John Quincy Adams* (Boston: Phillips, Sampson & Co., 1858).

19. *Evening Bulletin*, July 3, 1852; Robert V. Remini, *Henry Clay: Statesman for the Union* (New York: W. W. Norton, 1991), 778–86.

20. *Public Ledger*, March 13, 1857.

21. Gary B. Nash, *Forging Freedom: The Formation of Philadelphia's Black Community, 1720–1840* (Cambridge, Mass.: Harvard University Press, 1988), 246–79; *History of Pennsylvania Hall Which Was Destroyed by a Mob* (1838; reprint, New York: Negro University Press, 1969).

22. For references to the Declaration of Independence, see Howard Holman Bell, ed., *Minutes of the Proceedings of the National Negro Conventions, 1830–1864* (New York: Arno Press, 1969), 4, 9, 23. On the reaction against black migrants to Northern states, see James Oliver Horton and Lois E. Horton, *In Hope of Liberty: Culture, Community and Protest Among Northern Free Blacks, 1700–1860* (New York: Oxford University Press, 1997), 102–4.

23. Robert Purvis, "Appeal of Forty Thousand," in Herbert Aptheker, ed., *A Documentary History of the Negro People of the United States* (New York: Citadel Press, 1969), 176–86.

24. The quotation was attributed to *The Golden Legend*, by Wynkyn de Worde, a printer also known as Jan van Wynkyn, who worked in London from 1476 until his death in 1535. As published in the *Liberty Bell*, the quotation read: "It is said the evil spirytes that ben in the regyon, doubte moche when they here the Bells rongen: and this is the cause why the Bells ben rongen, whan grete tempeste and outrages of wether happen, to the end that the fiends and wycked spirytes should be abashed and flee."

25. *Liberty Bell*, 1841–63.

26. *History of Pennsylvania Hall*, 112.

27. Ibid., 151–52.

28. *Pa. Freeman*, August 22, 1844.

29. Ibid.; *Public Ledger*, August 19, 1844.

30. Frederick Douglass, "What to the Slave Is the Fourth of July?" in John W. Blassingame,

ed., *The Frederick Douglass Papers*, series 1, vol. 2 (New Haven, Conn.: Yale University Press, 1979), 359–88.

31. *Minutes and Proceedings of the First Annual Convention,* in Bell, 11. Also see Geneviève Fabre, "African-American Commemorative Celebrations in the Nineteenth Century," in Geneviève Fabre and Robert O'Meally, eds., *History and Memory in African-American Culture* (New York: Oxford University Press, 1994), 72–91.

32. Fugitive Slave Cases, 1850–1860, Circuit Court, Records of the U.S. District Court for the Eastern District of Pennsylvania (RG 21), NA, Mid-Atlantic Region.

33. Stanley W. Campbell, *The Slave Catchers: Enforcement of the Fugitive Slave Law, 1850–1860* (Chapel Hill: University of North Carolina Press, 1970), 110–47.

34. Because records of the U.S. District Court are incomplete, it is difficult to determine the total number of cases. Thirteen cases in Philadelphia between 1850 and 1860 are identified by Campbell, *The Slave Catchers,* 199–206.

35. *National Era,* January 2, 1851.

36. *Public Ledger*, October 18, 1850, October 19, 1850; *Evening Bulletin*, October 18, 1850, October 19, 1850.

37. *Evening Bulletin*, December 21, 1850; *Public Ledger*, December 23, 1850, December 24, 1850.

38. On the perception of Ingraham as a southern sympathizer, see Ellis P. Oberholtzer, *Philadelphia: A History of the City and Its People*, vol. 2 (Philadelphia: S. J. Clark Publishing Co., 1911), 349.

39. *Public Ledger*, January 25, 27, 1851.

40. *Pa. Freeman,* February 13, 1851; *Evening Bulletin,* February 10, 1851; *Public Ledger,* February 7, 8, 10, 1851.

41. *Evening Bulletin*, March 10, 11, 12, 13, 1851; *Public Ledger,* March 10, 1851.

42. Quoted in Jonathan Katz, *Resistance at Christiana: The Fugitive Slave Rebellion, Christiana, Pennsylvania, September 11, 1851* (New York: Thomas Y. Crowell, 1974), 143.

43. Quoted in W. U. Hensel, *The Christiana Riot and the Treason Trials of 1851* (Lancaster, Pa.: New Era Printing Co., 1911), 145.

44. *National Era*, November 27, 1851; Katz, *Resistance at Christiana,* 178–81; Hensel, *The Christiana Riot,* 83–84.

45. *Report of the Trial of Castner Hanway for Treason* (1852; reprint, Westport, Conn.: Negro Universities Press, 1970), 53–54.

46. Ibid., 198–99.

47. Ibid., 246–49; Katz, *Resistance at Christiana,* 230–42. State charges against the Christiana defendants were later dropped in a bargain with defense attorneys, to undo their filing of a charge of perjury against a federal marshal and his imprisonment under $1,000 bail.

48. *The Celebration of the eighty-third anniversary of the Declaration of American Independence, by the Banneker Institute, Philadelphia, July 4th, 1859* (Philadelphia: W. S. Young, Printer, 1859), Murray African-American Pamphlets, LC.

49. See Michael Feldberg, *The Turbulent Era: Riot and Disorder in Jacksonian America* (New York: Oxford University Press, 1985); Michael Feldberg, *The Philadelphia Riots of 1844: A Study of Ethnic Conflict* (Westport, Conn.: Greenwood Press, 1975); Elizabeth M. Geffen, "Industrial Development and Social Crisis, 1841–1854," in Russell F. Weigley, ed., *Philadelphia: A 300-Year History* (New York: W. W. Norton, 1982).

50. John Hancock Lee, *The Origins and Progress of the American Party in Politics* (Philadelphia: Elliott and Gihon, 1855), 14–16.

51. Ibid., 136–56.

52. *Public Ledger*, May 8, 9, 1844; Feldberg, *Philadelphia Riots*, 107–14.

53. Tyler Anbinder, *Nativism and Slavery: The Northern Know Nothings and the Politics of the 1850s* (New York: Oxford University Press, 1992), 44–47; Michael F. Holt, *The Rise and Fall of the American Whig Party: Jacksonian Politics and the Onset of the Civil War* (New York: Oxford University Press, 1999), 836–57.

54. Ibid., 53–55; *Public Ledger*, June 7, 9, 1854.

55. Frederick Anspach, *The Sons of the Sires* (Philadelphia: Lippincott, Grambo & Co., 1855), 15–16.

56. *Evening Bulletin*, June 28, 1858; *DAB*, vol. 4 (New York: Charles Scribner's Sons, 1930), 355–56.

57. Robert T. Conrad, ed., *Sanderson's Biography of the Signers to the Declaration of Independence* (Philadelphia: Thomas, Cowperthwait & Co., 1852), xvii–xxii.

58. Report of the Committee on City Property, December 26, 1849, in *Journal of the Select Council of the City of Philadelphia for 1849–1850* (Philadelphia: Crissy & Markley, 1850), appendix 24, 59.

59. *Evening Bulletin*, July 18, 1854, December 7, 1854; *Public Ledger,* August 19, 1854, August 29, 1854, October 27, 1854, November 29, 1854.

60. Between June and October 1854, council members submitted bills for more than $1,300 for cigars. *Public Ledger*, January 16, 1854.

61. R. A. Smith, *Philadelphia As It Is, in 1852* (Philadelphia: Lindsay and Blakiston, 1852), 23.

62. Edward William Watkin, *A Trip to the U.S. and Canada: In a Series of Letters* (London: W. H. Smith, 1852), 95.

63. On the redecoration project, see *Ordinances and Joint Resolutions of the Select and Common Councils of the Consolidated City of Philadelphia, From June Twelfth to December Thirty-First, 1854* (Philadelphia: W. H. Sickels, Printer, 1854), 47, 124, 161; *Ordinances and Joint Resolutions of the Select and Common Councils of the Consolidated City of Philadelphia, From January First to December Thirty-First, 1855* (Philadelphia: J. H. Jones & Co., Printers, 1855), 20, 69, 70; *Ordinances and Joint Resolutions of the Select and Common Councils of the Consolidated City of Philadelphia, From January First to December Thirty-First, 1855*, 143; *Public Ledger*, September 15, 1854, October 7, 1854, January 8, 1855, February 21,1855.

64. Exactly when and how the Liberty Bell cracked is unknown. The jagged "crack" most visible on the bell resulted from an 1846 attempt to repair it by drilling out and inserting bolts into a much less visible crack. The ringing of the repaired bell caused further damage. On February 26, 1846, the *Public Ledger* reported that "this venerable relic of the Revolution rang its last clear note on Monday last . . . and now hangs in the great city steeple irreparably cracked and forever dumb." After the Liberty Bell's installation in the Hall of Independence in 1852, visitation more than doubled, from 6,584 in 1851 to 16,533 in 1853. Figures published in *Public Ledger*, January 1, 1852, and January 14, 1854.

65. Lettie Smith's Diary, January 27, 1855, Newtown Historic Association, Newtown, Pa. I am indebted to Connie S. Griffith Houchins for this source.

66. Inscription on bell pedestal quoted in *Public Ledger*, February 21, 1855.

67. Lettie Smith's Diary, January 27, 1855.

68. *Public Ledger*, February 23, 1855.

69. See Patricia West, *Domesticating History: The Political Origins of America's House Museums* (Washington, D.C.: Smithsonian Institution Press, 1999), 1–37.

70. David W. Belisle, *History of Independence Hall: From the Earliest Period to the Present Time* (Philadelphia: James Challen & Son, 1859), 350–89.

71. Ibid.

72. George R. Prowell, *The History of Camden County, New Jersey* (Philadelphia: L. J. Richards & Co., 1886), 321.

73. Belisle, *History of Independence Hall,* 9–10.

74. Russell F. Weigley, "The Border City in Civil War, 1854–1865," in Weigley, ed., *Philadelphia*, 383–416.

75. Scharf and Westcott, *History of Philadelphia,* vol. 1, 738–40.

76. Ibid., vol. 1, 740–824; vol. 3, 1796.

77. *Evening Bulletin*, February 22, 1861.

78. *Public Ledger*, June 14, 1861; May 5, 1862, May 6, 1862, January 9, 1863; January 10, 1863; Scharf and Westcott, *History of Philadelphia,* vol. 1, 827.

79. *Public Ledger*, March 27, 1862.

80. *Evening Bulletin*, April 22, 1865.

81. Staff, INHP, *Historic Structures Report Part I on Independence Hall* (March 1959), and *Historic Structures Report Part II on Independence Hall* (April 1962); Edward M. Riley, "The Independence Hall Group," *Transactions of the American Philosophical Society* 43, part 1 (March 1953): 7–42; Dennis C. Kurjack, "Evolution of a Shrine," *PH* 21 (June 1954): 193–200.

82. See, for example, the biographical sketch of Robert C. Grier in Scharf and Westcott, *History of Philadelphia,* vol. 2, 1547–48.

Chapter 5. Legacy

1. *Fourth of July Souvenir, Containing a Succinct Account of the Celebration of the Fourth of July, 1866, Upon the Presentation of the State Flags Carried by the Pennsylvania Regiments During the Southern Rebellion* (Philadelphia: James Moore & Sons, 1866); *Public Ledger*, July 5, 1866; *Evening Bulletin*, July 5, 6, 1866.

2. See Robert Bellah, "Civil Religion in America," *Daedalus* (Winter 1967): 1–21; Russell E. Richey and Donald G. Jones, eds., *American Civil Religion* (New York: Harper & Row, 1974).

3. Dorothy Gondos Beers, "The Centennial City, 1865–1876," in Russell F. Weigley, ed., *Philadelphia: A 300-Year History* (New York: W. W. Norton, 1982), 419–20.

4. Michael P. McCarthy, "Traditions in Conflict: The Philadelphia City Hall Site Controversy," *PH* 57 (October 1990): 301–17; Howard Gillette Jr., "Philadelphia's City Hall: Monument to a New Political Machine," *PMHB* 97 (April 1973): 233–49. On considerations of new public buildings prior to the 1860s, see Journals of the Select and Common Councils for 1836–37, 1837–38, and 1849–50, PCA.

5. Max Page, "From 'Miserable Dens' to the 'Marble Monster': Historical Memory and

the Design of Courthouses in Nineteenth-Century Philadelphia," *PMHB* 119, no. 4 (October 1995): 317–19.

6. See, for example, *Evening Bulletin*, October 4, 1849.

7. *Journal of the Select Council of the City of Philadelphia From July 2, 1868 to January 1, 1869* (Philadelphia: E. C. Markley & Son, 1869), 345.

8. McCarthy, "Traditions in Conflict," 311.

9. *Press,* February 4, 1869, in George Canby, comp., *The Public Buildings*, HSP.

10. Ibid.

11. Sandra L. Tatman and Roger W. Moss, *Biographical Dictionary of Philadelphia Architects: 1700–1930* (Boston: G. K. Hall, 1985), 510–11; McCarthy, "Traditions in Conflict," 306.

12. E. Rogers, *Plan of the Proposed Alterations of the County Buildings,* wood engraving, LCP.

13. Report of Thomas U. Walter, chairman, Committee on Plans and Architecture, *Journal of the Select Council, July 2, 1868–Jan. 1, 1869*, appendix 195, 245.

14. Designs for Public Buildings on Independence Square (c. December 1869), Commissioners for the Erection of Public Buildings Records (RG 160), PCA.

15. The Public Buildings: An Appeal to the Legislature to Prevent the Desecration of Independence Square, March 1, 1870, in Canby, *The Public Buildings*, HSP.

16. Ibid.

17. *Evening Bulletin*, February 3, 1870, in Canby, *The Public Buildings,* HSP.

18. *Evening Bulletin*, March 1, 1870, in Canby, *The Public Buildings*, HSP.

19. More than 7,000 adult males signed the call for an election. More than 1,750 others signed petitions calling upon the state legislature to "prevent desecration of Independence Square." See petitions in House File, Records of General Assembly (RG 7), PSA.

20. *Journal of the Senate of the Commonwealth of Pennsylvania for the Session Begun at Harrisburg on the Fourth Day of January, 1870* (Harrisburg, Pa.: B. Singerly, 1870), 930, 938, 990; *Journal of the House of Representatives of the Commonwealth of Pennsylvania for the Session Begun at Harrisburg on the Fourth Day of January 1870* (Harrisburg, Pa.: B. Singerly, 1870), 183, 344, 640.

21. McCarthy, "Traditions in Conflict," 311.

22. Michael Kammen, *Mystic Chords of Memory: The Transformation of Tradition in American Culture* (New York: Vintage Books, 1991), 135–38.

23. James D. McCabe, *The Illustrated History of the Centennial Exhibition* (1876; reprint Philadelphia: National Publishing Company, 1976), 113–221. Also see Robert W. Rydell, *All the World's a Fair: Visions of Empire at American International Expositions, 1876–1916* (Chicago: University of Chicago Press, 1984), 9–37; Robert C. Post, *1876: A Centennial Exhibition* (Washington, D.C.: Smithsonian Institution Press, 1976).

24. As examples of Centennial guidebooks, see *Magee's Centennial Guide of Philadelphia* (Philadelphia: R. Magee & Son, 1876); Robert C. Ogden, *Philadelphia and the Centennial: How to See Them* (New York: Hurd and Houghton, 1876); *Frazier's Centennial Pocket Guide to Philadelphia* (Philadelphia: Frazier's, 1876).

25. Peter McCaffery, *When Bosses Ruled Philadelphia: The Emergence of the Republican Machine, 1867–1933* (University Park: Pennsylvania State University Press, 1993), 12–13.

26. *Public Ledger*, July 8, 11, 14, 16, 1870.

27. Judith Lazarus Goldberg, "Strikes, Organizing, and Change: The Knights of Labor in Philadelphia, 1869–1890" (Ph.D. diss., New York University, 1985), 74–75; *Public Ledger*, September 21, 1874.

28. *Digest of Laws and Ordinances Relating to the City of Philadelphia* (1872), 243.

29. Henry Samuel Morais, *The Jews of Philadelphia* (Philadelphia: Levytype Company, 1894), 392–94, 434, 464; Historical Society of Pennsylvania, *Guide to the Manuscript Collections of the Historical Society of Pennsylvania* (Philadelphia: Historical Society of Pennsylvania), 193.

30. John C. Milley, ed., *Treasures of Independence: Independence National Historical Park and Its Collections* (New York: Mayflower Books, 1980), 118.

31. Minutes, Board of Managers, National Museum, January 6, 1876, National Museum at Independence Hall Collection, Mary Johnson Brown Chew Collection, INHP (hereafter cited as Chew Collection, INHP).

32. Etting, *Historical Account of the Old State House,* 166–68.

33. John Savage, "Independence Hall and Independence Day," *Harper's New Monthly Magazine*, vol. 35, no. 206 (1867), 229.

34. Frank M. Etting, *An Historical Account of the Old State House Now Known as The Hall of Independence* (Boston: James R. Osgood and Company, 1876), 1.

35. Second Annual Report of the Committee on Restoration of Independence Hall, in *Second Annual Message of William S. Stokley, Mayor of the City of Philadelphia, With the Accompanying Documents, 14 May 1874* (Philadelphia: E. C. Markley & Son, Printers, 1874), 1011. On object-based knowledge promoted by other Philadelphia museums, see Steven Conn, *Museums and American Intellectual Life, 1876–1926* (Chicago: University of Chicago Press, 1998).

36. Etting, *Historical Account of the Old State House*, 165–66; "The Ethics of the Centennial," *Inquirer*, undated news clipping in scrapbook, Frank M. Etting Collection, HSP.

37. J. F. Hartranft to Frank M. Etting, June 1, 1875; Jno. W. Small to John F. Hartranft, April 19, 1875, Etting Collection, HSP.

38. Stephen W. Stathis, "Returning the Declaration of Independence to Philadelphia: An Exercise in Centennial Politics," *PMHB* 102 (January 1978): 167–83.

39. Use of other areas in the State House for museum purposes was outlined in an 1871 letter to Etting from Edward L. Henry, a New York artist who specialized in historical paintings. It is unclear whether Henry originated the ideas or was agreeing with a plan advanced by Etting. E. L. Henry to Frank M. Etting, July 8, 1871, Etting Collection, HSP.

40. The members of the Board of Managers were Lily Macalester Berghmans (resigned 1875), Agnes Irwin, Catherine Keppele Meredith, Julia Rush Biddle, Anne Hopkinson Foggo, Armine Nixon Hart, Cornelia Frances Taylor, Katharine Johnston Wharton, Alice Campbell Etting, Ann Ingersoll Hutchinson, Anna Riddle Scott, Sara Butler Wister, and Mary Johnson Brown Chew.

41. Patricia West, *Domesticating History: The Political Origins of America's House Museums* (Washington, D.C.: Smithsonian Institution Press, 1999), 1–37, 40–41.

42. Quoted in Frank M. Etting, Invitation, May 23, 1873, Chew Collection, INHP.

43. Quoted in *Philadelphia Bulletin*, October 25, 1873.

44. Frank Etting to the Board of Managers of the National Museum, October 2, 1874; Frank Etting to Lily Macalester Berghmans, October 26, 1874; Lily Macalester Berghmans to the

Committee on the Restoration on Independence Hall, December 8, 1874; Memorial of the Ladies Board of Managers of Independence Hall, undated draft; Frank Etting to Mary Chew, December 26, 1874, all in Chew Collection, INHP.

45. The National Museum, Independence Hall, invitation for deposits, January 18, 1875, Chew Collection, INHP.

46. *Second Report of the Board of Managers of the National Museum of Independence Hall*, October 15, 1875, Etting Collection, HSP.

47. H. A. Porcher to Mary Chew, December 31, 1873; Mary Caldwell to Sarah Butler Wister, November 23, 1873; Ellen Cale Long to Alice Campbell Etting, undated; Susan Waddell to Alice Campbell Etting, June 7, 1876, and March 30, 1876, Chew Collection, INHP.

48. National Museum Inventory, 1873–1877, Chew Collection, INHP; Second Annual Report of the Committee on Restoration, 1007–13.

49. Etting, *Historical Account of the Old State House,* 184–88; Frank M. Etting to William S. Stokley, September 22, 1875, Etting Collection, HSP.

50. *Sunday Times*, July 6, 1873, in scrapbook, Etting Collection, HSP. In preserving this clipping, Etting noted next to it, "This is preserved as a specimen. I am told subsequent issues kept up comments of a similar character."

51. Frank M. Etting, form letter to school teachers, June 2, 1874, Etting Collection, HSP.

52. *Public Ledger*, June 3, 1876, *Evening Bulletin*, July 14, 1876; *Going to the Centennial: A Guy to the Exhibition, Laughing Series No. 7, Bricktop Stories* (New York: Collin & Small, 1876).

53. Philadelphia *Press*, December 28, 29, 1875.

54. *Public Ledger*, July 13, 14, 1876; *Evening Bulletin*, July 14, 15, 1876; *Inquirer*, July 14, 1876.

55. See Minutes, Board of Managers, National Museum, 1873–97, and correspondence of Mary Chew, Chew Collection, INHP.

56. Wilfred Jordan and Carl Magee Kneass, *Catalogue of the Portraits and other Works of Art, Independence Hall, Philadelphia* (Philadelphia: Privately published, 1915), 17.

57. *Frank Leslie's Illustrated Newspaper*, January 22, 1876, 31; *Public Ledger*, December 31, 1875, January 1, 1876, January 3, 1876.

58. *Public Ledger*, May 30, 1876, June 3, 1876, June 8, 1876, June 15, 1876, July 1, 1873, July 3, 1873; Arthur H. Frazier, "Henry Seybert and the Centennial Clock and Bell at Independence Hall," *PMHB* 102 (January 1978): 40–58.

59. Elizabeth Cady Stanton, *Eighty Years and More, Reminiscences 1815–1897* (1898; Boston: Northeastern University Press, 1993), 307–21; Elizabeth Cady Stanton, Susan B. Anthony, and Matilda Joslyn Gage, eds., *History of Woman Suffrage* (Rochester, N.Y.: Susan B. Anthony, 1889), 31–34; *Public Ledger,* July 3, 1876.

60. *Evening Bulletin*, July 5, 1876.

61. Ida Husted Harper, *The Life and Work of Susan B. Anthony*, vol. 1 (Indianapolis: Hollenbeck Press, 1898), 474–81.

62. *Evening Bulletin*, July 5, 1876; *Public Ledger*, July 5, 1876.

63. See Cecilia Elizabeth O'Leary, *To Die For: The Paradox of American Patriotism* (Princeton, N.J.: Princeton University Press, 1999).

64. Goldberg, "Strikes, Organizing, and Change," 114–15; Harry D. Boonin, *The Jewish Quarter of Philadelphia: A History and Guide, 1881–1930* (Philadelphia: Jewish Walking

Tours of Philadelphia, 1999); W. E. B. DuBois, *The Philadelphia Negro* (Philadelphia: University of Pennsylvania Press, 1899).

65. Alan Axelrod, ed., *The Colonial Revival in America* (New York: W. W. Norton, 1985), especially Kenneth L. Ames, "Introduction," 1–14; Karal Ann Marling, *George Washington Slept Here: Colonial Revivals and American Culture, 1876–1986* (Cambridge, Mass.: Harvard University Press, 1988), 25–52.

66. Michael Kammen, *A Machine that Would Go of Itself: The Constitution in American Culture* (1986; New York: St. Martin's Press, 1994), 68–124.

67. *Evening Bulletin*, September 19, 1854.

68. *Public Ledger*, September 18, 1861.

69. Edward M. Riley, *Starting America: The Story of Independence Hall* (Washington, D.C.: National Park Service, 1954; reprint, Gettysburg, Pa.: Thomas Publications, 1990), 26–27.

70. Roger Lane, *William Dorsey's Philadelphia and Ours: On the Past and Future of the Black City in America* (Oxford: Oxford University Press, 1991), 82–83, 167; Harry C. Silcox, "Nineteenth-Century Philadelphia's Black Militant: Octavius V. Catto (1839–1871)," in Joe William Trotter, Jr., and Eric Ledell Smith, eds., *African Americans in Pennsylvania: Shifting Historical Perspectives* (University Park: Pennsylvania State University Press, 1997), 198–219.

71. Linda K. Kerber, *No Constitutional Right to Be Ladies: Women and the Obligations of Citizenship* (New York: Hill and Wang, 1998), 81–123.

72. Hampton L. Carson, ed., *History of the Celebration of the One Hundredth Anniversary of the Promulgation of the Constitution of the United States*, vol. II (Philadelphia: J. B. Lippincott, 1889); Lane, *William Dorsey's Philadelphia*, 28.

73. Carson, *History of the Celebration,* 251–99.

74. *Public Ledger,* September 17, 1887.

75. *Appendix to the Select Council*, February 17, 1917, in National Museum at Independence Hall Collection, William Staake Papers, INHP. On the Universal Peace Union, see the Baldwin-McDowell Papers, New York Public Library. On the law school in Congress Hall, see George E. Nitzsche, *University of Pennsylvania: Its History, Traditions, Buildings and Memorials,* 7th ed. (Philadelphia: International Printing Co., 1918), 167–68.

76. Charles B. Hosmer Jr., *Presence of the Past: A History of the Preservation Movement in the United States Before Williamsburg* (New York: G. P. Putnam's Sons, 1965), 29–122; Michael Holleran, *Boston's Changeful Times: Origins of Preservation and Planning in America* (Baltimore: Johns Hopkins University Press, 1998), 84–109; Lewis F. Fisher, *Saving San Antonio: The Precarious Preservation of a Heritage* (Lubbock: Texas Tech University Press, 1996), 40–44.

77. Hosmer, *Presence of the Past*, 88–90; Marling, *George Washington Slept Here*, 17–20.

78. See especially "Philadelphia: A Study in Morals," *New Englander and Yale Review* (January 1892): 51–62.

79. Hosmer, *Presence of the Past,* 86.

80. Ordinances published in *Evening Bulletin,* March 17, 1896.

81. Eugenia Washington, "History of the Organization of the Society of the Daughters of the American Revolution," presented at the Atlanta Exposition, October 18, 1895, in National Museum at Independence Hall Collection, Ellen Waln Harrison Manuscript Papers, INHP (hereafter cited as Harrison Papers, INHP); on DAR activism in historic preservation, see Polly Welts

Kaufman, *National Parks and the Woman's Voice: A History* (Albuquerque: University of New Mexico Press, 1996), 49–52.

82. J. E. Carpenter to Ellen Waln Harrison, December 10, 1895, Harrison Papers, INHP.

83. Cynthia A. Brandimarte, "'To Make the Whole World Homelike': Gender, Space, and America's Tea Room Movement," *WP*, 30, no. 1 (Spring 1995): 1–19.

84. Ellen Waln Harrison to Charles Henry Jones, December 4, 1895; Charles Henry Jones to Ellen Waln Harrison, December 5, 1895, Harrison Papers, INHP.

85. J. E. Carpenter to Select and Common Councils of the City of Philadelphia, December 12, 1895, Harrison Papers, INHP.

86. *Evening Bulletin,* February 5, 1896, March 17, 1896.

87. T. Mellon Rogers to Ellen Waln Harrison, October 26, 1896, Harrison Papers, INHP.

88. Hosmer, *Presence of the Past,* 87; *Evening Bulletin,* February 19, 1897; *Public Ledger*, February 20, 1897; *Inquirer*, February 20, 1897.

89. *Philadelphia Business Directory* (Philadelphia: C. E. Howe Co., 1895).

90. Hosmer, *Presence of the Past,* 199.

91. Horace Wells Sellers, speech to the Illuminating Engineering Society, n.d., AIA Papers, Philadelphia Athenaeum Architectural Archives.

92. T. Mellon Rogers Diary, March 14–July 4, 1898, INHP.

93. *Evening Bulletin*, July 2, 7, 1898; *Inquirer*, July 3, 1898.

94. *Evening Bulletin*, July 5, 1898.

95. *Evening Bulletin*, October 28, 1898.

96. Although most of the nineteenth-century history was stripped away, construction workers deposited one testimonial to their own history in the reconstructed arcades. Inside one wall, bricklayers encased a fruit jar with a letter telling the future about their wages, working conditions, and the outbreak of the Spanish-American War. See unidentified news clipping in Rogers Diary, April 20, 1898.

Chapter 6. Place and Symbol

1. *Public Ledger*, July 25, 1914. I am grateful to Gary Edwards of Oil City, Pennsylvania, for locating biographical information about Liberty Bell Cooper in local records.

2. The Liberty Bell's travels have been described heretofore at greatest length in Victor Rosewater, *The Liberty Bell: Its History and Significance* (New York: D. Appleton and Co., 1926) and in an internal National Park Service study, John C. Paige, *The Liberty Bell: A Special History Study*, ed. David Kimball (Denver: National Park Service, Department of the Interior, n.d.). A condensed version of the Park Service study, prepared for the tourist market, is David Kimball, *Venerable Relic: The Story of the Liberty Bell* (Philadelphia: Eastern National Park and Monument Association, 1989).

3. See, for example, John Bodnar, ed., *Bonds of Affection: Americans Define Their Patriotism* (Princeton, N.J.: Princeton University Press, 1996), and Cecilia Elizabeth O'Leary, *To Die For: The Paradox of American Patriotism* (Princeton, N.J.: Princeton University Press, 1999). The significance of the Liberty Bell in early twentieth-century patriotism was noted briefly in Merle Curti, *The Roots of American Loyalty* (New York: Columbia University Press, 1946), 134.

4. Benedict Anderson, *Imagined Communities: Reflections on the Origin and Spread of American Nationalism*, rev. ed. (New York: Verso, 1991).

5. *The Bell of Independence* (Philadelphia: Dunlap & Clarke, 1885); E. R. Gudehus and A. H. McOwen, *The Liberty Bell, Its History, Associations, and Home* (Philadelphia: Dunlap Printing Co., 1904, 1915); Charles S. Keyser, *The Liberty Bell, Independence Hall, Philadelphia* (Philadelphia: Allen, Lane & Scott's Printing House, 1893); Charles S. Keyser, *The Liberty Bell, Independence Hall, Philadelphia* (Philadelphia: Dunlap Printing Co., 1895, 1902, 1903).

6. On world's fairs in the United States, see Robert Rydell, *All the World's a Fair: Visions of Empire at American International Expositions, 1876–1916* (Chicago: University of Chicago Press, 1984), and Robert Rydell, John E. Findling, and Kimberly D. Pelle, *Fair America: World's Fairs in the United States* (Washington, D.C.: Smithsonian Institution Press, 2000).

7. Anne Sarah Rubin, "Seventy-six and Sixty-one: Confederates Remember the American Revolution," in W. Fitzhugh Brundage, ed., *Where These Memories Grow: History, Memory, and Southern Identity* (Chapel Hill: University of North Carolina Press, 2000), 85–105.

8. J. V. Guillotte to Mayor of Philadelphia, November 22, 1884, in *The Bell of Independence* (Philadelphia: Dunlap & Clarke, 1885), 6.

9. *Louisville* (Ky.) *Courier-Journal*, January 25, 1885; *Mobile* (Ala.) *Daily Register*, January 27, 1885; *New Orleans Daily Picayune*, January 27, 28, 29,1885; *Philadelphia Public Record*, June 18, 1885; *Washington* (D.C.) *Evening Star*, October 4, 1895; *Baltimore Sun*, January 5, 1895; *Richmond* (Va.) *Dispatch*, October 5, 6, 1895; *Knoxville* (Tenn.) *Journal*, October 7, 1895; *Atlanta Journal*, October 8, 9, 1895; *Harrisburg* (Pa.) *Patriot*, January 7, 1902; *Asheville* (N.C.) *Daily Gazette*, January 8, 1902; *Savannah* (Ga.) *Morning News,* January 8, 1902; *Charleston* (S.C.) *News & Courier*, January 10, 1902; *Dallas Morning News*, November 19, 1915; *New Orleans Times Picayune*, November 18, 19, 1915.

10. *New Orleans Daily Picayune*, January 27, 1885.

11. *Richmond Dispatch,* October 6, 1895.

12. *Philadelphia Record*, January 24, 1885; *Atlanta Journal*, October 8, 1895; *San Antonio Express*, November 18, 1915.

13. Leon F. Litwack, *Trouble in Mind: Black Southerners in the Age of Jim Crow* (New York: Alfred A. Knopf, 1998).

14. African American attendance at Liberty Bell appearances is noted in the *Nashville Daily American*, January 26, 1885; *Harrisburg Patriot*, April 26, 1893; *Baltimore Sun*, October 5, 1895; *Knoxville Journal*, October 6, 7, 1895; *Atlanta Journal*, October 10, 1895; *The State* (Columbia, S.C.), January 9, 1902; *Charleston News & Courier*, January 9, 1902; *New Haven* (Conn.) *Evening Register*, June 16, 1903; *Rocky Mountain News* (Denver, Colo.), July 11, 1915; *Tacoma* (Wash.) *Daily Ledger*, July 15, 1915; *San Antonio Express*, November 19, 1915; *Dallas Morning News*, November 19, 1915.

15. *Harper's Weekly,* June 27, 1885.

16. Kirk Savage, *Standing Soldiers, Kneeling Slaves: Race, War, and Monument in Nineteenth-Century America* (Princeton, N.J.: Princeton University Press, 1997).

17. W. Milton Lewis, "Pencilings," *The Freeman,* December 3, 1904.

18. As a reflection of the competing historical reputations of the two cities, see the speech of Hampton L. Carson, "In Defence of the Quaker City: Achievements of Philadelphia Contrasted with Boston," *Evening Bulletin*, July 5, 1898.

19. Boston *Daily Globe*, June 16, 18, 1903.

20. *Tacoma Daily Ledger*, July 14, 1915. Similar statements appear in the *Leavenworth* (Kans.) *Times,* July 9, 1915; *Nebraska State Journal* (Lincoln), July 10, 1915; *Deseret Evening News* (Salt Lake City), July 10, 12, 1915; *Tacoma Daily Ledger*, July 15, 1915; *Seattle Daily Times*, July 14, 1915; *Daily Oregon Statesman* (Salem), July 15, 1915; *San Francisco Chronicle*, July 16, 17, 1915, November 12, 1915; *Dallas Morning News*, November 19, 1915.

21. *Salt Lake City Tribune*, July 12, 1915.

22. *San Antonio Express*, November 17, 1915.

23. On the conception of relics as a bridge between past and present, see David Lowenthal, *The Past Is a Foreign Country* (Cambridge: Cambridge University Press, 1985).

24. *Kansas City Star*, July 8, 1915; other references to ancestors or hereditary societies appear in the *Indianapolis Journal*, April 29, 1893; *Chicago Daily Tribune,* April 29, 1893; *Washington Evening Star*, October 4, 1895; *Richmond Dispatch*, October 5, 6, 1895; *Knoxville Journal*, October 7, 8, 1895; *Charleston News & Courier*, January 31, 1896; *Harrisburg Patriot*, January 7, 1902; *Savannah Morning News*, January 8, 1902; *Hartford* (Conn.) *Daily Courant*, June 17, 1903; *Boston Daily Globe*, June 18, 1903; *Dubuque* (Iowa) *Daily Times*, June 8, 1904; *Chicago Daily Tribune*, July 7, 1915; *Leavenworth Times*, July 8, 1915; *Omaha* (Neb.) *Morning World Herald*, July 9, 1915; *Nebraska State Journal,* July 10, 1915; *Spokane* (Wash.) *Spokesman Review*, July 14, 1915; *Oregon Journal* (Portland), July 16, 1915; *Sacramento* (Calif.) *Union*, July 16, 1915; *San Francisco Chronicle*, November 12, 1915; *Louisville Courier-Journal*, November 22, 1915.

25. On the presence of recent immigrants in Liberty Bell crowds, see *Chicago Daily Tribune*, April 30, 1893, *Charleston News & Courier*, January 9, 1902; *Providence Daily Journal,* June 17, 1903; *Des Moines Register*, July 7, 8, 1915; *Rocky Mountain News*, July 11, 1915; *Deseret Evening News*, July 12, 1915; *Salt Lake City Tribune*, July 12, 1915; *Tacoma Daily Ledger*, July 15, 1915; *Oregon Journal*, July 15, 1915.

26. *Rocky Mountain News*, July 11, 1915; on souvenirs and photography also see *New Haven Evening Register*, June 16, 1903; *Boston Daily Globe*, June 18, 1903; *Des Moines Register*, July 8, 1915; *Leavenworth Times*, July 9, 1915; *Spokane Spokesman Review*, July 14, 1915.

27. On children's participation, see *Pittsburgh Dispatch*, January 24, 1885, April 27, 1893; *New Orleans Daily Picayune*, January 28, 1885; *Anderson* (Ind.) *Herald* reprinted in Indianapolis *Journal*, April 28, 1893; *Chicago Daily Tribune*, April 29, 1893; *Cincinnati* (Ohio) *Enquirer*, November 2, 3, 1893; *Wilmington* (Del.) *Every Evening*, October 4, 1895; *Baltimore Sun*, October 5, 1895; *Atlanta Journal*, October 7, 9, 1895; *Harrisburg Patriot*, January 7, 1902; *The State* (Columbia, S.C.), January 9, 1902; *Savannah Morning News*, January 9, 1902; *Charleston News & Courier*, January 8, 9, 1902; *Trenton* (N.J.) *Daily True American*, June 10, 1903; *New Haven Evening Register*, June 16, 1903; *Hartford Daily Courant*, June 17, 1903; *Providence Daily Journal*, June 17, 1903; *Boston Daily Globe*, June 18, 1903; *Rochester* (N.Y.) *Democrat & Chronicle*, June 5, 1904; *Milwaukee Sentinel*, June 6, 1904; *Dubuque Daily Times*, June 8, 1904; *Chicago Daily Tribune*, July 7, 1915; *Leavenworth Times*, July 9, 1915; *Rocky Mountain News*, July 11, 1915; *Oregon Journal*, July 15, 1915; *Daily Oregon Statesman*, July 16, 1915; *San Francisco Chronicle*, July 18, 1915; *Dallas Morning News*, November 19, 1915; Memphis (Tenn.) *Commercial Appeal*, November 21, 1915; *Indianapolis Star*, November 22, 1915; *Louisville Courier Journal*, November 23, 1915; *Cincinnati Enquirer*, November 23, 1915.

28. *Indianapolis Journal,* April 29, 1893.

29. *Chicago Daily Tribune,* April 29, 1893.

30. Ronald Millar, *Rocky Mountain News,* July 11, 1915.

31. On the enthusiasm for historical pageantry in this period, see David Glassberg, *American Historical Pageantry: The Uses of Tradition in the Early Twentieth Century* (Chapel Hill: University of North Carolina Press, 1990).

32. On civil religion, see Robert Bellah, "Civil Religion in America," *Daedalus* (Winter 1967): 1–21; Russell E. Richey and Donald G. Jones, eds., *American Civil Religion* (New York: Harper & Row, 1974).

33. Neil Harris, "John Philip Sousa and the Culture of Reassurance," in John Newsom, ed., *Perspectives on John Philip Sousa* (Washington, D.C.: Library of Congress, 1993), 11–41; Paul E. Bierley, *John Philip Sousa: American Phenomenon* (Englewood Cliffs, N.J.: Prentice-Hall, 1973), 58–61.

34. *Indianapolis Journal,* April 28, 1893.

35. Personification of the Bell appears in the *New Orleans Daily Picayune,* January 28, 1885; *Harrisburg Patriot,* April 25, 1893; *Pittsburgh Dispatch,* April 27, 1893; *Chicago Daily Tribune,* April 29, 1893; *Knoxville Journal,* October 7, 1895; *Atlanta Journal,* October 9, 1895; *Boston Daily Globe,* June 16, 1903; *Leavenworth Times,* July 9, 1915; *Omaha Morning World Herald,* July 10, 1915; *Deseret Evening News,* July 10, 1915. On the ritual of talking to the Bell, see *Omaha Morning World Herald,* July 8, 1915.

36. The role of newspapers in disseminating nationalism is demonstrated for an earlier period in American history by David Waldstreicher, *In the Midst of Perpetual Fetes: The Making of American Nationalism, 1776–1820* (Chapel Hill: University of North Carolina Press, 1997).

37. Such contrasts appear in reports of the *Nashville Daily American,* January 26, 1885; *Harrisburg Patriot,* April 26, 1893; *Chicago Daily Tribune,* April 30, 1893; *Baltimore Sun,* October 5, 1895; *Knoxville Journal,* October 6, 7 1895; *Atlanta Journal,* October 10, 1895; *Harrisburg Patriot,* January 7, 1902; *The State* (Columbia, S.C.), January 9, 1902; *Charleston News & Courier,* January 9, 1902; *New Haven Evening Register,* June 16, 1903; *Providence Daily Journal,* June 17, 1903; *Boston Daily Globe,* June 18, 1903; *St. Louis Palladium,* June 11, 1904; *Des Moines Register,* July 7, 8, 1915; *Rocky Mountain News,* July 11, 1915; *Deseret Evening News,* July 12, 1915; *Salt Lake City Tribune,* July 12, 1915; *Tacoma Daily Ledger,* July 15, 1915; *Oregon Journal,* July 15, 1915; *San Francisco Chronicle,* July 17, 1915; *San Antonio Express,* November 10, 1915; *Dallas Morning News,* November 19, 1915; *Pittsburgh Dispatch,* November 24, 1915; *Syracuse* (N.Y.) *Post-Standard,* November 26, 1915.

38. Boredom is mentioned in the *Des Moines Register,* July 8, 1915; disapproval of an African American child kissing the Bell in Arlington, Texas, is reported in the *San Antonio Express,* November 19, 1915.

39. *Atlanta Journal,* October 9, 1895.

40. *Atlanta Journal,* October 8, 1895; religious language in reference to the Liberty Bell also appears in the *Harrisburg Patriot,* April 26, 1893; *Indianapolis Journal,* April 29, 1893; *Washington Evening Star,* October 4, 1895; *Richmond Dispatch,* October 5, 1895; *Knoxville Journal,* October 7, 1895; *Boston Daily Globe,* June 16, 18, 1903; *Chicago Daily Tribune,* July 7, 1915; *Leavenworth Times,* July 9, 1915; *Nebraska State Journal,* July 10, 1915; *Rocky Mountain News,* July 9, 1915; *Spokane Spokesman Review,* July 12, 1915; *Louisville Courier Journal,* November 22, 1915.

41. Correspondence regarding this project organized by William O. McDowell of Newark, New Jersey, is preserved in the Baldwin-McDowell Papers, New York Public Library.

42. See, for example, *Washington Evening Star*, October 4, 1895; *Charleston News & Courier*, January 9, 1902; *St. Paul* (Minn.) *Pioneer Press*, June 6, 1904; *Salt Lake Tribune*, July 12, 1915.

43. *Atlanta Journal*, October 9, 1895.

44. Quoted and characterized in G. B. Sansom, *The Western World and Japan: A Study in the Interaction of European and Asiatic Cultures* (New York: Alfred A. Knopf, 1968), 411–15. I am grateful to Cornelius Kiley for bringing this novel to my attention.

45. William Francis Mannix, ed., *Memoirs of Li Hung-chang* (Boston: Houghton Mifflin, 1913); Samuel C. Chu, "Li Hung-chang: An Assessment," in Samuel C. Chu and Kwang-Ching Liu, eds., *Li Hung-change and China's Early Modernization* (Armonk, N.Y.: M. E. Sharpe, 1994), 286.

46. *Memoirs of Li Hung-chang*, 200.

47. *Tacoma Daily Ledger*, July 14, 1915.

48. *Oregon Journal*, July 15, 1915.

49. The Liberty Bell was especially prominent in Liberty Loan campaigns devised by the N. W. Ayer advertising firm, which had its headquarters on Washington Square in Philadelphia, close to Independence Hall and the Liberty Bell. See N. W. Ayer proof sheets, Smithsonian Institution Archives Center; Poster Collection, PSA; *Evening Bulletin*, April 5, 1918.

50. *Minneapolis Journal*, June 6, 1904.

51. *Deseret Morning News*, July 12, 1915.

52. *Wyoming Tribune*, July 12, 1915.

53. *Pennzoil: The First 100 Years* (Houston: Pennzoil, 1989), 18–22.

54. Joseph P. Eckhardt, *The King of the Movies: Film Pioneer Siegmund Lubin* (Madison, N.J.: Fairleigh Dickinson University Press, 1997).

55. Marshall Fey, *Slot Machines: A Pictorial History of the First Hundred Years*, 5th ed. (Reno, Nev.: Liberty Belle Books, 1997), 37–44, 85–89.

56. City of Philadelphia, *Annual Report of the Department of Public Works . . . 1915*, 404, PCA; *Evening Bulletin*, February 12, 1915.

57. *The State* (Columbia, S.C.), January 9, 1902; see also *Charleston News & Courier*, January 10, 1902.

58. *Public Ledger*, April 1, 1915, June 24, 1915; *Evening Bulletin*, October 24, 1915.

59. *Evening Bulletin*, September 21, 1920.

60. See, for example, *New Orleans Daily Picayune*, January 28, 1885; *Richmond Dispatch*, October 5, 1895; *Knoxville Journal*, October 7, 1895; *Dubuque Daily Times*, June 8, 1904.

61. *Copy of Petition of Thos. G. Morton, et al. vs. City of Philadelphia to Restrain the Loan of the "Old Liberty Bell" for the purposes of exhibition at the International Cotton Exposition at Atlanta, Ga.* (Philadelphia: Joint Special Committee of Councils of the City of Philadelphia on Atlanta Exposition, 1895).

62. W. H. Ball, Bureau of City Property Report, in City of Philadelphia, *Annual Report of the Department of Public Works for the Year Ending December 31, 1915*, 408, PCA.

63. *Evening Bulletin*, May 18, 1915, August 8, 1915, September 9, 1915.

64. Illinois Office of the Superintendent of Public Instruction, F. G. Blair, Superintendent of Public Instruction, State of Illinois, to Superintendents and Teachers, n.d., HSP.

65. *Evening Bulletin*, July 6, 13, 1922.

66. Arthur P. Dudden, "The City Embraces 'Normalcy,' 1919–1929," in Russell F. Weigley, ed., *Philadelphia: A 300-Year History* (New York: W. W. Norton, 1982), 571–75.

67. *Evening Bulletin*, January 1, 1926.

68. *Chestnut Street, Philadelphia* (Philadelphia: Thomson Printing Co., 1904), 8, 11–12.

69. Lloyd M. Abernethy, "Progressivism, 1905–1919," in Weigley, ed., *Philadelphia,* 562.

70. Lincoln Steffens, "Philadelphia: Corrupt and Contented," *McClure's* 21 (July 1903): 249–65.

71. "To Ask Councils for State House," *Record*, November 25, 1912.

72. Minutes of the Executive Committee of the Philadelphia Chapter, AIA, AIA Papers, Philadelphia Athenaeum Architectural Archives.

73. *Evening Bulletin,* January 20, 1917.

74. *Public Ledger*, November 22, 1912.

75. *Ordinances of the City of Philadelphia From January 1 to December 31, 1913 and Opinions by the City Solicitor* (Philadelphia: Dunlap Printing Co., 1914), 1; *Journal of the Select Council of the City of Philadelphia from September 19th, 1912 to December 30th, 1912,* vol. II (Philadelphia: George F. Lasher, 1912), 93, 104, 130–31, 176; *Journal of the Common Council of the City of Philadelphia From September 19 to December 30, 1912,* vol. II (Philadelphia: Dunlap Printing Co., 1913), 127, 216, 261.

76. Although the ordinance coincides with the women's use of the square, the new restrictions on public meetings were a reaction to the IWW request, not the suffrage activities. An indication of attitudes toward the suffragists is an editorial in the *Public Ledger*, which lamented that the ordinance governing Independence Square would prohibit even such "mild and innocuous" gatherings as the suffragists' convention. The newspaper said that banning all groups was the appropriate way to safeguard the square: "Independence Square is the property of Philadelphia, held in trust for Americans for all time. It is not a place for mass meetings or for utilitarian purpose, though the aim of those who use it may be beneficent and exalted." *Public Ledger*, November 22, 1912.

77. *Public Ledger*, November 22, 1912; *Evening Bulletin,* November 21, 1912.

78. *Public Ledger*, November 21, 1920, February 11, 1921.

79. *Evening Bulletin,* February 19, 24, 1921, March 2, 1921; *Public Ledger*, February 25, 1921, May 5, 1921.

80. League of Women Voters of Pennsylvania, "The Justice Bell," pamphlet in possession of the author; *Inquirer*, April 25, 1995.

81. *Annual Report of the Department of Public Works of the City of Philadelphia for the Year Ending December 31, 1914* (Philadelphia: City of Philadelphia, 1915), 656–57; *Annual Report of the Department of Public Works of the City of Philadelphia for the Year Ending December 31, 1916* (Philadelphia: City of Philadelphia, 1917)*,* 469, 473; *Annual Report of the Department of Public Works of the City of Philadelphia for the Year Ending December 13, 1913* (Philadelphia: City of Philadelphia, 1914), 309.

82. *Annual Report of the Department of Public Works . . . 1914*, 655; *Annual Report of the Department of Public Works . . . 1915,* 403; *Annual Report of the Department of Public Works . . . 1916,* 469.

83. A. S. Eisenhower, Bureau of City Property Report, in *Third Annual Message of Edwin*

S. Stuart, Mayor of the City of Philadelphia, vol. II (Philadelphia: Dunlap Printing Co., 1894), 308.

84. *Public Ledger*, October 15, 1923.

85. *Public Ledger*, July 25, 1914.

86. *Annual Report of the Department of Public Works of the City of Philadelphia for the Year Ending December 31, 1917* (Philadelphia: City of Philadelphia, 1918), 386.

87. Philadelphia War History Committee, *Philadelphia in the World War* (New York: Wynkoop Hallenbeck Crawford Co., 1922), 52, 646–48.

88. *Evening Bulletin,* April 8, 1917.

89. *Evening Bulletin,* April 10, 1918.

90. *Evening Bulletin,* June 17, 1918.

91. *Report of Committee on Preservation of Historic Monuments of the Philadelphia Chapter AIA*, August 31, 1918, and Henry T. MacNeill, *Survey of Independence Hall*, April-May 1918, AIA Papers, Philadelphia Athenaeum Architectural Archives.

92. Herbert Adolphus Miller, "What Woodrow Wilson and America Meant to Czechoslovakia," in Robert J. Kerner, ed., *Czechoslovakia: Twenty Years of Independence* (Berkeley: University of California Press, 1940), 83–86.

93. *Evening Bulletin,* October 23, 27, 1918; *Inquirer*, October 24, 25, 27, 1918.

94. *Evening Bulletin,* April 5, 1918, April 6, 1918; *Inquirer*, April 7, 1918

95. *Inquirer*, November 12, 1918.

96. Ibid.

97. *The World's Fair Album* (Chicago: Rand, McNally & Co., 1893).

98. *The Jamestown Exposition Illustrated* (New York: Isaac H. Blanchard Co., 1907). The building survived the exposition to become a museum for the Norfolk Naval Air Station.

99. Minutes, Pennsylvania State's World's Fair Commission, 1938–40, General Correspondence, Special Commissions (RG 25), PSA.

100. Mark Gelernter, *A History of American Architecture: Buildings in Their Cultural and Technological Context* (Hanover, N.H.: University Press of New England, 1999), 196–207; Carter Wiseman, *Shaping a Nation: Twentieth-Century American Architecture and Its Makers* (New York: W. W. Norton, 1998), 115–48.

101. Olof Z. Cervin, "The So-Called Colonial Architecture of the United States," in William Rotch Ware, ed., *The Georgian Period* (1898; reprint, New York: UPC Book Co., 1923). After its original publication in 1898, this collection of essays, plans, and photographs was reprinted in 1899, 1900, 1901, and 1923. A student's edition was issued in 1904.

102. J. Cayce Morrison, "School Construction and Modern Education," *Architectural Forum* (April 1929): 267–71.

103. Richard P. Dober, *Campus Architecture: Building in the Groves of Academe* (New York: McGraw-Hill, 1996); C. W. Short and R. Stanley-Brown, *Public Buildings: A Survey of Architecture of Projects Constructed by Federal and Other Governmental Bodies Between the Years 1933 and 1939 with the Assistance of the Public Works Administration* (Washington, D.C.: GPO, 1939).

104. Robert O. Derrick, interview by Kenneth N. Metcalf, June 17, 1957, transcript at Research Center, Henry Ford Museum and Greenfield Village; Geoffrey C. Upward, *A Home for Our Heritage: The Building and Growth of Greenfield Village and Henry Ford Museum, 1929–1979* (Dearborn, Mich.: Henry Ford Museum Press, 1979), 50; Steven Conn, *Museums*

and American Intellectual Life, 1876–1926 (Chicago: University of Chicago Press, 1998), 151–60.

105. James Playsted Wood, *The Curtis Magazines* (New York: Ronald Press, 1971), 53–57; *Public Ledger,* February 3, 1924.

106. Howell Louis Shay, "The New Independence Building," in *At the Historical Center of the United States* (Philadelphia: Independence Cos., 1925), 31–35.

107. Wood, *The Curtis Magazines,* 53–57.

108. Dunlea Hurley, *Panorama of a Century* (Philadelphia: Penn Mutual Life Insurance Co., 1947), not paginated; *Evening Bulletin,* August 14, 1930, March 31, 1950, June 17, 1970.

Chapter 7. Treasure

1. *Evening Bulletin,* June 5, 1924, May 27, 1926, November 18, 1928, April 3, 1929, November 27, 1929, October 13, 1936, June 21, 1937, September 4, 1937, October 6, 1937, May 28, 1941.

2. Christine Meisner Rosen, *The Limits of Power: Great Fires and the Process of City Growth in America* (Cambridge: Cambridge University Press, 1986).

3. Constance M. Greiff, *Independence: Creation of a National Park* (Philadelphia: University of Pennsylvania Press, 1987).

4. "Collective memory" refers to memory constructed by a group of individuals united within a specific time period and place. See Maurice Halbwachs, *The Collective Memory* (1950; reprint Harper & Row, 1980).

5. Lloyd M. Abernethy, "Progressivism, 1905–1919," in Russell F. Weigley, ed., *Philadelphia: A 300-Year History* (New York: W. W. Norton, 1982), 562.

6. Vincent B. Brecht, "George E. Nitzsche and the Independence Shrine," *The General Magazine and Historical Chronicle* (Spring–Summer 1955): 88–90, Isidor Ostroff Papers (hereafter Ostroff Papers), INHP.

7. Albert Kelsey, untitled manuscript, n.d., and Albert Kelsey and D. Knickerbacker Boyd, *Preliminary Study for the Dependencies and a New Setting for Independence Hall,* April 25, 1915, Independence Hall Association Papers (hereafter IHA Papers), INHP; *Evening Bulletin,* September 23, 1919.

8. *Inquirer,* November 15, 1922; *North American*, November 16, 1922, November 17, 1922, April 29, 1924; *Evening Bulletin,* May 1, 1924, in Independence Celebration Commission Scrapbooks (RG 25) PSA; *Cultural Landscape Report, Independence Mall* (June 1994), INHP.

9. Peter Hall, *Cities of Tomorrow: An Intellectual History of Urban Planning and Design in the Twentieth Century* (Oxford: Basil Blackwell, 1988).

10. David B. Brownlee, *Building the City Beautiful: The Benjamin Franklin Parkway and the Philadelphia Museum of Art* (Philadelphia: Philadelphia Museum of Art, 1989).

11. Walter S. Andariese, *History of the Benjamin Franklin Bridge* (Camden, N.J.: Delaware River Port Authority, 1981), 1–7, 35–36; *Record*, June 12, 1925; *Evening Bulletin,* January 28, 1922, April 7, 1924.

12. Seneca Egbert, "A Colonial Concourse," undated typescript, General Correspondence, IHA Papers; Seneca Egbert, typescript autobiography, July 30, 1914, in Seneca Egbert envelope, News Clippings Collection, UA; *Evening Bulletin,* April 13, 1936.

13. David Knickerbacker Boyd to George W. B. Hicks, December 8, 1928, and Boyd to

Seneca Egbert, May 12, 1930, General Correspondence, IHA Papers, INHP; Chestnut Street Business Men's Association Minutes, May 7, 1930, Chestnut Street Association Collection, UA; George E. Nitzsche, "A United States National Park in Philadelphia," *Pennsylvania Triangle*, April 1936, 10–11.

14. "Plan Bridge Artery," undated map in Approaches Folder, Benjamin Franklin Bridge File, News Clippings Collection, UA; *Evening Bulletin,* October 15, 1928, October 29, 1928, March 27, 1929, June 5, 1930, June 11, 1930, June 24, 1930, June 23, 1930, September 15, 1930, January 14, 1931.

15. Conditions in the area were documented by Seneca Egbert in a series of photographs in 1934. Photographs in General Correspondence, IHA Papers, INHP.

16. Abernethy, "Progressivism," 562.

17. Isidor Ostroff, interviewed by Eleanor Prescott, September 26, 1969, transcript, INHP.

18. U.S. Census, 1920.

19. *Evening Bulletin,* April 22, 1931, May 12, 1931, July 2, 1931, December 10, 1932.

20. *Record,* August 12, 1934; *Evening Bulletin,* August 4, 1934.

21. *Public Ledger*, August 2, 1931.

22. A. Lincoln Acker to Emerson C. Custis, April 19, 1933; A. Raymond Raff to Emerson C. Custis, April 29, 1941; Emerson C. Custis to James H. Neff, October 25, 1948, Official Papers, James H. Duff Papers (MG 190), PSA.

23. Michael Kammen, *Mystic Chords of Memory: The Transformation of Tradition in American Culture* (New York: Vintage Books, 1993), 299–309.

24. Charles B. Hosmer, Jr., *Preservation Comes of Age: From Williamsburg to the National Trust, 1926–1949,* vol. 1 (Charlottesville: University Press of Virginia, 1981).

25. John Bodnar, *Remaking America: Public Memory, Commemoration, and Patriotism in the Twentieth Century* (Princeton, N.J.: Princeton University Press, 1992), 170–205.

26. Franklin Delano Roosevelt, "New Conditions Impose New Requirements upon Government and Those Who Conduct Government" (Campaign Address on Progressive Government at the Commonwealth Club, San Francisco, Calif., September 23, 1932), in *The Public Papers and Addresses of Franklin D. Roosevelt,* vol. 1 (New York: Random House, 1938), 742–57.

27. Herbert Hoover, Campaign Speech at Madison Square Garden, New York City, October 31, 1932, in *The State Papers and Other Public Writings of Herbert Hoover*, vol. 2 (New York: Doubleday, Doran & Co., 1934), 408–28.

28. William E. Leuchtenburg, *Franklin D. Roosevelt and the New Deal, 1932–1940* (New York: Harper & Row, 1963).

29. C. W. Short and R. Stanley-Brown, *Public Buildings: A Survey of Architecture of Projects Constructed by Federal and Other Governmental Bodies Between the Years 1933 and 1939 with the Assistance of the Public Works Administration* (Washington, D.C.: GPO, 1939). Although the Public Works Administration did not dictate architects' choices of style for federally funded buildings, many buildings commissioned by the PWA were Georgian revival in design and therefore reminiscent of Independence Hall.

30. Correspondence and photographs on distribution of models in General Correspondence, 1935–38, Pennsylvania Constitution Commemorative Committee (RG 25), PSA (hereafter Constitution Committee Papers); additional photographs of model construction in Museum Extension Project Photographs (RG 13), PSA. Model dimensions in *Pittsburgh Sun-Telegraph*, September 5, 1937.

31. For a sampling of distribution, see Constitution Committee Papers, PSA.

32. *The WPA Guide to Philadelphia* (1937; reprint Philadelphia: University of Pennsylvania Press, 1988), 3.

33. Michael Kammen, *A Machine That Would Go of Itself: The Constitution in American Culture* (New York: St. Martin's Press, 1994), 282–312.

34. Clare Gerald Fenerty to Frank L. Devine, March 5,1936; George P. Darrow to Frank L. Devine, March 14, 1936; Frank L. Devine to Frank Smith, October 15, 1936, Constitution Committee Papers, PSA.

35. Christy poster in Poster Collection, PSA; Philadelphia commemoration programs in Constitution Committee Papers, PSA.

36. Sol Bloom to H. Ennis Jones, May 4, 1937, Constitution Committee Papers, PSA.

37. *Inquirer,* May 15, 1937.

38. *The History of the One Hundred and Fiftieth Anniversary, The Adoption of the Constitution of the United States*, typescript, Constitution Committee Papers, PSA.

39. *Celebration of the 150th Anniversary of the Constitution, May 14 to September 17, 1937*, program, Constitution Committee Papers, PSA.

40. *The History of the One Hundred and Fiftieth Anniversary, The Adoption of the Constitution of the United States,* typescript, and *Constitution Week*, program, Constitution Committee Papers, PSA.

41. Press release, May 18, 1938, Constitution Committee Papers, PSA.

42. *Report of Women's Activities During Celebration of 150th Birthday of the United States Constitution*, August 4, 1938, Constitution Committee Papers, PSA.

43. Edwin O. Lewis, interview by John Roberts, January 2, 1969, transcript, INHP.

44. Roy Larson, interview by John Roberts, January 25, 1969, transcript, INHP.

45. Ostroff interview.

46. *Record*, January 26, 1941.

47. Ostroff interview.

48. Raymond Pitcairn, *Walk Proudly Here, Americans* (Philadelphia: Privately published, 1940).

49. *Evening Bulletin,* November 21, 1965, July 12, 1966; *Inquirer,* July 13, 1966.

50. Pitcairn, *Walk Proudly Here,* 3, 13.

51. Raymond Pitcairn, "Some Notes on Independence Hall Booklet," typescript, July 1, 1942, General Correspondence, IHA Papers, INHP.

52. Committee on Conservation of Cultural Resources, National Resources Planning Board, "The Protection of America's Cultural Heritage," 1941, IHA Papers, INHP.

53. *Evening Bulletin,* April 18, 1942.

54. *Evening Bulletin*, December 12, 1941, December 14, 1941, January 28, 1942, February 3, 1942.

55. See extensive coverage in the *Evening Bulletin* and *Inquirer,* August–September 1942, May 1943, and June 1944.

56. Greiff, *Independence,* 44–45.

57. Halbwachs, *The Collective Memory.*

58. On the incorporation of the Independence Hall Association, see *Evening Bulletin*, October 18, 1942. Biographical information about the incorporators in newspaper articles in the *Evening Bulletin* News Clippings Collection, UA, and from biographical sketches in Herman LeRoy Collins and Wilfred Jordan, *Philadelphia: A Story of Progress*, vol. 4 (New York:

Lewis Historical Publishing Company, 1941). The incorporators were Add. B. Anderson, Edward M. Biddle, Arthur W. Binns, David K. Boyd, Edward C. Cardiner, William Innes Forbes, Charles Haydock, Charles F. Jenkins, John Story Jenks, Roy F. Larson, Edwin O. Lewis, William E. Lingelbach, Eleanor M. Lloyd, Sydney E. Martin, M. Joseph McCosker, Robert T. McCracken, Charles Abell Murphy, Roy F. Nichols, Thomas Ridgway, Bernard Samuel, Frank J. Smith, Joseph F. Stockwell, Charles L. Todd, Samuel Price Wetherill, Henry W. Wills, and Frances A. Wister.

59. Ostroff interview.

60. *Evening Bulletin,* July 1, 1942.

61. "Independence Hall: From Civic Center to National Shrine," exhibit program proof sheets, April 22– July 11, 1943; Independence Hall Association, "A National Historical Park in 'Old Philadelphia,'" typescript, September 24, 1943; Joseph Jackson, "Association Would Dignify Environs of Independence Hall," typescript, November 1943; Charles Haydock, "The Independence Hall Association," typescript, January 17, 1944, IHA Papers, INHP.

62. The legislative process is detailed in Greiff, *Independence,* 63–76.

63. Commonwealth of Pennsylvania, Governor's Office, Press Release, October 30, 1945, PSA.

64. *Evening Bulletin,* November 16, 1945.

65. Charles Haydock, "The Independence Hall Association," typescript, January 17, 1944, IHA Papers, INHP.

66. In total, the area within the designated park boundaries consisted of: the three city blocks between Walnut and Chestnut Streets from Second to Fifth Streets, excluding the Customs House; a mall from Walnut Street to Manning; the site of Benjamin Franklin's home, long demolished, between Market and Chestnut Streets and Third and Fourth Streets; and a lot adjacent to Christ Church at Second and Market Streets. See "Appendix A: Legislation" in *Draft General Management Plan, Environmental Impact Statement* (Philadelphia: Independence National Historical Park, 1995), 219.

67. Public Law 795, June 28, 1948.

68. James Holston and Arjun Appadurai, "Cities and Citizenship," *Public Culture* 8 (Winter 1996): 187–204.

69. John H. Campbell, *History of the Society of the Friendly Sons of St. Patrick for the Relief of Emigrants from Ireland of Philadelphia* (Philadelphia: Friendly Sons of St. Patrick, 1952), 76–83. The Barry Statue in Philadelphia corresponds with similar statue projects in other cities at this time. See Bodnar, *Remaking America,* 65–70.

70. "Barry Day" and "Barry Statue" envelopes, News Clippings Collection, UA.

71. Anne C. Loveland, *Emblem of Liberty: The Image of Lafayette in the American Mind* (Baton Rouge: Louisiana State University Press, 1971), 133–60.

72. *Ordinances of the City of Philadelphia From January 1 to December 31, 1913 and Opinions by the City Solicitor* (Philadelphia: Dunlap Printing Co., 1914), 1; *Journal of the Select Council of the City of Philadelphia from September 19th, 1912 to December 30th, 1912,* Vol. II (Philadelphia: George F. Lasher, 1912), 93, 104, 130–31, 176; *Journal of the Common Council of the City of Philadelphia From September 19 to December 30, 1912,* vol. II (Philadelphia: Dunlap Printing Co., 1913), 127, 216, 261.

73. "Pulaski Day" envelopes, News Clippings Collection, UA.

74. Claudia L. Bushman, *America Discovers Columbus: How an Italian Explorer Became an American Hero* (Hanover, N.H.: University Press of New England, 1992); "Columbus Day" envelopes, News Clippings Collection, UA. A Columbus Day parade and ceremony

remained a fixture of the Independence Hall calendar until the early 1970s, when the city's statue of Christopher Columbus was moved from Fairmount Park to heavily Italian South Philadelphia, where it became the new focal point for Columbus Day.

75. German-Americans, who had traditionally gone to Valley Forge to honor Friedrich von Steuben's role in training Washington's troops, added a parade and program at Independence Hall in the mid-1960s. About the same time, the Puerto Rican community instituted a parade to Independence Hall as a culminating event of an annual Puerto Rican Week celebration. See Protection—Special Events Files (1966–74), Administration Records, INHP.

76. James G. Spady, "Richard Robert Wright Sr.," in Rayford W. Logan and Michael R. Winston, eds., *Dictionary of American Negro Biography* (New York: W. W. Norton, 1982), 674–75.

77. William H. Wiggins, Jr., *O Freedom! Afro-American Emancipation Celebrations* (Knoxville: University of Tennessee Press, 1987). See pp. 20–24 for the author's description of the National Freedom Day commemoration in Philadelphia in 1973.

78. Richard Robert Wright, Sr., "Banker Works to Make Feb. 1 a National Holiday," *Philadelphia Tribune*, November 1, 1941; also *Tribune,* November 8, 1941, November 15, 1941, November 29, 1941, December 13, 1941, December 20, 1941, December 27, 1941, January 31, 1942, February 7, 1942.

79. Elizabeth Ross Haynes, *The Black Boy of Atlanta* (Boston: House of Edinboro, 1952), 209–10; Richard Robert Wright, Sr., "Banker Works to Make February 1 a National Holiday," *Philadelphia Tribune*, November 1, 1941; *Tribune*, October 25, 1941.

80. *Tribune,* January 31, 1942.

81. *Tribune*, February 7, 1942; *National Freedom Day Album*, General Correspondence, Edward Martin Papers (MG 156), PSA.

82. Articles about the Freedom Day commemoration appeared nearly every year in the *Philadelphia Tribune*, beginning in 1942. Programs from the event exist in the Protection-Special Events Files, Administration Records, INHP. For a history of National Freedom Day, 1942–1997, see Charlene Mires, "The Difference This Day Makes," *Pennsylvania Heritage* (Winter 1998): 4–11.

83. *Myerson v. Samuel,* Civil Action 7863, U.S. District Court, Eastern District of Pennsylvania (1947).

84. *Myerson v. Samuel,* Civil Action 7863, U.S. District Court, Eastern District of Pennsylvania (1947).

85. *Evening Bulletin*, November 2, 1947.

86. *Reilly v. Samuel,* Civil Action 8039, U.S. District Court, Eastern District of Pennsylvania (1947).

87. *Evening Bulletin*, February 1, 1948, February 19, 1941, March 11, 1948.

88. J. David Stern, *Memoirs of a Maverick Publisher* (New York: Simon & Schuster, 1962), 84.

89. Ibid., 70.

90. "Philadelphia—Home of the United Nations," *Record,* March 5, 1945.

91. J. David Stern to Franklin D. Roosevelt, March 3, 1945, John G. Herndon United Nations Papers, HSP.

92. See daily coverage in the *Record*, March 1945.

93. Mrs. L. B. Taylor, "Think of the Drawbacks," *Record,* March 10, 1945; J. H. Kavanagh, "Audacious Bid," *Record,* March 14, 1945.

94. "Philadelphia: Cradle of Liberty," Free Library of Philadelphia Brochures Collection, UA.

95. *Philadelphia: Cradle of Liberty* (Philadelphia: Citizens Committee of the City of Philadelphia in the Commonwealth of Pennsylvania, 1945).

96. United Nations, *Report by the Executive Committee to the Preparatory Commission*, November 12, 1945, 115.

97. Elton Atwater, "Philadelphia's Quest to Become the Permanent Headquarters of the United Nations," *PMHB* (April 1976): 243–57.

98. United Nations, *Report by the Executive Committee to the Preparatory Commission*, November 12, 1945, 121, 125.

99. United Nations, *Journal of the Preparatory Commission*, November 24–December 24, 1945, 32–33, 36, 84–85.

100. John Robbins Hart to John G. Herndon, November 19, 1945, John G. Herndon United Nations Papers, HSP; Robert Gray Taylor to Edward Martin, January 14, 1946; *Easton's Invitation to the United Nations*; Commissioners of Pike County to Dr. Stoyan Gavrilovic, January 18, 1946; Robert A. Pfeiffle to Edward Martin, January 17, 1946; Montgomery F. Crowe and R. Leroy Dengler to Edward Martin, November 20, 1946, Official Papers, Edward Martin Papers (MG 156), PSA.

101. Halbwachs, *The Collective Memory.*

102. The endurance of memory through artifacts is argued by Alan Radley, "Artefacts, Memory and the Shape of the Past," in David Middleton and Derek Edwards, eds., *Collective Remembering* (London: Sage Publications, 1990), 46–59.

103. On distinguishing characteristics of past and present, see David Lowenthal, *The Past Is a Foreign Country* (Cambridge: Cambridge University Press, 1985), 52–63.

Chapter 8. Anchor

1. *Evening Bulletin*, June 13, 1954. Visitation statistics in this chapter are derived from Visitor Statistics Correspondence and Historian's Monthly Reports, Office of History Records, INHP. On the Cold War context of the American family during the 1950s, see Elaine Tyler May, *Homeward Bound: American Families in the Cold War Era* (New York: Basic Books, 1988); Wendy Kozol, *Life's America: Family and Nation in Postwar Journalism* (Philadelphia: Temple University Press, 1994); Stephanie Coontz, *The Way We Never Were: American Families and the Nostalgia Trap* (New York: Basic Books, 1992).

2. On consensus historians, see John Higham, *History: Professional Scholarship in America*, updated paperback ed. (Baltimore: Johns Hopkins University Press, 1989), 212–32; Stephen J. Whitfield, *The Culture of the Cold War* (Baltimore: Johns Hopkins University Press, 1991), 53–71.

3. Dennis R. Judd and Susan S. Fainstein, "Global Forces, Local Strategies, and Urban Tourism," in Judd and Fainstein, eds., *The Tourist City* (New Haven: Yale University Press, 1999); Whitfield, *Culture of the Cold War,* 71–72.

4. The most thorough account of the early years of Independence National Historical Park is Constance Greiff, *Independence: The Creation of a National Park* (Philadelphia: University of Pennsylvania Press, 1987). This institutional history details the work of the National Park Service, but pays less attention to vernacular activities and the creation of Independence Mall.

5. *Evening Bulletin,* June 2, 1951.

6. *Evening Bulletin,* September 23, 1953, December 27, 1954, April 27, 1954.

7. For discussion of these issues in New York City earlier in the century, see Max Page, *The Creative Destruction of Manhattan, 1900–1940* (Chicago: University of Chicago Press, 1999).

8. House of Representatives, 80th Congress, 2nd Session, Committee on Public Lands Report 1819, "Providing for the Establishment of the Independence National Historical Park," April 26, 1948.

9. Ibid.

10. Ibid.

11. "Planning and Development in Philadelphia," special issue of *Journal of the American Institute of Planners* (August 1960).

12. See Edmund N. Bacon, *Design of Cities* (New York: Viking Penguin, 1967); Alexander Garvin, *The American City: What Works, What Doesn't* (New York: McGraw-Hill, 1996).

13. *Inquirer,* May 4, 1955.

14. J. Thomas Scharf and Thompson Westcott, *History of Philadelphia, 1609–1884,* vol. 1 (Philadelphia: L. H. Evarts, 1884), 703, 721–22.

15. William E. Lingelbach, "Historic Philadelphia Redevelopment and Conservation," in *The Independence National Historical Park and Independence Hall in Historic Philadelphia* (Philadelphia: Independence Hall Association, 1951), 7.

16. *The Industries of Pennsylvania* (Philadelphia: R. Edwards, 1881); Walter Licht, *Industrializing America: The Nineteenth Century* (Baltimore: Johns Hopkins University Press, 1995), 30–35.

17. Greiff, *Independence,* 49–52.

18. *Evening Bulletin,* May 11, 1967.

19. *Inquirer,* June 24, 1955.

20. *Inquirer,* August 8, 9, 1955; *Evening Bulletin,* August 10, 12, 1955.

21. S. Polinow, "In Defense of Vagrants at Independence Mall," *Evening Bulletin,* August 24, 1955.

22. Edward M. Riley, "Interpretation," reported dated 1952, in *Master Plan Development Outline, Independence Historical Park Project* (1954), 87, Planning Records, INHP.

23. "Introduction," *Master Plan Development Outline, Independence Historical Park Project* (1954), Planning Records, INHP.

24. Public Law 795, 80th Congress, June 28, 1948.

25. *Master Plan Development Outline* (1954), 3–4.

26. Deborah C. Andrews, "Bank Buildings in Nineteenth-Century Philadelphia," in William Cutler III and Howard Gillette, Jr., eds., *The Divided Metropolis: Social and Spatial Dimensions of Philadelphia, 1800–1975.*

27. Greiff, *Independence,* 77–112; Charles E. Peterson, "Ante-Bellum Skyscraper," *JSAH* 9 (October 1950): 27–28, and "Penn Mutual Building, Philadelphia, 1850–51," *JSAH* 9 (December 1950): 24–25; Webster, *Philadelphia Preserved,* 80–81, 87.

28. Valerie Sue Pace, "Society Hill, Philadelphia: Historic Preservation and Urban Renewal in Washington Square East" (Ph.D. diss., University of Minnesota, 1976).

29. G. Edwin Brumbaugh, "Independence Hall Area: Rebirth of the Old City," *JAIA* (September 1957): 298.

30. *Evening Bulletin,* December 2, 1958, September 14, 1960.

31. Pace, "Society Hill," 135–37.

32. *Evening Bulletin,* July 25, 1971.

33. Pennsylvania Department of Commerce, News Release 524, in News Clippings Collection, Box 110, Folder 6, UA.

34. *Evening Bulletin,* October 11, 1961, December 7, 1961.

35. "Independence Hall Never Had It So Good," *Philadelphia Inquirer Magazine,* July 4, 1965; *Evening Bulletin,* December 26, 1965, May 29, 1966, December 4, 1966, May 9, 1969, January 4, 1972.

36. "A Report to the National Security Council by the Executive Secretary (James S. Lay Jr.), April 14, 1950" (National Security Council Document 68), in *Foreign Relations of the United States,* I (1950), 235–93.

37. On the national phenomenon of Cold War pageantry, see Richard M. Fried, *The Russians Are Coming! The Russians Are Coming! Pageantry and Patriotism in Cold-War America* (New York: Oxford University Press, 1998).

38. Preservation and use are stated priorities of the national park system. See William C. Everhart, *The National Park Service* (New York: Praeger, 1972), 80–98.

39. John A. Jakle, *The Tourist: Travel in Twentieth-Century North America* (Lincoln: University of Nebraska Press, 1985), 185–98.

40. Visitor Statistics Correspondence and Historian's Monthly Reports, Office of History Records, INHP.

41. Michael Kammen, *Mystic Chords of Memory: The Transformation of Tradition in American Culture* (New York: Alfred A. Knopf, 1991), 551–52, 573–81; Pauline Maier, *American Scripture: Making the Declaration of Independence* (New York: Alfred A. Knopf, 1997). On increasing tourism, see Gilbert C. Fite, *Mount Rushmore* (Norman: University of Oklahoma Press, 1952); Aubrey L. Haines, *The Yellowstone Story*, vol. 2 (Yellowstone National Park, Wyo.: Yellowstone Library and Museum Association, 1977), 478–80.

42. For a detailed account of the research process, see Greiff, *Independence,* 113–87, and Historian's Monthly Reports, 1951–74, Office of History Records, INHP.

43. Historic Research Master File, INHP.

44. Edward M. Riley, *Starting America: The Story of Independence Hall* (Washington, D.C.: National Park Service, 1954).

45. James M. Mulcahy, "*Congress Voting Independence*: The Trumbull and Pine-Savage Paintings," *PMHB* 80 (January 1956): 74–91.

46. Greiff, *Independence,* 144–45.

47. Historian's Monthly Reports, April 1952, May 1952, Office of History Records, INHP.

48. "Facts on the Changes in the Assembly Room, Independence Hall," undated memorandum, Office of History Records, INHP; *Evening Bulletin*, December 4, 1964, July 4, 1965; Greiff, *Independence,*125–60.

49. Independence National Historical Park Project, *Interpretive (Guide) Manual* (March 1952), 24, Office of History Records, INHP; Freeman Tilden, *Interpreting our Heritage* (Chapel Hill: University of North Carolina Press, 1957), 78–83; William J. Lewis, *Interpreting for Park Visitors* (Philadelphia: Eastern Acorn Press, 1986).

50. U.S. Department of the Interior, National Park Service, *Interpretive Survey: Independence National Historical Park* (June 1959), 8–11, Administrative Interpretive Division Records, INHP.

51. *Master Plan Development Outline* (1954), 89–90.

52. Tilden, *Interpreting Our Heritage*.

53. John C. Milley, ed., *Treasures of Independence: Independence National Historical Park and Its Collections* (New York: Mayflower Books, 1980), 23, 104.

54. Ibid., 20.

55. Sample talks, Office of History Records, INHP; Hugh Scott, "There's Something New at Independence Hall," *Today, the Philadelphia Inquirer Magazine*, December 10, 1961.

56. *All Around the Town* script, May 31, 1952, TV & Radio Scripts and Correspondence, Office of History Records, INHP.

57. Historian's Monthly Reports, July 1954, November 1956, Office of History Records, INHP.

58. *Home* script, October 22, 1956, TV & Radio Scripts and Correspondence, Office of History Records, INHP. Ellipses in original.

59. Independence Hall Film Strip Project, revised script, February 25, 1954, Office of History Records, INHP.

60. On origins of Cold War pageantry, see Fried, *The Russians Are Coming!* especially 87–98. Records of daily events at Independence Hall are in Protection Special Events Reports, 1951–1974, Administration Records, INHP.

61. On Captive Nations Week, see *Evening Bulletin*, July 12, 1960, July 1, 1961, July 20, 1964, July 19, 1965, July 9, 1966, July 17, 1967, July 22, 1968, July 13, 1970.

62. Daniel Tobin to Region Five Superintendents, August 26, 1958, and Superintendent INHP to Region Five Director, September 9, 1958, Protection Special Events Reports, 1958–59, Administrative Records, INHP; Historian's Monthly Reports, 1951–1960, Office of History; Protection Special Events Reports, 1951–1974, Administration Records, INHP; Ronald F. Lee, *Public Use of the National Park System, 1872–2000* (Washington, D.C.: U.S. Department of the Interior, 1968), 58.

63. *Evening Bulletin*, August 24, 1951, December 1, 1965.

64. *Evening Bulletin*, January 9, 1948, July 15, 1950.

65. *Evening Bulletin,* May 10, 1950.

66. *Evening Bulletin*, January 9, 1951; *New York Times*, January 8, 1967.

67. Protection Special Events Reports, 1958–59, Administrative Records, INHP.

68. *Evening Bulletin*, June 19, 1968.

69. *Evening Bulletin*, November 21, 1970.

70. *Independence Hall*, Independence Hall of Chicago—Miscellaneous Pamphlets, Chicago Historical Society; Sidney L. DeLove, *The Quiet Betrayal* (Chicago: Independence Hall of Chicago, 1960); *Chicago Daily News*, February 28, 1957; *Sun-Times,* October 30, 1971; *Tribune*, October 30, 1971.

71. "Address at Independence Hall, Philadelphia, July 4, 1962," in *Public Papers of the Presidents of the United States, John F. Kennedy, January 1 to December 31, 1962* (Washington, D.C.: GPO, 1963), 278–79.

72. The dialectic of "official" and "vernacular" memory is developed in John Bodnar, *Remaking America: Public Memory, Commemoration, and Patriotism in the Twentieth Century* (Princeton, N.J.: Princeton University Press, 1992), following on use of the terms by Susan G. Davis, *Parades and Power: Street Theatre in Nineteenth-Century Philadelphia* (Berkeley: University of California Press, 1986).

73. On relics as objects of reassurance, see David Lowenthal, *The Past Is a Foreign Country* (Cambridge: Cambridge University Press, 1985), 191–95.

Chapter 9. Prism

1. The Independence Day commemoration took place on July 5, 1965, because the Fourth of July fell on a Sunday. For control center activities, see Protection Special Events Reports, 1964–65, Administrative Records, INHP; on breakdown of the 1950s consensus, see Maurice Isserman and Michael Kazin, *America Divided: The Civil War of the 1960s* (New York: Oxford University Press, 2000).

2. On the Lincoln Memorial, see Scott A. Sandage, "A Marble House Divided: The Lincoln Memorial, the Civil Rights Movement, and the Politics of Memory, 1939–1963," *JAH* 80 (June 1993): 135–67.

3. Steven Kuromiya, ed., *1968 Collegiate Guide to Greater Philadelphia* (Philadelphia: Collegiate Guide to Greater Philadelphia, 1967), 21.

4. NAACP, Philadelphia Branch, *Let Freedom Ring*, event program, May 17, 1958, Protection Special Events Reports, 1956–65, Administration Records, INHP; on the Cold War context of such events, see Mary L. Dudziak, *Cold War Civil Rights: Race and the Image of American Democracy* (Princeton: Princeton University Press, 2000).

5. Events listed in Protection Special Events Reports, 1956–65, Administration Records, INHP.

6. *Evening Bulletin,* September 22, 1963.

7. NAACP, University of Pennsylvania, *Demonstration at Independence Hall*, typescript, March 12, 1965, Special Events Reports, Office of History Records, INHP.

8. *Evening Bulletin,* March 12, 1965.

9. *Evening Bulletin,* March 13, 1965.

10. Lenora E. Berson, *Case Study of Riot: The Philadelphia Story* (New York: Institute of Human Relations Press, 1966); Joseph S. Clark, Jr., and Dennis J. Clark, "Rally and Relapse, 1946–1968," in Russell F. Weigley, ed., *Philadelphia: A 300-Year History* (New York: W. W. Norton, 1982), 676.

11. *Evening Bulletin*, February 16, 1965, February 17, 1965, February 28, 1965, May 18, 1965, June 15, 1965.

12. Dennis C. Kurjack to Superintendent, INHP, April 12, 1965, Protection Special Events Reports, 1956–65, Administration Records, INHP.

13. *Evening Bulletin,* March 16, 1965.

14. *Philadelphia Tribune*, July 6, 1965, July 12, 1969; *Inquirer,* July 6, 1967; *Evening Bulletin,* July 19, 1970; Marc Stein, "Sex Politics in the City of Sisterly and Brotherly Loves," *Radical History Review* (Spring 1994): 82–83, and *City of Sisterly and Brotherly Loves: Lesbian and Gay Philadelphia, 1945–1972* (Chicago: University of Chicago Press, 2000).

15. *Inquirer*, July 6, 1967.

16. "Why Are Homosexual American Citizens Picketing at Independence Hall on July 4?" typescript, July 4, 1965, Special Events Reports, Office of History Records, INHP.

17. On conservatism, see John A. Andrew III, *The Other Side of the Sixties: Young Americans for Freedom and the Rise of Conservative Politics* (New Brunswick, N.J.: Rutgers University Press, 1997); Godfrey Hodgson, *The World Turned Right Side Up: A History of the Conservative Ascendancy in America* (New York: Houghton Mifflin, 1996).

18. On decline of Cold War pageantry elsewhere by the late 1950s, see Richard M. Fried, *The Russians Are Coming! The Russians Are Coming! Pageantry and Patriotism in Cold-War America* (New York: Oxford University Press, 1998), 139.

19. *Dedication Day—Viet Nam*, event schedule, October 23, 1965, Protection Special Events Reports, 1956–65, Administration Records, INHP; *Evening Bulletin,* October 24, 1965.

20. *Light Up for Freedom Rally*, event poster, January 8, 1966, Protection Special Events Reports, 1966–74, Administration Records, INHP; *Evening Bulletin,* January 9, 1966.

21. *Inquirer,* August 7, 1966; *Evening Bulletin,* August 7, 1966.

22. Protection Special Events Reports, 1969–1970, Administration Records, INHP; *Evening Bulletin*, September 15, 1969, September 19, 1969.

23. Protection Special Events Reports, 1966–67, Administration Records, INHP; *Evening Bulletin*, May 15, 1967, May 24, 1967.

24. Special Events Reports, Office of History Records, INHP.

25. Knott's Berry Farm, "Building Independence Hall," <http://www.knotts.com/mplace/shows/indehall/build.htm>, April 10, 2002.

26. John Maass, "Architecture and Americanism, or Pastiches of Independence Hall," *Historic Preservation* (April-June 1970): 24.

27. Lorrie Barofsky to Dennis Kurjack, June 17, 1959, TV & Radio Scripts and Correspondence, Office of History Records, INHP.

28. *Evening Bulletin*, March 30, 1958, February 27, 1967, May 10, 1968; *Inquirer,* February 28, 1969.

29. *Evening Bulletin*, August 3, 1957, October 23, 1960.

30. *Evening Bulletin*, May 8, 1968, August 27, 1968.

31. Reports and programs of Freedom Week activities in Protection Special Events Reports, Administration Records, INHP.

32. Archibald MacLeish, "The American Bell," in *Let Freedom Ring* (New York: American Heritage, 1962), 50–61; *Evening Bulletin*, February 4, 1960, June 22, 1962, June 28, 1962; *Daily News*, June 8, 1962; *Inquirer*, July 3, 1962.

33. *Evening Bulletin*, September 4, 1968.

34. Sound and light show visitor surveys, 1968, Administration Records, INHP. The show continued at Independence Hall through the summer of 1975, getting a boost in 1970 with more dramatic special effects and a new script created by a television writer.

35. *Master Plan for Independence National Historical Park* (May 1968), INHP.

36. *Master Plan for Independence National Historical Park* (1971), INHP.

37. Constance M. Greiff, *Independence: The Creation of a National Park* (Philadelphia: University of Pennsylvania Press, 1987), 125–60.

38. *Daily News*, March 13, 1973; *Evening Bulletin*, May 27, 1973; for a critical view, see Willard Randall, "A Hammerlock on History," *Today, the Philadelphia Inquirer Sunday Magazine*, July 8, 1973.

39. *Interpretive Survey* (June 1959), INHP.

40. *Master Plan Development Outline* (March 1954), INHP.

41. Stephanie G. Wolf, "The Bicentennial City," in Russell F. Weigley, ed., *Philadelphia: A 300-Year History* (New York: W. W. Norton, 1982), 725–31.

42. American Revolution Bicentennial Administration, *The Bicentennial of the United States of America: A Final Report to the People*, vol. 1 (Washington, D.C.: GPO, 1977), 54, 74, 139, 246.

43. Greiff, *Independence*, 233–55.

44. *Evening Bulletin,* February 5, 1972.

45. Greiff, *Independence,* 205–32; *Evening Bulletin,* February 4, 1972, February 7, 1972, February 11, 1972, February 25, 1972, April 14, 1972; *Inquirer,* December 7, 1972, December 14, 1972, February 6, 1973.

46. *Daily News,* May 18, 1972; *Evening Bulletin,* June 27, 1972, September 21, 1973, *Evening Bulletin,* August 23, 1974.

47. *Daily News,* March 7, 1975; *Inquirer,* December 31, 1975.

48. Greiff, *Independence,* 231; *Evening Bulletin,* December 31, 1975.

49. *Inquirer,* December 21, 1975; *Evening Bulletin,* December 14, 1975, January 1, 1976.

50. *Evening Bulletin,* January 2, 1976.

51. Hobart G. Cawood, Superintendent's Annual Report, March 10, 1977, Bicentennial Records, INHP.

52. On "relics" as bridges between past and present, see David Lowenthal, *The Past Is a Foreign Country* (Cambridge: Cambridge University Press, 1985).

53. On the opposition of official and vernacular memory, see John Bodnar, *Remaking America: Public Memory, Commemoration, and Patriotism in the Twentieth Century* (Princeton, N.J.: Princeton University Press, 1995).

54. On "site of memory," see Pierre Nora, *Realms of Memory: The Construction of the French Past,* vol. 1 (New York: Columbia University Press, 1996), 1–20. On the triggering of memory, see David Thelen, "Introduction: Memory and American History," in Thelen, ed., *Memory and American History* (Bloomington: Indiana University Press, 1990), vii-xix.

Chapter 10. Memory

1. Hans-Georg Gadamer, "The Ontological Foundation of the Occasional and the Decorative," in Neil Leach, ed., *Rethinking Architecture: A Reader in Cultural Theory* (London: Routledge, 1997), 134.

2. *General Management Plan, Independence National Historical Park* (1997), 30, INHP.

3. Comparisons to other sites are based on 2000 figures due to the disruption in tourism that followed the terrorist attacks on the United States on September 11, 2001. In 2000, Independence Hall had 822,070 visitors, while the Liberty Bell Pavilion had 1,580,622; in 1999, the totals were 802,208 for the Hall and 1,638,733 for the bell; in 1998, 800,304 for the Hall and 1,659,488 for the bell. In 2001, due to the decline of tourism and increased security that followed September 11, visitation declined 9.71 percent at Independence Hall and 25.41 percent at the Liberty Bell compared to the year before. See Independence National Historical Park Visitor Use Data, <http://www.nps.gov/inde>, April 10, 2002. Other National Park Service statistics from NPS Visitation Database, <http://www.nps.gov>, April 10, 2002.

4. World Heritage Nomination Form for Independence Hall, October 24, 1979, INHP.

5. *Superintendent's 2002 Compendium of Designations, Closures, Permit Requirements and Other Restrictions,* 16–17, INHP.

6. Ibid., 19.

7. *Inquirer,* July 5, 1992, November 8, 1995, November 10, 1995, July 4, 1999.

INDEX

ACKNOWLEDGMENTS

Assembling a history of Independence Hall that extends beyond the eighteenth century involved investigating the depths of many libraries, museums, and archives. This research was supported by generous grants from the Pennsylvania Historical and Museum Commission, the Henry F. du Pont Winterthur Museum and Library, Temple University, Villanova University, and the National Endowment for the Humanities. Many archivists, librarians, and curators were supportive research partners. They include especially archivist Karen Stevens at Independence National Historical Park as well as the staffs of the Urban Archives at Temple University, the Pennsylvania State Archives and Museum, the Historical Society of Pennsylvania, the Winterthur Museum and Library, the Library Company of Philadelphia, the Philadelphia City Archives, the University of Pennsylvania Archives, the Athenaeum of Philadelphia, the National Archives, and the Library of Congress. Present and former staff members at Independence National Historical Park were unfailingly generous with their time and expertise. For this, I thank Karie Diethorn, Anna Coxe Toogood, Doris Devine Fanelli, Penelope Hartshorne Batcheler, Frances Delmar, Joanne Blacoe, Robert Leone, Andrea Ashby Leraris, and the many ranger interpreters at Independence Hall and the Liberty Bell.

Many others have enriched this book through their enthusiasm and critiques. These include especially Allen F. Davis, who encouraged the project from the beginning and read more versions of the manuscript than either of us cares to remember. At the University of Pennsylvania Press, I was fortunate to work with Robert Lockhart, an editor whose devotion to his craft and deep knowledge of American history and culture made this book immeasurably better. Others who assisted by lending their expertise in their specialties to reviewing all or parts this work include: William W. Cutler III, Herbert Ershkowitz, Marc Gallicchio, Howard Gillette, David Glassberg, Karen Kauffman, Catherine Kerrison, Seth Koven, Jennifer Lawrence, Lawrence Little, Emmet McLaughlin, Gary Nash, Miles Orvell, William Pencak, Paige Roberts, Billy G. Smith, Mark Sullivan, Morris Vogel, Stephanie Yuhl, participants in the Temple University dissertation colloquium, and anonymous reviewers for *Pennsylvania History: A Journal of Mid-Atlantic Studies*, *The Public Historian*, and the University of Pennsylvania Press.

In addition to those already named, I was assisted by individuals who retrieved materials from distant places or brought documents and artifacts to my attention. They include John Cirilli, Jane Dye, Gary Edwards, Dinah Hale, Steve Hale, Connie S. Griffith Houchins, Cornelius Kiley, Catherine Mires, Cathleen Nista, Katherine Parkin, Joe Pixler, and members of the H-Net discussion groups for American Studies and local history. Students at Temple, LaSalle, and Villanova Universities and teachers in the summer workshops of the Independence Park Institute contributed to this book through their questions and observations about American history, which stimulated my thinking about communication of the past.

Portions of this book appeared previously. I am grateful to the Pennsylvania Historical Association for permission granted to incorporate material previously published as "Slavery, Nativism, and the Forgotten History of Independence Hall," *Pennsylvania History: A Journal of Mid-Atlantic Studies* 67 (Autumn 2000): 481–502, and to the University of California Press for permission to incorporate material published previously as "In the Shadow of Independence Hall: Vernacular Activities and the Meanings of Historic Places," *The Public Historian* 21 (Spring 1999): 49–64.

Finally, I thank friends and family who tolerated my single-mindedness for the duration of this project. This work of history and memory has much to do with an early appreciation for historic places cultivated by my father, Charles Wilson Mires, a Civil War enthusiast who had a penchant for photographing his children in front of cannons and for seeking ancestors among the tombstones of Ohio cemeteries. This book is an extension of his vocation, resting on memories of the historic places we visited together and many others that he did not get to see.